THE

WILDFIRE
——READER——

A CENTURY OF FAILED FOREST POLICY

EDITED BY
GEORGE WUERTHNER

 **ISLAND**PRESS

WASHINGTON ❖ COVELO ❖ LONDON

Our major goal in creating this book is to promote a greater appreciation of the role of wildfire on the landscape, to challenge commonly held assumptions about wildfire, and to encourage development of an ecologically based wildfire policy for public lands. As with any natural resource issue, various interpretations and conclusions are possible, even from the same research. We therefore felt it important to include a variety of voices on the subject of wildfire ecology and policy. Participation in this book by authors or photographers should not be interpreted as an endorsement of any particular agenda or ideology by them, nor should the inclusion of any author or photographer be interpreted as an endorsement by the Foundation for Deep Ecology of any particular political agenda or ideology.

—The Editor

DEDICATION

To Summer, Stratton, and all future generations. May there always be wild places for children and fires to roam.

Grateful acknowledgment is made to the following for permission to reprint copyrighted material. Portions of "The Fire of Life" were adapted from *Tending Fire: Coping with America's Wildland Fires* by Stephen Pyne, Shearwater Books/Island Press, 2004. "Fire and Native Peoples" was adapted from "The Myth of the Humanized Landscape," originally published in *Natural Areas Journal* 18, no. 3 (July 1998) and in *Wild Earth* (fall 1999). "Conventional Salvage Logging" was adapted from "Salvage Logging," originally published in *International Journal of Ecoforestry* 12, no. 1 (1996): 176–178.

LIBRARY OF CONGRESS CATALOGING-IN-PUBLICATION DATA
The wildfire reader : a century of failed forest policy /
edited by George Wuerthner.
  p.   cm.
Includes bibliographical references and index.
ISBN 1-59726-087-8 (pbk. : alk. paper)
1. Wildfires—United States—History. 2. Forest fires—United States—History.
3. Fire ecology—United States—History. 4. Forest policy—United States—History.
SD421.3.W54   2006
333.750973—dc22   2005032567

Printed in the United States on acid-free recycled paper, of which 30 percent is post-consumer waste.

Published by the Foundation for Deep Ecology by arrangement with Island Press.
Foundation for Deep Ecology
Building 1062, Fort Cronkhite
Sausalito, California 94965

Cover photograph by John McColgan/National Interagency Fire Center
Cover design by Roberto Carra

10 9 8 7 6 5 4 3 2 1

CONTENTS

Essays that do not carry an author's name were written by the editor.

INTRODUCTION

The Nez Perce National Forest in Idaho is rich country, a productive landscape defined by exquisite forests. Among the crumpled hills and steep mountains lies a diversity of trees usually seen only among the giants of the Pacific Coast. Here, 500 miles from the sea, such a forest seems particularly astounding, both for the size of its trees and for its contrasts. There are hillsides brown with golden grass in late summer, punctured with the orange-red boles of big-bellied ponderosa pine. These dry hills often cradle a damp valley through which runs an icy creek lined with verdant pockets of massive cedars surrounded by a thick understory of lacy, spreading sword fern fronds. Between these two extremes one can find growing among the Nez Perce's mountain folds the tall, straight boles of white pine—once used for the masts of clipper ships that plied the Pacific Ocean—or the corky-barked Douglas-fir, the delicate-needled western larch, and dense, hairy thickets of lodgepole pine, among others. And each of these tree species, to one extent or another, is dependent on, or adapted to, wildfire.

Wildfire is to the Nez Perce what rain is to the rainforest. It shapes, sculpts, prunes, cleans, and sustains these magnificent forests. Wildfire often determines which trees are found where, their age, their general health, and the composition of codominant species. I got to know the intimate wrinkles of these mountains in college. Like a lot of young men who loved the woods, I worked during the summer months for the U.S. Forest Service. One summer I landed a job as forestry technician on a timber crew with the Nez Perce National Forest. Our task was to gather data on tree species composition, growth rates, and other general ecological and physical data useful for forest planning, including where to place future timber-cutting units.

I rather enjoyed the timber stand surveys, as they were called. We tramped through the deep, lichen-draped forest, and at predetermined sites we noted all the species of trees, ground cover associations, slope, and terrain within a study plot. The pay was generous enough for a college student, and the fringe benefits were priceless—a lot of exercise, fresh air, and a chance to walk through the woods admiring the forest.

Toward the end of summer our stand survey crew was shifted to marking timber sales. We would march through the forest, paint cans in hand, spraying "leave" trees, or in some cases, "cut" trees, each a different color of paint depending on the prescription of the sale. Sometimes the agency would be telling loggers to cut specific trees, though more often they were permitted to cut everything except a few "leave" trees that were considered desirable for reseeding a site or because they were to serve some wildlife benefit.

I had less enthusiasm for the timber sale marking. I had a vague, uneasy feeling that by marking timber sales, I was contributing not only to the death of individual trees, but to the destruction of the forest ecosystem. I'd often heard from my forestry professors and coworkers that logging merely replaces natural processes like fire. After all, they would remind me, fire kills trees, but the forest grows back, so what's the difference if loggers cut the trees—the Forest Service replants new ones. These platitudes of industrial logic never quite sat well with me. Even then, I had inklings that the evenly spaced rows of single-species tree plantations cut on predetermined rotations were not the same as a naturally sustained forest.

Despite these qualms, I went forward with my task of tree marking, permitting these pundits' presumed greater knowledge of forestry to assuage my reservations. Often the timber sale prescription required us to mark the biggest trees for cutting. These were the most economically valuable, and in the Forest Service parlance of the time, they were "overmature" and "decadent." The general perception among foresters was that these trees had outlived their usefulness, and the sooner we got them out of the forest, the better. The forest would be "healthier" once these ancient trees were removed. Though I had no reason to object to the process then, I later learned that the extraction of the largest, most fire-resistant trees actually contributed to the unhealthy forests that we have today.

Fortunately, as the summer turned to autumn, there were a growing number of wildfires burning around the West. A shortage of trained firefighters allowed the Forest Service to reassign other workers to the fire lines to assist in containing blazes. So it was with real relief that I learned that my crew was taken off the timber sale marking assignment and put to work fighting fires. At least now, I thought, I could do something useful and ecologically ethical like saving the forest from the "destructive" effects of fire.

After a couple of days of instruction in basic firefighting safety and techniques, my crew was assigned to the less dangerous task of "mop-up" duties. We patrolled existing fire lines looking for the occasional smoking stump or active small blazes, which we were to extinguish before they could grow into large fires again. There was no doubt in my mind as I "attacked" the small smokes and burning embers along the fire line that I was "saving" the forest from destruction. I never suspected that by shoveling dirt on these blazes, I was thwarting one of nature's most important agents of renewal. I felt good about my contribution to the safety, long life, and good health of the forest. I slept well at night knowing I had put in a good day doing something worthwhile.

A number of years later, I worked as a biologist with the Bureau of Land Management. Again, a hot, dry summer led to widespread fires around the West, and all agency personnel were given the opportunity to work on fires. By the middle of August, nearly all the able-bodied people in the office were already out working on fire crews, and I was asked to do my share and work on a fire as well.

As before, I had the task of doing mop-up. But in the intervening years, I had grown less certain that stopping fires was always a good thing. My ecological training and my own observations gleaned from many years out in the woods had given rise to doubt that fires were all "destructive." Already I was beginning to believe that maybe we should just leave fires alone.

Out on the fire line I reached one particular blazing piece of wood and began to shovel dirt on the orange flames. But as I quenched the glowing red embers, I began to wonder whether I was like the old wolf hunters who rode through the West, righteously killing predators to make the land safe for cows, elk, and deer. I paused in my work. Leaning on my shovel, I watched the last crimson embers die in the burning log. Tilting back my yellow hard hat, I looked up at the surrounding snags, blackened tree trunks, and gray ash, and instead of seeing death and destruction, I saw the promise of a new forest. Suddenly I realized that in my urge to "save" the trees from fire, I was helping to destroy the forest. With that insight, I went back to the fire boss, handed him my shovel, and asked to be taken off the fire. I never again fought a fire.

▼

The realization that wildfire can be an important ecological agent for forest renewal has had greater symbolic implications for me. Over the years I have come to be more and more skeptical of our ability to manage and control anything in nature. It seems that no matter how much we learn, we never fully understand the complexities of ecosystems.[1] This philosophical split is part of a larger schism that I feel permeates our society and culture, which sees itself as apart from nature, rather than dependent upon nature. This dichotomy exists in our relationship to wildfire as well. Our attempt to control wildfire is really an attempt to control the wild, and as in every attempt we have made to control the wild, whether it is to control wild rivers with dams or to control predators, we have learned to our chagrin that we have not really controlled anything. As we discuss in this book, even the assumption that we should reduce or limit big blazes is one that all do not share. There should be a place for large fires on the landscape, and we should not assume that it is desirable to control them all.

How we relate to wildfire is part of a schism in the conservation movement as well. Some advocate human control of nature and genuinely believe we know enough to manage the cows, the forests, the predators, and so forth, to achieve a "better world." Yet to my mind, even the attempt to control such natural processes and landscapes smacks of great human conceit. This hubris in respect to nature—of which our relationship to wildfire is only one clear manifestation—is the driving force behind the ecological collapse we are witnessing all around us, from the depletion of our fish stocks to species extinctions, to tropical deforestation, to desertification, to give only a few examples.

I admit that we all try to manipulate the environment to a degree. I heat my house to keep out the cold. I smack the mosquito that is biting my arm. But I do not advocate warming up the globe to reduce my heating bill, nor do I support draining swamps to eliminate mosquitoes. Landscape or global treatments involve too many variables for me to feel comfortable advocating any kind of long-term manipulation. At best, I support restoration of some ecological processes like fire or predators and feel we must allow these natural forces to determine what the "right" amount of anything is to the greatest degree possible.

We have looked upon wildfire in the same way countless generations viewed wolves—as evil forces that "destroyed" deer herds and livestock, and that were thus in need of control and extirpation if possible. Though attitudes toward predators like wolves have improved to the point that we now accept the idea that there is value to maintaining wolves, many still view wolf restoration as appropriate only to national parks or other special lands we have set aside for nature, rather than allowing wolves to assume their important ecological role as a top predator across the landscape.[2] Even more importantly for our development of a mature and healthy relationship to nature, the next step in this process is that we must allow wolves to be wild, not radio-collared creatures that are tracked, moved, or killed at our whim. Our attitudes toward wildfire have evolved in a similar way, and to a similar point.

Today we tolerate wildfire under very precise conditions designed to ensure that they do not burn great numbers of acres, thus limiting their ecological influence in the process. This is not unlike our current attitude toward wolves. We often kill wolves that stray beyond the bounds of protected landscapes like Yellowstone and "manage" wolves if their numbers rise beyond what we consider to be an acceptable level. We usually permit wildfires to burn unimpeded only in some national parks and wilderness areas, but we still attempt to "kill" fires elsewhere, even when there is no immediate threat to human settlement or life.

Since the time I laid down my shovel and walked away from firefighting, I have come to view with skepticism most fire suppression as nothing more than "predator control" for forests. And I am equally dubious about forest thinning/salvage logging proposals in the name of "protecting" forest health. It seems that logging is nearly always the solution to whatever ails the forest, much as people once thought that nearly all disease was a consequence of bad blood. Our understanding of ecology is not much more advanced than our understanding of human health in the days when leeches were used to bleed the body. Again and again, the lesson I have taken from the study of ecology is one overriding fact: we continually believe we know how to manage nature, only later to learn how misguided our understanding of how things work turned out to be. There are many examples of this from the scientific literature.[3]

Let me be up-front and admit my bias: I believe that nature should be the final arbitrator in the "management" of our wildlands. There is room for some flexibility in the approaches society may adopt to solve the problems we have created with past land management— and the different authors in this volume provide a variety of perspectives on this issue—but there is ultimately agreement among us that the final goal is to arrive at a point where we can learn to live with wildfire, rather than being continuously at "war" with it.

There may be a place for thinning trees near communities where a major fire is unacceptable, but only after other options such as prescribed fire, natural fire, and even insects and drought are unable to adequately address the perceived problem. I worry, however, that thinning will become—by political default, if not by general consensus of ecologists—the dominant mechanism for land restoration that motivates most federal and state land management agencies because it promises the least controversy and potentially the most commercial applications available to land agencies. The goal of this book is to raise a lot of questions and cautionary remarks in this debate.

This is not to suggest that I advocate a complete policy of no wildfire management on all lands, or that, by default, I want to let fires burn up homes and communities. Indeed, I believe there are plenty of opportunities for individuals to take responsible, proactive steps to minimize the threat of fire to personal property, such as reducing fuels near homes and communities, and to minimize new fire hazards by controlling urban sprawl—issues that we discuss in this book. Nevertheless, there is an enormous difference between changing policies to minimize fire hazard to homes and communities and advocating control and manipulation of forest ecosystems across vast swaths of the landscape.

A good analogy can be found in how different people approach the issue of river floods. An interventionist approach sees the "flood" as a problem, and seeks to control the river through dams, riprap, levees, and channelization. An alternative, noninterventionist approach recognizes that a healthy river occasionally floods, and that even massive floods are equally as important to river ecology as "normal" flows, and are thus desirable. A proactive solution is therefore to prohibit home construction in river floodplains.

There is general agreement that past land management activities such as fire suppression, logging, and livestock grazing have severely altered the natural fire regimes in some forest ecosystems—especially in many of the ponderosa pine forests of the West. These changes have created a potential problem of unnaturally intense blazes. Various authors in this volume discuss these ecosystem changes and their ecological consequences. However, what we do in response to these changes is still a matter of debate, which I hope this book will further stimulate. In some instances, moderate amounts of thinning, followed by prescribed burning, done strategically, can potentially alter fire severity at stand and landscape levels and even lead to the restoration of a natural fire regime. Nevertheless, the precautionary principle suggests that we should act with prudence in any significant human manipulation of the landscape. In the end, the goal should always be to return as much of the "management" of the landscape as possible back to nature.

Equally as important, unless activities that have contributed to the altered fire regimes in the first place—again, fire suppression, commercial logging, and livestock grazing—are terminated so that natural fire regimes can be reestablished, any area thinned today will need to be thinned again in the future, creating never-ending intrusions into the landscape.

▼

While this book is about fire policy and fire ecology, it is also a discussion of a much larger philosophical debate over the ultimate role and influence humans should have on natural landscapes. Part One presents responses to a number of common misconceptions, or myths, about fire ecology and fire behavior. Part Two explores the human relationship to wildfire, including historical, political, and media portrayals of wildfire and personal reflections about fire and humans. Part Three deals with the ecological attributes of fire in various landscapes, including chaparral, ponderosa pine, mixed-conifer, and eastern wood-lands, among others.

Part Four critiques the notion that logging is ecologically similar to fire and, more importantly, argues that salvage logging after a burn is particularly harmful and has no place in forest management. Part Five looks at the ways in which wildfire has given rise to a new fire-indus-trial complex and exposes the economic forces that drive fire suppres-sion—much to the detriment of the forest and taxpayers. Part Six offers alternatives to current misguided fire policies—including chang-ing the way we build our communities and altering our perception of wildfire so that we can allow it to be restored across the landscape. Part Seven lays out the case for retiring Smokey Bear and creating new poli-cies that promote living with wildfire rather than against wildfire.

In the end, I hope that, like Aldo Leopold, who came to "think like a mountain" in respect to wolves, we can begin to think like a moun-tain when it comes to wildfire. If we truly begin to think like a moun-tain, we will come to celebrate wildfire and to welcome its presence on our landscapes. And if we make this transition in thought and action toward restoration of a natural fire regime, toward seeing fire within a larger human-natural system, we will move closer to a healthier human and natural world that will enrich us all—not just those within the fire-industrial complex.

Part One

WILDFIRE MYTHS

Myths are often perpetuated to promote a particular worldview. The worldview held by most people and, in some cases, created by special interests, is that fire is something to be feared, controlled, and suppressed. Seen through this lens, wildfires are viewed as destructive events rather than natural processes of rejuvenation and regeneration. In this section we challenge several of the major misconceptions about wildfire and refute them based on a knowledge of wildfire's important ecological role in the landscape.

MYTH

FIRE IS BAD
AND NEEDS TO BE SUPPRESSED

TRUTH

Fire is an elemental and critical ecological force in nature. Many plants and wildlife species depend on fire to create important habitat, provide nutrients, eliminate competitors, and propagate progeny. In many ecosystems, including much of the arid West, biological decomposition is slow because of limited moisture and generally unfavorable temperatures. In these ecosystems, fire is often the alternative decomposer that releases bound-up nutrients, making them available for future plant growth. Fires also produce snags, down woody debris, and other structural components of the landscape that provide home and food for many species.

Because fire is such an important and widely distributed natural phenomenon, few ecosystems suffer long-term harm as a consequence of blazes. Indeed, for those forests adapted to periodic fire, fire suppression—rather than fire itself, as often portrayed in the media—changes ecosystems in ways that are detrimental to the landscape and ecological health.

There will always be places where humans do not and cannot tolerate fire. However, over much of the landscape where important human values are not jeopardized, a policy of aggressive fire suppression is not only detrimental to long-term ecosystem health, but also economically suspect. Indeed, suppression only delays, rather than prevents, future fires, since without blazes, fuels continue to build until their energy is released by decomposition. Fire suppression is like buying on a credit card—at some point there is payback.

MYTH

BIG FIRES ARE THE RESULT
OF TOO MUCH FUEL

TRUTH

While fuel is a key ingredient for any blaze, and fuel accumulations can exacerbate fire intensity, most large blazes result from drought and wind—not fuels. Yet because fuel treatments are emphasized in management prescriptions, the general public is led to believe that fuels are the driving force in large blazes and, by inference, that fuel reduction through tree thinning will prevent large fires. This myth ignores the fact that some ecosystems—such as the lodgepole pine forests of Yellowstone and the Douglas-fir forests of the Cascades—are characterized by large but infrequent stand-replacing fires, a point of reference that is often omitted in media accounts.

Without drought and wind, there can be an immense amount of fuel in the form of down woody debris, as in the rainforests of southeast Alaska, but almost no fires. On the other hand, under drought conditions, even young, recently regenerating clearcuts will burn, and burn intensively.

Even ecosystems such as the ponderosa pine forests of the Southwest—which were, to the best of our knowledge, historically dominated by small, "cool" fires—have experienced occasional climatic conditions of drought and wind that permitted numerous small blazes to coalesce into one large blaze or several large blazes. Fuel reductions through thinning may make it easier to control and contain a fire in some situations, but under extreme climatic conditions, wind and drought—not fuels—will be the driving force behind the flames.

MYTH

LOGGING MIMICS FIRE

TRUTH

Many timber companies and logging proponents argue that removing trees mechanically through logging differs little from "thinning" of the forest by fire. Yet there are substantial ecological differences between commercial logging operations and fire. The biggest difference between the two is the removal of woody debris. Logging removes trees from the forest ecosystem. By contrast, after a fire, trees killed by heat or flames remain a resource for decades. These snags supply homes for countless cavity-dwelling species, from flying squirrels to bluebirds. The dead trees also furnish food for beetles, fungi, and other decomposers. When snags fall to the ground, they provide room and board for a new set of species. Fallen snags also act as natural water bars, reducing erosion. If the trees happen to fall into a stream, they help to stabilize stream channel morphology, reduce water erosion, and provide cover for fish and aquatic insects. Fire also produces ash, a natural fertilizer, and releases nutrients bound up in plant material so they are available for new growth. Finally, the heat and smoke from fires can kill some plant pathogens.

In addition to these structural differences, logging has other negative consequences that make it differ drastically from fire. Logging can introduce insects, tree diseases, or exotic weeds into an area through logging equipment, which also compacts soils and may increase erosion. Roads created by logging open up areas for more hunting, poaching, off-road vehicles, and other human uses.

MYTH

BIG FIRES CAN BE STOPPED

TRUTH

Many agencies promote the notion that fire suppression can halt large blazes. What in fact happens far too often is that the conditions that allow a blaze to rage change—it rains or snows, or the wind dies down—and the fire is controlled and extinguished. For instance, it was snow in September, not the suppression efforts of 10,000 firefighters, that ultimately quenched the historic 1988 Yellowstone fires. Fire suppression agencies are sometimes quick to take credit for stopping a fire when, in fact, the fire was destined to die of natural causes anyway.

Large blazes are similar to large floods on rivers—they are an ecologically critical force of nature that shapes natural ecosystems. Most large blazes are seen as "bad" and viewed as destructive by the public and many land management agencies because they are resistant to human efforts to control them; however, from an ecological perspective, large blazes, particularly in ecosystems dominated by stand-replacement fires, are well within the normal range of variability. Trying to stop large blazes—if this is even possible, and it often is not—is like trying to keep a river from flooding. In the effort to dam rivers, we have destroyed river channel function and aquatic ecosystem health. Similarly, trying to stop large blazes is futile and ecologically destructive.

Far too often, because we automatically assume that big fires are bad, we don't even stop to ask whether there may be some important ecological role for them to play.

MYTH

FIRE "DESTROYS" FORESTS
AND WILDLIFE

TRUTH

Fire no more destroys the forest in fire-prone ecosystems than rain destroys the rainforest. But because we tend to equate a charred forest with a charred, burned-out house, we unwittingly cling to the view that fires destroy the forest. Images of Bambi running away from a forest fire add to our conviction that fires must be destructive to wildlife. Yet fire is such a pervasive element of so many natural ecosystems that plants and animals have mechanisms that allow them to cope with fire, and often even thrive on fire.

In fire-adapted ecosystems, most species have evolved ways of avoiding or surviving a fire. Some shrubs and trees sprout from their roots after the tops are killed by a blaze. Others have seeds that germinate only after being heated.

Wildlife is equally at home in fire-charred landscapes. Since the timing of most western fires occurs in summer after nesting birds have fledged, few birds are hurt by flames. Smaller mammals such as ground squirrels or mice hide in burrows in the soil, which is an excellent insulator. Large animals such as elk and deer merely walk or bound away from the flames. In fact, the biggest threat to larger animals comes not from fire, but from the smoke that can sometimes suffocate them. Of course, fires do hurt or kill some animals—however, Bambi movies aside, the actual number of animals directly killed by flames is generally small.

MYTH

FIRE "STERILIZES" THE LAND

TRUTH

The idea that fires "sterilize" the landscape is perpetuated by the news media, which seek out the most dramatic and stark landscapes to characterize a fire. Indeed, most people are surprised to see snags in the aftermath of a blaze since they are conditioned to believe that fires vaporize all living matter. Most fires in the West are not so hot that they completely burn up trees and shrubs, and few blazes actually sterilize soils. Furthermore, since most fires burn in a mosaic pattern of varying fire intensity, many areas are simply not burned at all or are only lightly brushed by fire.

Very hot blazes can cause localized mortality for underground roots, seeds, mycorrhizae, and soil microfauna. Intense blazes can also cause soils to develop a hydrophobic layer, or water-impervious cap, that prevents moisture from soaking into the soil. The cap is formed when organic compounds in the trees or plants coat soil particles so their ability to absorb water is reduced. Such occurrences are relatively rare, occurring within certain ecosystem types or where unusual conditions such as a massive blowdown create an exceptionally high fuel load, leading to abnormally hot blazes. The hydrophobic effects last only a few seasons before natural weathering begins to break them down, permitting normal water infiltration. In sum, soils "sterilized" by fire make up a very small percentage of any fire, or of annual acreage burned, and the sterilization effects are ephemeral.

MYTH

NORTH AMERICAN LANDSCAPES WERE WIDELY MANAGED BY NATIVE AMERICAN FIRE USE

TRUTH

The idea that Native Americans "managed" North American ecosystems with fire is a widely held myth with a grain of truth to it, but which is generalized to cover much too great an area. Some perpetuate the idea to justify current landscape manipulations, such as massive tree-thinning programs, by suggesting that these management activities are not significantly different from Native American practices prior to Euro-American intervention. Others use this myth to deconstruct the idea that any landscapes were "wild" or unmanaged.

It is true that many low-elevation valley grasslands were maintained or created by Indian-set fires. However, most Indian burns were very local—such as the burning of a particular favorite camping spot, or as a pasture for horses near a major encampment. Indian fires were not a significant influence on the wider landscape.

At higher, wetter elevations around the West, the vegetation remains lush and green so late into the summer that, in effect, these lands are "fireproof" and burn only under extraordinary conditions. They are "asbestos" forests, and human influences on fire frequency here were negligible.

Even where Native Americans could be seen as responsible for many fires, it is debatable whether these blazes were in addition to, or merely took the place of, natural fires. In much of the West, lightning strikes are more than sufficient to account for nearly all observed fire intervals, regardless of human influences.

MYTH

LIVESTOCK GRAZING
CAN PREVENT FIRES

TRUTH

Some livestock proponents argue that livestock grazing, by reducing fine fuels, can prevent fires. This assertion has several flaws. First, it assumes that fires are undesirable and need to be prevented—an assumption not shared by many ecologists.

Second, anecdotal evidence suggests that livestock grazing does not significantly reduce large blazes. During periods of drought, forage production, which is directly related to soil moisture, is significantly reduced. As a consequence, livestock consume most of the available forage, leaving little fuel. Yet the largest range fires occur during these same drought periods. How can that be? The answer is that livestock do not necessarily remove all vegetation. They may consume the grasses, but not the sagebrush, which remains to carry a flame. In addition, large blazes are driven by wind and drought, and during these conditions, any residual vegetation—no matter how little— burns briskly.

Lastly, even if livestock grazing were able to reduce fires, and this was deemed desirable, other consequences resulting from the presence of livestock make the "cure" worse than the "disease." Livestock spread exotic plants like cheatgrass that are actually more fire-prone than native grasses. Livestock also compact soils, increase soil erosion, pollute water, degrade riparian areas, compete with native herbivores for forage, and jeopardize predator populations as a result of livestock-induced predator control. The end result of all these negative environmental consequences is far worse, in the view of many ecologists, than the occasional blaze.

MYTH

SALVAGE LOGGING AFTER A FIRE
IS NECESSARY TO RESTORE FORESTS

TRUTH

Salvage logging—the removal of burned trees after a fire under the presumption that it will hasten forest recovery—is a myth perpetuated by the timber industry. Forests have evolved over millennia to regenerate themselves after a blaze. Certain species, particularly nitrogen-fixing plants, often colonize burned sites immediately after a fire. Short-circuiting this process by cutting and planting trees may ultimately bankrupt the forest ecosystem due to a reduction in nutrient replacement.

We are taught to believe that something "dead" is useless, forgetting that many species find food and shelter in dead trees. Removal of burned trees takes away many valuable forest legacies, including nutrients bound up in trees that would otherwise remain on-site and provide for the next generation of trees. Logging also removes snags, and the potential woody debris that creates habitat for fish and other aquatic organisms. Snags even create a microclimate that fosters tree regeneration, slowing wind, providing shade, and reducing soil moisture losses. Many animals, such as woodpeckers and flying squirrels, use snags for homes and food.

Salvage logging also potentially facilitates the spread of exotic weeds and plant diseases that are carried on logging equipment. The creation of logging roads may increase siltation in streams through erosion and runoff, and also may increase access for hunters, trappers, and poachers—all with potential negative impacts on wildlife.

MYTH

PRESCRIBED BURNING IS AN ADEQUATE SUBSTITUTE FOR WILDFIRE

TRUTH

Prescribed burning is the intentional lighting of fires under controlled conditions. While an important tool in restoring fire to the landscape, and as a mechanism of reducing fuels near communities or other targeted areas where wildfire would be undesirable, prescribed burning alone is not an adequate substitute for natural wildfire.

First, the conditions under which prescribed fires are set are often less than ideal for the rapid spread of a blaze. As a consequence, the amount of acreage burned, even under an aggressive prescribed burning program, is far less than what would burn under ideal fire conditions. In terms of fuel reduction or even mimicking historic fire regimes, prescribed burning often falls far short. Second, because prescribed burns are intentionally set when control is possible, the timing is often different from that of natural fires. For instance, in many areas prescribed burns are set in the spring, when soil moisture is higher—just when young birds and small mammals are more vulnerable to blazes, and just when plants are beginning to green up. A fire at this time can do more damage to an ecosystem than much larger blazes during the normal fire season. Third, the vast acreage that would need to be burned annually to make any substantial reduction in fuel accumulation—in the millions of acres—would require a huge fire control force to implement. The costs would be far greater than allowing natural fires to burn.

Part Two

WILDFIRE

PERSPECTIVES AND VISIONS

INTRODUCTION

Humans and Fire

Humans and fire go together like people and dogs. In fact, before
we domesticated the dog, we likely domesticated fire. Fire is also
the first natural phenomenon we learned to control. Fire was used in
warfare, to clear brush, to favor plants that we or our prey ate, and it
allowed us to eat certain foods that otherwise would be poisonous,
unpalatable, or even inedible without cooking. The control of fire was
a critical step in our dominance of the planet. Human history and fire
history are intertwined and complex. Reflecting our relationship to fire
and its complexity, each of the authors in Part Two provides a different point of view on fire, including historical, biological, philosophical,
political, and personal perspectives.

In his many books and essays on fire, historian Stephen Pyne
argues that it was fire as much as social organization and tools that
permitted our species to dominate the globe. Without fire to warm our
tents, huts, and caves, it would have been difficult for us to penetrate
the colder regions of the Northern and Southern hemispheres. Here
Pyne further explores the coevolution of humans and fire in a provoca-
tive essay suggesting that fire should be seen as a biological and cultural agent.

Mollie Matteson, a former Forest Service wilderness ranger, writes
about the experience of wildfire as part of a spiritual knowledge that
should be preserved as much as the scenery, wildlife, or any other component of a natural area.

While humans have used fire to modify the landscape to suit their
needs, the question of whether this influence has significantly altered
the planet is the subject of ongoing debate. Geographer Tom Vale takes
a critical look at the cultural use of fire by Native Americans in terms
of how and to what degree it may have shaped the plant communities
of the West. This issue is especially important to understand as we try
to restore fire to the landscape. Is human intervention necessary to re-
create historic fire patterns, or are natural ignitions from lightning and

other sources sufficient to account for past fire frequency and spatial scale?

Joe Fox, a former wildland firefighter and smokejumper, explores the motivations that draw people into becoming smokejumpers and explores the conflicts of the work. Ironically, as Fox acknowledges in his essay, the control of wildland fire by firefighters like himself destroys the very wildness they seek to find in these remote hinterlands.

However, the vast majority of people do not see fire as anything but a destructive force. Few feel the magic and awe in the surging power of a firestorm or the beauty of a glowing flame. Because of the often-adversarial relationship humans have with fire, it is not surprising that we tend to speak of it in negative terms. The short sidebar "Incendiary Language" describes how the pejorative language used in connection with fire affects our perception of fire as good, bad, or neutral. Conrad Smith examines how journalists often ignore the ecological role of fire and instead exploit the fear of fire to sell news. Part of the problem, Smith points out, is that most journalists do not seek out scientific information about fire ecology. Often, because they lack an informed background, they don't know the right questions to ask, or how to frame the issue of wildfire in such a way that the public's understanding of fire is improved. This lack of ecological understanding is also influenced by the language we use to describe fires.

Les AuCoin, a former U.S. congressman, explains how and why politicians are often eager to exploit a blaze to garner votes or funding for their local economy. From an insider's perspective, AuCoin uncovers the politics of fire and how the public's fear of flames is used to manipulate support for unnecessary and often uneconomic solutions, such as the Bush administration's Healthy Forests Initiative.

Lastly, poet Gary Snyder, who lives among the pine forests of the Sierra Nevada, tells his own story of how he and his neighbors are learning to live with fire, describing what will hopefully become a widely accepted new paradigm for how humans can coexist with, rather than fight against, fire.

THE FIRE OF LIFE

Thinking About the Biological Basis for Fire

STEPHEN J. PYNE, PH.D.

FIRE IS A CREATION OF LIFE: *the oxygen, the fuel, and, with human-ity, the spark that combustion requires all come from the living world. Yet we continue to imagine burning as simply a physical force against which we should muster physical counterforces. This is inad-equate. We need, rather, a properly biological theory of fire.*

▼

How should we think about fire? The question is trickier than it might seem, for fire synthesizes its surroundings; it takes its char-acter from its context. Like the other elements of the Ancients—earth, water, air—fire's manifestation depends on its setting. However, unlike them, fire is not a substance but a reaction, and unlike the others, its environs make its very existence possible. Describe fire's setting, and you describe fire. Control that setting, and you control fire. To imagine fire is to imagine fire's context. The most elemental failure of contem-porary fire management is finally a failure of that imagination.

The traditional prism for conceptualizing fire is physical: it should be more deeply biological. The traditional prism of fire protection is to envision fire within a hierarchy of physical frames. Life matters because it spawns fuels and complicates predictions of what will hap-pen after the flames have passed, but grand physical parameters really control fire, and they must be countered by physical forces of equal magnitude. The ecological equivalent is to consider fire as a "distur-bance," part of a suite of outside agencies that intrude upon, upset, or shatter biotas. Flame becomes a kind of heat-flux hammer, whose impact is measured by comparing the eco-edifice that existed before its blows with the shards that survive.

It is possible, however—perhaps essential—to turn this conventional conception inside out. One can, instead, define fire as primarily a phenomenon of the biosphere, subject to biological controls both tiny and huge, with the well-known physical constraints internal and secondary to that scaffolding. The old expression that such-and-such a disease spread like wildfire would be reversed to read that such-and-such a fire spread like a disease, a contagion of combustion. Fire more resembles severe acute respiratory syndrome (SARS) or a bark beetle epidemic than a clearcut. Such a reconception could better accommodate the enormous diversity in what burns, how it burns, and what effects the burning yields.

HOW LIFE MADE FIRE

The larger justification for this construct goes like this. Fire is a creation of the living world. Life supplies its oxygen, life furnishes its fuel, and through ourselves, life kindles most ignitions. Wind, lightning, drought, upper-level highs, El Niño–Southern Oscillation (wet/dry) episodes, ridges and ravines—in the absence of life, such physical parameters constrain nothing but themselves. They exercise influence only through the medium of a biosphere that makes combustion possible and that profoundly shapes its properties. This is not a plea for a vague Gaian fire, or a metaphysical appeal to life forces. It simply states a reality lost in the fury of quenching flames, forecasting winds, and chopping "fuel." Wind, ice, landslides, floods—all such disturbances can occur without a particle of life present. Fire cannot. Its power resides in its power to propagate, and the power to propagate requires transmission through a biotic medium. No life, no fire. While we speak loosely of solar, nuclear, or volcanic "fires," these expressions are metaphors for things that appear bright and hot. They are not founded on a chemistry of combustion.

Real fire—the oxidation of hydrocarbons—is a creation of life. Real combustion takes apart what photosynthesis puts together. It is among the most elemental of biochemical reactions; when it occurs in cells, we call it respiration, and when it occurs on landscapes, we call it fire. At every scale, a suite of biological controls can shape how combustion's core chemistry behaves. From the level of molecules and mitochondria to individual particles to landscape patches to the planet itself as an abode for fire—genetic, ecological, and evolutionary processes sculpt what kind of fire exists, when, and where. Pick almost any aspect of Earthly fire, and its biological character is fundamental, for without life, fire would not exist. Moreover, a biological theory of fire would reserve pride of place to ourselves as uniquely fire creatures, as the one species to claim a monopoly over fire's direct manipulation. Fire ecology, as presently conceived, encompasses only a fraction of what a general theory of fire biology would embrace. Such a redefinition of fire as a subject would allow for a redefinition of fire as a problem.

HOW THE BIOLOGY OF FIRE SHOULD SHAPE THE MANAGEMENT OF FIRE

What would such a biologically based theory of fire mean in practice? For actual firefighting, it might mean little. Suppressing the intermix fire along the urban fringe will still depend on simple, mechanical treatments like raking needles and shearing off "ladder" fuels. Firefights will still resort to water, pulaskis, and retardants in an effort to break the chain of combustion chemistry. But the context of protection could shift from simple mechanical tools to more ecological engineering, from confronting flame to controlling the fuels that shape flame—which is to say, to assuring that fire has the right habitat to do the biological work required of it without damaging humanity's own habitations. Certainly, reintroducing fire to a landscape that has lost it is akin to reintroducing a lost species; fire can only thrive if it has the proper setting. What is likely is that the search for a suitable biologically based strategy will integrate fire management with everything else that happens on the land.

It is improbable that the search for biological controls would plunge into the molecular level—it is hard to conceive of genetically modified fuels, for example—but in principle it is possible in ways that one cannot so imagine a genetically modified flood or ice storm. A biological theory could, however, redefine prescribed fire away from simple hazard reduction, as though fire were merely a flaming woodchipper. What matters is not merely fire's physical rearrangement of biomass but its biochemical reactions. The purpose of prescribed burning is to ensure that fire does the ecological work demanded of it;

the purpose of fuel management is to get that fire. (If all one wants is fuel reduction, there are plenty of techniques available other than burning.)

A biological theory of fire could recharter fire as a *bio*technology, one in which "control" depends on context. Some fires do behave as mechanical implements—a candle, say, or a blowtorch. But fires in the landscape take on the properties of their setting. A fire in agricultural fallow more resembles a sheep dog or a milk cow, a domesticated creature. A prescribed fire in wildlands is a captured ecological process, akin to a grizzly bear trained to dance. The mantra that "fire is a tool" contains little of these nuances, suggesting that one could substitute an ax or bulldozer for flame. One can't. Truly biotechnological treatments would thus range beyond slashing and fuel reduction burning, for whatever shapes fire's surroundings shapes fire, and fire's effects will vary with the biotic medium that sustains it. Integrated pest management is a better model of fire management than traditional firefighting.

A genuinely biological theory of fire would reposition our conception of what we ought to do (and not do) to promote fires we want and to prevent those we don't. It would encourage some big fires (of any provenance) because, in certain places, they are necessary, doing ecological work that nothing else can. But such a theory would also boost small fires (of any provenance) because they may be useful in smaller sites as a kind of fire gardening, an alternative to mindless mowing and the application of chemical herbicides and pesticides, allowing us to reinstate flame into vernacular as well as monumental landscapes. A biological theory of fire would reclassify such sites as fire niches and opportunities, while a mechanical conception lashed to the political constraints of the public lands would necessarily overlook such sites or view them only as points of infection from which wildfire might escape.

HOW PEOPLE COMPLETE THE CYCLE OF FIRE

More profoundly, a biological theory of fire would allow a place for ourselves as an ecological presence—in fact, as the biosphere's designated fire agent. Landscapes forged in anthropogenic fire would be the norm for understanding, and sites from which humans have chosen to absent themselves would become, properly, ecological outliers. No place is truly exempt from what people choose to do or not do regarding fire. Declaring places that are currently emptied of people as a core model for fire ecology belongs with physicists addicted to ideal frictionless surfaces; it simplifies the equations but does not describe the real world. For fire ecology as a form of scholarship it may make more sense to reverse past traditions: instead of beginning with a "wild" landscape and putting people in, it would be truer to begin with people and their fires and then see what happens when people and their fires are removed. The arguments for such a recentering of fire theory (or refocusing, *focus* being the Latin word for hearth) are two—one theoretical, the other practical.

The theoretical case is that we hold a species monopoly over fire's manipulation, that we very nearly close the circle of life for fire's cycle. Other creatures knock over trees, dig holes in the ground, eat plants, hunt: we do fire. This is who we are as ecological agents. We may choose to remove ourselves from the scene in select wilderness areas, but this is our choice, not a natural state for humanity, who tend to fill up (and overflow) every place they can get to. Removing ourselves from theory, however, is nonsense. No one would argue that we ought to delete lightning from fire ecology models because it complicates ignition rhythms, yet humans start many more fires than lightning. No one would suggest that we erase grazers and browsers from models of fire-frequented ecosystems since they muddy the fuel scene, yet people affect "fuels" far more than any other organism. No comprehensive theory can ignore how we conceive of the world and our place in it, any more than a grand unified theory of physics can ignore gravity, however inconvenient to quantum calculations. A biological theory of fire demands a place for ourselves.

The practical issue is that fire ecology includes the flow of ideas and information as much as carbon, and that institutions structure landscapes as fully as mountains and seasons. Because humans are such powerful fire agents—starting and stopping ignitions, forever fiddling with fuels—the means by which they decide what to do powerfully influence how fire appears on the land. People choose fire practices on the basis of what they know, and they act on those choices through institutions. The programmatic crashes in fire management that followed the 1988 Yellowstone fires illustrate nicely how a fire's effects can be broadcast through journals, reports, and government bureaus as well as through air, water, and soil. Whether they read the scene correctly or not, agencies shut down reforms and forced natural fire programs to start anew. Fire officers from Siberia to South Africa reconsidered their policies and practices in the light of how they understood (or misunderstood) what had happened in Yellowstone. By such means, landscapes far removed from the Northern Rockies felt the impact of Yellowstone's burns. This is as real as fire ecology gets.

Such a reconception of fire ecology that allows for—indeed, mandates—humanity's presence also creates a place for information. Ideas, data, misperceptions, beliefs—all these mold how people behave, directly with fire or indirectly with the landscape through which fire must act. Increasingly, information is the power behind fire applications. For decades, fire management has resembled a commodity economy, a coarse exchange between money and burned area. More and more, however, it has re-created itself as a kind of service economy, for which information has become the specie of circulation. Although the likely prospect is that fire management must become more, not less, intensive in the future, increased intensity need not simply mean more axes and pumps. It should mean denser data and contextual knowledge that can guide more specific decisions about particular places. Intensity of management will depend on intensity of information.

Lightning, torch, furnace; smoking snag, flaming fallow, combusting coal—through the agency of humanity as a fire creature these share a plenum of burning, an ultimately common ecology of fire, linked not only by the chemistry of oxidation but by our agency as fire creatures. Industrial combustion, in particular, exists only because humans tend it, and it interacts with other varieties of combustion through the medium of human societies.

It is more than odd that a creature with a species monopoly over fire should deny its own presence in theories about fire ecology, yet that has been the case, in good part because fire scholarship has meant fire science, and fire science has meant fire physics. The American fascination with wilderness has further clouded the issue by suggesting that fire ecology could be best understood in wilderness, unencumbered by human finagling, privileging wilderness fire as an archetype instead of an outlier. Permitting a place for ourselves would permit industrial fire to join the constellation of earthly combustion. Since today industrial fire is the dark attractor of planetary combustion, the deep driver of how and why fire looks as it does on Earth, this is not a trivial consideration. Without industrial fire, conceptions of fire ecology are both inept and incomplete.

Not least, industrial fire, which seems so abstracted from the living world, and which, encased in machines, would seem to argue powerfully for the physical character of fire, in fact challenges the assumption that physical parameters are paramount. The composite burning of both living and especially fossil biomass is progressing to the point that it is perturbing the global climate. At its core, global warming is a question of combustion, and of people. Which is to say that even climate can no longer be considered an absolute, a physical condition beyond the realm of anthropogenic fire practices to influence.

That is why the fire of life is more than a cliché or a metaphor of convenience. It is how we must reconceptualize those fires we want, those we dread, and those we hope to understand.

A SPIRAL DANCE

The Necessity of Fire to Wildness

MOLLIE MATTESON

WILDFIRE IS A KEY ECOLOGICAL PROCESS *in many natural communities. But it is also much more. Symbolically, fire epitomizes change and transformation, the unpredictable and uncontrollable essence of nature. Fire is wildness in motion. Human attempts to suppress fire threaten the spirit of wildness in nature, and the spirit of wildness in ourselves. At stake is nothing less than the connection of our own essential nature to that of Earth.*

▼

A swirling of wind, the darkening horizon. Heat. Air. Electricity. A storm sweeps across the parched land. A sudden surge of tremendous voltage, the sundering of air from air, the flashing path of light and heat. Sky to earth, earth to sky, an unbearably brilliant river of electrons flows back and forth in a fraction of a second. What is above roars and rumbles and builds momentum for the next explosive dive. What is below will receive the next transfusion of white-hot energy.

Somewhere in a forest below the vast western sky, this is the moment of death and the moment of birth. If the tinder is dry, the oils potent and volatile, the fuel abundant, a lightning bolt may become an agent of change. Heat becomes light, light becomes heat, heat becomes flame, flame unravels the molecules of a standing forest. A forest becomes a forest-on-fire.

The tempo of engagement increases exponentially. Molecules of oxygen and the carbon-based molecules of life move from their chemical slow waltz into a frenetic tarantella. Wind meets leaf, flame wraps stem, air heats and expands, rolling over the contours and curves of the recumbent Earth. Burning, the forest reveals itself in a new way. Its natural history—past fires, blowdowns, beetle kills, new growth and old growth, disease, disturbance, and change of all kinds and at all scales—interacts with this fierce and fast courier. The fire shifts, it grows or shrinks, in accord with the conditions of the moment and the many layers of past physical and biological events.

Few natural phenomena epitomize so spectacularly as wildfire the intimate connection between the raw elements and laws of the universe, and the complexity, adaptability, and resilience of life. Fire, where it is a dominant feature in a natural system, is as much a part of what defines a place as the community of species that live there, the topography, and the regional climate. Fire is also a force that defies easy mastery by humans. Fire is wild, it resists control, it cannot be manipulated or suppressed over the long term without significant, often unpredictable, consequences for the natural world and for people.

Both metaphorically and ecologically, fire is a transformative process. And yet it is in transformation that the whole is maintained. A fire-evolved natural system, whether it is a ponderosa pine forest in the Southwest, chaparral scrub in southern California, or a spruce-fir forest in the boreal north, is a spiral dance of recurring themes and patterns, vibrations and frequencies, particular structures, species, chemical reactions, nutrient and energy flows, directed and disciplined by the powerful, periodic appearance of fire.

Whether fire burns through a natural community once every 3 to 5 years on average, as in some southwestern ponderosa pine forests, or once every 200 to 400 years, as in the lodgepole pine forests of the Yellowstone Plateau, fire is the essential rhythm-keeper, the percussive element that sets the beat for the movement of life.

▼

In 1988, I was a wilderness ranger on the Gallatin National Forest, part of the Greater Yellowstone Ecosystem, in southwest Montana. It was my fourth summer of this work, and my second year on the Gallatin. My duties were simple. I hiked the trails and did light trail maintenance; I talked to backpackers and horse riders about "wilderness etiquette" and no-trace camping; I posted informational placards at trailheads, and generally patrolled the backcountry to ensure that all was well. Though I enjoyed the "visitor contact" aspect of my work well enough, I loved my job for the freedom it allowed me to be out in the mountains and to spend much of my time alone.

Since my first wilderness summer in Olympic National Park in the Pacific Northwest—an eager easterner dazzled by the big trees, the glaciers, the impossibly steep and endless mountains—I'd been impelled by something I could not fully articulate but which seemed vital and irresistible. I blazed up the trails and often left them for the high, wide spaces of the alpine zone. In the Wind River Range of Wyoming, I'd dashed up a forested trail during a thunderstorm so I could watch lightning flash about the circular theater of a rocky, treeless basin.

Ever since childhood, electrical storms excited something wordless and wondering in me, and in the Rockies in the summertime I found the perfect combination of high, dramatic mountains and frequent, intense, and cathartic storms. From the gradual building of the alabaster cloud pillars, to the increasingly restless, searching winds, and on to fury, explosion, hail and rain, and the release of titanic energies—it was an external elemental drama that mirrored the weather chamber of my heart. The passion of the earth was my own.

That second summer on the Gallatin began unremarkably. April and May were wetter than normal according to climate records, but by June the Yellowstone area was in a serious drought. Dry lightning sparked fires in the parched forests, but as is typical with most years, many of these wildfires went out on their own. What looked to be a somewhat more active fire season in mid-July shifted only a week or so later into something big and theatrical enough to draw national media attention. A number of dramatic days marked the last couple of months of that historic summer, but "Black Saturday" stood out: on August 20, more than 150,000 acres burned. Gale-force winds drove the flames, making the efforts of hundreds of firefighters, battalions of bulldozers, airplanes, helicopters and other machinery, and all the time-tested tactics of seasoned fire bosses pale into complete irrelevance.

As a Forest Service employee, my ranger duties that summer were increasingly shifted from backcountry to "frontcountry." As the fires heated up, Forest Service restrictions, and eventually an edict handed down from Montana's governor, closed the public lands to most recreational access. While no one could stop the lightning strikes, government could attempt to limit the numbers and activities of people, who through carelessness or stupidity or plain bad luck were the cause of some of the most severe fires of the year. By mid-August, instead of rambling on the trails and in the mountain meadows, I was mostly sitting in my truck, either driving around or staking out the entry points to key Forest Service roads.

One hot and windy afternoon, I was parked at a pullout in Paradise Valley watching a black bank of smoke and ash roiling over the ragged, silhouetted peaks of the Absaroka Range. The valley was wrapped in a surreal grayness, and the sun, the ultimate source of all this unleashed, hungry energy, was barred from view. The world had become a thick, dark, restless place, and there was no escaping the sense that the work and will of human beings were tiny, almost whimsical impulses in a universe moved by vast, ungraspable forces. I sensed that year that I had been graced with a rare privilege. A prolonged and grand spectacle of that sort comes once only every few centuries.

▼

Ultimately, just seven fires were responsible for 95 percent of the burned acreage in the Yellowstone ecosystem, and of these, three were human caused. Though I was a relative newcomer to the region in 1988, without years of memories to place against the sudden and dramatic changes that were wrought that summer, I can still go to particular sites in the park and recall the place as it was, before and after. There is not the feel of strangeness as there was the first few times I toured the park following the historic fires. But memory, nonetheless, seems to be a process of calling up snapshots or still images of the past, rather than moving pictures. There is the "old normal," and the "new normal," and while, if we are open-minded enough, we can allow ourselves to transition from one reality to the other, we struggle to see the process of change itself as the norm.

An attachment to averages and a steady-state way of being seems to run deep, at least in the Western mind. We like to think that the rules of existence put boundaries on events, on behavior, on the circumstances of time and chance. Yet, while much of life is lived within the neighborhood of the mean, by definition the unlikely or the infrequent does occasionally occur. In these "crisis" moments, we are apt to think something is unnatural and wrong. We want to stop it as soon as we can, and make sure it never happens again. But the constancy of change is a lesson that comes to all of us repeatedly, despite our individual and collective efforts to avoid this teaching.

The terror of wildness is its ability to toss us on our butts despite all our planning, intelligence, technology, and even good intentions. Life will kill you; one absolute certainty. Yet every day we resist. One could say that nearly the whole of modern technological society is dedicated to the attempt to overcome this truth.

But we are also in love with wildness. Certainly our affection for nature can be seen in a thousand ways on a daily basis, from our gardens, to our pets, to the popularity of visiting national parks and engaging in various recreational pursuits such as fishing or birdwatching. But these relatively docile expressions of our connection to the more-than-human world are not the whole of it. The yearning for life lived closer to the edge is manifested in sports such as mountaineering and whitewater kayaking, and in solo journeys across wild lands and the still-untamed oceans. The thrill of terrain that is hostile to human comfort or even survival is irrational, yet even the less adventurous among our species are tantalized and moved by the sight of ragged snow-draped mountains, precipitous canyons, and boiling volcanic craters. Such scenes stun, provoke, and hold our attention far beyond their actual relevance to our daily lives. Why?

Despite our predilections for ease and security, we are also fascinated with the kind of nature—and the experience of nature—that can overpower us. We not only appreciate a sense of awe, we actively seek it. Among the richest, most profound experiences that any of us as human beings may have are those in which we feel small, vulnerable, and yet strangely at peace, in the presence of something greater. It is the very mystery and irreducibility of that which is before us or which surrounds us that inspires our joy and reverence. In some, this feeling for the wild, natural world is fleeting. In others, it is a passion to shape an entire life. This spectrum of belief and experience is perhaps no different from any other aspect of human character and behavior, like varying degrees of proficiency in verbal expression, or athleticism. But I would argue that there is an undeniable element in the human spirit that longs for the wild, and in our quest for the security of the steady state in our external environment we are robbing our world of its power to awe us. We are diminishing our own inner world. That is the spiritual tragedy, to match the shackling and domestication of the wild earth.

Wildfire, storms, and other intense, violent natural events trigger the deepest instincts in our hearts. We are witness to something utterly foreign, without reason or explanation, something that blatantly belies the orderliness of our manufactured world. We are stunned into wonder.

▼

To speak in the most bold and generalizing terms, the arc of human existence has been one of ever-greater facility at the control of nature, yet accompanied—perhaps inextricably—by ever more grandiose and lethal hubris. The story is old, the lessons as elusive today as when Icarus fell to earth, the wax on his wings melted by the sun, a consequence of technological overreach and unheeding overconfidence.

The human impulse toward greater command over the uncertainty and limitations of life always begins with ideals and good intentions. Knowledge. Safety. Prosperity. With regard to the history of fire suppression in the West, the ostensible reasons for fighting fire are obvious, with antecedents as old as humanity itself: protection of home and family, and safeguarding of an economic resource.

Yet, if this were all that motivated the attempt to quell wildfire, there would not be an entire army of firefighters dispatched every summer to put out fires in remote, unpopulated locations on public lands, and in places where the cost of suppressing fire far exceeds any economic value that might be lost if fires were allowed to burn. When every year hundreds of firefighters are transported to the edge of active fires, rather than evacuating the few people that might be in harm's way, the logic of preserving human health and safety begins to crumble. Throughout the West, modest investments in proactively preparing fire-prone communities, such as clearing limited areas around the perimeters of towns, or requiring homeowners to put metal roofs on their houses, are nearly always far more effective defenses against human casualties and property loss than dumping firefighters into the middle of conflagrations thousands of acres in size and expecting them to put out the flames with their shovels. When periodically a "tragic" accident occurs, with young firefighters suddenly overrun by fire and smoke and unable to flee or take shelter, there are calls for reform, for alternatives to this costly, dangerous, and unnecessary government program. But true change cannot come without a change of heart.

The problems of fire suppression in the West—ecological, fiscal, or in terms of the cost to safety and human health—are not traceable, ultimately, to ineffective technology, poor budgeting, or bad judgment on the part of fire bosses placing their firefighters in the field. What is wrong with fire suppression is what is wrong with every other zealous, arrogant, and reckless approach to making the planet over to suit narrow human interests. It is extreme, it is based on a fundamental hostility to the natural world, and its unintended, unforeseen consequences are frighteningly expensive, environmentally destructive, and probably far worse, in the end, than the "problem" that was supposed to be solved.

But beyond even this, the dilemma of 100 years of fire suppression—and the ongoing attempt to actively, intrusively manage millions of acres of forests and other fire-associated ecosystems on western lands—is about the suppression of wildness. This is not so much an ecological or scientific problem as is it a spiritual crisis. Thus it is with all battles in the war against wild nature. Not so very different are the wars we have carried out against wolves, mountain lions, and other predators, or the ways we've attempted to imprison and enslave rivers with systems of dams, levees, and other barriers.

We are left not only with new dilemmas we had not anticipated, but with a kind of pervasive dullness. The world simplified and made safer is no longer so interesting, nor so beautiful. If we are sensitive and curious, we notice not only the obvious scars of human control but the subtle absences. We notice that even after a fire, a forest silhouetted in the moonlight is a lovely and magical place. In contrast, no matter how luminescent the sky above, a forest raked by bulldozers and explosive lines and dotted with chain-sawed stumps will not appear ethereal. It is, at best, a wounded landscape, awaiting the balm of time.

Fire destroys and it transforms. Metaphorically, it seems initially a process of erasure. Yet, fire is the active memory of an ecosystem, touching what is, and remembering, renewing, and recycling what time otherwise might have taken away. Wildfire is as much a part of our western forests as the trees themselves. Much the same could be said of other fire-associated natural communities.

Thus it comes down to this: If what we wish for are wild forests, with all that implies in terms of diversity, beauty, and self-regulation, we will not attempt to control that which defines the essence of their wildness. And if we think we can have all the loveliness, magic, and awe-inspiring power of our natural landscapes—their spiritual aspects, in short—while at the same time dictating energy flow and the basic dynamics of change upon them through our rapacity or our management, or both—we are arrogant fools.

The attempt to end wildfire, or even to merely tame it, is misguided on ecological grounds. But beyond this error is another one, harder to recognize, but no less tragic in its implications for our human future. Kill what is wild in the world, and we kill what is wild in us. What is wild in us is hard to name, because as with all wild things, it is elusive. Yet, to say it is our genius, our spark, our wonder, and our capacity for ecstasy is to come close. It is our longing for connection. Some would call it our soul.

FIRE AND NATIVE PEOPLES

A Natural or Humanized Landscape?

THOMAS R. VALE, PH.D.

THE ONCE-POPULAR VISION OF THE PRE-EUROPEAN *United States as "pristine," as a natural landscape, has been largely replaced by the view that the precontact country was "humanized" by native peoples. While having merit, the contemporary emphasis on ubiquitous human agency is overstated: large parts of the United States, particularly in the American West, may have been essentially natural, their landscapes characterized by processes of nature rather than people.*

▼

A human society hewed from a state of nature, from a wild landscape, from a wilderness—for two centuries, this vision had been central to the creation myth of the United States. Increasingly over the last decades, however, this image has been challenged, even rejected, and replaced by the conviction that the pre-European landscape of the country was modified by Native Americans.[1] Tilling rows of maize and squash, raising houses of mud bricks or tree bark, constructing mounds and terraces, harvesting wild rice and acorns, hunting deer and rabbits, digging fern roots for fiber or cutting shrub stems for arrow shafts, igniting fires over prairie, chaparral, and forest—all of these activities are seen as having altered nature, creating a humanized landscape. The old vision of the great American wilderness has been declared a falsehood, and to the degree that we continue to believe in such an ideal, we are told that we embrace a myth, the "myth of the pristine landscape."[2]

Certainly, the older wilderness imagery needed qualification—Native Americans did affect biodiversity at the local scale and, in some areas, probably modified ecosystems at the regional scale. But to portray the continent at the time of European contact, from the Atlantic to the Pacific and from the Great Lakes to the Rio Grande, as a vast scene of agricultural fields, expansive villages, raised terraces, carefully tended plants, coppiced shrubs, depressed game numbers, and burned-over forest—in total, a landscape so altered that its characteristics were a consequence more of human agency than of natural process—is to engage in blanket imagery of another sort. Lest we be labeled antiquarian for holding onto an idée fixe, perhaps we desert our former convictions too unequivocally in our rush to embrace this "idée nouveau." We have simply replaced the old myth with a new one: the "myth of the humanized landscape."

The replacement of one landscape vision by another is eased by the ambiguity of the critical, defining words.[3] For example, *pristine* could mean no human effect or simply little human impact. It might generate a mental image of a landscape without any humans in view, or one with people but whose presence modifies the scene only minimally. It could stress either ecological criteria—have humans changed the characteristics of nature?—or psychological/humanistic standards—does the landscape mean anything, regardless of the degree to which people have modified natural features, to those who interact with it? It could connote an objectified and distanced natural scene or a landscape of home. Endless debate reverberates among those with differing meanings in mind. Whatever the intellectual virtues of that debate, a common and casual definition will be pursued here: a *"state of nature," a "pristine landscape," a "wilderness condition" means, simply, that the fundamental characteristics of vegetation, wildlife, landform, soil, hydrology, and climate are those of natural, nonhuman processes, and that these conditions would exist whether or not humans are present.* Given this criterion, a landscape might be judged, through empirical and scientific effort, to be, in whole or in part, pristine or humanized.

Assessments to understand where, how, and to what degree the pre-European landscape was a product of people and their activities need to be undertaken, unencumbered by commitment to a notion of the ubiquity of human agency. For some areas, this empirical assessment will be easier than for others; for many places, serious ambiguities will remain. I would guess, nonetheless, that the evidence will suggest that the model of the pristine landscape will have applicability in certain locales—most likely (although not exclusively) in the western states, where, compared with the eastern parts of the country, smaller numbers of nonagricultural peoples inhabited landscapes more prone to lightning fires. More specifically (although not restrictively), I might further predict that the American wilderness will remain most appropriate as a vision in those very areas long admired for their perceived character as "natural," the units of the national park system and the wilderness areas on the national forests—disproportionately represented by landscapes of high elevation, of mountain and ice, of rock and canyon, of low biological productivity, of flammable vegetation, of only seasonal human occupancy. Whether they actually represent pristine conditions and whether landscapes of other characteristics truly were humanized are matters to be evaluated with scientific assessment.

ECOLOGICAL UNDERSTANDING: A NATURAL YOSEMITE?

A place to explore the applicability of the dichotomous views of "pristine" and "humanized" landscapes is one of the icons of protected nature, Yosemite National Park. My purpose here is not to make a full assessment of Yosemite, declaring it to be natural; rather, it is to suggest, judging from existent knowledge, that the Yosemite landscape at the time of European contact could well have been mostly pristine, mostly a product of natural, rather than human, processes, or, at the very least, that its landscape was a mixture of pristine and humanized conditions.

The contrary perspective, the belief that Yosemite of either 1492 or 1851 (the year of its formal discovery by outsiders) was a humanized landscape, has become the conventional wisdom. Landscape scholar Kenneth Olwig, for example, talks of the "environmental stewardship" of "Indian gamekeepers" who regularly burned Yosemite Valley not only to improve habitat for certain mammals, but also for "field games."[4] (Olwig, then, makes Yosemite analogous to Three Rivers Stadium or Lambeau Field!) Similarly, cultural historian Rebecca Solnit describes the landscape of Yosemite Valley as "transformed" by the native Miwok people, who both "burned the meadows" and "gathered its largesse . . . there never was a wholly 'natural' landscape there."[5] Perhaps ethnoecologist N. Kat Anderson and ethnobotanist Gary Nabhan express the most strident view:

> These Yosemite landscapes [were] shaped by centuries of Indian
> burning, pruning, sowing, weeding, coppicing, tillage, and selec-
> tive harvesting. . . . Not only the Yosemite trails [John Muir]
> walked upon but the vegetation mosaic he walked through were
> the legacy of Miwok subsistence ecology.[6]

Native Americans themselves espouse the dogma; after describing former Indian villages in Yosemite Valley, a modern Miwok proclaims his
people's devotion to "care of the land . . . the so-called wilderness was
being looked after by the Indians for thousands of years."[7]

These assertions of widespread humanization are questionable.
First, they focus on the small valley called Yosemite, rather than the
expansive mountainous landscape that surrounds it. The 1,813 hectares
comprising Yosemite Valley—one of the few areas in the park where
Indians occupied permanent settlements—are not characteristic of
most of the 303,305 hectares of Yosemite National Park, through
which Indians passed as transients or entered only seasonally; even if
Indian activities "transformed" the valley, it is not necessarily the case
that such transformation occurred elsewhere.

Second, the mere acts of "pruning" a bigleaf maple (*Acer macro-
phyllum*) "so that it will produce straight, sienna-hued sprouts" or digging "rhizomes of a bracken fern"[8] do not necessarily mean that
Yosemite Valley's fundamental ecological character or basic landscape
appearance was altered from what would have existed in the absence
of these subsistence people. On the other hand, a definition of wilderness that precludes any human imprint whatsoever, however modest,
would render Yosemite Valley as humanized by these activities.

A third observation involves the reference to a human activity
that is always the crucial cog in the humanized landscape argument—
Indian burning. Clearly, the Miwok set fires in Yosemite Valley. To
note this, however, is not sufficient to support the claim that such
burning altered the fundamental character of the landscape, either in
the valley or in the park more generally. A more accurate assessment
should ask whether the human ignitions were in addition to, rather
than a substitution for, natural ignitions, and whether fires set by
Indians changed the landscape from that which otherwise would have
existed.

For Yosemite, even a cursory look at appropriate ecological data suggests that the pre-European fire regime in the national park might be mostly attributable to natural factors. Almost two-thirds (61.2 percent) of the park area—the higher-elevation red fir (*Abies magnifica*) and lodgepole pine (*Pinus contorta*) forests, and all of the subalpine and alpine environments—burned rarely, if at all, in spite of fairly common lightning ignitions;[9] this absence of fire suggests that the condition of the vegetation—a natural factor—determined the fire regime, not the number or the source of ignitions. The lower-elevation chaparral and mixed-conifer forest (totaling 37.8 percent of the park area) burned frequently, with return times of a decade or two documented for these vegetation types both in Yosemite and elsewhere in the Sierra Nevada.[10] Over the last 2,000 years, in the southern Sierra, tree-ring analysis indicates temporal variability in these fire frequencies, with burning closely tracking weather conditions—an indication that natural factors, not humans, determined fire occurrence.[11]

Over the last century, in Yosemite National Park, the formal record of lightning fires suggests that natural ignitions might account for the fire regime: For the period 1930–1983, in the lower-elevation vegetation types of the park, fires averaged 187 per decade (as mentioned above, 10 years is the approximate return time for fires in these types); actual fires might have been more numerous, moreover, because of less sophisticated detection methods in the 1930s and 1940s.[12] Lightning fires in the national forests adjacent to Yosemite's western boundary (the forests include the same vegetation types that occur in the park, although the proportion of low-elevation forest and brush is larger) add to the total number of ignitions that might have burned park land in the absence of fire suppression: 475 per decade for the Stanislaus National Forest and 977 per decade for the Sierra National Forest.[13] Even without fire suppression, not all of these ignitions would have resulted in large areas of burned landscape, with previously burned vegetation a critical constraint to the spread of fires,[14] a fact that again hints that natural factors determined the basic fire regime. Overall, then, the number of ignitions from lightning was high; whether ignitions caused by Native Americans altered the natural fire regime in Yosemite in a way that changed the fundamental appearance of the landscape, either regionally or locally, is a question.

Still, it may be possible that small areas were burned more frequently by the Miwok, resulting in local humanized landscapes;
Yosemite and Hetch Hetchy valleys would have been the most likely
such locales. Perhaps the valley bottom meadows and the surrounding
forests, close to permanent settlements, burned more frequently as a
consequence of Indian ignitions than did the regional vegetation; such
a pattern of increased burning close to Indian villages would be consistent with at least some interpretations elsewhere.[15] As in other matters of Indian impacts, empirical work could help resolve the question
of the spatial patterns of naturalness in the landscape.

Other Miwok activities may or may not have altered the basic
character of the Yosemite landscape. The agricultural plots and constructed earthworks that characterized the native cultures in the mid-
western prairies and some of the eastern forests of the United States
were not elements of the indigenous people of Yosemite. Their dependence on the acorns of the oaks, especially those of California black oak
(*Quercus kelloggii*), is indisputable, although even if the Miwok
planted and tended the oak groves, it was an activity restricted to a
modest part of Yosemite Valley and perhaps a few other locales elsewhere. Local modifications to the forms of some shrubs or the occurrences of certain herbaceous species would similarly seem most likely
near villages. The Miwok hunted deer and other mammals, but
whether such harvesting changed the long-term numbers of animals or
whether those altered populations in turn influenced the vegetation
cover would be speculation.

An unequivocal alteration of the park landscape associated with
native peoples was the building of settlement structures. Certainly,
some villages were impressively substantial—bark-covered shelters in
winter; cone-shaped brush shelters in summer; "large, semi-subter-
ranean dance or assembly houses, forty to fifty feet in diameter, dug to
a depth of three or four feet"; circular sweathouses; granaries for acorn
storage; and small conical grinding houses.[16] Such settlements were,
nevertheless, restricted to a few locales in the lower-elevation environments of the park, particularly parts of Yosemite and Hetch Hetchy
valleys, Wawona, Big Meadow, and Lake Eleanor.[17] Even within
Yosemite Valley, village sites seem to have been highly localized; the
largest was "below Yosemite Falls and stretched southwest for three-

fourths of a mile"; other settlements lay just to the east, "in the largest tract of open, level ground . . . at the mouth of Indian Canyon."[18]

Away from these village sites, occupancy was ephemeral. Archaeological surveys have found artifacts—typically projectile points, other rock tools, and features associated with seed grinding—in many locales elsewhere in the park. Archaeologist James Bennyhoff in his classic survey of the archaeological resources of Yosemite, identified former Indian camp sites, occupied only temporarily and seasonally, by the presence of obsidian flakes on the ground surface and the lack of numerous mortar holes (which for him suggested a house or village); he documented 188 such "camp" sites in the park, mostly in the higher elevations.[19] The total area represented by all of these 188 sites was less than 260 hectares, compared with about 187,800 hectares of high-elevation terrain in the park; these Indian camp sites may be comparable to the area used by campers in the Yosemite backcountry today. Moreover, the environmental alteration of most of these camping locations was modest: Two-thirds of these sites necessitated a "lengthy search . . . to obtain any sizeable sample of obsidian flakes," indicating to Bennyhoff a "small camp" used infrequently. In sum, humanized settlements, whether villages or camp sites—however important from an archaeological perspective, however effective in evoking a sense of the Miwok past—were obviously extremely localized.

In total, the map of Yosemite National Park reflects a mixed picture of "pristine" and "humanized" landscapes. Village sites were substantially humanized by the everyday life of Indians; groves of oaks or stands of bracken fern may have been modified in form or extent, for variable lengths of time, by native peoples; some areas of low-elevation meadows and forests could have been altered by Miwok burning, although lightning fires seem adequate to account for the pre-European fire regime; the middle and higher elevations, by contrast, were changed only superficially by Indian peoples. Even given the most generous interpretation of what was "humanized," much of the park was "natural"—in the sense that its landscape characteristics were determined by natural processes. With a more conservative interpretation of "humanized," most of Yosemite was natural, was wilderness.

Overall, then, the model of primeval nature—a nature molded by nonhuman forces—seems realistic for at least part, and perhaps much, of Yosemite National Park. In other landscapes, it may or may not be applicable. The landscapes of villages and agricultural fields in parts of the East and Southwest clearly were humanized—the characteristics of such areas were substantially modified from what would have existed in the absence of humans.[20] So too, for the tallgrass prairie and savannah of the Upper Midwest, where the frequent burning essential to the maintenance of those systems seems to have required Indian ignitions.[21] The pine forests of the Southeast, where lightning fires are more common than in the Northeast, present a more ambiguous situation—might the pre-European fire regime have been controlled by natural processes, or was it partly influenced by Indian burning? Other parts of the eastern forests may have been changed from what would have existed in the absence of Native Americans,[22] but the impacts of indigenous peoples "were still localized. . . . [with large areas] almost devoid of Indian activity."[23] The grasslands on the Great Plains existed even before the arrival of humans on the continent,[24] indicating that the basic ecosystem structure of that large area was not a consequence of Native American activity. Within the nonagricultural, sparsely settled forests of the West, the fire regimes— whether very infrequent crown fires or more common ground fires[25]— easily might have been a consequence of natural, rather than human, processes. The same seems likely for the West's vast shrubby vegetation types. The general point, then, is that the pre-European landscape of the United States was not monolithically humanized, not "a managed landscape, much of its look and ecology the product of the human presence,"[26] but, rather, a patchwork, a mosaic, at varying scales, of pristine and humanized conditions. A natural American wilderness, an environment fundamentally molded by nature, did exist. Just where and how much is an ecological question, subject to empirical investigation.

SOCIAL IDEOLOGY: RATIONALE FOR THE HUMANIZED LANDSCAPE

The desire to see a humanized landscape in the pre-European scene, whether in Yosemite or elsewhere, may be prompted by commitment to a certain social ideology. Several concerns manifest that commitment.

First, to envision the impacts of Native Americans as ubiquitous and fundamental is to grant them their basic humanity, to make them one with other people, particularly those who have transformed the country's landscapes over the last 200 years.[27] Second, to see indigenous Americans as modifiers of the landscape of 1492 also incorporates them into history, recognizing their presence and completing the view of the past.[28] Third, this historical inclusion legitimizes the native peoples' claims, both legal and emotional, to the land.[29] Fourth, the assertion that pre-European people humanized the landscape reinforces the argument favoring active ecosystem manipulation and undermines "natural regulation."[30]

A fifth intellectual stance asserts that Native Americans—whether pre-European or contemporary—and nonnatives view the wild landscape in distinctive ways. These differing perspectives are sometimes characterized as polar opposites, contrasting through the seeing of a detached, objective wilderness—a landscape of recreation—and through the viewing of personal, subjective home—a landscape of everyday living. Such a polarity frames many modern issues involving people and nature: the absence of "land wisdom" among those in modern society and the "stewardship" among indigenous peoples;[31] the seeing of nature only in wilderness, which remains distant and apart, and the ignoring of nature in the familiar and everyday;[32] the culturally learned aesthetic reaction to place—associated with the visual sense, public symbolism, and scenes that command human attention—and the personally experienced "field of care" reaction to place—linked to various senses, private familiarity, and settings that evoke individual affection.[33]

MODERN WILDERNESS:
A LANDSCAPE FOR RECREATION OR AS HOME?

For some observers, the concerns stemming from social ideology so dominate the interpretation of contemporary wilderness that any enthusiasm for the pristine or the natural suggests superficiality, relegating that enthusiasm to the impulse for recreation rather than for everyday living. But such characterization belittles the diversity of the modern experience. The contemporary visitors to Yosemite, for example, include those for whom the wild landscape, through all the senses, is intimately known and emotively valued. Examples from written sources, even in just the last few years, abound.

Ranger-naturalist Will Neeley reflects that "the mountains have become familiar and have revealed pattern and form . . . never before have I felt so at ease with them. . . . I was intoxicated with [them]."[34] His fellow naturalist Carl Sharsmith developed "a love of nature so cultivated, so refined, so carved by wind and shined by dew that it has become a treasure."[35] Yosemite artist Steven Lyman "knew the value of time in a place . . . to be comfortable in the adversity of the elements, which he saw as natural processes to experience and embrace."[36] Concessionaire worker Howard Weamer "wondered last night, watching the ridge go black and white in the dusk, whether I had seen it too often . . . [but] it's still very exciting, just familiar."[37] Long-time Yosemite author Shirley Sargent, thinking back to her childhood, formed a multisensed image of a distant landscape of affection: "It was felt in the cool July breeze, seen in the expansive, river-cut meadows . . . heard in the sound of rushing water, bird-cry and wind . . . scented in the pine-needled image of the Sierra."[38]

Summer visitors from a variety of non-Indian cultures similarly express the warmth that comes from knowing the Yosemite landscape; a volunteer laborer "having been enriched by Yosemite many years . . . [found] it was a pleasure 'to give something back,'"[39] and a journal writer found herself "reminiscing about the mountain terrain that our group has moved through—and that has moved through me."[40] Can John Muir's knowledge of, and bonding to, the Yosemite landscape be ignored? Or David Brower's?[41] Might I include my own familiarity with and love of this special place?[42] The failure to recognize such reactions stigmatizes contemporary people, leaving the wilderness landscape forever removed from intimate human knowledge and warmth, leaving the wilderness visitor forever "a person who does not belong, a stranger in Paradise."[43] Such omission creates a stereotype no more valid than that of the uncaring savage: For at least some, perhaps many, Americans, even those lacking an Indian heritage, wilderness is a part of home.

A MIDDLE GROUND

The pre-European landscape of North America was both pristine and humanized, varying through space and time, varying in degrees of conformity to the extreme conditions of the purely naturalistic and the purely anthropogenic. Similarly, the present-day wilderness is both a landscape for "the stranger in Paradise" and a home place, a "field of care." It is oversimplification to treat the two dichotomies of pristine/humanized and stranger/homebody as if they were categorically exclusive, as if we were choosing up sides for a game of kickball. Decisions about the management of our natural areas should involve a thoroughness of context that recognizes the ecological models of both the pristine and humanized landscapes, and attempts to disentangle the applicability of each through ecological assessment—as well as the humanistic reactions—in all of their varied richness, whether in the past or the present—to wildness, to naturalness. We need more than blind and unthinking allegiances to ecological myth or social ideology.

COYOTE WILDFIRE

Evolving Firefighters into Fire Guiders

JOE FOX, PH.D.

WHY DO MANY FIREFIGHTERS KNOWINGLY PARTICIPATE *in work that may be destructive to the wildlands they love? Perhaps they are similar in effect and spirit to earlier explorers who naively tamed the wilderness. Although dispatched to domesticate wildfire, many wildland firefighters hope for the day they can turn the work that they love toward restoring natural fire in the places they revere.*

▼

*C*resting a battered ridgeline we plunge into shambled canyons of Salmon River country during late August of the last century. We follow the wispy trails of smoke from the spur ridge. Faces pressed against the small windows of our ancient DC-3, we peer down onto this fire. Each smokejumper calculates a thousand elements of logistics and the tactics of attack, escape, vanquish, and return home. Lazily circling this fire—our prey—the airplane's broad buzzard wings fan the sky above while its shadow bumps the rocks and trees of the gnarled terrain below. For a while we didn't believe we would find this little "two-manner" fire, but as we got closer, we could see it stirring in its refuge. If left alone, this fire could become a destructive dragon, possibly reaching cataclysmic proportions. Presently, it is a hatchling—a pathetic little fire absurdly and optimistically gnawing on the base of a big ponderosa pine, scavenging abundant downfall, and gobbling up the too-slowly rotting duff. We have successfully hunted this fire. Now we are going to kill it.*

Our airplane pitches and yaws, batted by thunder cells and the plural effects of unstable air flowing over mountain country. A cacophony of engine roar and howling torrent of air claws through the gape of our large open door. We descend to take a low pass 100 feet above

treetop to stare this fire in the eye, to get its mark, to measure its feroc-
ity and potential. The spotter juts his head out into the slipstream. The
first jumper stands above him, at the threshold. One unmatched
g-force, one erratic buffet, and either could careen out of the door.
Their parachutes would not open in time.

I think of those unresolved questions that entangle us in justifications
for our perilous work. We jumpers have endless conversations about
the work we do during the long nights of watching a vast, dying wildfire hiss and spark into a hundred thousand twinkling embers that
reflect the inscrutable starry night. We recognize two elements of a
blunt syllogism that challenges the work we do; yet we can't seem to
muscle out the consequences that should direct our destiny. First, we
acknowledge that we cherish the wildlands and love the work we do.
Second, we recognize that, as initial attack specialists, we are the tip of
the spear for fire suppression policy. When we indiscriminately suppress fires, we destroy the positive effects of fire regimes that promote
a low fuel load in wildlands. We destroy those beneficial fires that
merely prune the branches of large trees and kill the overcrowded competing brush and small trees. The cumulative effects of our successful
work may be contributing to unnatural catastrophic wildfires that
threaten to vaporize our beloved forests.

Ergo, should we abandon the work we love because that work
helps to destroy the places we love? Instead we ask introspective questions that avoid contemplation of duty and consequences. What draws
us to this sort of job in this sort of place? What sort of people are we
wildland firefighters?

Our antediluvian DC-3, stalwart mule of World War II, pulls up and
ascends. G-forces drain every sense of strength from our bodies and
make our heavy padded protective jump gear seem like tight swaddling
clothes. The spotter barks observations to the pilot through the micro-
phone in his helmet. He and the first jumper shout above the roar of
wind and engine. They make decisions about fire suppression tactics,
the jump spot, how many will jump, and where the smokejumpers will
hike out after the fire is dead. The spotter jerks up four fingers, catch-
ing the fixed gaze of the anticipating smokejumpers. A four-manner. I
am number three on the jump list, so I will be leaping this fire.

The spotter drops to his hands and knees and with his head out of the open door aligns the pilot to fly over the jump spot. He drops several drift streamers—each 20 feet of brightly colored crepe paper weighted with a few ounces of sand. By measuring the drift from where the streamers were dropped to where they land, the spotter judges how far to carry the jumpers into the wind past the jump spot before signaling them to jump. I look hard at the jump spot as we pass over it. It's the best clearing nearest the fire. Yet it is filled with huge boulders and scattered logs, and is punctuated by broken dead trees that marshal an angry fortress defiant against our aerial invasion. Hefty snags and tall, brittle-looking trees surround the clearing. Brutal. Because the thunder cells are so close, the airplane is bucking like a horse with a burr under its saddle. I pull on my fireproof Nomex gloves, snap my personal gear bag onto my body harness so that it tethers at my thighs, squeeze on my crash helmet, and close its steel mesh visor. I hook my static line, the tether that jerks open the parachute as we jump, to the overhead cable. Then I slouch toward the open door.

We are reminded of the forces that draw us into this work every time the chaotic sirens wail, triggering our automatic rush to put on gear and go whooping to board the thundering airplane. Our work propels us across the threshold that rifts civilization from the wildlands. Jaunting deep into the wilderness, we easily forget the equivocal nature of our mission and the decisiveness of our dispatch. Journeying to this fire, we bounced along craggy Rocky Mountain peaks until we reached the deep gorges of the Salmon River. There we saw the rumpled landscape of timeless rocks and steep slopes piled into a blood-red horizon. En route to other fires in Oregon and Washington we have seen distant majestic forests mantling stunning volcanoes that cleave azure skies. Sometimes we see elk herds undulate directly below. In Alaska we have seen the endless oxbows of the Yukon River braiding the soft verdant carpet of tundra and myriads of conical spruce trees scattered below. Occasionally we see wolves so absorbed in their hunt that they seem oblivious to the blare of low-flying aircraft. In Utah, New Mexico, and Colorado we see wind-eroded red rock, forests covering the flat mesas above, the tawny desert yawning out below—all beneath a universe of omnipotent sky.

There are four reasons why wildland firefighters are drawn to this job, although each may prioritize the motives differently. One is the hero status. The public recognizes that the constant and intense danger of the work requires sustained bravery matched by few other jobs. Then there is the camaraderie. Strong and deep friendships are natural outcomes of the exigencies and hardships. And there is the money. A wildland firefighter can sometimes make over $20,000 in a four-month season. (Ironically, this is also about the cost of two and a half fire retardant drops, or eight hours of helicopter flight time.) And finally, there is the idealism—the sense that we enter the wilderness with a selfless, communal purpose. To many firefighters this is the driving motivation above all else. To go to these wild places and see these sights makes the heart soar and the mind forever grateful. Yearning souls behold the sacred.

The airplane crabs and rolls, then straightens for the final run. The first jumper stands poised in the three-by-five-foot open door. Tense and ready, he is like a sprinter in the blocks. Behind him, his jump partner tries to hold his position amid the turmoil of the lunging airplane. The spotter pulls in his head, removes his hand from the first jumper's left foot, pauses a couple of seconds, then slaps the jumper on the back of the thigh. Out leaps the first jumper. His vault explodes through the obliterating slipstream. The shearing static line answers with an immediate crack. The second jumper follows within three seconds. The spotter shoots his head out again to gauge their descent and progress. The assistant spotter heaves in the parachute deployment bags, like a fisherman pulling up a heavy net. I wait for the signal from the spotter, then place my foot at the threshold and watch the prior jumpers desperately try to get into the jump spot as the airplane hooks around and levels out. On the next pass my partner and I will hurtle out the door through the violent pressure seal of the slipstream into a searing bright sky and fall to a jagged earth below.

What sort of people are we wildland firefighters? We find no escape from the consequences of our work. Every remote biome we enter suffers the impact of our fire suppression. We tangle with the ethical dilemmas in the rooty kinnikinnick thickets of Idaho and Montana. We ponder their ramifications in the smoldering peat bogs of the Alaskan tundra. We wrestle with them again in the thorny, flinty terrain of Utah pinyon-juniper-sagebrush territory.

Perhaps we are the wanderers of *Moby Dick*: when we feel that "cold November" in our souls, we must take to the air and hunt fires, like hunting mammoth whales, to refrain from knocking the hats off of every stranger we meet on the street. Sometimes I think our work may fit the phylogeny of Frederick Jackson Turner's *The Frontier in American History*. Turner suggested that the frontier served as an outlet for those malcontents who could not suffer the restraints of civilization, and mapped out a sort of Heisenberg-uncertainty-principle irony: to experience the untamed lands one has to touch them; when touched they change, so one cannot experience again the unadulterated phenomenon. Reflecting this irony, perhaps we wildland firefighters also generate that from which we seek to escape. Many thoughtful wildland firefighters loathe the stultifying aspects of civilization, and to flee its goading miseries we must plunge into the purity of the wilderness. But our fire suppression transforms the wilderness into the managed landscapes we love less and makes it more readily accessible to other tribulations of civilization.

The plane wobbles, bounces, and then powers up to prevent stalling. "Get ready, get set!" shouts the spotter. His slap on the back of my thigh triggers my bolt out through the concussion of the slipstream. I hold a tight position—knees slightly bent, feet down, chin on chest, hands on reserve—all while wind, speed, and gravity tear at me. "Four, five . . ." As I count, the parachute opens like a rifle shot, jerking me upward. I look up into the billowing material to find the reassurance of a proper opening—that no great rifts have formed, no material has ripped away.

Pulling the toggles to steer my parachute, I turn the chute around and view my jump partner behind me. He is twisted. His shroud lines, stretching from his body harness to his canopy, have coiled into a tight cable. Instead of an ice cream cone, he silhouettes as a mushroom. Because he cannot steer, it is not a good situation. I toggle and steer my parachute to test the wind drift. I am not drifting down as quickly as I should be. I am in an updraft—an inevitable part of thunder cells. The two jumpers who leapt before us have overrun the jump spot. One chute is high in a tree; the other is scattered in broken snags near the ground. I face into the wind and hold. My jump partner untwists and does the same. As we approach the edge of the jump spot, we hit a severe downdraft—another inevitable part of thunder cells. The jump spot becomes an impossibility as we sink so rapidly. Despite desperate attempts at steering, we are pretty much just aerial plankton. To hit the ground descending at this rate risks serious injury.

The trees that await my landing are a mixed blessing. They could cushion my fall. However, they present an extreme danger: a collision with a tall tree could collapse the parachute and cause me to free-fall to the ground. Branches and needles suddenly envelope me. I hear limbs snapping and tearing my parachute. I'm jerked one way and then the other. Debris hails down on me and a good-three-inch-diameter branch slaps the top of my helmet. I shout out to let my jump partner know my location. He hoots in response. We're both treed-up.

I clear loose branches and shroud lines away from me and reach into my right pant-leg pocket to pull out 10 feet of the 120-foot letdown line. I thread it under my leg, through the friction links sewn on my protective jumper pants, and then to the parachute risers that connect the shroud lines to my body harness. Opening my quick-release fasteners frees me of the parachute, and I rappel down the letdown line 70 feet to the ground. I hustle out of my jump gear, grab my personal gear bag, and sprint to the jump spot.

Here the DC-3 strafes in, 100 feet above the treetops, and kicks cargo. The quick-deployment cargo chutes immediately snap open. The rectangular cardboard cargo boxes that hold our tools, food, water, and sleeping bags resemble floating coffins as they descend, but to us they look like Christmas presents drifting under billows of colorful ribbons and bows. Most of the cargo boxes hit the ground, but a couple of the five-gallon water boxes hang up in trees that surround the jump spot.

What sort of people are we wildland firefighters? Some are compulsive adrenaline junkies I call "thrill riders." To the thrill riders everything about wildland firefighting is exciting. The next fire is the steeper ski run, the swifter rapids, the harder rock climb. Those that remain thrill riders throughout their wildfire careers seldom have any interest in exploring the consequences of their work. They fail to ponder the rightness of what they do, or whether they should be doing it. They just don't care about such things, so they remain guiltless.

Other wildland firefighters I call "good soldiers." They are similar in makeup to policemen, urban firefighters, and military servicemen. "Good soldiers" are proud to be protectors of the public's wildlands. They assume that wildland fire management policy is ideal, and that their leaders always know exactly what should be done. Duty dictates adherence to protocol. They are rarely at a loss as to what to think or do and remain untroubled when protocol contradicts itself, because they often fail to see the inconsistency. Given a few years on the job, however, many good soldiers become cynical about management's motives, decisions, and intelligence. They, as do many of the thrill riders, slip over into the group I call the "wilderness wanderers."

The ethos of the wilderness wanderers is wrapped up in their relationship with unbounded wilds. Perhaps they need permission to encroach there, or need a mission to rationalize their intrusion into aboriginal country. Wilderness wanderers have spent many meditative hours gazing down at pristine wildlands from low-flying aircraft. To their secular spirituality the rough-hewn mountain peaks rising above piles of imperfect forests, the gnarled snags with perching hawks and eagles, and the relentless underbrush are mystic temples embodying the sacred. As they grow older, wilderness wanderers begin to hate the savage gapes of roads that forever scar the mountainsides. Many wildland firefighters become at some level wilderness wanderers, tethered to the life of entering sacred landscapes with a shared purpose.

At the jump spot, we quickly cut open the cargo boxes and grab food, water, and pulaskis, the favored hand tool of wildland firefighters, as it combines an ax with a grubbing hoe. Then we head to the fire. The first jumper is the fire boss for this incident. He radios the spotter in the airplane, relates our size-up of the fire, and determines the amount of people or supplies needed. We first go after places that appear to have the most potential for spreading fire. Using a chain saw or the ax end of the pulaski, we cut away ladder fuels that could route fire to the forest canopy—brush and small trees and the lower branches of larger trees. We cool down hot and sparking piles of burning downfall with showers of dirt. Then we use the grub end of the pulaski to dig out the fire line. We clear away organic debris and surround the fire with a shallow, one-foot-wide trench dug down to mineral soil. This is nearly the toughest part of firefighting, surpassed only by the packout with our 120 pounds of jump gear, cargo, and tools.

If we are not too exhausted by rooty soil, deep duff, or losing the fire to the heat of the day, wind, and low humidity, we sometimes discuss academic concepts while we work. Topics we don't have time for in graduate school. Yet these issues seem to mingle in the empyreal vapor released by wildfires.

Here is the irony. We wilderness wanderers imagine we can escape the deadening travails of civilization by leaping into wildlands. Yet we irrevocably trammel the wilderness through our suppression activities. And we know this. Fire suppression alters wildlands and begins to convert them into the insufferable managed landscapes we seek to evade. Why do we persist?

Firefighters who recognize this irony but won't reconcile it may be similar to introspective, maturing hunters who are on the verge of giving up hunting. Such hunters may be finding it harder to rationalize what they do, but they are not yet able to give up the adrenaline rush, the personal challenge of endurance and skill, the moment of fatal decision, and, for some, the final conversation with their prey, in which they ask permission to take its life.

At our wildfire as evening approaches, we break out our fusees, hand-held flares designed to quickly ignite dry plant material, and burn out vegetated areas to complete our fire line with a circle of black, burnt ashes, almost doubling the size of the original fire. Once the fire line is secure, we converge on our camp to set up our rain shelters and cook some grub. The sun slides under the mountain's shoulder and brings on the hour of the pearl. As is often the case, our camp occupies the only semiflat places on these burning slopes and is as messy as a teenager's bedroom, strewn with cans of food, cargo, and tools. After we eat, we are very, very happy. We joke, discuss, and then return to the fire line to patrol, mop up, and look for hotspots.

As the night deepens into the witching hour, the smoke wanes, and the fire begins to die. Mountain breezes shift, bringing a cold shudder to us. The fire struggles in short, shallow, swirling breaths. We walk

through the fire's domain and pile logs to build huge bonfires that con-
sume the scattered, smoldering fuel. For a few brief hours the fire
revives in the disjunct intensity of a score of these glinting bonfires. We
ramble amid this swirling, sparking chaos like howling fire demons
and hoist a salute to the spirit and dignity of this wildfire. Crackling
and hissing, embers chase the stars into the sky. The distant moun-
tainsides seem to grow and loom. The surrounding forest seems to
coagulate into a mysterious unity. As our bonfires regress, we have a
conversation with this dying wildfire. We thank it for bringing us to this
place of unique beauty and serenity. We assure it that it will come
again. We ask it for permission to do what we do.

Could we firefighters be like the federal hunter in Aldo Leopold's *Sand
County Almanac* who kills the last grizzly bear in New Mexico? Do we
kill off the fierce greenfire in the wolf's eye? No. Wildfires are more like
coyotes than grizzly bears or wolves. Wildfires seem to be multiplying
in the urban-wildland interface. The more we hunt them, the harder
they are to exterminate. Wildfires will gnaw off their own legs to get
out of our traps. They have learned to feed on the detritus of mangled
ecosystems. This knowledge of wildfire as coyote is the justification
some firefighters use to escape responsibility for what they do. It
doesn't matter whether this particular wildfire is suppressed because
wildfire will continue to return until the fuel is depleted.

This Br'er Rabbit–Br'er Fox joke is on fire management: *Oh,
whatever you do, don't throw us into those wildland fires!* The more
we put 'em out, the more they reappear and the more we take those
wild rides into the wildlands. However, fire management plays the
same game. Fire suppression gives midlevel bureaucrats the brief
opportunity to assume the rank of a general at war, commanding hundreds of wildland warriors, dispatching an air force, and spending a
million dollars a day. That job is a whole lot more fun than arguing
with scruffy biologists over logging plans. So perhaps this joke is really
on the taxpayers. They pay the mounting costs of a fire suppression
strategy that simply breeds more coyote wildfires across the landscape.

The next day we do the tedious work of an undertaker. We make sure
this dead fire is laid out in the way our bosses would want to see it. We
process any heat or embers so the carcass won't spawn any other new

fires. There is a whole manual of protocol to prevent a "reburn." We faithfully use "wilderness tactics" or "minimum impact suppression tactics." We try to disguise our work so it is hard to notice from an airplane, and hard to recognize a year from now if a hiker stumbles across this spot. We scatter the piles of brush and small trees we created while making the fire line, and mutilate the chain-saw cuts we made in downfall, so the place will look more untouched. We climb trees and pull out the parachutes, even if they are 100 feet up. Every lick of trash is burned or packed away. We intend to leave only footprints and a mineral-soil fire line.

Our exit from this fire through the wilderness becomes the final segment of this mission. On this fire we are lucky. A helicopter with a longline and net is coming in to pick up our packout bags. Carrying a 120-pound pack over several miles of rugged terrain is a torturous experience. Now we can stroll out toting a 30-pound personal gear bag and enjoy our final day immersed in this awesome wilderness.

Envision firefighters evolving into fire guiders. Firefighters can begin a new legacy by becoming fire specialists skilled at monitoring backcountry wildland fires, and even igniting them when conditions are appropriate. When lightning naturally kindles tinder in the hinterlands, erstwhile firefighters could nurture these coyote wildfires to run yapping, crackling, smoking through the wildlands. Wildland fireguider specialists could beckon these coyote wildfires, herd them around as best they could—or at least ameliorate some of their mischief—and restore these distorted lands to their fire-hardied origins. Wildland firefighters would then also be doing something truly worthy.

Government hunters gave way to government biologists, who now signal alarms when commodity extraction schemes menace habitats for threatened wildlife. The skills and spirit of the hunter remain present in the biologist. So, too, the skills and spirit of firefighters can remain intimate to a new generation of fire specialists. Agencies and others have been busy doing "prescribed fires" for years. However, these are scheduled and well-planned events, often burdened with the inflexibility of bureaucratic inertia. Now a new coterie of wildland fire guiders is beginning to exploit the opportunity of natural ignition to burn a predetermined amount of acreage.

A distant smoke column in the backcountry would still induce a frantic dispatch to the site. However, now these fire guiders can allow the wildland fire to grow larger. With drip torches and fusees, they burn from ridgetops or other natural fire barriers and secure the fire perimeter to ensure that the fire does not meander beyond the predetermined area. They easily contain the fire within boundaries by using the knowledge and techniques of fire suppression, such as patrolling for spots outside the main fire, "cold trailing" (ensuring the fire's blackened-ash edge is dead out), and "hotspotting" (cooling down hot areas by throwing on dirt or separating fuel). If necessary, when ambient conditions change, they use "minimum impact suppression tactics" to cool down sections of the fire.

The National Park Service has been developing these techniques, known as "wildland fire use," and their fire monitors are growing richer in experience. Although the public would listen to ground-level wildland firefighters speaking about reforming fire management policy, these firefighters are not yet speaking loudly. It is time to make this new vision mainstream. When aberrant fuel loads are reduced to acceptable levels by years of such work, then wildland fire specialists can enter the wilderness with a selfless, communal purpose to observe wild-running coyote wildfires romping through a fire-permeable landscape. Perhaps my children will some day enter the wilderness, stare a coyote wildfire in the eye, get its mark, measure its ferocity and potential, and leave it alone to an uncontorted destiny as a hundred thousand twinkling embers reflect the inscrutable starry night.

INCENDIARY LANGUAGE

How Words Affect Perception

Words frame an issue, and affect our perception of it. In subtle and not so subtle ways, the language we use to describe wildfires affects our perception of these events. When the media, politicians, and even some ecologists describe wildfire and its effects, pejorative language is the norm. How often have you heard a TV reporter or government official describe how a wildfire was "catastrophic" or "destroyed" so many acres of land? We are told that the blaze "incinerated," "blackened," or "devastated" the forest, leaving nothing but "charred snags." Furthermore, the language used in describing wildfires is often militaristic, with "firefighters" "battling" the fire "front," thus casting wildfire as an "enemy" to be subdued.

Our human-centered view of wildfire and the language we use to describe it often hinder us from appreciating the positive role of fire in natural ecosystems. Fires may "destroy" homes, but it's questionable whether they "destroy" the forest. Because we speak of wildfire in terms of something to be "fought," to "suppress," and to "control," we automatically portray fire as a negative force.

Unless we change the language we use to describe wildfire, we may never get away from the perception that it is harmful and undesirable. Talking about wildfire in nonjudgmental language is probably not possible, but if we must err, let us err on the side of ecological health. It will be a welcome day when the media and government officials talk about how fires "restored" the landscape, "created" so many acres of new wildlife habitat, "released" nutrients, and "reestablished" a plant or animal community. At the very least, such terms would be far more accurate than language that casts fire as persona non grata in the ecological family of events.

HOT NEWS

Media Coverage of Wildfire

CONRAD SMITH, PH.D.

MOST OF US GET OUR INFORMATION ABOUT WILDFIRE *from the news media rather than from direct observation. News reports from Yellowstone in 1988 portrayed the wildfires there as "raging" disasters that "menaced," "devastated," and "destroyed" forests—language that obfuscates the ecological role of wildfire in shaping the American West. Stories about catastrophic events tend to include scientific context when scientists themselves are proactive, or "enterprising," as news sources.*

▼

Wildfire was not a big story before World War II. Now it is. In 1937, when 15 firefighters received fatal burns fighting a wildfire near Yellowstone National Park in an effort to save trees for logging, the *New York Times* described their deaths in two stories comprising 980 words, stories buried on pages 8[1] and 23.[2] Each death got 65 words. More than half a century later, in 1994, when 14 firefighters burned to death protecting woodland homes west of Glenwood Springs, Colorado, the *New York Times* described the event on its front page on July 8 and again on July 9, and in four additional stories on those inside pages in the days following the deaths—a total of 5,020 words, or 358 words per death.[3] This greater attention to fallen firefighters suggests that people who fight wildfires have more public importance now than in 1937, and the more prominent 1994 story placement indicates that wildfires have more news value today than before World War II. Why the change?

Events in 1949, 1988, and 1994 altered journalists' perspectives on wildfire. A 1949 fire in Mann Gulch near the Missouri River in Montana killed 12 smokejumpers, the first on-the-job deaths of the professionally trained firefighters who emerged after World War II. Because Norman Maclean described this event so well in *Young Men and Fire*, I will limit myself here to the observation that men jumping from airplanes to fight fires is more interesting to journalists than the 15 Civilian Conservation Corps men who died fighting the 1937 Yellowstone wildfire after being called away from their regular work of building picnic tables in Forest Service campgrounds.

The Yellowstone fires of 1988 increased the degree to which wild-fires are reported as a natural biological process, although the social impacts of wildfire remain the primary focus. The 1994 deaths of 14 firefighters on Storm King Mountain in Colorado focused federal land agencies and journalists on the reality that young men and women had been giving up their lives to save houses threatened by wildland fire.

THE YELLOWSTONE FIRES OF 1988

During the slow-news summer of 1988, Yellowstone National Park, a national icon, seemed threatened by large fires that again and again in August burned with more intensity than worst-case predictions made by the country's most respected wildfire analysts. The park's pre-scribed natural fire policy, under which lightning-caused fires were ini-tially allowed to burn if they did not threaten developed areas, was sus-pended on July 21 because of drought conditions and increasing fire activity. The fires' intensity subsided during the first three weeks of August, but flared up again toward the end of the month.

In the ensuing national media onslaught of late August and early September, NBC News alone had 23 people in and near Yellowstone reporting on the fires. On September 9, NBC Nightly News showed pic-tures of a charred moonscape as correspondent Roger O'Neil told view-ers: "This is what's left of Yellowstone tonight." Urban journalists in Yellowstone's rural setting often followed the lead of some park-area merchants and their political representatives, who used the park's ear-lier prescribed natural burn policy as an explanation for why the fires were still burning more than a month after they became national news. Scientists who study wildfire, however, concluded that about the same number of acres would have burned even if all of the 1988 fires had been fought immediately.[4]

Fires of similar intensity had burned through Yellowstone's lodge-pole pine forests many times before Europeans arrived to observe them.[5] Public interest in the 1988 fires offered an opportunity for journalists to explain the historical and ecological context in which the fires burned, but few who reported the story had the knowledge to do so. The majority of the 936 news accounts about the Yellowstone-area fires that appeared during 1988 in three Yellowstone-area newspapers, in three nationally known newspapers, and in the evening newscasts of the three television networks focused on the fires themselves rather than on the ecological context in which they burned.[6]

Only one of the 936 stories—published in December 1988, after the fires were out—provided a detailed description of the scientific foundation of Yellowstone's prescribed natural fire policy.[7] Six paragraphs of this *New York Times Magazine* story, by well-known environmental writer Peter Matthiessen, traced the evolution of Yellowstone's fire policy through its roots in the cessation of predator control in the 1930s and the National Park Service's natural regulation philosophy, based on the 1963 Leopold Report, which recommended that natural ecosystems should be re-created within the national parks.[8]

Before 1988, the primary source of information about wildfire for many journalists and other Americans was the Smokey Bear public education campaign. This effort, designed to reduce forest fires caused by humans, implied that wildfire is always harmful because it destroys forests. Many Americans were also influenced by the Disney animated movie *Bambi*, which has been described by wilderness scholar Roderick Nash as doing "more to shape American attitudes towards fire in wilderness ecosystems than all the scientific papers ever published on the subject."[9] Naturally these aspects of popular culture influenced journalists as well as their readers and viewers.

My surveys of journalists who covered the Yellowstone fires in 1988, and of the sources named in their stories, indicated that many in each group believed the Yellowstone fires were poorly reported.[10] The most common complaints among the journalists themselves were that the reporting was exaggerated or sensationalized, and that the stories did not provide enough information about the political or geographical context in which the fires burned. Reporters tended to blame poor coverage on ignorance, preconceived notions about fire, logistical problems with access and communications, deadline pressure, and on sometimes-inept Park Service fire information officials.

Four panels of wildfire experts whom I asked to evaluate network television stories about the Yellowstone fires concluded that those broadcast during the height of the 1988 coverage were less accurate than stories that aired before and after the peak coverage period.[11] The network correspondents who did the largest number of television stories about the fires for ABC,[12] CBS,[13] and NBC[14] each acknowledged in retrospect that their 1988 stories exaggerated the impact of the fires. This kind of introspection within the journalistic community, described eloquently in a *Washington Post* opinion piece by one of the journalists who covered the fires,[15] appears to have resulted in more thoughtful wildfire reporting in subsequent years.

In 1989, for example, reporters from the television networks and from nationally known newspapers and magazines returned to Yellowstone to assess how the park looked after the 1988 fires. In 1993, reporters again returned for five-year-retrospective stories about the fires. Some of the post-1988 news accounts addressed ecological aspects of wildfire. Because these stories were features produced under less time pressure than hard news written under tight deadlines, they offered journalists more opportunity to explore the scientific aspects of wildfire.

THE STORM KING MOUNTAIN FIRE OF 1994

In early July 1994, thousands of lightning strikes ignited numerous wildfires in western Colorado. One of those, initially too small to be considered worthy of attention from scarce firefighting resources, was attacked by firefighters after some residents of a small housing development, a few miles west of the fire and surrounded by forest, complained to the White River National Forest supervisor's office in nearby Glenwood Springs (the fire itself was on land administered by the Bureau of Land Management). High winds from a cold front on July 6 caused this fire to explode, killing 14 of the firefighters. This human sacrifice to save houses that were destined to burn because of their location focused media attention on the value of human life relative to the value of houses built where they should not be.[16] The risk of fire to homes made of fuel built among forest fuels has appropriately been compared to the risk of flood damage to houses built on floodplains.

NEWS, CONTEXT, ACCURACY, AND THE SOCIOLOGY OF JOURNALISM

Journalists have been criticized for making factual errors, for exaggerating and sensationalizing events, and for not providing enough context in their stories. Understanding some of the workplace constraints inherent in news work can help explain why these problems occur.

Media scholar James Carey has suggested that it is uncharitable to criticize daily news reports for their lack of context.[17] That is perhaps the most common complaint about how journalists report events. Most journalists place a high value on factual accuracy, but accuracy alone does not necessarily characterize good reporting. Describing the number of acres charred does not explain why wildfires are burning; the social, economic, or ecological impact of the flames on the burned areas; or the political ramifications of the fires. In my surveys, reporters who covered the 1988 Yellowstone fires, as well as those reporters' sources, were more critical of omitted information and missing data than of factual errors in stories about the fires.

Several scientific studies suggest that omitted facts and lack of context are more serious journalistic shortcomings than overt factual errors.[18] The scholarly literature on reporting also suggests that news accounts are socially constructed realities designed to meet the needs of the journalistic workplace rather than objective accounts of issues and events.[19]

In an ideal world, reporters' news sources would be chosen entirely by the relative expertise of those sources. More often in the daily grind of journalism, however, sources are chosen for their accessibility rather than their knowledge.[20] Sources eager to influence how journalists report events often succeed in doing so.[21] Media research also indicates that science and technology are more poorly reported than other topics.[22] In part this is because newspapers tend to give science a low priority,[23] and because scientific ignorance is widespread.[24]

Most scholars who study wildfire examine it as a natural rather than a social phenomenon. But the research cited above suggests that most journalists are better equipped to report the social impact of wildfire than its role in shaping and maintaining natural landscapes, that news sources named in stories about wildfire will be selected more for their availability than expertise, and that the most available news sources will have opportunities to exert considerable influence on how the relevant stories are framed.

My own research indicates that fewer than 5 percent of 589 American newspaper and magazine stories about the 1988 Yellowstone fires published during the subsequent five years contained any kind of ecological information in the first three paragraphs. Of these 29 stories, only 5 went beyond descriptions of immediate fire effects to explain the long-term role of fire in forest ecosystems. Readers hungry for scientific information clearly did not get very much of it from these 589 wildfire stories. This raises two questions: (1) Why did the media pay so little attention to the scientific aspects of a story with so much scientific potential, and (2) is it reasonable to expect more?

DETERMINANTS OF HOW CATASTROPHIC EVENTS ARE REPORTED

Media coverage of catastrophic events seems largely a function of five factors: (1) the amount of enterprise exhibited by potential news sources, (2) the degree to which elements of the story resonate with cultural norms, (3) the salience of relevant issues, (4) the newness of the event, and (5) the degree to which the setting for the story is rural or urban. I derive this conclusion from my research on how the media reported the 1988 Yellowstone fires[25] and three other major stories: the 1989 *Exxon Valdez* oil spill in Alaska,[26] the 1989 Loma Prieta earthquake in California,[27] and climatologist Iben Browning's unscientific projection that an earthquake would strike New Madrid, Missouri, on or about December 3, 1990.[28]

Source Enterprise

One of the traditions of journalism is that reporters attribute information to named sources. As observers cited above have noted, news is weighted toward sources eager to be heard. Sociologists Harvey Molotch and Marilyn Lester described news coverage as a battle among sources with vested interests to define events in self-serving ways.[29] Communications scientist Robert Entman suggested that journalistic practices make it so easy to manipulate news that public officials who talk honestly with reporters do so at their own peril.[30] Because of deadlines, there is often not enough time for even the most conscientious reporter to find the best sources. This journalistic fact of life makes reporters vulnerable to the most easily accessible sources, especially during crisis stories, such as those about wildfires or earthquakes.

The "source enterprise" factor describes the degree to which news sources successfully court media attention. Success is measured by the degree to which resulting stories legitimize the source-generated viewpoints and news angles. For example, a representative of an environmental advocacy group who sought media attention would rate high on source enterprise if the resulting story focused on environmental aspects of the event. A politician who sought media attention to portray wildfire as an economic disaster would display high source enterprise if the resulting news account took that perspective. Consider the following examples.

After the *Exxon Valdez* oil spill in March 1989, the State of Alaska, which received much of its revenue from oil and which had approved the ineffective oil spill contingency plan, launched a successful propaganda effort to portray itself as the innocent victim of Exxon. Alaska commissioner of environmental conservation Dennis Kelso and Coast Guard commandant Admiral Paul Yost delivered sound bites that made good copy and obscured the culpability of each government body in the lax enforcement of safety standards and oversight of preparedness for large spills.[31] Exxon was less skilled in dealing with reporters, exacerbating its public relations problems.

After the October 1989 Loma Prieta earthquake, U.S. Geological Survey (USGS) geologists in Menlo Park, California, who had been courting reporters for 25 years,[32] rated news coverage of that event much more accurate and complete than did seismic engineers, who had not sought media attention in any organized way.[33] This suggests that scientists who seek out journalists get more accurate coverage than those who do not.

Although Iben Browning had no standing as a seismologist and only one supporter among academic seismologists, his unscientific earthquake prediction for the New Madrid fault was often reported as scientifically credible until the USGS intervened, releasing a report by a committee of 11 respected scientists that discredited Browning's prediction.[34] Statistical analysis by the author indicated that this source enterprise by the USGS was the single largest factor explaining the variance in the accuracy of news accounts about Browning's prediction.[35]

In 1988 coverage of the Yellowstone fires, federal agencies were relatively unsuccessful in their attempts to influence reporters in ways that focused attention on the natural role of fire in forest ecosystems. But about half of the expert sources named in post-1988 stories about the fires were associated with Yellowstone National Park, suggesting renewed opportunity for federal agencies to influence coverage. Although many of the stories were ecologically superficial, most expressed more positive attitudes toward the park than did stories published in August and September of 1988.

But the Intermountain Fire Sciences Laboratory in Missoula, described twice in the 1988 stories about the Yellowstone fires,[36] was mentioned only once among the 29 post-1988 stories that had ecological content in the first three paragraphs.[37] If the fire sciences lab had been cultivating media contacts for a quarter century as had the USGS geologists in Menlo Park, coverage of the 1988 fires and their aftermath might have turned out differently.

Cultural Resonance

If the message offered by news sources resonates with widely accepted cultural values (e.g., Bambi terrorized by fire; Smokey Bear's admonitions that fire is bad), it will take less enterprise to influence reporters than if the perspective offered by sources contradicts popular wisdom.

Because journalists hold oil companies in low esteem,[38] and because the drunken sailor is a part of maritime myth, the perspectives that alcohol caused the wreck of the *Exxon Valdez* and that the company was responsible for failed efforts to contain the spilled oil resonated with cultural values. Other causes identified by the National Transportation Safety Board, such as poor Coast Guard oversight, resonated less with popular conceptions and received less media attention, independent of efforts by news sources to influence coverage. Because Alaska symbolized uncorrupted wilderness for many Americans,[39] the idea that the state bore no responsibility for the spill or the unsuccessful cleanup efforts resonated with popular wisdom. For that reason, the state could get favorable coverage with considerably less enterprise than Exxon.

Most of the damage from the Loma Prieta earthquake occurred outside San Francisco in places such as Oakland, Santa Cruz, and Watsonville. But San Francisco is better known than the other cities, and the 1906 earthquake there is part of our cultural lore. Thus, because San Francisco is a familiar reference and resonates with our knowledge of earthquakes, media accounts of the 1989 earthquake focused on San Francisco far more often than the distribution of seismological effects would have suggested.

Iben Browning's New Madrid earthquake prediction resonated with the cultural myth that earthquakes can be accurately predicted. Perhaps for that reason, inaccurate reports that Browning had earlier predicted the Loma Prieta earthquake and the eruption of Mount St. Helens were initially described by journalists as fact without being investigated.

Because we are culturally conditioned to think of fire as destructive, it will take no source enterprise to persuade journalists to portray wildfire pejoratively. In the face of this widespread conception, source enterprise is particularly important in communicating the biological context of wildfire to reporters. If agency managers and fire information officers are content to answer reporters' questions without actively providing scientific information about wildfire, they will unwittingly reinforce the Smokey Bear message that fire is always bad.

Issue Salience

The salience of an issue or event—the degree to which it captures our attention—is another factor that influences how events are reported. Thus wildfires in Yellowstone National Park, which is widely known, received considerably more media attention than equally intense fires in lesser-known areas, such as the 1988 Canyon Creek Fire in the Scapegoat Wilderness between Missoula and Great Falls, Montana.

Of the stories discussed here, the earthquake stories probably have the highest cultural resonance. Because most of us drive over bridges and on freeways, we can relate personally to stories about how those structures collapsed and killed people. Iben Browning's dubious prediction—a 50-50 chance of a major earthquake near New Madrid within two days of December 3, 1990—had greater specificity than USGS predictions that estimated the probability of a Bay Area earthquake over a period of three decades. The Browning prediction was therefore more journalistically salient and received greater coverage.

The Alaska oil spill and Yellowstone wildfires were salient in symbolic ways. Each symbolized the corruption of innocence by outside forces. Alaska, the pristine last frontier, and Yellowstone, the crown jewel of the national park system, were portrayed as innocent victims of bad management by inept administrators. In Alaska, journalists increased issue salience by portraying environmental damage in terms of doomed sea otters instead of explaining that the real threat was that mortality among less charismatic species in some parts of a complex aquatic ecosystem might eventually affect other parts of that system. In Yellowstone, issue salience was greater because journalists focused on national icons presumably threatened (e.g., Old Faithful geyser) and on presumably terrorized megafauna rather than on less charismatic stands of lodgepole pine, which are evolutionarily adapted to wildfire.

Wildfire ecology probably has considerably less salience than threatened national icons and allegedly inept land managers, and is therefore much less likely to be the focus of stories about wildfire.

Newness

Where a wildfire has burned since yesterday, who or what is now most at threat, and the most recent administrative actions, will always be newer than ecological issues, and therefore more newsworthy. After the *Exxon Valdez* oil spill in Alaska, stories about the day's events (sea otters rescued, beaches cleaned) and symbols (oiled shorelines and wildlife) were always more newsworthy than information that would help to prevent future spills. After the 1989 Loma Prieta earthquake in California, stories about damage and victims were always more newsworthy than information about past zoning decisions and funding cutbacks that assured widespread damage to buildings and roads. Stories about Iben Browning's New Madrid earthquake prediction focused on public reactions to it rather than on its scientific merit.

The Urban Rube

Most of journalism is practiced in urban areas. In 1988, I would have said that wildfires burn in rural places, though later wildfires in the

Oakland/Berkeley Hills (October 1991) and Los Alamos (May 2000) have tempered that observation. Urban reporters are generally better qualified to report urban than rural phenomena, and generally more interested in urban events. Urban crime, politics, and scandal are appropriate staples of news, because cities are where most of us live.

We've all heard stories about the country rube who goes to the big city and gets taken because he doesn't know the ways of the city. You can take the boy out of the country, and so forth. But the same concept works in reverse when urban journalists report rural events. A reporter who is quite sophisticated about the subtleties of Washington politics may be completely out of his or her element in a story about federal lands in rural areas. Thus Bill Greenwood, Washington correspondent for ABC, reported in 1988: "There's no doubt the flames [in Yellowstone] will cost the timber industry tens of millions of dollars."[40] Greenwood was apparently unaware that timber harvest is not allowed in national parks.

In Valdez, Alaska, reporters from prestigious national news organizations generally knew much less about the background and issues relevant to the *Exxon Valdez* oil spill than did their counterparts from Alaska-based news organizations. In California, Bay Area reporters generally had lived through other earthquakes, and many had working relationships with USGS scientists in Menlo Park. Reporters who flew to San Francisco from other urban areas had fewer bearings and were more likely to buy into the myth that earthquakes are somehow more dangerous than other natural disasters, such as the hurricanes that sweep through the Southeast every few years.

The New Madrid fault, which traverses a predominantly rural area, was the focus in 1990 of stereotypical stories about simple folks in small-town America and their fears about the great earthquake. In Alaska, stories about the *Exxon Valdez* oil spill perpetuated myths about the primitive lifestyles of native peoples, portraying them as less assimilated into the cultural mainstream than they really were. In Yellowstone, many reporters used urban concepts to explain rural fires. If the fires were still burning, the thinking appears to have been, somebody must have screwed up. By the same logic that fires can destroy buildings, they can "destroy" rural landscapes.

Having offered my theoretical explanation of why the media

reported so little and, in some cases, so superficially about wildfire ecology in Yellowstone after the 1988 fires, I now come to the second question: Is it reasonable to expect more? My conclusion is that the practical constraints on journalists are such that reporting on wildfire ecology and other scientific subjects will not change very much until scientists and other expert sources take a considerably more active role in cultivating reporters and actively educating them about both the methods and results of their research.

DON'T GET HOSED

How Political Framing Influences Fire Policy

LES AUCOIN

THE BUSH WHITE HOUSE CAREFULLY CHOSE *the phrase "healthy forests" to characterize its effort to increase logging in the public's national forests. It was a masterpiece of political "framing" — the art of creating a central organizing idea or context for an issue through use of selection, emphasis, exclusion, and elaboration. "Healthy forests" evokes a sense of environmental protection and personal safety at a time of deep fear of wildland fire.*

▼

"The fire is destroying Yellowstone—destroying it—and the Park Service is just sitting around, letting it happen!" Congressman Ralph Regula, a senior Republican from Ohio, was flushed with rage in the hearing room of the House Interior and Related Agencies Appropriations Subcommittee in Washington, D.C., that morning in June 1988.[1]

Then Regula delivered the coup de grâce—a fact so awful that it would surely seal his argument: "It's so bad, the park's rivers are running *black!*" A collective gasp filled the hearing room. Yellowstone Park—the crown jewel in the national park system, the world's first national park—was being "devastated."

But the Yellowstone fires were not destroying this fire-adapted landscape any more than similar conflagrations had done over millennia. Throughout history, fire has worked through western forests, giving them a chance to reset nature's clock and renew themselves. But it is a rare politician who understands wildfire ecology, and few if any scientists of any kind serve in the Congress. This may explain why politics tends to produce decision makers who, with several notable exceptions, seek to fireproof the forests—through thinning if they can, or, if they cannot, through salvage logging. At its core, American politics is anthropocentric—human centered, not nature centered. Worse for the environment, politics abhors a vacuum. Faced with a massive natural disturbance like a wildlands fire, politicians cannot just sit idly by. No sir, they've got to get out that good wrench and be seen as fixing the problem! This is especially true in the age of the modern media—the 24/7 "infotainment industry" that looks for drama and action and showers coverage on politicians who provide them.

In 1988, the national news media chased a perfect storm: five fires had erupted in Yellowstone while the Park Service operated under a 16-year-old policy of letting fires run their course in fire-adapted ecosystems. For the infotainment industry, this was as good as it gets: the equivalent of the burning of Rome and the discovery of covert pyromaniacs rolled into one. Unburdened by scientific knowledge, reporters and politicians pummeled the Park Service in an echo chamber of escalating criticism.[2] Montana senator Max Baucus, a Democrat, took the U.S. Senate floor to declare that the national fire policy was "responsible for much of the injury caused by this year's forest fires."[3] Then-senator Malcolm Wallop, a Republican from Wyoming, demanded the firing of National Park Service director William Penn Mott, a fellow Republican, saying: "He continues to celebrate [the fires] while all the rest of us are suffering."[4]

The Park Service's fire policy, however, was based on peer-reviewed science, which showed how fire had shaped the Yellowstone landscape and its biota for millennia. Many of Yellowstone's plant species are fire adapted. The cones of lodgepole pine, a species that makes up nearly 80 percent of Yellowstone's forests, are a good example. Sealed by resin, they crack in the intense heat of fire and release seeds to begin life afresh.

But try to explain these facts to a television news reporter who operates on 10-second sound bites. Or to a congressman or senator who makes a political living off of them. On the tube, that great arbiter of modern American reality, Yellowstone scientists and managers came off as ostrich-headed bumblers muttering a language from another world.

It was a rout. Science was mugged by politics as whipped-up TV viewers across the nation flooded the offices of their senators and representatives with one message: suppress the fires without further delay. On

July 21, as the flames began to expand rapidly, the Park Service lifted its natural fire policy. The agency's decision was partly a capitulation to overwhelming political pressure, especially from western senators, who have disproportionate power in the Congress because senators are elected two to a state, regardless of a state's population. In fairness, the decision was also based on the intensity of the fire, which raced across the crowns of trees, shooting out firebrands up to a mile ahead of the front and threatening nearby human populations outside the park.

But if the Park Service thought that its about-face would still its critics, it was wrong. Detractors refused to believe Interior Secretary Don Hodel when he told Congress that he had suspended the "let burn" policy. Meanwhile, Hodel's decision incited criticism from Park Service fire scientists,[5] independent wildfire biologists, and environmentalists, who believe that bulldozers and other firefighting equipment cause more harm to a landscape than wildland fire.

Today, in 2005, the Park Service's natural fire policy—long since reinstated and adjusted to better protect human populations and property—has worked successfully on subsequent fires in Yellowstone. Nevertheless, the political storm caused by the 1988 fire gave a strong hand to logging advocates on all federal lands, who make the argument that dead trees ought to be logged instead of "wasted," although nothing in nature is ever wasted.

The lesson is unmistakable: the media thrive on drama, especially fear,[6] while the political marketplace almost always operates on the understanding that there is profit in satisfying the crowd.

Today, 17 years after the fire reset nature's clock, Yellowstone's plants are brimming with youthful vigor. Independent scientists report that although flames consumed aboveground parts of grasses and forbs, the belowground root systems remained unharmed.[7] Researchers Jay Anderson of Idaho State University, William Romme of Colorado State University, and other scientists have documented the Greater Yellowstone Ecosystem's remarkable but not unexpected recovery.[8] Vegetation in most burned areas quickly regenerated. Water flows have increased in many streams without causing the severe erosion that some feared. Fish and other forms of aquatic life are abundant again. Mammal populations are still healthy—albeit reapportioned to conform to natural habitat changes.

Writing for the *High Country News* in October 1994, reporter Michael Hofferber described the park's incredible resiliency just six years after the fire:

> Crouched over a metal screen like a gold rush prospector and peering through its grid at the forest floor, [researcher] Cindi Persichetty calls out what she sees through each square-inch opening: "Line four: moss, moss, litter, seedling, seedling, seedling." Another Idaho State University graduate student, Mike O'Hara, sits on a log recording the findings on a clipboard. The charred remains of lodgepole pine loom above them, groaning in the morning breeze that rises off the Madison River in Yellowstone National Park. The forest floor is carpeted with thousands of bright green seedlings, each less than a foot high.[9]

Findings of this kind prompt John Varley, director of the Yellowstone Center for Resources, to observe that a forest's rebirth after a fire disturbance can leave the ecosystem and its biodiversity healthier than they were before the flames erupted. Overwhelmingly, conservation biologists agree with him.

Yet, since the 1988 Yellowstone fires, the rush to "fix" the wildland fire problem has escalated across the West. Oregon's July 2002 Biscuit Fire showed that naïveté, lack of knowledge, and deception still underscore public debate. Although climate change, fire suppression, and logging are among the primary agents in transforming western forests into tinderboxes,[10] the timber industry and the Forest Service's "solution" is to ramp up logging.[11]

The Biscuit Fire was the nation's largest in the summer of 2002 and the largest in Oregon's history. When, after 120 days, it finally died, its outer boundary encompassed nearly 500,000 acres, including the fabled Kalmiopsis Wilderness and 160,000 acres of roadless areas.[12] But the fire did not burn all of those acres. It left a mosaic of live and burned trees, and many forest stands inside the "burn" were untouched.

President George W. Bush cited the Biscuit Fire as an example of why he has given a green light to the timber industry to mow through forest stands across the West. Traveling to Medford, Oregon, in 2002 while the Biscuit blazed, the president announced a plan he said would reduce the number of conflagrations. He called it his "Healthy Forests Initiative." The program was enacted into law on December 3, 2003, as the Healthy Forest Restoration Act. It relies on the timber industry to "thin" forests in the deep outback and exempts this logging from the National Forest Management Act, the Appeals Reform Act, and the National Environmental Policy Act—laws that Congressman Mark Udall, among others, describes as the fundamental laws of sound forest management.[13]

A further, conspicuous problem with the Healthy Forest Restoration Act is that the timber industry is not exactly a philanthropic movement. When it "thins" trees, it expects to make a profit. Thus, it must cut big (commercially valuable) trees to offset the cost of thinning smaller ones. The president's plan, then, means loggers are taking large, fire-resistant trees and leaving smaller trees, which are more susceptible to fire. An examination of Oregon's 2002 Tiller Fire demonstrated the shortcoming of this tactic: the most severely burned places were previously logged tracts in which older, larger trees had been replaced with plantations of smaller trees.[14]

These facts were smothered in the congressional debate on the president's misleadingly named plan; the bill sailed through the House on a vote of 256–170 and cleared the Senate by 80–14. What political factors were at work? Mainly the "Mr. Goodwrench" syndrome, in which pressured legislators feel compelled to act as problem solvers even through they may be making matters worse.

Ignorance or avoidance of environmental knowledge is one thing. A deliberate frontal attack on forest science is another. The Healthy Forests Initiative was developed by individuals who used fear of wildland fire to increase logging and mask their dismantling of President Bill Clinton's science-based 1993 Northwest Forest Plan.[15] The Clinton plan reduced the public timber cut in the region by 75 percent to protect viable populations of the spotted owl and other wildlife, which were threatened by logging and habitat loss.[16]

For the 2005 Biscuit Fire "restoration" alone, the Bush administration's Final Environmental Impact Statement (FEIS) called for a "salvage" of 372 million board feet of timber—some 170 million board feet more than the normal yearly cut on the public lands of Oregon and Washington combined. Leading biological experts contend that postfire logging can be more harmful than fire.[17] Heavy equipment damages delicate, traumatized soils; log skidding creates erosion and river siltation; and removal of fallen trees robs the soil of nutrients and destroys woody debris needed as a lifeboat for dependent species until the regenerating forest begins to produce its own "new" large dead wood structures, typically a century later.[18] Logging trucks carry the seeds of noxious weeds that, in the absence of postfire competition, multiply rapidly and choke natural vegetation. The Biscuit EIS also targeted 8,173 acres of inventoried roadless areas for industrial logging.

Mark Rey, the U.S. undersecretary of agriculture, is President Bush's top political appointee for the Forest Service and was responsible for overseeing the Healthy Forests Initiative. From the mid-1980s to the early 1990s, Rey was a top lobbyist for the American Timber and Pulp Association, the largest timber industry trade association in the nation.[19] In that role he tried in vain to stop logging curtailments called for in the Northwest Forest Plan. Today, under the rubric of "forest health," he has succeeded where he failed throughout the 1990s. He has also weakened the Clinton administration's roadless forest protections in Oregon and elsewhere.[20]

How is it, one might ask, that legislation like the Bush administration's so-called Healthy Forests Initiative can sail through Congress when polls consistently show strong public support for a sound and healthy environment?[21] The answer is "framing"—the art of creating a central organizing idea or context for an event or proposal and suggesting the issue through use of selection, emphasis, exclusion, and elaboration.[22] This is why the Bush White House chose the phrase "healthy forests" to characterize its effort to increase logging in the public's national forests. A masterpiece of Orwellian doublespeak, "healthy forests" evokes a sense of environmental protection and personal safety at a time of deep fear of wildland fire. (Remember, in Abraham Maslow's hierarchy of human needs, safety is a fundamental human requirement.)

Successful framing is a powerful tool in molding political opinion. An experiment described by Thomas E. Patterson, professor of political science at Syracuse University's Maxwell School of Citizenship and Public Affairs, illustrates this point:

Cognitive psychologists Daniel Kahneman and Amos Tversky told a group of subjects to imagine that an unusual disease was expected to kill six hundred people and then asked them to choose between treatment A, which was expected to save two hundred, and treatment B, which offered a one-third probability of saving all six hundred and a two-thirds probability of saving none of them. By 72 percent to 28 percent, the subjects preferred treatment A. A matched group of subjects was provided the same information about the disease and asked to choose between treatment A, under which four hundred were expected to die, and treatment B, which offered a one-third probability that nobody would die and a two-thirds probability that all six hundred would die. In this case, treatment B was preferred 78 percent to 22 percent. The choice given to both groups was identical, but one choice was framed in terms of the number of people who would live if the action were taken, and the second one was framed in terms of the number who would die. By altering the way in which the choice was framed, people's preferences were completely changed.[23]

The broadcast media, which Americans depend on for most of their news,[24] play a major role in communicating politically framed issues. This has had an unfortunate impact on political discourse—in part because nuance and analysis are difficult to fit into an average 10-second sound bite. These media, especially television, tend to favor attention-getting political frames rather than ones that elucidate issues.[25] In the modern symbiosis between the media and elected officials, many politicians, needing attention for personal advancement, are loath to challenge political frames communicated by the media.

To be sure, past government policy on the land and its natural processes has produced some notable ecological achievements—the Wilderness Act; the Clean Air, Clean Water, and Alaska National Interest Land Conservation acts; the establishment of national parks; the creation of the Environmental Protection Agency; and many others. But much of today's sophisticated antienvironmental framing is built atop a history of human domination of nature that Roderick Nash describes so well in his seminal book *Wilderness and the American*

Mind. From the first light of time, through the mid-19th-century period of Manifest Destiny, the New Deal, and into the modern age, Nash describes American self-identity as forged in no small part by taming the frontiers and, when the chips were down, by placing humans above nature—not as a part of it.[26]

In this spirit, wildland fire in the West—and the threat of it—seem to have created a reflexive impulse for logging, and to make the most of it, the Bush administration has lifted bedrock environmental laws that protect the health of the nation's forests. Perhaps the words of Alexis de Tocqueville, sharing his perspective on America some 170 years ago, best pertain to the agenda of politicians who seek to reverse many hard-won gains in the science of forest ecology: "They may be said not to perceive the mighty forests that surround them till they fall beneath the hatchet."[27]

LIFETIMES WITH FIRE

A Place in the Wildland Interface

GARY SNYDER

IN A SENSE, THE WHOLE BIOSPHERE IS *fire adapted. We walk the line between revering and treasuring what is, and letting go: taking destruction, loss, and drastic change in our daily stride. This is an account of fire in the woods, fire in the stove, fighting fires, and setting fires, with the gossip and tools that go with it all, in the social and political heat of our times.*

▼

In 1969 I packed my books and robes, and with my young family sailed back to California from ten years in Japan. When I first moved to a piece of Sierra mountain forestland the next summer, I wouldn't let even a tractor drive over it. Except for a couple of very ancient logging tracks that evolved into an access road, I wouldn't take a truck into the woods. We built a house that summer. We felled trees for posts and beams using an old Royal Chinook two-man falling saw and then barked the logs with large draw knives. They were not skidded or trucked to the building site, but carried by crews of strong young men and women using rope slings and little oak-pole yokes. The three-month job—the workers were mostly just out of college, and a only a few had architecture and building skills—was done entirely with hand tools. Our ridge had no grid power available, and we had no generator. The rocky road ran across a barren mile of ancient rounded riverbed stone laid open by hydraulic mining in the 1870s. The building site was beyond the diggings and back in the forest 3 miles from the paved road and the mailbox. Town was 25 miles away across a 1,200-foot-deep river canyon.

Twelve years later I took a trip back to Japan to visit Buddhist monk and artist friends. I also looked at the new farming and forestry.

Small gas engines had taken over what oxen or humans had done before. Ingenious tillers, small precise rice thrasher-huskers, a variety of weed whackers, beautiful tiny trucks, brightly colored miniature backhoes and excavators, and everyone using them without the least sign of guilt or stress. I thought, if the four-stroke engine (and the two-stroke) had a place even in the Asian scheme of things, maybe they'd work for me as well.

Our roads have not improved yet and there's still no grid power. Though I have stayed mostly with hand tools, over the years since, we have gone from kerosene lamps to solar panels with a backup generator. I take my 4-wheel pickup into the woods for firewood, and our homestead is now a hybrid of 19th- and 21st-century technologies. There's a wood-burning kitchen range and two large wood-burning heating stoves, but we also use laptop computers, have a fax and a copying machine, and buck the big down oak rounds with a large Husqvarna and a small Stihl chain saw.

Every summer season I do a bit more work clearing back the underbrush (ceanothus and manzanita) from under the trees, and every winter I burn the brush piles. California and southern Oregon forests are fire adapted and are tuned to fairly regular low-level wildfires sweeping through. But then a few summers back it seemed the wildfires got hotter and the roads and houses closer, and some big plans for firebreaks were designed by the California Department of Forestry and Fire Protection (CDF).

I'd prefer to clear the understory fuel the natural way, with fire. I stood watch on a prescribed burn a few years back on mostly Bureau of Land Management forest, with the planned burn zone overlapping onto an adjacent private parcel. The fire torched up a few big trees and burned a lot of underbrush down to ash. It was scary, but the fire chief assured us everything was okay. Bulldozer operators were on alert, ready to come if needed; and so were the CDF pilots at the county airport with their spotter and tanker planes. The burn went well all day. There were some complaints about the smoke, and that's one problem with prescribed burns—the air quality goes down, and newcomers don't like it. But the bigger problem is, eight years later, that the site is getting brushy again. It needs a follow-up burn, and we don't know if we'll ever be able to do it. "The window of safety is too small." So maybe mechanical crunching is another answer.

In 1952 and 1953 I worked on fire lookouts in the Skagit District of the Mount Baker National Forest in the northern Washington Cascades. Crater Mountain first and then Sourdough. Those were the first jobs I'd held that I felt had some virtue. Finally, guarding against forest fires, I had found Right Occupation. I congratulated myself, as I stood up there above the clouds memorizing various peaks and watersheds, for finding a job that didn't contribute to the Cold War and the wasteful modern economy. The joke's on me 50 years later, to be knowing about how much of the fire suppression ideology was wrong-headed and how it has contributed to our current problems.

I fought on a few fire lines back in the fifties, too—as I was working alternately in logging camps and on lookouts or trail crews. I'd be carrying the little backpack pump full of water with its trombone-slide handle, and always toting a duff hoe. Fire in the very high mountains is most commonly caused by lightning. A lively lightning storm passes over, lasts all night, and hundreds of strikes are visible. Flashes light up the whole sky with their distant forks and prongs. Every once in a while a strike goes to ground, and even from a distance you can see a little fire blossom and bloom where it has started a spot fire, becoming a distant light that usually soon is quenched (rains come with storms). A dry lightning storm is what's dangerous—you might have hundreds of spot fires going at the same time. A few of those would still be going at dawn, and you'd take a reading on them with the Osborne Fire Finder, then radio in the bearing and describe the drainage. Fifty years ago, the crews hiked in with the help of a pack string. There were only a few smokejumpers then.

In 1954 I was working as a choker setter on a logging crew at the Warm Springs Indian Reservation in Oregon. A light plane crashed in the nearby hills and started a fire. They drafted a bunch of us off the crew and we hiked in, along with some Forest Service boys; half of our logging crew were local Wasco and Warm Springs Indians. The fire had spread to about two acres, but it was slow, and overcast and finally drizzly, so it wasn't hard to put it out. The pilot had been killed.

Fifty years later, I have three of that same type of backpack pump, all in good condition, under the eaves near the tool shed door. They are filled with water and kept covered with cloth to protect them from the sun. A duff hoe (called a "McCloud" in California) hangs on a bracket, and next to that in the woodshed there's a whole section full of hoes, shovels, and a few extra fire rakes. The classic wildfire fighter's tool, a pulaski, hangs in the shop. In the open porch space of the house is a line of wood pegs holding work clothes, but one peg is reserved for fire-fighting clothes: ragged old Wild Ass logger jeans on a hanger, with a Nomex fire coat and yellow helmet, and a full canteen looped on as well. In one Nomex coat pocket are the firefighting goggles, and in the big pocket is a pair of work gloves.

There are several hundred families living in the pine-oak zone on this Sierra ridge. Higher up is national forest and heavy winter snow; lower down, the blue oak, grass, and gray pine country that once was hot and droughty ranchland but now is either air force base or becoming air-conditioned new development. At our higher forest elevation, most of the community seems to feel that we should be prepared to step out the door anytime to help hold the fire line till the forestry crew trucks (men and women) come. There would be help from air tanker planes and backup bulldozers eventually, too, but if there are big fires going elsewhere in California, thousands of firefighters and all the equipment might be there instead. So then it's us and our small but dedicated volunteer fire department.

In the Yuba country's forested areas, there are plenty of firefighting protocols in place: the San Juan Ridge Volunteer Fire Department, the U.S. Forest Service, the Bureau of Land Management, the California Department of Forestry, and the really local citizens with their Yuba Watershed Institute. There have been several little fires my family and I took care of ourselves. Like one time a tree only a few hundred feet from the house took a lightning strike, and the lower trunk and forest floor around were quietly burning. I saw the flickering light against the window. At 3:00 a.m. we went out and doused it with our backpack pumps, and went back to bed. We checked it again and doubled the width of the fire line at dawn.

Those of us who live in the actual wildland interface know and respect the public land agencies. But in the last decade some sort of semiretired population of right-wing suburbanites has also moved into the lower elevations, many of them expecting their neighbors to be like minded. This faux-conservative ideology includes a habit of nasty attacks on the county land use planners, animosity in principle against the Forest Service (and especially *biologists*!), and a deep distrust of the California Department of Forestry because they require "logging plans" and also they might want you to clear more brush around your house for fire safety reasons—"but it's PRIVATE PROPERTY," gasp! And some of them have convinced themselves that the volunteer fire department is secretly run by former hippies. All is not bliss in the rural counties. I say "faux conservative" because true conservatives believe in conservation.

Back to fires: When there's a suspicious smoke, the spotter plane takes off and cruises over, and if it's not just somebody's transgressive brush pile, tanker bombers might go out on it right away. If it looks needed, the bulldozer trailer hauler will start moving in that direction. CDF stations are staffed with crews all summer. They have admirable fire trucks, and they'll be there pronto. Still, in a place maybe 25 miles or more from a fire station, if there's a fire started, you're the one to hold it in check and maybe even get it out.

I had an education that pulled together a combination of labor in the woods and on the farm, U.S. Forest Service seasonal work, and a college major in native North American ethnology with a good dose of art, philosophy, and world history. My readings on native California cultures, and then doing backcountry trail crew work for Yosemite National Park, helped me realize that fire was not an enemy but should be a partner. The huge Sierra Nevada range, from the timberline high country down to the oak-and-grass foothills, is all one big fire-adapted ecosystem, and a century of fire suppression—mostly the government's idea—has somewhat messed things up. I wrote the following poem in 1971:

CONTROL BURN

What the Indians
here
used to do, was,
to burn out the brush every year.
in the woods, up the gorges,
keeping the oak and the pine stands
tall and clear
with grasses
and kitkitdizze under them,

never enough fuel there
that a fire could crown.

Now, manzanita,
(a fine bush in its right)
crowds up under the new trees
mixed up with logging slash
and a fire can wipe out all.

Fire is an old story.
I would like,
with a sense of helpful order,
with respect for laws
of nature,
to help my land
with a burn, a hot clean
burn.
     (manzanita seeds will only open
     after a fire passes over
     or once passed through a bear)

And then
it would be more
like,
when it belonged to the Indians

Before.

          —from *Turtle Island*, 1974

—Nowadays they would call it a "prescribed burn" instead of a "control burn"—and it's true you can't always control it. The "Indians" in this particular "here" were the Nisenan.

    The Tahoe National Forest boundary is just a few miles east of where we live. From there and over the Sierra crest clear to Nevada it is a checkerboard of public land and Sierra Pacific Industry lands, section by section. A 28,000-acre fire went through there in early fall 2001. Recovery and salvage logging arguments have been divisive, and the Washington, D.C., agriculture brass has been putting pressure on the Forest Service line officers to cut more timber. In summer 2002, the Biscuit Fire in southwest Oregon swept over half a million acres, largely in the drainage of the lower Rogue. It got national coverage. Next came the always-contentious plans for "salvage logging." The media fell into line, and much of the public has been sweet-talked into thinking cutting merchantable trees contributes to "forest health."

Three points: First, that media reporting on wildfires is usually off the mark. It rarely tells us whether the fire is in brush, grass, or forest, and if in forest, what type. TV reporting might say "ten thousand acres were destroyed," when the truth is that fire intensity is highly variable, and islands of green, patches of barely scorched trees, and totally scorched stands create what foresters might well call a healthy mosaic. A good percentage of Oregon's Biscuit Fire was probably a good thing.

Second, as for the intensely burned areas, the outstanding forest ecologist Jerry Franklin had this to say in his "Comments" on the Draft Environmental Impact Statement for the planned recovery project in the Rogue River National Forest's Biscuit Fire area:

> Salvage logging of large snags and down boles does not contribute to recovery of late-successional forest habitat; in fact, the only activity more antithetical to the recovery process would be removal of surviving green trees from burned sites. Large snags and logs of decay resistant species, such as Douglas-fir and cedars, are critical as early and late successional wildlife habitat as well as for sustaining key ecological processes associated with nutrient, hydrologic, and energy cycles.

and

> Slow re-establishment of forest cover is common following natural stand-replacement disturbances in the Pacific Northwest. . . . This circumstance provides valuable habitat for early-successional species, particularly animals that require snags and logs and diverse plant resources, and for many ecosystem processes. Fifty years for natural re-establishment of forest cover is not a particularly long period; many 19th and early 20th century burns are still not fully reforested.

and finally,

In fact, naturally disturbed habitat that is undergoing slow natural reforestation—without salvage or planting—is the rarest of the forest habitat conditions in the Pacific Northwest. Yet, it is increasingly evident from research, such as at Mount St. Helens, that such large, slowly reforesting disturbed areas are important hotspots of regional biodiversity.

—January 20, 2004

This is bold and visionary science, and contains the hope that both the Forest Service and the forest industry might learn to slow down and go more at the magisterial pace of the life of a forest. The bottom line for all talk of forest sustainability is holding to an undiminished quality of soil and the maintenance of the entire diverse array of wildlife species in full interaction. In earlier times, no matter what the bug kills, fires, or blowdowns, the ecosystems slowly and peacefully adapted and recovered. After all, until recently the entire Human Project too was a lot more leisurely and measured.

The third point, then, is: We shouldn't use a forest fire's aftermath as a cover for further logging. What's called "salvage logging" should be prudent, honest, and quick. The "quick" part is difficult to achieve though, because the U.S. Forest Service has a miserable record of not being clear and aboveboard about its motivations and practices, and the skeptical environmental critics are always planning to take the Forest Service to court, so almost any recovery plan tends to end up in appeals.

Here in the Sierra we live with the threat of fire six months of the year—miles of forest stretching in every direction from our clearing. Over the last 35 years we've taken out the biggest manzanita for several hundred yards, and thinned out a bit of the pine, oak, and madrone canopy. But any fire with enough wind behind it to crown could still overwhelm our little place—four outbuildings, a small barn converted to a seriously useful library and gear room, and a 1,700-square-foot handmade house—and hundreds of square miles beyond.

I saw, and most of my neighbors saw, that our hand clearing work was too slow, and that prescribed burns were also too slow and chancy. Even so, it was a big step to let a big tracked excavator with the "brontosaurus" thrasher head go down our ridge through the oak and pine woods, crunching all the old-growth manzanita (leaving the pine and the oak) and spitting out wood shards everywhere, leaving big tracks in the duff. This for a fuel break to help slow down a wildfire: not just for my place, but for all the forests to the north of me, on both private and public land.

Looking back on it later and recalling travels in the Chobe Forest of Botswana in the early nineties, I can see it's not unlike the way the mopane groves look after a herd of elephants has browsed through, breaking limbs and thrashing the trees to get the leaves. Mother Nature allows for a bit of rough sex, it seems.

Our balance here with this mostly wild ecosystem is the same balance that we would hope for the whole North American West. We'd like to see the forests be a mix of mature and all-age trees cleared out or underburned enough to be able to take the flames when they do come, and big and diverse enough to quickly recover from all but the very worst fires. This is doable—but it sickens one to see whatever clueless administration that is passing through use fear of fire to warp public policy in favor of more exploitation, more industry, and more restrictive law. It is an exact parallel of the use of "terrorism" to warp American values and circumvent our Constitution to justify aggressive foreign policy and to promote again the sick fantasy of a global American empire.

Fire can be a tool and a friend. I've always cooked on wood, outdoors and in. For several decades we had an open firepit in the center of the house—for heat, and for keeping a big hanging iron water kettle hot. The kitchen range was made in St. Louis in 1910 with curvy floral art nouveau motifs. There's also an outside kitchen area with a stone fire circle with forked sticks and crossbar, iron cookpots neatly hanging; a wood-fired sauna bath with a wood-burning stove from the Nippa Company of Bruce Crossing, Michigan—last we heard, the only company still making wood-burning sauna stoves in North America. My sons and daughters learned kindling splitting, fire laying, and feeding the wood as part of daily life.

Now that the center firepit is gone, the main heating stove's an Irish Waterford with a round stone watchtower (for Vikings?) as its symbol, cast into a side panel. The other's a Danish Lange. Along one side it has a cast bas-relief of a stag with a crucifix between its antlers.

The kitchen range: You start the fire going with some dry pine splits, then slip in dry oak to stabilize it and bring the heat up. If needed, you can flash the heat up higher with more pine, then slow it down with a chunk of green oak. Those are old kitchen cooking tips I learned orally from elders.

We use a short-handled hatchet, a graceful slender-handled Hudson Bay ax, a full-length poll ax, and a double-bitted ax for specific tasks. For green wood bucking there's a swede saw, a two-man saw, a small Stihl chain saw, and the big Husqvarna chain saw. For limbing the trees up there are two pole-mounted pruning saws. For splitting, use the double jack with a 10-pound head, and a set of wedges. Also a 12-pound maul. You need at least five wedges for going at it: two for working around from the top, and at least two more for opening it on the sides when it gets sticky. I've used hydraulic splitters too, and they are fast, but there's a lot of setup time. Every year we put five or six cords of oak and pine into the woodsheds, all of it from down and dead trees, and no sign of it ever running short. New trees grow, old trees drop, spring after spring.

▼

The firebreak is in. Sixteen acres of forest and brushland were thinned and brushed, in a long skinny swath, with some watershed improvement and firefighting funds helping pay the bill.

But there will always be brush piles too. Year after year in the Sierra summer, we work with ax and saw taking off limbs and knocking down manzanita, ceanothus, and too-dense pine, fir, or cedar saplings. We drag the limbs and little trees and pile them in an opening. When it gets to be fall, we scythe or duff-hoe back the weeds around them, and make a mineral-earth fire line to be ready for winter burning. (Bailey's in Laytonville sells wide rolls of tough brown paper to put over your brush piles, and this will keep them dry through the first sprinkles of fall rain so that they'll light more easily. Since it's paper you won't be burning the quickly shredding black 4-mil plastic.)

You have to look for proper burning weather, just as with prescribed burns. Not too dry, not too windy, not too wet, not too hot. The very best is when you've had dry weather and can now see the rain clouds definitely coming. It has been a good burn day when the big pile burns to the ground and is still hot enough to keep burning up limb ends from around the edges when you throw them back. Then comes the rain, but still it all burns to ash. No further spreading or underground simmering can take place.

One late November day, I stand by a 12-foot-high burning brush pile, well dressed for it, gloves and goggles, face hot, sprinkles of rain starting to play on my helmet, old boots that I could risk to singe a bit on the embers. A thermos of coffee on a stump. Clouds darkening up from the west, a breeze, a Pacific storm headed this way. Let the flames finish their work—a few more limb ends and stubs around the edge to clean up, a few more dumb thoughts and failed ideas to discard—I think: this has gone on for many lives!

> How many times
> > have I thrown you
> > > back on the fire

Part Three

FIRE ECOLOGY

STORIES AND STUDIES

INTRODUCTION

Fire-Adapted Landscapes

A merica's landscape is shaped by fire. Fire helps to maintain the tallgrass prairies in the Midwest, the open beauty of the south-western ponderosa pine forests, and the grass and chaparral that cloak California's golden hills. Fire-recycled nutrients create new wildlife habitat, and fire helps to break apart rocks to form new soil. Fire even influences landscapes we may not at first believe to have had their origin in blazes. The wet redwood forests of California and the Douglas-fir forests of the Pacific Northwest may not appear to be fire-dependent ecosystems, yet both of them are influenced by fire.

Not all ecosystems are influenced to the same degree by fire, nor in the same way. These differences are important in determining public policy toward fire. To that end, this section presents stories and studies that provide an overview of how fire interacts differently in a variety of landscapes.

In the first essay, I look at the 1988 blazes in Yellowstone National Park that ultimately rejuvenated its landscape. The Yellowstone Plateau is dominated by lodgepole pine forests, which throughout time have been characterized by stand-replacement blazes that kill most of the mature trees. Today, Yellowstone has a vigorous even-aged forest that will set up the park for the next big blaze years from now.

In contrast to the stand-replacement fire regime of Yellowstone, the forests of California's Sierra Nevada—perhaps the most diverse and beautiful in the United States—are characterized by a variety of fire regimes. The majority of these forests experience what are known as mixed-severity fire regimes—that is, a mosaic ranging from light burning of the understory to crown fires that may kill all trees in an area. In his essay, Jan van Wagtendonk speaks of the Sierra as "forests born to burn," yet decades of fire suppression have changed their fire regime, resulting in the thickening of forest stands and the dangerous accumulation of fuels.

Next, Jon Keeley and CJ Fotheringham examine southern

California chaparral wildfires, large, high-intensity fires that frequently threaten dwellings at the wildland-urban interface. The authors argue that these fires are chiefly driven by extreme wind conditions, not fuels, and that unlike many western forests, where fire restoration is needed to reduce fire hazard and return natural processes, California shrublands need greater protection from an increasing onslaught of fires, fuel modification at the wildland-urban interface, and better land use planning.

Dominick DellaSala then provides an overview of fire in the Klamath-Siskiyou ecoregion along the California-Oregon border, an ecosystem that has largely been shaped by fire. He discusses how logging and fire suppression, acting alone or together, have transformed the fire mosaic of this biologically diverse area from fire-adapted systems to fire-prone landscapes, priming the fire pump for uncharacteristically severe wildfires.

Tom Ribe tells the story of fire in the Southwestern ponderosa pine forests of New Mexico and Arizona. Here, frequent but low-intensity blazes have crept through the understory of grasses, killing most of the younger trees and eliminating competition for the larger mature trees, with the result that stand-replacement crown fires are rare events.

Most people do not think of the East as fire-prone, and for the most part it is not, but some of its ecosystems are largely shaped by fire, including the piney woods of the South and the red pines of the Great Lakes states, among others. I provide a brief look at these fire landscapes.

Across the country, the timing, intensity, and size of any particular blaze is strongly influenced by present vegetative communities, past fire history, regional climatic conditions, and topography. As a consequence, broad characterizations often do not represent unique fire patterns in certain regional landscapes. Like the quip that all politics are local, all fire regimes also depend on local conditions.

THE YELLOWSTONE FIRES OF 1988

A Living Wilderness

GEORGE WUERTHNER

THE 1988 FIRES IN YELLOWSTONE NATIONAL PARK *captivated the nation with numerous reports that the park was "destroyed" and that somehow the large blazes were the fault of Park Service management. But large stand-replacement fires are the norm for the lodgepole pine forests that dominate Yellowstone and occur whenever drought combines with high wind—the conditions prevailing in Yellowstone the summer of 1988.*

▼

Yellowstone National Park is an internationally known icon. The 2.2-million-acre park lies at the core of the 28-million-acre Greater Yellowstone Ecosystem.[1] Established in 1872, Yellowstone was the first national park in the world. It is one of the few parts of the West that have never undergone commercial cattle grazing. It was the first place where the nation sought to save an endangered species (wild bison) from extinction, and was later central to the recovery of regional populations of grizzly bear and gray wolf. Yellowstone was also the first place in the country where underground water sources for thermal features were given protection from exploitation.

The large fires that ran across the Greater Yellowstone Ecosystem in the summer of 1988 were the largest in the region since the great 1910 blazes that burned more than 3 million acres in northern Idaho and western Montana. Because of their dramatic size and Yellowstone's international stature, the 1988 fires captured public attention and media headlines. The fires, collectively called the Yellowstone Park Fire by the media, actually involved more than eight major blazes and many smaller ones.[2] The eight largest blazes—known as the North Fork, Fan, Hell Roaring, Storm Creek, Clover-Mist, Red Snake Complex, Mink, and Huck fires—were unprecedented in size, larger than any previous blazes experienced by park visitors in recent history, though well within the norm for the ecosystem. The North Fork blaze, for instance, ran across 531,182 acres.[3] In total, more than 2.2 million acres in the Greater Yellowstone Ecosystem burned, with about 793,000 of these acres (36 percent) within Yellowstone National Park borders.[4]

The park's fame, combined with the unprecedented size of the fires, impelled a major firefighting effort. At the height of the fires, more than 9,000 firefighters were employed in the park, including more than 4,000 military personnel. By November, when the last flame was extinguished, over 25,000 firefighters had been deployed at one time or another to contain the blazes, and more than $120 million had been spent.[5] Some 665 miles of hand-cut fire lines and 137 miles of bulldozer lines had been constructed in a vain effort to control the blazes.[6]

Most media accounts portrayed the burned park and surrounding lands as a "natural disaster" that "devastated" the park's beauty and natural environment.[7] There was little attempt to put the fires in an ecological context, and most media sources were nearby residents and businesspeople, not fire ecologists or others with an understanding of fire's role in the ecosystem. In a study of 589 media reports about the fires, journalism professor Conrad Smith found that only 29 included ecological information in the first three paragraphs.[8]

The news media and many politicians asserted that Yellowstone had been "damaged," "devastated," or "destroyed" by the massive fires.[9] However, stand-replacement crown fires are the norm for the lodgepole pine forests that dominate Yellowstone.[10] Low-intensity/high-frequency fire regimes, such as those found in ponderosa pine forests, can be suppressed under most circumstances.[11] Stand-replacement crown blazes are difficult to stop, however, and impossible to control when terrain, weather, and wind act in concert.

Some critics maintained that prescribed burns or fires purposefully set during less severe conditions could have reduced fuels and thus prevented the large blazes of 1988. But modeling by fire researcher James Brown of the U.S. Forest Service Intermountain Research Station concluded that prescribed fire is impractical for Yellowstone. In most years, few if any acres would burn in the park's forested areas because of the naturally moist summer conditions, and the window for any prescribed burning would be extremely small—generally the month of August, when visitation to the park is greatest. Furthermore, prescribed burns would need to blaze across 50,000 acres a year every year for decades to have any effect on fuel loading.[12]

Contrary to media hysteria about what reporters deemed the Park Service's "let burn" policy, most of the 1988 fires were fought from their inception, including the North Fork Fire, which began when a woodcutter tossed a cigarette just outside the park borders, starting what eventually became the single largest fire of that summer. Nevertheless, media coverage of the Yellowstone 1988 blazes had a chilling effect on wildfire policy throughout the country. For instance, in 1988, 26 national parks, including Yellowstone, had prescribed natural burn policies that permitted naturally ignited fires (most lightning caused) to burn under specific prescribed circumstances. After 1988, most such fire programs were weakened or canceled. The average annual acreage burned on national park lands fell from 32,135 acres per year in 1983–1988 to 3,708 acres per year in 1990–1994.[13] As of 2005, suppression of fires is the norm, even on national park lands and within wilderness areas, where natural ecological processes like wildfire are supposed to be given a free hand.

The truth about the 1988 fires is that Yellowstone was not "damaged," "devastated," or "destroyed" by these blazes; rather, the park and the Greater Yellowstone Ecosystem were rejuvenated and restored by wildfire. Indeed, the 1988 fires demonstrated that Yellowstone was still functioning properly and could accommodate landscape-scale disturbances.[14]

THE HISTORY OF FIRE IN YELLOWSTONE

On most federally managed lands, fire was initially viewed as a threat. Yellowstone's creation as a national park in 1872 resulted in few immediate changes in management. The National Park Service and its ranger force were not established until 1916, and at first Yellowstone was largely neglected, with little human intervention in processes like fire. In 1886, the U.S. Army was deployed to the park to patrol and protect the park features. This work included the suppression of fires.

Fire suppression continued after the National Park Service took over management of the park from the army in 1916. However, records of fires suppressed were limited to occasional ranger reports until a formal record system was established in 1931. In that summer, an 18,000-acre blaze reinvigorated the area around Heart Lake. This blaze was eventually quelled by rain, not firefighters. It was only after World War II that equipment improvements and modern air transport made parkwide suppression of fires effective. Yet just as fire suppression activities were becoming effective, major philosophical changes within the Park Service led to questioning the wisdom of putting out all blazes.

Beginning in the 1930s, ideas about park management began to change from interventionist management to guardianship of natural processes. One of the first modifications in management resulting from this shift was the termination of the park's predator control policies. In the 1960s, Yellowstone stopped feeding bears along roadsides and at garbage dumps in an effort to force the bears into more natural feeding and travel patterns. About the same time, the park also terminated fish stocking and instituted preservation of native fish populations.

Along with all these other philosophical and management changes, park ecologists called into question the continued suppression of fires. Recognizing that fire had an important role to play in the ecosystem, Yellowstone was one of the first national parks to establish and implement a fire program that permitted lightning-caused wildfires to burn without an immediate suppression response. In the first 16 years (1972–1987) of this new fire policy, only 15 Yellowstone blazes grew larger than 100 acres. And the single greatest acreage that burned in any one year during the period this policy was in force was only a bit more than 20,000 acres.

The dearth of large fires in Yellowstone during those years contributed to the sense that the fires of 1988 were "abnormal." However, research done in the park before and after the fires demonstrated that large stand-replacement blazes are typical for this ecosystem. Ecologists Bill Romme and Don Despain's study of 320,000 acres in Yellowstone's subalpine forests found that fires burned in this region on average every 300 to 400 years. Indeed, they found that less than 10 percent of the watershed had burned in the previous 350 years, with the last major fires occurring between 1690 and 1740.[15] A more extensive 17,000-year fire history of the park, reconstructed through

study of charcoal and pollen from lakebed samples, found that periodic large blazes are completely normal[16] and well within the expected
"historic range of variability." And research on charcoal found in
debris flows (sediments washed down from the mountains by intense
thunderstorms) within the park confirmed that stand-replacement
fires are common.[17] Indeed, Yellowstone's basic ecology is driven by
large wildfires.[18]

FIRE ECOLOGY IN YELLOWSTONE

Yellowstone Park is composed primarily of volcanic rock, erupted by
numerous volcanoes over the centuries. Indeed, the central portion of
Yellowstone is an immense collapsed caldera more than 45 miles
across.[19] This volcanic history profoundly influences vegetation in the
region. Greater Yellowstone Ecosystem soils formed from andesite
have a higher nutrient level and better water-holding ability than the
coarser-textured, nutrient-poor rhyolite-based soils that are also common here.[20] Consequently, different forest communities are found on
these soils: lodgepole pine tends to dominate the drier rhyolite-derived
soils, whereas spruce-fir communities develop into old-growth forests
on soils formed from andesite.[21] Forests on good soils developed from
andesite bedrock produce more fuels than those on poor soils developed on rhyolite, yet rhyolite is the most common bedrock in the park.
The limited fuels, particularly on rhyolite soils, contribute to the
"asbestos" reputation of Yellowstone's forests.

The abundance of lodgepole pine also affects fire behavior in the
park. Lodgepole pine forests are slow to accumulate litter that promotes blazes, and self-pruning of lower branches effectively restricts
movement of surface fires into the crowns of trees. Most of Yellowstone
National Park is clothed with dense forests of lodgepole pine. Yet some
60 percent of the forest stands in Yellowstone's forested habitat would
eventually become nearly pure stands of subalpine fir were it not for
fires that favor pine. Lodgepole pine is seral (successional) to subalpine fir; but because of stand-replacement blazes, most of
Yellowstone's forested habitat consists of pine, not fir.[22] In other words,
in the absence of wildfire, most of the Yellowstone Plateau would eventually be dominated by subalpine fir. But this doesn't happen, because

fire tends to favor lodgepole pine, and lodgepole forests burn infrequently, creating naturally long intervals between fire events.

Data compiled by ecologist Don Despain[23] show that in the 15
years prior to 1988—during which Yellowstone managers allowed
most wildfires to burn without suppression—only 16 percent of the
blazes grew larger than 5 acres in size; the vast majority (84 percent)
were naturally extinguished after burning only a few acres. There are
good reasons for these observations.

First, crown fires, or stand-replacement blazes, require understory
fuels to heat the crowns of trees to the ignition point. Young lodgepole
pine forests have very little undergrowth and fuel to carry a blaze, in
part because the young pines can't grow in the shade of mature trees.
Subalpine fir, however, is shade-tolerant and readily grows in the
understory of lodgepole pine forests. It also maintains its lower
branches, providing an ideal conduit for flames to travel from the
ground into the tops of trees. In addition, subalpine fir resins are very
flammable. Even a green subalpine fir will burn with gusto under
droughty conditions. However, it takes about 150 years for fir to
become established beneath lodgepole pine, and another 150 years of
slow growth before these fir trees are sufficiently large to reach up into
to the canopy of the pines.[24] For this reason, only fires in mature lodgepole stands with a good understory of fir are likely to "crown" and
become stand-replacement blazes.

CLIMATE/WEATHER INFLUENCES
ON FIRE NUMBER AND SIZE

Another reason large blazes are relatively infrequent events in
Yellowstone has to do with moisture. In wet years, there are essentially
no fires in Yellowstone. Most of Yellowstone is high country, with an
average elevation of 8,000 feet. Snow comes early and leaves late
across much of the park. In some years, snowpack lingers into June or
even early July. As a consequence, soils and fuels are saturated well
into summer, and vegetation remains lush and green until late August,
by which time new snow begins to accumulate in higher elevations.

How wet or dry any particular year or series of years may be is
related to Pacific Decadal Oscillations and El Niño effects—patterns of

climate variability associated with fluctuating ocean temperatures. When both these effects occur together in the northern Rockies, large fires are likely because of the resulting dry weather.[25] Indeed, large-scale climatic changes over the past 17,000 years have shown that an upswing in fires accompanies periods of drought, while cooler, wetter summer conditions lead to reduced numbers of fires.[26]

CONDITIONS CONTRIBUTING TO BIG BLAZES

Fire intensity and behavior are driven by three main factors: weather, terrain, and fuels. Of these three, weather is by far the most important. If it's dry, hot, and windy, any fire will burn with great fury.[27] The summer of 1988 was not just any summer. It was the driest ever recorded in Yellowstone, with virtually no moisture during July and August. Relative humidity was below 20 percent most of the summer and reached a record low of 6 percent at Tower Falls on August 22.[28] The drop in relative humidity dried out park vegetation. By mid-July, the moisture content of grasses and litter on the ground was only 2 to 3 percent, that of down trees 7 percent. By comparison, kiln-dried lumber has a moisture content of 12 percent. Low fuel moisture caused fires to burn well into the night instead of "dying down" nightly, as is typical of most blazes under less severe drought conditions.[29]

Because of the low moisture content of vegetation and the continuing drought, the Park Service suspended its prescribed natural fire policies in midsummer. Beginning July 21, when fewer than 17,000 acres within the park had burned, all fires were fought as soon as they were detected. In 1988, a total of 248 fires started in the Greater Yellowstone Ecosystem (which includes Yellowstone National Park and much of the surrounding national forest); 50 of those were in Yellowstone National Park. Only 31 of these were permitted to burn— thus the vast majority of blazes were fought from their inception,[30] and yet more than a million acres were rejuvenated by fire.

However, drought isn't the only factor that made the summer of 1988 exceptional in recent memory. A key ingredient for large blazes—assuming the presence of an ignition source like lightning—is wind.[31] The 1988 Yellowstone fires demonstrated how critical wind and regional drought are to the development of large blazes.[32] Though older stands of lodgepole with understory of subalpine fir are more likely to crown and burn than younger stands, that generalization did not hold in the summer of 1988: high winds that blew across the Yellowstone Plateau pushed flames through all forest age classes.[33]

What many citizens did not understand, and what media accounts often did not reflect, is how much regional climatic and local weather conditions influenced and affected the 1988 fires—as they do all large fires. Low humidity, even at night, joined with high winds to advance the flames, throwing firebrands as much as a mile in advance of fire fronts and torching new fires. Nearly half of all acreage affected by the fires occurred on just four days when winds were exceptionally high. For instance, on August 20, high winds pushed the fires across 150,000 acres in a single day.[34] And on September 6 and 7 the Clover-Mist Fire raced 14 miles down Jones Creek just east of the park border and burned 37,000 acres.[35]

Unfortunately, the public has been led to believe that modern fire-fighting techniques and equipment can control fires. This is true under ordinary fire conditions; however, when drought and wind coincide, the best firefighters can do is to get out of the way. Close scrutiny of media and official reports shows that the majority of big blazes are contained when weather conditions change. One Yellowstone firefighter unwittingly revealed this connection when he noted in his official report on a fire fought in the 1930s: "Finally got the fire under control—had a hell of a time breaking camp in the rain." In 1988, it was again a change in the weather that finally brought the fires' spread to a halt when, on September 11, snowfall, not firefighters, brought the blazes under control.

EFFECTS OF FIRE ON YELLOWSTONE

Despite the huge acreage affected, very little long-term damage was incurred by the park and its facilities. Some 67 structures were destroyed, but wildlife casualties were relatively light, given the magnitude of the fires: only 345 elk (of an estimated 40,000–50,000), 36 deer, 12 moose, 6 black bears, and 9 bison died as result of the fires.[36] The enduring drought and its effects on plant growth actually had a greater impact on park wildlife than the fires. Measured summer forage production in 1988 was less than 50 percent of normal years.[37] Far greater numbers of large mammals starved because of reduced forage production than died in the blazes.

Researchers also studied the effects of the fires on watersheds and fisheries. Initially the loss of vegetation caused significant sedimentation and debris flow into park streams and rivers. However, such debris flows must be viewed within a historical context. Sedimentation records from the Holocene to the present show that approximately 30 percent of the deposits in alluvial fans are the result of past fires.[38]

The loss of forested cover increased solar radiation and snowmelt in affected drainages and led to higher runoff, but overall, the effects on peak flows in major park rivers were slight. Measurement of flows on the Yellowstone River at Corwin Springs, Montana, just outside the park, showed an increase of only 4 to 5 percent. However, the loss of tree cover and subsequent reduction in tree use of soil moisture led to an increase in summer and fall flows—a time when water flows are critical to fish populations.[39] The loss of vegetation also led to higher soil erosion levels. However, erosion generally peaks within 10 years of a blaze, as vegetation reclaims the site, and much sediment is trapped behind fallen logs.[40]

Crown fires like those in Yellowstone also create what is termed "coarse woody debris." These logs are very important to postfire recovery. When they fall across a slope, they trap sediment. When they fall into a stream, they stabilize the banks and slow the velocity of water, reducing flood-induced channel erosion. They also are important habitat for fish. Furthermore, these snags and logs are a long-term resource that may last up to 100 years after a fire. A comparison with clearcut sites in Wyoming found that logged sites provided 50 percent less coarse woody debris than unlogged sites,[41] a fact with important implications for postfire salvage logging proposals.

The fires were found to have minimum impact on fish, except in the smallest drainages, and within a year, fish populations reestablished themselves in streams. No effects on fisheries in the larger rivers in the park were observed.[42] The long-term effects of the fires on the park's meadows and grasslands were minimal. Since heat from fires rises, most plant roots are protected by soils. Hence, grasses and flowers in meadows were unaffected by the blazes. Indeed, in years following the fires, spectacular wildflower displays were evident in these areas.

Forested areas have also seen regeneration of new trees. Lodgepole pine is well adapted to the Yellowstone fire regime. Since it has a thin bark that provides little protection against blazes, most mature lodgepole are killed by fire, except in the lowest-intensity burns. However, they possess several attributes that permit them to readily compete and colonize burned sites.[43] Most lodgepole pines in Yellowstone have serotinous cones. Waxy coatings on the scales hold seeds inside the cones—sometimes for up to 75 years. When heated, the cone scales open, releasing the seeds. Although the degree of serotiny varies across the Yellowstone landscape,[44] and from region to region (e.g., serotiny is less common in Sierra Nevada lodgepole forests), as a generalization, fire improves seed cast and recolonization of lodgepole pine forests. Few severely burned sites were far from potential seed sources. Studying the aftermath of the Yellowstone fires of 1988, researchers found the majority of severely burned areas were within 600 feet of unburned or lightly burned areas.[45] Nearly all forested areas in the park are in varying stages of reforestation.

In the Yellowstone region, fires also played an unexpected role in the establishment of new aspen clones.[46] Prior to the Yellowstone fires, aspen were thought to only reproduce in the Rockies via sprouting from existing root systems, creating genetically identical clones. Aspen seeds are tiny and have almost no food reserves. They require bare mineral soil and high soil moisture to successfully germinate. In most places where such moist conditions are found, existing vegetation precludes any seedling establishment. However, immediately after the large blazes of 1988, new aspen seedlings were observed throughout the Yellowstone Plateau, often far from any known root source or existing aspen grove. It is thought that the severity of drought and large extent of the fires burned away litter in moist areas that normally would not burn— except under severe fire conditions. And these areas became prime sites for aspen seedlings to successfully colonize.[47] As in the past, many of these aspen shoots were browsed by elk, moose, and other mammals; however, in yet another ecological benefit of the blazes, as trees killed by the fires began to fall, they created barriers to browsing that may allow the establishment of new aspen stands throughout the park over time.[48]

(The reintroduction of wolves in Yellowstone National Park—which keep the elk and moose moving—is also theorized to have benefited aspen establishment and regeneration.)

Another effect of the large blazes that raced across Yellowstone was the increase of heterogeneity in the vegetative landscape. Fires rarely kill all trees across the landscape, even in stand-replacement blazes. Rather, the fires hop and skip across the landscape—as a consequence of topographical and terrain features, wind patterns, time of day when the fire moved through the area, and fuel loading, including stand age—to create a mosaic of unburned, lightly burned, and severely burned patches.[49] Since younger stands of lodgepole pine have lesser amounts of fine and ladder fuels than older more mature stands, past fires can influence where, when, and how intense future blazes will burn.[50]

YELLOWSTONE AS PRESERVER OF WILDFIRE

While park protection is critical to preservation of wildlife, geothermal features, and scenery, what Yellowstone does better than nearly any other landscape in the temperate world is to protect the wild—the wild in fire and the wild in the landscape. Fire is to the Greater Yellowstone Ecosystem what the wolf is to Yellowstone's elk herds—a major evolutionary force that maintains the wild nature and ecosystem integrity of the park. And just as with the wolf, which is critical to the wild behavior and nature of its prey, if we are to truly preserve wildness as an essential element of the landscape, then we must provide space for wildfire to "live" unimpeded with a minimum amount of interference from humans. In the Greater Yellowstone Ecosystem we have such a space.

FIRE ECOLOGY OF THE SIERRA NEVADA

Forests Born to Burn

JAN W. VAN WAGTENDONK, PH.D.

FIRE ALWAYS HAS BEEN AND ALWAYS WILL BE *an ecological force in the Sierra Nevada. Decades of fire suppression have changed this role, allowing stands to thicken and fuels to accumulate, especially in the foothills and lower montane zone, where developments are increasing. We can either manage and live with fire on our terms or let fire dictate the terms. The choice is ours.*

▼

John Muir named the Sierra Nevada the Range of Light; a better name might have been the Range of Fire. Fire has been an ecological force in the Sierra Nevada since the retreat of the glaciers over 10,000 years ago. Flammable fuels, abundant ignition sources, and hot, dry summers combine to produce conditions conducive for an active fire role. While this role has varied over the millennia as these factors, especially climate, have changed, fire continues to be a significant ecological process today, shaping the vegetation and other ecosystem components. In order for humans to coexist with fire, land management activities must include the use of fire along with traditional suppression activities.

PHYSICAL GEOGRAPHY

Extending for more than 400 miles along the eastern side of California, the Sierra Nevada form a massive westward-sloping block with a steep eastern escarpment. This block of the earth's crust broke free along a bounding eastern fault line and has been uplifted and tilted.[1] The relatively moderate western slope of the Sierra Nevada is incised with a series of steep river canyons, from the Feather River in the north to the Kern River in the south. As the mountain block was uplifted, the rivers cut deeper and deeper into underlying rock.[2] Glaciers continued the erosion process by stripping the overlying metamorphic rocks from the granitic intrusions below, exposing large expanses of the core through-out the range.[3] The foothills are gently rolling, with both broad and narrow valleys. At the midelevations, landforms include canyons and broad ridges that run primarily from east-northeast to west-southwest. Rugged mountainous terrain dominates the landscape at the higher elevations, reaching over 14,000 feet at the southern end of the range.

CLIMATE PATTERNS

The pattern of weather in the Sierra Nevada is influenced by its topog-raphy and geographic position relative to California's Central Valley, the Coast Ranges, and the Pacific Ocean. The primary sources of pre-cipitation are winter storms that move in from the North Pacific and cross the Coast Ranges and Central Valley before reaching the Sierra Nevada. As the air masses move up the gentle western slope, precipi-tation increases and, at the higher elevations, falls as snow. By the time it has crossed the Sierra Nevada crest, the air mass has lost most of its moisture, and precipitation decreases sharply. Precipitation also decreases from north to south, with nearly twice as much falling in the northern Sierra Nevada as does in the south. Mean annual precipita-tion ranges from a low of 10 inches at the western edge of the foothills to over 80 inches north of Lake Tahoe. More than half of the total pre-cipitation falls in January, February, and March, much of it as snow. Summer precipitation is associated with afternoon thunderstorms and subtropical storms moving up from the Gulf of California.

Sierra Nevada temperatures are generally warm in the summer and cool in the winter. At one weather station at 5,400 feet in the northern Sierra Nevada, the maximum normal daily temperature occurs in July at 77 degrees Fahrenheit, while the minimum daily nor-mal of 30 degrees occurs in January. The record high temperature was 93 degrees in September, and the record low was 5 degrees in January. Temperatures decrease as latitude and elevation increase. Relative humidity mirrors temperature, with the normal 10:00 a.m. relative humidity highest in January at 60 percent and lowest in July at 30 per-cent. Extremely low relative humidity is common in the summer. Southwest- and west-facing slopes, particularly those associated with steep canyons, receive disproportionately large amounts of afternoon solar radiation, making them hotter and drier in the summer than the north-, northeast-, and east-facing slopes. Such high temperatures and low humidities ensure that fires are able to burn every summer.

Wind speeds and direction are variable throughout the Sierra Nevada. During the fire season, winds are associated with frontal passages, thunderstorms, and diurnal heating and cooling. Up-canyon winds in the morning are particularly effective in spreading fires as the day begins to warm. At the northern Sierra Nevada weather station, winds average 7 miles per hour but have been recorded as high as 70 miles per hour out of the north during October.

Lightning is pervasive in the Sierra Nevada, occurring in every month and on every square mile, with over 210,000 strikes from 1985 through 2000.[4] There are spatial and temporal patterns, however. The highest concentration of lightning strikes occurs just east of the crest in the central part of the range. There is a strong correlation between the number of lightning strikes and elevation, with strikes increasing with elevation. Summer afternoon heating of slopes causes uplift of moist air masses in the mountains and results in the development of thunderstorms. Ridgetops receive more strikes than valley bottoms. The greatest number of strikes occurs in the afternoon in July and August. At all elevations, there are a sufficient number of lightning strikes to act as ignition sources for naturally occurring fires.

THE ROLE OF FIRE IN SIERRA NEVADA ECOSYSTEMS

The vegetation of the Sierra Nevada is as variable as its topography and climate. In response to actual evapotranspiration and the available water budget, the vegetation forms six broad ecological zones that roughly correspond with elevation.[5] These zones are arranged in elevation belts from the Central Valley up to the Sierra Nevada crest and back down to the Great Basin. The bands increase in elevation from the northern to the southern Sierra Nevada.

Foothill Shrub and Woodland

The foothill shrub and woodland zone covers nearly 6,000 square miles from the lowest foothills at 500 feet to occasional stands at 8,000 feet, reaching a maximum extent between 1,000 and 1,500 feet.[6] The primary vegetation types in this zone are foothill pine–interior live oak woodlands, mixed-hardwood woodlands, and chaparral shrublands.

Fire regimes in the foothill zone vary with topography and vegetation. Before the era of fire suppression, in the lower portions with gentler topography, the oak grassland savannah areas burned frequently and with low to moderate intensity. Fire season began in early summer and extended to fall. Steeper areas dominated by chaparral and scattered trees or pockets of conifers burned less frequently and with higher-intensity crown fires, resulting in severe effects to vegetation. These are amongst the driest areas in the Sierra Nevada, with less than 25 inches of average annual precipitation. Because of the high number of species with fire-enhanced responses, such as vigorous sprouting and seeds that require heat to germinate, the vegetation overall is resilient to high-severity fires, although shifts in the abundance of different vegetation types have occurred naturally and as a result of fire suppression.

Lower Montane Forest

The lower montane forest occupies over 8,000 square miles, primarily on the west side of the Sierra Nevada just above the foothill zone.[7] This forest is the most prevalent ecological zone in the range. Although some stands may occur as high as 11,000 feet, the greatest occupied area is between 5,000 and 5,500 feet. Major vegetation types include California black oak, ponderosa pine, white fir–mixed conifer, Douglas-fir–mixed conifer, and mixed-evergreen forests. Interspersed within the forests are chaparral stands, riparian forests, and meadows and seeps.

Historically, fire was generally frequent in the lower montane zone, with return intervals ranging from 2 years on average at the landscape scale to 20 years at the stand level.[8] There was noticeable variation in fire pattern with latitude and elevation, related to shifts in fire season and precipitation. Drier areas with longer fire seasons experienced the most frequent and regular fires. These areas are most prevalent in the southern and central Sierra Nevada, as well as throughout the range on south aspects, ridges, and lower elevations, and tend to be dominated or codominated by ponderosa pine and California black oak. Throughout the zone, relatively cooler and wetter sites have had frequent but less regular fire and are more likely to have a presence or dominance of Douglas-fir and white fir. Historically, fire patterns and vegetation interactions also varied at fine spatial scales for all portions of this zone. Open or more variable forest structure likely occurred as a result of more frequent fire. Not only did fire with different return interval patterns favor different species, it also affected forest structure by thinning the young trees, leaving a patchier or more open forest, and selectively retaining larger, fire-resistant trees.[9]

Upper Montane Forest

The upper montane forest covers more than 4,000 square miles and extends from as low as 2,500 feet to as high as 11,500 feet.[10] It is most widely spread between 6,500 and 7,000 feet, where it covers 700 square miles. Forests within this zone include extensive stands of red fir, along with occasional stands of western white pine. Woodlands with Jeffrey pine and mountain juniper occupy exposed ridges, while meadows and quaking aspen stands occur in moist areas.

Fire regimes in the upper montane forests have not been significantly affected by fire suppression. Although the forest receives a proportionally higher number of lightning strikes on a per area basis than the lower montane forest, fewer fires result.[11] Lightning is often accompanied with rain, and the fuel beds of short needles compacted by the previous winter's snow are not easily ignited. Those fires that do occur are usually of low intensity and spread slowly through the landscape, except under extreme weather conditions. Natural fuel breaks such as rock outcrops and moist meadows prevent extensive fires from occurring.[12] Fire regimes tend to be more variable in frequency and severity than those in the lower montane forest. Median fire return interval estimates calculated from fire scars range from 12 to 69 years.[13] Data from lightning fires allowed to burn under prescribed conditions in Yosemite National Park suggest that in upper montane red fir forest, the fire rotation—that is, the number of years it would take to burn the forest at the current rate—is 163 years.[14] Occasional crown fires occur in red fir stands, but normally fires spread slowly because of compact surface fuels and the prevalence of natural terrain breaks.

Subalpine Forest

The subalpine forest zone ranges from 5,500 to 11,500 feet and reaches its maximum extent between 9,500 and 10,000 feet.[15] It

includes 2,000 square miles and consists of lodgepole pine and mountain hemlock forests; limber pine, foxtail pine, and whitebark pine
woodlands; and numerous large meadow complexes.

Although lightning strikes are plentiful in the subalpine forest
zone, ignitions are infrequent, and fire suppression has had little
impact. Between 1930 and 1993, in Yosemite National Park's subalpine forest zone, lightning caused only 341 fires, and those fires
burned only 6,000 acres, primarily in the lodgepole pine forest.[16]
Between 1972 and 1993, when lightning fires were allowed to burn
under prescribed conditions, only six fires in lodgepole pine grew larger
than 300 acres. When fires occur in lodgepole pine forests, the more
prolifically seeding pines replace encroaching red firs and mountain
hemlocks. In areas where lodgepole pines have invaded meadows, fires
will kill back the trees.[17] Stand-replacing fires are rare, but when they
do occur, lodgepole pines become reestablished from the released
seeds. The fire return interval in lodgepole pine has been estimated to
be several hundred years.[18] Data from fires that have burned in
Yosemite's wildland fire use zone, where lightning fires are allowed to
burn under prescribed conditions, suggest a fire rotation of 579
years.[19] In any case, fires are rare and are usually light to moderately
severe.

Alpine Meadow and Shrubland

Sitting astride the crest of the Sierra Nevada is the nearly 1,700-
square-mile alpine meadow and shrubland ecological zone.[20] This zone
extends from 7,000 feet in the northern Sierra Nevada to 14,500 feet
in the south, with most of the area between 11,000 and 11,500 feet.
Alpine fell fields—containing grasses, sedges, and herbs—and willow
shrublands are the dominant vegetation types.

The short growing season produces little biomass, and fuels are
sparse. Lightning strikes occur regularly in the alpine zone but result
in few fires. Weather, coincident with lightning, is usually not conducive for fire ignition or spread. Fires are so infrequent that they
probably did not play a role in the evolutionary development of the
plants that occur in the alpine zone. The 70-year record of lightning
fires in Yosemite's alpine zone includes only eight fires, burning a total
of 28 acres, primarily in a single fire.[21]

Eastside Forest and Woodland

On the eastern side of the Sierra Nevada, Jeffrey pine, white fir, and mixed-conifer forests and single-leaf pinyon woodlands cover a total of 1,500 square miles.[22] The zone ranges in elevation from 3,500 to 9,500 feet and is most prevalent between 5,000 and 5,500 feet.

Fire regimes vary with both vegetation type and landscape location. Historically, the most frequent and lowest-intensity fires occurred in the lower-elevation, open, pine-dominated areas of this zone. On less productive portions of the zone south of Yosemite, Jeffrey pine woodlands likely had fire regimes similar to those described for upper montane Jeffrey pine woodlands. In the Lake Tahoe basin, mean fire return intervals ranged from 22 to 122 years across sample areas of several acres for Jeffrey pine and white fir stands on the drier east shore.[23] White fir forests occurred in a mosaic, with chaparral on the more mesic sites on north slopes and at higher elevations. Fire regimes included a greater variety of severities, owing, in part, to less consistent fire intervals and patterns. The fire season was primarily from summer through fall, with longer seasons at lowest elevations in open pine forests.

THE HISTORY OF FIRE IN THE SIERRA NEVADA

The earliest evidence of the presence of fire in the Sierra Nevada can be seen in lake sediments over 16,000 years old in Yosemite National Park.[24] Charcoal fragments in sediment cores from seven meadows, from Yosemite south to Sequoia National Park, occur as early as 10,000 years B.P. and continue to the present.[25] Six separate peaks in charcoal deposits were recorded between 8,700 and 800 years B.P. in multiple meadows some distance apart. Five of these peaks occurred after 4,500 B.P. Such increases in charcoal abundance above the background level indicate large individual fires or fire periods. Charcoal was less prevalent in the early Holocene than in the late Holocene, suggesting that the climate was drier during the earlier period and that the forests were too open to carry large fires.[26]

Fire scars offer another source of documentation for the historical role of fire. Fire scar records from seven mixed-conifer stands between 4,300 and 5,600 feet on the western slope of the Sierra Nevada, between the Feather River on the north and the San Joaquin River on the south, indicate that fire return intervals ranged from 7 to 9 years during the period from 1380 to 1920.[27] In a study area 30 miles west of Lake Tahoe, fire scars dating from 1649 through 1921 showed median fire intervals of between 5 and 15 years.[28] Farther south, in Kings Canyon National Park, fires scarred trees in mixed coniferous forests between 5,600 and 6,900 feet every 7 years on west-facing slopes and every 16 years on east-facing slopes.[29]

Fire scar records from five giant sequoia groves located from Yosemite to south of Sequoia National Park confirm the presence of fire in the Sierra Nevada for the past 3,000 years, with the earliest recorded fire in 1125 B.C.[30] Regionally, according to climate reconstructions determined from a different set of trees, synchronous fire occurrence was inversely related to annual precipitation amount. The scars showed that extensive fires burned every 3.4 to 7.7 years during the cool period between A.D. 500 and 800, and every 2.2 to 3.7 years during the warm period from A.D. 1000 to 1300. After 1300, fire return intervals increased, except for short periods, during the 1600s for one grove and during the 1700s for two other groves.[31] Fire-free intervals ranged from 15 to 30 years during the long-interval period, and were always less than 13 years during the short-interval years.

Ignitions by Native Americans were also a source of fires, possibly as early as 9,000 years ago.[32] Native American use of fire was extensive and had specific cultural purposes, such as cultivating basketry materials.[33] It is currently not possible to distinguish charcoal deposits or fire scars caused by lightning fires from those caused by Native American ignitions. However, some scientists have attributed a decline in pine pollen in Yosemite Valley sediments, along with a simultaneous increase in oak pollen and charcoal in those sediments, to expanding populations of aboriginal inhabitants 650 years ago.[34] Similarly, burning by aboriginals cannot be ruled out as the cause of an increase in charcoal beginning 4,500 years ago.[35] It is reasonable to assume that the contribution of ignitions by Native Americans was significant but that it varied over the spectrum of inhabited landscapes.[36]

The arrival of European Americans in the Sierra Nevada in the mid-19th century affected fire regimes in several ways. Native Americans were often driven from their lands, and diseases brought from Europe decimated their populations. As a result, use of fire by

Native Americans was greatly reduced. During the 1860s, settlers further exacerbated the situation by introducing cattle and sheep to the Sierra Nevada, setting fires in attempts to improve the range, and excluding fires from other areas to protect timber and watershed values.

Of all the activities affecting fire regimes, the exclusion of fire by organized government suppression forces has had the greatest effect. Beginning in the late 1890s, the U.S. Army attempted to extinguish all fires within Yosemite and Sequoia national parks. When the Forest Service was established in 1905, it developed both a theoretical basis for systematic fire suppression and considerable expertise to execute that theory on national forests.[37] This expertise was expanded to the fledgling National Park Service when it was established in 1916. Fire control remained the dominant management practice throughout the Sierra Nevada until the late 1960s. Fire exclusion resulted in an increase in accumulated surface debris and density of shrubs and understory trees. Although the number of fires and the total area burned decreased between 1908 and 1968, the proportion of the yearly area burned by the largest fire each year increased.[38] Suppression forces were able to extinguish most fires while they were small but during extreme weather conditions they were unable to control the large ones.

Fire Management

Homeowners and land managers in the Sierra Nevada have a choice when dealing with the fuels that have accumulated as a result of decades of fire exclusion. They can either actively treat fuels, or wait for a wildfire to treat fuels for them. Since the late 1960s, the National Park Service in Yosemite, Sequoia, and Kings Canyon national parks has taken an active approach to fuels management. Following early research by university scientists,[39] the National Park Service changed its fire policy in 1968 to allow the use of prescribed fires deliberately set by managers, and to allow fires of natural origin to burn under prescribed conditions—the latter known as "wildland fire use." The Forest Service followed suit in 1974, changing from a policy of fire control to one of fire management.[40] As a result, fire was reintroduced to the Sierra Nevada landscape through programs of prescribed burning and wildland fire use.[41]

For much of the Sierra Nevada, however, fire suppression is still the rule, resulting in a change in fire regime from less frequent, low-intensity fires to frequent large fires.[42] Fuel accumulations, brush, small trees, and dense forests produce very different conditions for the inevitable fire that occurs, whether from lightning or human sources. These landscape-scale changes are characterized by departures from the natural fire return interval—the number of years between successive naturally occurring fires for a given vegetation type. Prior to the exclusion of fire, intervals between fires ranged from a few years in lower montane forests to centuries in subalpine forests.

The Ecological Basis for Fire Management Programs

Interruption of the natural fire regime, reflected in departures from normal fire return intervals, is a major challenge for Yosemite National Park's fire management program.[43] Areas that have missed multiple fire return intervals are more susceptible to stand-replacing wildland fires, which are uncommon in natural surface-burning fire regimes. The goal of Yosemite's fire program is to restore and maintain the natural range of variability in fire regime through focusing fire treatments on areas with greater fire return interval departures.

To analyze fire return interval departures in Yosemite National Park, fire managers use a geographic information system (GIS) model based on a method originally developed in Sequoia and Kings Canyon national parks.[44] This model combines information on fire history and fire ecology to assess the ecological condition of all vegetation communities, using departures from the natural fire return intervals as an indicator of change. The analysis consists of four steps: (1) vegetation types are defined on the basis of similar fuels and fire behavior; (2) fire return intervals based on fire scar studies are assigned to each type of vegetation;[45] (3) the number of years since an area last burned is determined from fire history maps dating back to 1930;[46] and (4) departures from the natural fire interval are calculated using the return interval. Landscape-scale changes in the fire regime are characterized by an analysis of departures from the fire return interval had fires been allowed to burn naturally.[47] In general, the further vegetation communities depart from their natural fire regimes, the more unnatural conditions prevail and the higher the risk of the occurrence of a stand-replacement wildland fire that is not natural to surface-burning fire regimes.

The analysis showed that 74 percent of vegetation had missed no more than two median return intervals and is considered to be in acceptable ecological condition (that is little to no deviation from natural fire regime) as of the year 2000. These areas are expected to remain in acceptable ecological condition as long as the natural fire regime is maintained. Another 1 percent of the vegetation showed significant deviation from natural conditions, and 25 percent of the acres are considered highly compromised by past fire suppression. Most of the deviation from natural conditions occurs in the lower- to mid-elevation conifer forests, including the giant sequoia groves.

Yosemite National Park's Current Fire Management Program

The fire return interval departure analysis was used extensively in the development of Yosemite National Park's current fire management program.[48] Although the nature and extent of the unnatural buildup of fuels had long been recognized, the maps depicting the results of the analysis reinforced this recognition and communicated the extent and severity of the problem.

For prescribed burning operations, the fire return interval departure analysis is being used to prioritize areas for treatment; those with the highest departure values are being burned first. In the wildland fire use zone, the analysis highlights areas where intensive monitoring might be necessary because of unnaturally high fuel accumulations or dense stands. Similarly, the analysis aids fire suppression operations by indicating where wildland fires might be expected to be more intense than under natural conditions, and helps to set priorities for fuel treatments in the wildland-urban interface.

Yosemite National Park's current fire management program builds on the accomplishments of the past three decades. The prescribed burning and wildland fire use programs, begun in 1970 and 1972, respectively, ushered in the era of fire management. Since the beginning of the program, managers have ignited over 200 prescribed fires, and those fires have burned more than 48,000 acres. Most of the prescribed burning has been in white fir and ponderosa pine forests, where fuel conditions have been affected by fire exclusion in the past.

Fourteen of the prescribed fires were more 1,000 acres in size, and one exceeded 5,000 acres. The wildland fire use program has burned more than 80,000 acres in over 600 different fires, the largest of which were the 8,800-acre LeConte Fire in 1999 and the 7,200-acre Hoover Fire in 2001.

Fire suppression remains an integral part of the fire management program in Yosemite, for suppression remains critical in areas where fuel accumulations are outside of their natural range. All human-caused fires are extinguished upon detection, as are lightning fires outside of the wildland fire use zone. Occasional fires inside the use zone are suppressed because prescribed conditions are not met.

THE FUTURE OF FIRE IN THE SIERRA NEVADA

Many issues face private property owners, land managers, and the public in the Sierra Nevada as a result of changed fire regimes and human population growth.[49] Primary among the issues is the accumulation of fuels, both on the ground and in tree canopies. Dealing with these fuels has been complicated by increased development in wildland areas, endangered species, and air quality considerations.

As we have learned, the fuels issue is most acute in the foothill zone, where chaparral fuels are particularly flammable, and in the lower montane zone, where fire return intervals are short. The effects of fire exclusion are less pronounced in the upper montane, subalpine, and alpine zones because fire return intervals are longer. However, as in the foothill and lower montane zones, short fire return intervals and fire exclusion efforts are becoming an issue in the eastside zone.

The population of the Sierra Nevada more than doubled between 1970 and 2000, much of this growth occurring in the foothill, lower montane, and eastside zones. The other zones are primarily federal lands, and, with the exception of the Lake Tahoe area, there are few opportunities for private development. The central Sierra Nevada contains one of the largest mixes of homes in wildlands in California. As a result, fire patterns are changed, and restoration and fuels reduction activities are restricted. Chaparral in the Sierra Nevada foothills grows quickly, and, consequently, maintenance of fuel reduction areas needs to be more frequent and is more costly. Property owners demand that fire suppression forces protect their homes first, diverting firefighters from protecting forests and shrublands. Commonly, millions of dollars are spent to save hundred-thousand-dollar structures while tens of millions of dollars of magnificent forests are being lost.

Each new catastrophic fire increases the clamor to do something about fuels. Homeowners expect fire and land management agencies to act, yet are often unwilling to accept some of the responsibility themselves. The most immediate problem exists around developments, and areas of high societal values, such as cultural sites and endangered species habitats. Mechanical removal of understory trees followed by prescribed burning is the most likely method to succeed in these areas. Where houses have encroached into shrublands, removal of shrubs up to 100 feet from houses may be necessary. Less compelling are treatments in remote areas where there is less development and access is difficult. Prescribed burning and the use of naturally occurring fires are more appropriate in areas beyond the urban-wildland interface. The call to thin forests to prevent catastrophic fires has confused the issue. Only on rare occasions can a fire move independently through the crowns of trees without a surface fire to feed it. Thinning forests to prevent crown fires without treating surface fuels is ecologically inappropriate and economically unjustifiable. A combination of treatments is most likely to be effective.

Many at-risk species occur in the Sierra Nevada, and some of these, including the Pacific fisher, American marten, and California spotted owl, are dependent on fire-maintained habitats. Concurrent changes in fire regimes and vegetation in the lower-elevation portions of the Sierra Nevada foothill and lower montane zones have resulted in regionwide changes in wildlife habitat. The question becomes how to restore natural fire regimes without adversely affecting at-risk species and their habitats. To do nothing only makes the situation worse, predisposing the species and habitats to destruction by catastrophic fire. These species evolved with fire, and the answer must include fire. Care must be taken, however, to ensure that fragmented populations are not adversely affected by fire treatment activities.

Among the biggest impediments to conducting prescribed burns or allowing wildland fires to burn under prescribed conditions in the Sierra Nevada are restrictions on air quality. Smoke is a by-product of burning, whether it comes from a prescribed fire, a wildland fire burning under prescribed conditions, or a wildfire. Society is faced with deciding to accept periodic episodes of low concentrations of smoke from managed fires or heavy doses from wildfires. Either reduced emission restrictions for wildland management activities or exemptions for federal agencies from local air pollution control district regulations will be necessary if fire is to be allowed to play its natural role in the Sierra Nevada.

The success of our fire management in the Sierra Nevada is contingent upon our ability and willingness to keep fire as an integral part of these ecosystems. Not to do so is to doom ourselves to failure. Fire is inevitable, and we can only try to manage in harmony with fire.

WILDFIRE MANAGEMENT ON A HUMAN-DOMINATED LANDSCAPE

California Chaparral Wildfires

JON E. KEELEY, PH.D., AND CJ FOTHERINGHAM

CATASTROPHIC WILDFIRES ARE AN OUTCOME *of the California vegetation and climate. These fires are driven by severe weather, and fire management is unable to prevent or stop them. Unlike many western forests, where fire restoration is needed to reduce fire hazard and return natural processes, California shrublands need greater protection from an increasing onslaught of fires. Fuel modification at the wildland-urban interface and better land planning are important future needs.*

▼

Since 1970, 12 of the nation's 15 most destructive wildfires have occurred in California, costing the insurance industry $4.8 billion,[1] the most destructive being the firestorms of October 2003 (see Box 1). That California leads the nation in fire losses is not surprising since, with more than 33 million people, it is the most populous state in the nation. Almost all of these fires have occurred in shrublands rather than in forests, which should also not be surprising since chaparral is the most extensive vegetation type in California, covering over 8.8 million acres (3.6 million hectares),[2] or one-twelfth of the state, and is a highly flammable plant community. Relative to the national focus on western forests, there is need for greater attention on the California wildfire problem, not just because it accounts for most of the losses in property and lives in the nation, but also because fire management practices appropriate for other parts of the country often are inappropriate for this region.

BOX 1. OCTOBER 2003 WILDFIRES
IN SOUTHERN CALIFORNIA

The southern California fires of late October 2003 were the largest fire event in California's recent history. In over a half-dozen separate fires, more than 742,000 acres (364,000 hectares) of wildlands burned, in many cases through a complex mosaic of urban and wildland fragments, as well as across the well-defined and extensive wildland-urban boundary. A total of 3,361 homes and 26 lives were lost in this event, which stands as one of the costliest disasters in California, exceeding previous fires, earthquakes, and other natural disasters.

The October 2003 fires burned through diverse plant communities, but the proportion of different vegetation types burned was not reflected in the media coverage, which made it appear as though most were forest fires. This mistaken image was undoubtedly due to the fact that some of the fires burned in unnaturally intense and spectacular crown fires in forests with important recreational value and relatively high-density housing. However, coniferous forests made up only about 5 percent of the total acreage burned.[1] Most of the burned landscape was chaparral shrublands, and nearly all of the loss of property and lives was due to these shrubland fires. Nonetheless, this important fact did not prevent exploitation of the disaster by timber advocates as further justification for extensive forest thinning or clearcutting.[2]

San Diego County suffered the most from these shrubland fires, especially the Cedar Fire (center outline, Figure 1), which at 273,230 acres (110,620 hectares) is the largest fire in official California records dating back to circa 1910.[3] The fires burned through a mosaic of young and old fuel classes, and the behavior of the fires was largely dictated by the powerful Santa Ana winds. Despite extreme fire conditions, the public expected fire suppression forces to directly attack these infernos. Illustrative of the misunderstanding associated with the causes of these fires was the claim by one major insurance company that policyholders who lost property did so, not because of unavoidable aspects of weather, fuels, or other attributes of the fire, but because of mishandling of the fire by agencies with firefighting jurisdiction.[4]

FIGURE 1. Fuel ages burned by Santa Ana wind-driven fires in San Diego County, California, October 2003

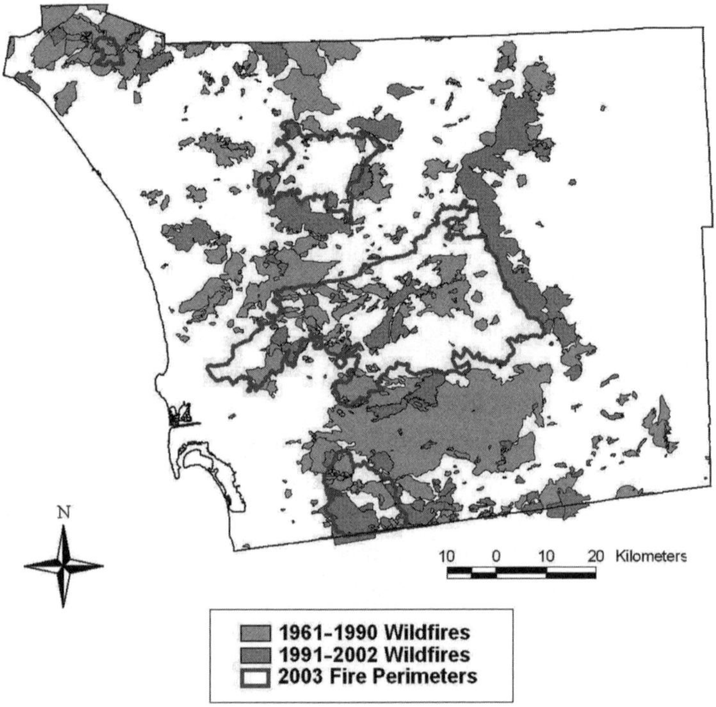

Outlines, *from top to bottom:* Roblar Fire, Paradise Fire, Cedar Fire, Otay Fire.

Source: Adapted from J. E. Keeley, CJ Fotheringham, and M. Moritz, "Lessons from the 2003 Wildfires in Southern California," *Journal of Forestry* 102, no. 7 (2004): 26–31.

FIRE REGIMES AND FIRE MANAGEMENT OPTIONS

The term *fire regime* refers to the types of fuels consumed (surface or canopy fuels) and the intensity, frequency, and seasonality of fires in an area; the fire regime in any particular place is dictated by climatic factors, the fuel characteristics of the vegetation, and the pattern of natural lightning and human ignitions. Understanding the fire regime of an area is critical to developing an effective management policy, and the diversity of fire regimes over the North American landscape means that there can be no single model of how fire managers should approach fire hazard. Two examples illustrate this point: the ponderosa pine forests of the southwestern United States and California's chaparral shrublands. Historically, fires in southwestern ponderosa pine forests typically burned in frequent, low-intensity surface fires that, because of widely spaced canopies and sparse, patchy understory fuels, burned only as high-intensity crown fires on a limited spatial scale.[3] In contrast, chaparral shrublands always burn in high-intensity crown fires that typically kill all aboveground biomass, and low-intensity chaparral surface fires are unknown.

One critically important difference between these extremes is that a century of fire suppression policy has been very effective at excluding fires from many forests in the western United States, but not from southern California shrublands (see Box 2). Before we consider chaparral, however, it will be instructive to understand the factors contributing to fire suppression impacts in forests. Certain attributes of western forests allow rapid fire suppression: mountain climates have a much shorter fire season; ignitions are commonly from lightning, under weather conditions not usually conducive to rapid fire spread; and fires typically spread by surface fuels, which produce lower flame lengths. Over much of the 20th century, these characteristics have led to highly successful fire suppression, equivalent to fire exclusion, over much of the West.

Consequently, western forests now have an unnatural accumulation of surface fuels, and an increased density of young, shade-tolerant trees. Increased density of young trees is perhaps the more serious problem because these saplings act as ladder fuels that change fire behavior from surface fires to lethal crown fires. In addition to fire suppression, heavy livestock grazing has also contributed to fire exclusion by reducing herbaceous fuels in some forest types.[4] While fire exclusion has contributed to these dangerous fuel conditions throughout the western United States, other land use practices such as logging have also played a role. Logging encourages the dense ingrowth of young trees and increases surface fuels from slash left on the site. In fact, one recent study of factors determining fire severity after a large northern California fire attributed more fire damage to past timber practices than to fire exclusion.[5] In contrast to the situation in western forests,

---

BOX 2. CONTRASTING FIRE REGIMES

Western U.S. conifer forests have had a long history of mostly low-severity fires, as revealed in studies relating annual tree rings to fire scars embedded in the wood. Such fire records are possible wherever low-severity fires scar but do not kill trees.

Throughout the western United States, researchers have investigated literally thousands of tree records, which have revealed a remarkably similar pattern from New Mexico to California. Prior to the 20th century, forest fires were frequent, occurring every 10 to 20 years, but since the beginning of fire suppression activities in the early 1900s, tree rings show almost no fire scars.[1] In these forests, a century of fire suppression has succeeded in excluding fire.

In contrast, shrubland fires are always lethal crown fires that eliminate any records of past fires. The U.S. Forest Service and other agencies, however, have very good written records that are relatively accurate indications of 20th-century shrubland burning patterns. Those records show that in coastal California, substantial acreage has burned every decade throughout the century, indicating that fire suppression policies have never excluded fire from these landscapes. The written records also demonstrate a fire rotation interval in coastal California shrublands of 30 to 40 years for much of the 20th century.[2] It is doubtful that fires were ever much more frequent, since 20 to 30 years is near the limit of fire tolerance for many of the dominant native shrubs.

California shrublands have not experienced fire exclusion,[6] nor are fuel levels outside the historical range of variability.[7]

Shrubland Fires

In California, most large and deadly fires are chaparral fires, and we must understand their causal factors if we are to reduce the losses from such catastrophic events. The solution is not simply to allocate more resources to fire management activities. Indeed, for the latter half of the 20th century, every decade has been followed by a decade of increased expenditures on fire suppression activities, yet each decade has also been followed by one of increased losses in property and lives.[8]

One of the major reasons for the inability of fire managers to stop losses from chaparral fires is that for most of the last several decades, both scientists and managers have approached chaparral management with a one-size-fits-all model. It seemed intuitive that if fire suppression had excluded fires from ponderosa pine forests and had created a dangerous fuel buildup, other landscapes with a similar fire suppression policy would experience the same unnatural fuel buildup. However, we now know that in coastal California's chaparral landscapes, fire suppression policy cannot be equated with fire exclusion (see Box 2), and that for most of the 20th century, California's chaparral shrublands have burned at close to or higher than natural frequencies.[9]

It is now becoming clear that the age and spatial pattern of fuels are minor factors controlling the ultimate size of chaparral fires (see Box 1 and Figure 1). Indeed, fire frequency analysis in chaparral from northern Baja California to Monterey has shown no strong relationship between fuel age and fire probabilities.[10] Instead, in nearly all areas, the hazard of burning increases only moderately with time since the last fire. A more localized investigation of historical burning patterns in Los Angeles County found a similar pattern, but with an increasing probability of burning during the first two decades after the last fire.[11] However, the apparent resistance to burning by young age classes exhibits a strong interaction with fire weather conditions; although the probability that fires will burn out in young age classes during moderate weather is high, under severe winds, fires readily spread through young stands of chaparral.[12]

The reason fuels play only a minor role in controlling large fires in southern California chaparral is because this region has the worst fire climate in the country, with extreme winds capable of overcoming any potential fuel limitation (see Box 3). These winds, known as Santa Anas in southern California and as Diablo winds in the San Francisco area, result in stormlike conditions producing wildfires commonly referred to as "firestorms." Under these conditions firefighters are forced into defensive actions until the weather changes. In the Santa Monica National Recreation Area northwest of Los Angeles, the 12 largest wildfires in recorded history ranged in size from 16,000 to

BOX 3. SANTA ANA WIND-DRIVEN FIRES

Southern California has the worst fire climate in the country, largely because of the regular autumn foehn winds, known as Santa Anas.[1] Although massive wildfires anywhere in the world are usually driven by severe fire weather, such conditions are generally not annual events. Southern California is an anomaly, and severe fire weather conditions occur every autumn. Lasting from a few days to a week or more, a high-pressure cell over the Great Basin, coupled with a low-pressure trough off the Pacific Coast, leads to very high offshore winds (60–100 km/hr) with a relative humidity of below 10 percent. Under these conditions firefighters are forced into defensive action that includes evacuating homes ahead of the fire front and protecting property on the periphery. Fire containment does not occur until the weather changes.

43,000 acres (6,700–17,400 hectares), and all were autumn fires driven by Santa Ana winds.[13] In other parts of southern California, large fires are usually associated with Santa Ana wind conditions, and the very destructive ones nearly always are (see Table 1).

Further illustrative of the overriding importance of these winds is the relationship between large fires and drought. Throughout the western United States, large fires are usually restricted to periods of extreme drought.[14] However, in southern California, Santa Ana winds are just as likely to cause a large fire during a wet year as during a dry year.[15] Antecedent climate does appear to play a role in that it increases the length of the fire season, because large fires over 5,000 hectares that occur outside the Santa Ana season take place only during drought.

THREE KEY POINTS ABOUT CHAPARRAL FIRE MANAGEMENT

- Large, high-intensity wildfires are a natural feature of chaparral landscapes. They occurred prior to Euro-American settlement and will take place again in the future.

TABLE 1. Recent major fires in San Diego County

Most destructive fires occur during severe autumn Santa Ana wind conditions. Even in non–Santa Ana wind conditions, however, weather is still a contributing factor—for example, the July 2002 Pines Fire occurred during a heat spell and was accompanied by gusting winds.

| | | | LOST | |
Fire	Month/Year	Acres	Structures	Lives
*Cedar	Oct. 2003	281,000	2,232	14
*Laguna	Oct. 1970	190,000	382	5
*Paradise	Oct. 2003	56,600	169	2
*Harmony	Oct. 1996	8,600	122	1
Pines	July 2002	61,690	45	0
*Gavilan	Feb. 2002	6,000	43	0
*Viejas	Dec. 2001	10,350	23	0
La Jolla	Sept. 1999	7,800	2	1

Source: U.S. Forest Service fire records for the Cleveland National Forest, California. Acreage approximate.

*Santa Ana wind-driven fires.

- Twentieth-century fire management practices have been ineffective in preventing chaparral wildfires.
- We need to view chaparral fires as we do other uncontrollable natural disasters and to focus on developing human infrastructure capable of minimizing their damage.

HISTORY OF LARGE CHAPARRAL FIRES

The 2003 firestorms (see Box 1) were natural events that have been repeated on the California landscape for eons. Studies of charcoal depositions extracted from ocean bottom sediment cores off the coast of Santa Barbara have found that the frequency of large fires has not changed in the past 500 years.[16] Indian legends from tribes in the vicinity of the current San Diego County also describe a mass migration of local tribes due to a massive wildfire.[17]

Although the October 2003 Cedar Fire (see Box 1) was the largest in California since official fire records have been kept, historical accounts portray even larger fire events. A *Los Angeles Times* article on September 27, 1889, described a fire near Santa Ana three times larger than the recent Cedar Fire: "The fire which has been burning for the past few days still continues in the canyons. The burned and burning district now extends over 100 miles north to south, and is 10 to 18 miles in width." In fact, collectively, fires in southern California during late September 1889 exceeded all of the October 2003 acreage burned; another fire ignited that same week in September 1889 in San Diego County, near Escondido, and in two days the same Santa Ana winds blew it all the way to downtown San Diego,[18] a distance roughly equal to the long axis of the 2003 Cedar Fire. Other large 19th-century fires are known from other counties in coastal California.[19]

While large wildfires were reported throughout southern California during the 19th and early 20th centuries, it was only in the latter half of the 20th century that they routinely resulted in major loss of property and lives.[20] The primary reason for this development was not a change in fire behavior but rather the fact that California's population had grown exponentially.[21] As a consequence, urban sprawl placed huge populations adjacent to watersheds of dangerous fuels. In addition, because 95 to 99 percent of all fires on these chaparral landscapes are started by people, as populations grew, fire frequency increased (see Figure 2), which in turn increased the chances of ignitions during Santa Ana wind events. Prior to the entrance of Native Americans into North America, lightning was a potential source of ignition for Santa Ana wind-driven fires since there is significant overlap in their seasonal distribution; thus such fires were likely a natural feature of this landscape, albeit at a lower frequency than observed today.[22]

The key point here is that massive fires have occurred at periodic intervals in the past and likely will occur again in the future. It may be more useful from a planning and management perspective to see these events as we currently view 100-year flood events or other such cyclical disasters.

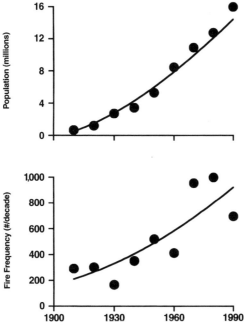

FIGURE 2. Fire frequency and population growth in southern California, 1910–1990

Source: J. E. Keeley and CJ Fotheringham, "Historic Fire Regime in Southern California Shrublands," *Conservation Biology* 15 (2001): 1536–1548; J. E. Keeley and CJ Fotheringham, "Impact of Past, Present, and Future Fire Regimes on North American Mediterranean Shrublands," in *Fire and Climatic Change in Temperate Ecosystems of the Western Americas,* ed. T. T. Veblen, W. L. Baker, G. Montenegro, and T. W. Swetnam (New York: Springer, 2003), pp. 218–262.

TWENTIETH-CENTURY SHRUBLAND FIRE MANAGEMENT PRACTICES

For the past several decades, southern California shrubland fire management has been based on the philosophy that prefire fuel management practices can control the ultimate size of these massive fire events. On California shrubland landscapes, the preferred treatment has long been prescription burning, applied on a rotational basis so that a mosaic of different-age fuels is created. These fuel modification treatments were expected to prevent large wildfires by creating mosaics that included patches of young fuel, which theoretically were expected to act as barriers to fire spread. However, over the past several decades, this management philosophy has not been effective at eliminating large, catastrophic fires.

Some would argue that the failure to eliminate catastrophic shrubland fires is due to inadequate funding of fuel treatments, coupled with restrictions on prescribed burning related to strict air quality standards and the danger of burning in wildland-urban mosaics. While these concerns are real,[23] nothing about the future economic outlook or environmental restrictions suggests that these limitations are likely to change, and we have good reason to believe that even if greater fuel modifications were possible, the hazard of catastrophic fires would not diminish.

The extent to which landscape-level fuel treatments are effective in shrubland fire is mainly a function of weather conditions during the fire event. The evidence is overwhelming that under extreme fire weather conditions such as the autumn Santa Ana winds, young fuels (Figure 1), or even fuel breaks, will not act as barriers to fire spread.[24] This is quite evident for southern California's October 2003 wind-driven wildfires (see Box 1). Crossing nearly the entire width of San Diego County's east-west burning Cedar Fire were substantial swaths of vegetation less than 10 years of age, not just in one, but in two parts of that fire (Figure 1).[25] Burning in San Diego County at the same time was the Otay Fire, which exhibited the same phenomenon: the fire burned through thousands of acres on which the vegetation was only 7 years of age. The primary reason young fuels cannot act as a barrier to fire spread under such severe weather conditions is that if high winds do not drive the fire through the fuels, the winds will spread the fire around them, or lift and carry firebrands over them to spread the fire a half-mile or more beyond the active front.

WHAT IS THE APPROPRIATE FUTURE FIRE MANAGEMENT STRATEGY?

Prefire fuel modifications will undoubtedly remain an important part of the southern California fire management arsenal, but their applica-

tion needs to be carefully considered if they are to be effective and provide benefits equal to or exceeding their cost.[26] For example, fires
burning under moderately calm wind conditions and high humidity
have been observed to burn out when the fire encounters young fuels,
and such fires are less likely to spread firebrands beyond these barriers. These fires, however, seldom present major problems for firefighting crews and do not pose a major threat to the loss of property and
lives (see Table 1). Thus, serious attention needs to be paid to whether
or not fuel treatments are cost-effective for these fires.

The key to effective use of prefire fuel modifications in crown fire
ecosystems such as chaparral is their strategic placement. Under
severe weather, lower fuel loads will not stop the spread of fire, but
they do reduce fire intensity and thus provide defensible space for fire
suppression crews. The chief benefit of prefire fuel manipulations in
crown fire ecosystems is the enhancement of firefighter safety, and
strategic placement is therefore critical to the success of these measures. However, much of the southern California shrubland landscape
is far too steep to provide defensible space regardless of fuel structure,
and thus fuel manipulations in these areas are unlikely to provide economically viable benefits. We suggest that fuel manipulations will be
most cost-effective when focused on the wildland-urban interface.
Homes are often lost during severe fire weather because firefighters
refuse to enter areas that lack a buffer zone of reduced fuels sufficient
to provide defensible space.

How Do We Measure Fire Management Success?

In terms of management goals, the metric for fuels treatments on these
shrubland landscapes needs to change from simply measuring "acres
treated" to consideration of their strategic placement. This change in
management philosophy is being recommended by the Santa Monica
Mountains National Recreation Area, the largest National Park Service
unit in southern California.[27]

To accurately measure the success of fuel treatments, studies need
to take a close look at the role of prefire fuel treatments versus weather
during the fire. For example, in the Cedar Fire (see Box 1), fuel breaks
were not effective at preventing major structural losses in adjacent
subdivisions (see Table 1) because of the severe weather conditions

during the early stages of the fire. In contrast, prefire fuel treatments northwest of the town of Pine Valley in eastern San Diego County may have saved that community from destruction by the Cedar Fire. However, the fire front threatened Pine Valley after the Santa Ana winds had died down and after the onshore breezes had brought cooler temperatures and higher humidity. If weather conditions had not improved, the fuel treatment area would have provided less of a barrier to fire spread into the community; that particular fuel treatment prescription therefore may not be an adequate standard for other fires threatening Pine Valley.

One justification for rotational prescription burning is that maintaining a large fraction of the landscape in young fuel-age classes reduces fire severity and thus enhances vegetation recovery. However, extensive studies of postfire recovery following the 1993 fires in southern California found that the impact of high-severity fires was variable, with both positive and negative effects on postfire recovery.[28] Five years postfire, researchers could find little discernable difference in chaparral recovery between high- and low-severity burn sites.[29] It would therefore be premature at this point to conduct expensive fuel treatments with the expectation of producing major improvements in postfire recovery of vegetation.

Another resource benefit of fuel treatments has long been thought to be their ability to reduce postfire flooding and sediment loss.[30] Presumably, if watersheds in proximity to urban environments were to receive prescription burning on a rotational basis, only a small portion of each watershed would lose excessive amounts of debris at any given time, and thus flooding and debris flow hazards would be reduced. However, any such patchwork of age classes is still vulnerable to large-scale Santa Ana wind-driven wildfires.[31] (See Box 1 and Figure 1.)

Alternatively, it has been suggested that, regardless of the size of burned patches, burning watersheds on a 5-year rotational interval would greatly reduce the immediate postfire sediment loss.[32] In the long run, however, this approach may not be cost-effective for several reasons. One critical determinant of sediment loss is the magnitude of precipitation in the first postfire year.[33] If rainfall is light, sediment loss is minimal, regardless of prefire stand age. But when burning is followed by a winter of high rainfall, sediment losses are considerable.

Prescription burning at 5-year intervals greatly increases the probability of a fire being followed by an El Niño year of high rainfall, as contrasted with the probability of an El Niño year following a fire at its more natural return interval of 35 years. Cumulative sediment loss over the long term would also be much greater for 5-year burn intervals since such intervals would mean multiple peak discharges, as opposed to a single peak discharge over a 35-year burn interval. More important than any of these factors is that burning at 5-year intervals will almost certainly result in type conversion of native shrublands to alien grasses and forbs,[34] which would greatly increase the chances of slope failure in these steep watersheds.[35]

Resource Damage from Fire Management Practices

Fire management decisions often have negative effects on natural resources, but agencies differ in their ability to integrate fire and resource issues. Many local California fire departments as well as the California Department of Forestry and Fire Protection have reducing fire hazard as an overriding mandate; resource issues are often not primary concerns. Even in federal agencies more directly concerned with resource management, such as the U.S. Forest Service and the National Park Service, because of the complexities of modern management practices, fire management decisions are not always closely linked to resource management. As a consequence, fire managers are sometimes unaware of resource threats posed by fire management practices.[36]

Fire suppression and prefire fuel manipulations are management practices that have ecological equivalents in the roles played by equilibrium and disequilibrium processes in natural ecosystems. Fire suppression attempts to maintain ecosystem equilibrium by preventing disturbance, whereas prefire fuel manipulations introduce disequilibrium. Understanding how our management practices might simulate natural ecosystem processes may be an important step toward more effective adaptive management.

In forested environments such as ponderosa pine ecosystems, some of the dominant species have a reproductive cycle dependent on disturbance, and therefore the equilibrium conditions created by successful fire suppression have very negative impacts on the long-term sustainability of these forests.

In contrast, for many shrubland ecosystems, fire suppression policy, despite valiant efforts, has been unable to keep up with the ever-increasing frequency of fires on these human-dominated landscapes (see Figure 2). As a result, shrubland ecosystems have been exposed to an unusually high frequency of disturbance. Most casual observers see little problem with this kind of disturbance because shrublands are classically described as "fire-type" or "fire-adapted" ecosystems. However, it is a misnomer to describe the species in these communities as "fire adapted." Species are not adapted to fire per se, but rather are adapted to a fire regime that includes a particular range of fire frequencies, seasonality, and fire intensities. Deviations from this regime can threaten the persistence of many native species.

The primary threat to native species comes from the fact that fires create an ecological disequilibrium that can be exploited by many aggressive alien weeds. The dense canopy cover of undisturbed shrublands readily shades out herbaceous alien plants; after a fire, the extent to which aliens invade is dependent on a race between alien seeds reaching the site and shrub canopy recovery.[37] Following every fire, shrublands undergo a developmental period in which native plant populations recover dormant seed banks and transport photosynthetic products to tubers, bulbs, and corms. Repeat fires with insufficient recovery periods between them will result in limited native shrub recovery, creating an ecological vacuum rapidly filled by alien weeds. This "type conversion" from native shrubs to alien herbaceous vegetation can have a profound impact on many ecological processes.

Such type conversion has already occurred over a quarter or more of the current wildland landscape in coastal California, beginning with the earliest human occupation of the region.[38] While fire suppression activities have failed to exclude fire from this landscape, they almost certainly have prevented massive landscape changes that might have occurred if the exponentially increasing rate of human-ignited fires during the 20th century had been left unabated.[39] Although the rate of type conversion is not currently being monitored, it appears to the authors of this essay that it is happening at an ever-increasing rate in southern California. These landscapes are currently challenged with far too much fire, and any management practices that create disequilibrium conditions, such as fuel reduction projects, must evaluate the potential negative impacts of these practices—particularly alien plant invasion.

CHANGING OUR PERSPECTIVE ON FIRE

Californians need to embrace a different model of how to view fires on chaparral landscapes. Our response needs to be tempered by the realization that fires are natural events that cannot be eliminated from California shrublands. We can learn much from the science of earthquake or other natural disaster management: no one pretends we can stop earthquakes—rather, we engineer infrastructure to minimize their impact.

We need to closely evaluate human development practices that place people at serious risk to destructive wildfires. The primary shortcoming of California's fire management agencies has been the failure to adequately convey to the public their inability to stop massive Santa Ana wind-driven fires. For much of the past half-century, public agencies have held the false belief that how or where they allowed new developments to be built was irrelevant to fire safety—largely because of assurances that fire managers could prevent fires from burning across the wildland-urban interface. Undoubtedly there has been substantial pressure on fire managers to convey an overly confident image, and not to highlight their limitations.

Future development in California needs to closely involve fire managers at the planning stage. In addition, communities need to take greater responsibility for creating defensible fire-safe zones through placement of greenbelt infrastructure, such as golf courses and parks, between wildlands and homes.

FIRE IN THE KLAMATH-SISKIYOU ECOREGION

Protecting and Restoring the Fire Mosaic

DOMINICK A. DELLASALA, PH.D.

FIRE'S VARIED INFLUENCE IN THE KLAMATH-SISKIYOU ecoregion has created a rich and diverse mosaic of plant communities in continuous recovery from fire. Decades of logging, road building, fire suppression, livestock grazing, and, more recently, climate change have disrupted the fire mosaic. Fire management policy is now at a historic crossroads. Sustainable landscapes and beneficial relationships with fire are only possible through a new approach to fire management that recognizes its keystone role in shaping rich and healthy landscapes.

▼

The Klamath-Siskiyou ecoregion of southwest Oregon and northwest California is one of the most diverse temperate forest regions on Earth.[1] To the locals, the ecoregion goes by many names: the Klamath Knot, for its hodgepodge of mountain ranges; State of Jefferson, for a local secession movement popularized in 1941; and Bigfoot Country, for the reputed sightings and mythical connection this creature inspires in indigenous communities. To biogeographers and conservationists, however, this area has many accolades, including designation as a World Wildlife Fund/World Conservation Union global center of plant diversity, a World Wildlife Fund Global 200 ecoregion, and proposed United Nations Educational, Scientific, and Cultural Organization (UNESCO) designation as a biosphere reserve.[2]

Fire's presence is strikingly obvious in shaping the ecology here. A wide assortment of plant communities influenced by fire blankets these mountains with chaparral, semiarid oak woodlands, mixed-conifer and mixed-evergreen forests, Jeffrey pine savannah, and verdant temperate rainforests.[3] Remarkably, many of these communities can be found growing on the same hillside owing to differences in soils, position along the slope, elevation above sea level, moisture tolerance, and, of course, fire.[4]

Historically, early Native Americans deliberately set fires for a variety of cultural benefits. Indian tribes along the Klamath and Rogue rivers used rotational burning, setting fires every three to five years to maintain forest openings that benefited deer and elk.[5] They also used fire regularly to stimulate growth of plants for baskets, foods, and medicinal herbs.

Today, the fire regime (severity and frequency of fires) in the Klamath-Siskiyou is remarkably spotty.[6] Fires of variable frequency— ranging from every 5 to every 75 years or more—and variable severity, ranging from ground-burning and understory fires to conflagrations, create a quiltlike tapestry, or mosaic, of plant communities in different stages of postfire recovery (the "fire mosaic"). In this fashion, a single fire is made up of a mixture of varying proportions of low, moderate, and high severity influenced by the interplay of geography (coast versus inland), vegetation, topography (slope and elevation), and climate.[7] The mixture of fire severities contributes to the fire mosaic in different ways, with the high-severity portion generating a coarse-grained heterogeneity expressed as a patchiness of plant communities at the landscape scale and the low-severity component contributing to fine-grained heterogeneity expressed through site-specific (or local) differences in plant communities.

Fire-created mosaics can persist for decades in continuous flux as plant communities recover from one fire to the next through a procession of successional changes. Fire passing through an area periodically resets the successional clock to early pioneering plants consisting of fire-adapted grasses, flowering plants, mosses, and ground-dwelling shrubs. However, over time, burned landscapes progress from pioneer stage (with a few scattered live trees) to forest wherever site conditions support forest as the potential natural vegetation. If succession is uninterrupted by another fire, it may be decades to more than a century before the forest canopy completely envelopes the hardwood and shrub understory.[8] This combination of very tall conifers with lower-growing hardwoods and understory shrubs is diagnostic of the mixed-evergreen forests of the ecoregion, forests exceptionally rich in plant and wildlife species. Thus, every plant community in the fire mosaic is at some successional stage in recovery in response to fire's chaotic resetting of the successional "clock."

Over decades to centuries, repeating fires have sculpted a landscape of chaparral, oak woodland, and multiaged forests.[9] Because of topographic differences, some areas—mainly those along streamsides, valley bottoms, the lower third of mountain slopes, ravines, and north- and east-facing slopes—escape fire for decades to centuries. Here individual trees reach gigantic proportions, overshadowing their neighbors where they persist either as members of dense forests or as widely scattered trees embedded in a sea of shrubs.[10] Regional fluctuations in climate and weather influence fire's periodicity, with more fire events during fuel-desiccating periods. In this fashion, vegetation, climate/weather, and topography interact to control fire behavior. The warming and drying climate of the late 20th and early 21st centuries is now poised to tilt the fire behavior dynamic to the point where a greater proportion of high-severity fires could become the norm,[11] regardless of efforts by forest managers to manipulate fuels and vegetation.

Many plant species of the Klamath-Siskiyou are finely tuned to periodic fires of mixed severity. Conifers like knobcone pine depend on fire to burst open seed-bearing cones that are quickly deposited in charred soils. Shrubs such as manzanita and *ceanothus* persist even after the hottest fires because their seeds lie buried within the soil. These postfire pioneers begin the process of recovery by "fixing" nitrogen in the soils; some species develop symbiotic relationships with mycorrhizal fungi that attach themselves to the shrubs' roots, where they aid in transport of nutrients and the spread of fungal mats to nearby tree seedlings. Even some wetlands are shaped by fire.

The insect-eating cobra lily is a species uniquely adapted to nitrogen-deficient soils of the fen wetlands of the Klamath-Siskiyou ecoregion. The fens that this insectivorous plant occupy contain one of the most distinctive plant communities of the Siskiyou Mountains, with five endemic plants found nowhere else in the world: Waldo gentian, Oregon willow-herb, large-flowered rush-lily, purple-flowered rush-lily, and western bog violet are the fen's must prized possessions.[12]

The cobra lily's "appetite" for nitrogen is due to the absence of this essential nutrient from the chemically complex ultramafic soils of the area. Ultramafic bedrock is an important mountain-forming rock consisting of serpentinite and peridotite rocks and soils that, from a plant's perspective, are deficient in vital minerals like calcium, nitrogen, phosphorus, and potassium, yet naturally toxic (to plants) in iron, magnesium, chromium, cobalt, and nickel.[13] The cobra lily gets a booster shot of nitrogen in an otherwise nitrogen-deficient environment by acting as a living "roach motel." With its drooping appendages, the insectivorous plant lures unsuspecting insects into its ominously shaped "hood." The insects work their way down a long tubular stem lined with stiff, reflexed "hairs." Once the insects are inside, symbiotic bacteria begin extracting nitrogen from their nitrogen-rich exoskeletons by devouring their trapped carcasses. As ground-burning fires periodically pass through the area, they cleanse out competing shrubs and pines, maintaining open conditions suitable for the cobra lily and its unique co-inhabitants. In the absence of fire, azaleas and pines shade out the light-demanding carnivorous plants and their fire-adapted neighbors.

UNDER SMOKEY'S WATCH ("ONLY YOU CAN PREVENT FOREST FIRES" — BUT SHOULD WE?)

The fire mosaic of the Klamath-Siskiyou is different today than when encountered by early Native Americans. A century of landscape degradation caused by industrial-scale fire suppression and other factors has discombobulated the fire-mosaic dynamic. Fire intervention takes many forms, and its degree varies within the Klamath-Siskiyou ecoregion and across the West. Most approaches center on treating fuels (a symptom, not a cause) with some of the same causal agents—suppression and more logging—that have transformed the fire mosaic into a proverbial ticking firebomb.

With the arrival of the iconic image Smokey Bear over 60 years ago, the U.S. Forest Service finally had a symbol for its 1935 fire suppression policy of "every fire out by 10 a.m." following its detection.[14] Wildfires were and still are attacked with military precision. Post–World War II fire suppression technology improved firefighting dramatically, with the unintended consequence of altering the composition and structure of fire-adapted plant communities, mainly in low-elevation areas close to towns and settlements. Fire-resistant communities would soon be replaced by fire-intolerant, shade-loving trees and shrubs codesigned by logging and fire suppression. For example, many forests in the Klamath-Siskiyou ecoregion have been forced to skip fire cycles. With heavy ground fuels and high densities of small, fire-intolerant, and shade-loving trees and shrubs prospering under Smokey's watch, some of the ecoregion's forests are now poised for uncharacteristically severe fires. In short, military precision in shutting off the fire "valve" has come with enormous consequences to the health, resiliency, and the landscape patch-iness of the fire mosaic that we are only now beginning to understand.

FALL OF THE FIRE-RESISTANT GIANTS

Politically charged rhetoric and fire phobia have shaped today's fire debate, leading to sweeping policy changes predicated on a strategy that can never succeed ecologically. The public's fear of fire became the opportunity for timber interests to capture the fire debate through a deeply entrenched agenda centered on more logging. The debate over fire reached an apex in 1995 when President Clinton signed into law the Emergency Supplemental Appropriations and Rescissions Act. Dubbed the "Salvage Rider," this bill ushered in a wave of changes to forest management that were anything but healthy for fire-adapted forests.[15] Recent legislation, the Healthy Forest Restoration Act of 2003, signed into law by President George W. Bush, continues this mis-guided fire policy by seeking to fireproof forests through some of the same factors—logging and fire suppression—that have transformed them into today's tinderboxes.[16]

Building on the public's fear of fire, President Bush visited the Rogue Valley of southwest Oregon at the height of the state's largest fire, the Biscuit Fire of 2002, to announce major policy changes ostensibly aimed at thinning overgrown woods in the name of fire prevention. What the president did not say, however, was that the "thinning" was to be paid for mainly by logging the last of the fire-resistant giants. Ironically, the new policy could reverse many of the beneficial effects of the fire mosaic. Instead of clearing away small trees and underbrush as many fires do, logging removes the fire-resistant giants, leaving behind piles of small trees, branches, and brush as kindling for the next fire.

Many fire ecologists have noted that large trees are insurance for the future—they are critical to ecosystem health.[17] The thick, corky bark of large sugar pine and ponderosa pine confers a resistance to low- to moderate-severity fires, similar to the fiberglass insulation in a home. It takes over 100 years for trees, particularly large pines, to acquire these fire-insulating properties. But once present, a mature pine can survive up to an hour of moderate-intensity fire at its base.[18]

Today's forests have fewer large trees and much greater numbers of small ones, in some places planted in dense rows as tree farms. In sum, logging and fire suppression acting alone or together have transformed the fire mosaic from fire-adapted systems to fire-prone landscapes, priming the fire pump for uncharacteristically severe wildfires.

Across the dry interior West, high tree densities, principally caused by past timber management and decades of fire suppression, are a major contributor to today's heightened fire severity.[19] Typically, when fire hits densely stocked tree plantations, it encounters a continuous layer of ground and near-surface fuels that contribute to rapid fire spread and consumption of tree crowns. Closer to home and since the first satellites began snapping images of spaceship Earth, including the Klamath-Siskiyou, in the 1970s, more than 50,000 acres of forests have been cut down each year.[20] The rate and scale of logging far eclipsed the magnitude and type of ecosystem change caused by fire over the same time frame. Even during high-severity fires, pockets of large trees and understory plants survive as seed banks. The survivors of fire "lifeboat" the recovering burned forest as their seeds propagate burned areas.[21] As the forest recovers, the survivors act as biological "legacies," transferring their life-giving recovery functions to the burned forest within which they are embedded.

Legacy trees provide many recovery functions vital to postfire recovering forests, including:

- Shade and relatively moist microclimates for seedling propagation. Burned forests with large live and dead trees have soil temperatures several degrees cooler than similar forests that have been logged.
- Habitat for scores of insect-eating bats, birds, and parasitic wasps that help keep destructive insects at bay following fires.
- Stabilization of soils from erosion by "anchoring" them through the tree's extensive root mass.

• Pockets of seed sources that act as recolonization sites for plant propagules and habitat for wildlife involved in seed dispersal.
• Energy and nutrient pathways as dead trees are processed by decomposers and minerals returned to soils.
• Fish-hiding and spawning cover from logs that fall into streams.[22]

Even the dead trees retain their recovery functions for decades to centuries in the fire mosaic. Depending on the species, dead legacy trees (or snags) can remain upright for decades. When they eventually fall over from natural causes (rot, insect damage, lightning, wind, etc.), the downed logs provide essential nutrients for a developing forest as they act as nurseries for new seedlings. Downed logs are eventually transformed into organically rich humus by an army of decomposers, a process that takes centuries before the decaying log's presence is slowly erased. In sum, a biologically diverse and healthy forest could not exist without its legacy components, and even the dead ones experience a second life as they lifeboat the burned area through recovery. In almost Zen-like fashion, the cyclical nature of life and death is joined at the hip by fire. Logging that removes legacy trees, replacing them with flammable and biologically impoverished tree farms, interrupts these important recovery functions. The same satellite images of the ecoregion reveal that tree plantations burn at much higher severities than do natural forests.[23] In fact, logging and conversion to tree plantations have set the stage for a dangerous wildfire-logging-wildfire feedback loop whereby forests burn and are then logged and planted to tree plantations, only to burn even hotter in the next fire. Despite arguments made by the timber industry and proponents of the Healthy Forest Restoration Act, logging will not fireproof forests.

ROADS AS FIRE FUSES, PLANTATIONS AS FIREBOMBS

More than 30,000 miles of roads crisscross the fire mosaic of the Klamath-Siskiyou ecoregion.[24] This spaghetti-like network of roads is enough to complete 50 round-trips across the entire north-south distance of Oregon. Roads act as pathways for fire ignitions—because they provide access to forests, where people may set fires, by accident or arson—and also for the invasion of fire-prone alien species. The ignition pathway of roads may combine with the flammability of tree plantations much in the same way as fuse is to bomb. However, the relationship between fire and roads is a difficult one for the public and many politicians to grasp. On the one hand, access during fire is important in setting up defensible space for firefighters to conduct suppression activities, including setting backburns to prevent fires from reaching timber or houses. On the other hand, the contribution of roads to fire ignitions is seldom considered in fire planning. Instead, most fire managers focus on hazardous fuels (flammable vegetation) rather than ignition sources. Managers involved in fire planning need to take off their fuel blinders and weigh the benefits of road access against the significant risks associated with roads as conduits for fire ignition and exotic weeds. This means developing a transportation plan that strategically targets some roads for seasonal closure and obliteration. Moreover, through a prioritization process, managers can identify the intersection of high road densities (human-related ignition sources) and high fuel loads (hazardous fuels) to determine where risk reduction treatments like thinning small trees and closing roads seasonally would be most effective. Often, this intersection occurs at the wildland-urban interface (the place where human homes abut forests) and should be the target of fire risk reduction treatments.[25] Common sense, supported by fire science, indicates that treating fuels near forest homes is prudent insurance for reducing the risk of uncharacteristic fire events.

CATTLE AS CONTRIBUTING AGENTS OF FIRE-PRONENESS

The reduction in biomass of fine plant fuels (native grasses and forbs) by livestock grazing has reduced fire frequency and increased tree invasion in parts of the West.[26] Livestock grazing exposes mineral soils to rapidly advancing exotic weeds and conifers that can overtake native plant communities. The effects of cattle can be particularly damaging to fire mosaics. Over the years, cows can remove fine fuels associated with ground-burning fires while avoiding less palatable shrubs and small trees. The result is a landscape where fire, instead of being carried along the ground by native grasses, can be passed like a baton from flammable shrubs to tree crowns. When combined with fire suppression, cattle can be a major factor involved in the loss and degradation of many fire-adapted native pine-oak woodlands and oak savannahs.[27]

THE SISKIYOU WILD RIVERS AREA

The Siskiyou Wild Rivers area of about a million acres in the southwest corner of Oregon is a hotspot of the ecoregion's outstanding biodiversity. With its beacon the Kalmiopsis Wilderness, some of the most remote and rugged terrain along the Pacific Coast occurs here, including five national wild and scenic rivers and nine candidates for wild and scenic designation, 27 botanically significant designations, the headwaters of the Chetco and Smith rivers, the Smith River National Recreation Area, and the National Wild and Scenic Illinois River and its tributaries. The Siskiyou Wild Rivers area was proposed as a national monument in 2000 for its extraordinary biodiversity. The area derives its scenic values from its remarkable emerald green waters, which are colored by bedrock deposition from the area's exceptionally high concentration of serpentine peridotite. In terms of fire, the Siskiyou Wild Rivers area is the Yellowstone of the Pacific Coast, with fire returning every 5 to 75 years to make its mark on a stunningly complex and botanically diverse landscape.

The Siskiyou Wild Rivers area also is the Pacific Coast's "outback," as it contains the largest complex of undeveloped roadless lands from Baja California to Canada. Roadless areas are strongholds for endangered salmon and rare, endemic conifers like the Port Orford cedar. The cedar, in particular, is a "keystone" species (i.e., essential to the health and survival of many species), providing shaded stream banks and cool waters for spawning salmon and stream-dwelling amphibians, and anchoring stream banks through its fibrous roots. However, the cedar is being devastated by an exotic root-rot fungus whose spores hitch a ride on the undercarriage of muddy logging trucks, which pick them up in wet areas and deposit them in streams; the spores then float downstream, affixing themselves to the roots of other cedars along the way.[28] Notably, the healthiest populations of both cedar and salmon are in roadless areas, free of vehicular traffic and the deadly fungal spores.[29]

The Biscuit Fire Mosaic

The summer of 2002 produced record-breaking triple-digit temperatures in southwest Oregon's Siskiyou Mountains. Forests were already stressed by heat and low humidity from two successive dry summers, with the driest summer on record in 2001. Fire danger gauges in the Siskiyous in early July 2002 were at peak levels, uncharacteristically high for this time of the year and a predictor of large fire events. During the week of July 12–15, 12,000 lightning strikes were recorded throughout Oregon, igniting 375 fires. Of these, 240 were on federal lands in southwest Oregon, and 16 of these 240 grew to be larger than 100 acres.[30] The biggest fire in Oregon's history would soon follow from lightning strikes during a two-day period in that same week.

On July 12–13, lightning triggered five small fires in the Kalmiopsis Wilderness and South Kalmiopsis Roadless Area. Specifically, the fire began in the Sourdough Camp of the North Fork of the Smith River within the South Kalmiopsis Roadless Area and in the Florence Creek drainage of the Kalmiopsis Wilderness. Some of the smaller fires would join up as the Sour-Biscuit and Florence fires, and eventually these would merge to become the Biscuit.

The Biscuit Fire of 2002 was a terrain- and weather-driven event. Bulldozers, fire lines, and air tankers were no match for high winds, regional drought, and steep canyons. What began as small lightning-triggered fires was, within 10 days, in places a huge blaze racing up hillsides. A week after the Siskiyou fires began, crews were assigned to a fire that was building beyond suppression capabilities.

Over a three-day period (July 25–27), the fire grew at an alarming rate of 60,000 acres each day, spewing firebrands miles ahead of advancing flames. A fire plume was reported topping out at 30,000 feet, where smoke plunged through the atmosphere, and atmospheric temperature differences created a downward pressure gradient that pushed the fire up steep canyons. High winds combined with steep slopes to precook soils and vegetation ahead of approaching flames. The Florence and Sour-Biscuit fires would take advantage of these conditions to merge on August 6. By then, the towns of Cave Junction, Selma, Galice, and surrounding communities were placed on 30-minute evacuation notice while fire crews bulldozed fire lines and lit backburns. The cooler, moister conditions of the Pacific Coast fog belt would act as a natural barrier to prevent the fire from reaching coastal communities. In the end, the Biscuit Fire would burn for 120 days across nearly 500,000 acres, performing many of the same ecosystem functions that its predecessors had done countless times before. It was eventually declared "controlled" on November 8 as fall rains began in earnest.[31]

According to Forest Service figures, during the peak of the blaze, 7,000 firefighters and support personnel were engaged at a record-breaking cost of over $150 million, the largest and most costly fire suppression ever undertaken. During the fire, crews bulldozed over 400 miles of fire lines, while air tankers and helicopters dumped tons of fire retardants. Based on estimates from fire ecologists, approximately one-third of the fire was the result of backburns ignited during extreme meterological conditions to prevent the fire from spilling over into populated areas to the east as well as along the western fire perimeter, where timber was a concern.[32]

While the media portrayed the Biscuit Fire as a "catastrophic" event that "scorched" nearly half a million acres and the Forest Service claimed that the Biscuit was unusually severe, the fire actually burned in a mixed-severity pattern typical of the western Siskiyous. In fact, using Forest Service estimates of vegetation mortality derived from satellite images taken before and after the fire, 57 percent of the fire area had no or low vegetation damage, 25 percent had moderate damage (all vegetation dead but needles and leaves remain), and 18 percent had high damage (trees dead with few or no needles or leaves, primarily from crown fires).[33] Although comparing fire severities among fire events is confounded by differences in how researchers estimate severity and the degree of backburning influences, these estimates are within the range of mixed-severity proportions reported elsewhere in the Klamath-Siskiyou ecoregion since at least 1977.[34] Thus, contrary to assertions that the Biscuit Fire produced a "charred moonscape," the fire effects appear to have been within the range of fire's varied effects.

Recovery After the Fire

Photographs taken one to two years after the Biscuit burn reveal a classic fire mosaic pattern with examples of low-, moderate-, and high-severity fire at the landscape level. Wildflowers and pioneering mosses carpeted charred soils, jump-starting the process of renewal. Rare plants like Sadler's oak, endemic to the Siskiyous, sprouted from burned stumps, extracting life from the lifeless. Important shrub species like the nitrogen-fixing ceanothus and the mycorrhizal-symbiotic manzanita sprang from the ashes, preparing soils for a procession of plant changes that in places will eventually give rise to a mixed-evergreen forest. A bumper crop of whitish flowers was produced by crimson-colored Pacific madrone, a hardwood tree that survived the fire, exposing its bright red berries to a cadre of seed-dispersing birds and small rodents. Cobra lily fens punctuated burned fens with renewed vigor since competing azaleas had been cleared out by low-burning fire. Jeffrey pine savannahs unveiled an aromatic display of wildflowers, including rare species of Calochortus. At higher elevations, seeds of pinecones burst open by hot flames were consumed by voracious flocks of pine siskins, which occasionally pooped the seeds onto charred soils. Even in high-severity burn areas, small islands of live trees clung to life, performing legacy functions with clockwork efficiency. In fact, according to a computer mapping analysis by scientists from the Conservation Biology Institute, over 90 percent of burned areas were within 660 feet of patches of live trees that act as natural seed banks—the "Johnny Appleseeds" of the recovering forest.[35] Contrary to fire propaganda, the Biscuit Fire was not a catastrophe but a force of nature, sculpting the area's magnificent fire-dependent ecology as had its many predecessors.

DEATH OF THE FIRE MOSAIC BY A THOUSAND CUTS

As of 2004, the Siskiyou Wild Rivers area has been caught in the crosshairs of a national debate on what to do with large postfire recovering landscapes. Almost immediately after the Biscuit Fire, the Forest Service began planning for "restorative" and economic activities in burned areas, vowing to stay out of roadless areas and old-growth reserves but proposing alternatives amounting to 100 million board feet of timber (the equivalent of approximately 20,000 fully loaded logging trucks, each carrying 5,000 board feet). However, soon after, foresters from Oregon State University submitted a report (known as the Sessions report, after the lead author) to the Forest Service estimating that over 2 billion board feet (400,000 logging trucks' worth) was available from the fire area. The Sessions report delayed the planning process and triggered a public outcry as the Forest Service inserted two additional logging alternatives into its environmental impact statement, dramatically increasing the proposed volume to over 500 million board feet (100,000 logging trucks' worth).[36] The additional logging alternatives proposed by the Forest Service called for five times the initial volume proposed by the agency in its original scoping (agency scoping is done prior to an environmental assessment to help draft the range of alternatives); most of the added volume would come from sensitive watersheds, roadless areas, and old-growth reserves.[37]

Largely because of agency errors in timber estimates, the proposed logging project was later modified to 372 million board feet, one of the largest logging projects on federal lands in recent times. In the final analysis, the scale of the logging project amounted to over 20 times the average estimated logging rate in the Siskiyous since the listing of the northern spotted owl as a threatened species in 1990.

In addition, the Forest Service has proposed planting approximately 25,400 acres for "future commercial wood production and late-successional habitat."[38] This combination of tree planting and salvage logging could set into motion the wildfire-logging-wildfire feedback loop already reported for the Marbled Mountains just to the south.[39] The Sessions report argued that the "window of opportunity" for recovering forests after the burn was closing fast and that intervention was the best means for leapfrogging nature's persistent but slower succession of brushy field to forest. Global climate change was turned into justification for planting trees since it was argued that forests would take too long (100 years) to recover in drier climates dominated by brush—even though this is the typical successional sequence responsible for the mixed-evergreen forests of these mountains.[40]

Salvage Logging

While there is much to learn about the specifics of postfire logging impacts, a growing body of literature indicates this activity is usually damaging to postfire recovery.[41] Salvage logging removes the recovering forest's legacies, leaving behind flammable slash to contribute to future fire spread. In fact, the 1987 Silver Fire, which raced through a portion of the same landscape as did the Biscuit, and the 2002 Biscuit Fire offer opportunities for scientists to compare notes. Where these two fires overlapped, fire severity was over twice as high in areas that had been logged postfire as in those that had not.[42] Other scientists report that the removal of more than 25 to 40 percent of the standing volume of trees in an area could trigger sediment delivery to creeks.[43] This is why scientists have proposed strict guidelines for postfire logging to minimize environmental damages, including: (1) avoiding steep slopes (generally greater than a 40 percent grade); (2) staying out of roadless areas, old-growth reserves, and streamside habitats; (3) retaining all large-diameter and old trees (greater than 20 inches diameter at breast height, and more than 150 years old); and (4) avoiding fragile, intensely burned soils.[44] If the Forest Service were to adhere to these guidelines, the volume of trees logged from the Biscuit Fire would be drastically reduced, but the ecological damage would be minimized.

Conifer Planting and Reseeding

Often forest crews rush into a burn area to stock it with trees grown at nurseries under controlled environmental conditions. While some foresters argue that this is necessary for producing a "forest" rather than a brush field,[45] an engineered forest is no substitute for nature's varied gene pool, which has provided the evolutionary cradle for well-adapted recovery sequences inherent to the fire mosaic. The Klamath-Siskiyou ecoregion, and the western Siskiyous in particular, have periodically experienced climatic changes dating back millions of years. Numerous species have survived these changes as relicts of bygone epochs, such as Port Orford cedar and Brewer's spruce, or have found refuge within the area's varied climate. While there will be winners and losers in a changing global climate, the region's complex terrain and corresponding climatic gradients combined with a varied gene pool provide conditions for many species to weather the coming climate storm. It is naive to think that a forest and its complex gene pool can be engineered for any purpose other than commodity-producing forestry. Proponents of intensive engineering of the fire mosaic should heed the humbling words of former Forest Service chief Jack Ward Thomas: "Ecosystems are not only complex, they are more complex than we can imagine." This is true for all levels of biological diversity, from gene pool to species to communities to ecosystems to fire mosaic to biosphere. The Yellowstone of the West Coast is no place for widespread tree farms or poorly conceived engineering experiments in salvage logging as proposed by the Forest Service and their backers in the timber industry.

Late-Successional Logging

Another assertion is that salvage logging can accelerate recovery of old-growth forests by bypassing earlier successional steps and is needed to restore habitat for the threatened northern spotted owl.[46] This claim is based on the assumption that logging dead trees followed by planting conifers is preferred over natural recovery and that revenues from dead trees are needed to pay for purported "restorative" activities. However, this approach could in fact have the opposite effect by damaging recovering soils, inhibiting natural postfire recovery processes, and removing the recovering forests' legacies—particularly the large dead and living trees. Further, evidence from spotted owl monitoring in northern California indicates that the owl's reproductive fitness is best served in the fire mosaic.[47] One of the primary prey items of the northern spotted owl, the dusky woodrat, thrives in young recovering forests; yet in the Pacific Northwest, naturally recovering forests following fire are even sparser than old-growth forests.[48] Thus, the fire mosaic produces everything the owl needs—young naturally recovering forests that offer a select food menu and older fire-surviving legacies that provide proper bedroom conditions.

Removal of Biological Legacies

Contrary to pro-salvage logging assertions, insect outbreaks are not an eventuality following fire, and salvage logging of biological legacies has limited effect on outbreaks. According to Forest Service documents, there was no buildup of insect populations in the Biscuit area prior to the fire,[49] and other than populations of woodboring beetles just east of the burn area, there do not seem to be any population buildups within the immediate area. In fact, the natural mosaic of young and old forests combined with legacies within recovering forests may be the best remedy for dealing with insect outbreaks.[50] The recovering fire mosaic of young and old forest provides habitat for scores of insect-eating bats, birds, and parasitic wasps that serve to increase the period between outbreaks while dampening their effects. Removing legacy components and simplifying postfire landscapes by planting tree farms has the opposite effect by eliminating habitat for these natural enemies of destructive insects.[51]

LEARNING FROM THE FIRE MOSAIC

If the current fire-phobic paradigm continues, future generations will face a landscape that is more (not less) prone to fire and devoid of many essential postfire recovery processes provided by the unique and biologically rich fire-created mosaic. Each fire season, we struggle for a magic bullet to the fire crisis, applying one-size-fits-all strategies to a Rubik's Cube of pre- and postfire problems caused by the very same factors used in the presumed "cure." If we are to live sustainably and safely in fire habitat, we must work with, rather than against nature and draw lessons from the fire mosaic. For humans, fire, and natural ecosystems to coexist, we must:

- **Recognize that forests cannot be "fireproofed," particularly not through logging.** This does not mean that some forms of logging have no place in restoring fire mosaics. When judiciously applied, tree thinning can reduce ladder fuels (small- to medium-size trees that can transfer flames from the ground to taller adjacent trees), particularly in artificially dense situations such as heavily stocked tree plantations, fire-suppressed forests, and brushy areas near homes. Thinning projects should focus on small trees and brush and should be followed with well-managed prescribed fire to mimic wildland fires where appropriate.

Removal of small fire-prone trees can then be used as restoration by-products for rural forest workers—nature and humans working together rather than at odds.

- **Retain all large fire-resistant trees.** A forest will not recover to prefire levels of biological complexity and resiliency in the absence of legacies. All large live and dead trees (greater than 20 inches diameter at breast height) should be maintained, particularly where these trees often are fire's only survivors.

- **Protect roadless areas and old-growth reserves and allow them to recover on their own.** These areas are strongholds for salmon, threatened and endangered species, and other rare and unique plant and wildlife communities and need to be fully protected, particularly since the large size and remoteness of some of these areas offer the best opportunities to maintain remnants of the historic fire mosaic.

- **Do no harm in postfire recovery management.** The Hippocratic oath should be the standard by which we evaluate postfire recovery projects. That is, the burden of proof should be on those who wish to salvage-log and plant: they must demonstrate that such activities will not jeopardize natural recovery and that they are needed ecologically.

- **Protect representative areas of large postfire recovering landscapes.** There are few areas of untouched postfire recovering landscapes in the West. Even in many wilderness areas, suppression has altered fire-recovery processes. Places as diverse as the Siskiyous warrant increased levels of precaution with respect to postfire recovery. We know very little about how such areas recover from fire, and studies conducted following the Yellowstone 1988 fires have shown that recovery can be surprisingly rapid and prolific.[52] The Siskiyou Wild Rivers area has enormous potential for natural postfire recovery that rivals Yellowstone, and it should be studied as a large Research Natural Area or biological preserve.

- **Thin fire-prone tree plantations.** Defuse the plantation firebomb in at least four ways: (1) stop the conversion of native forests to firebombs; (2) plant small trees in low densities and avoid dense rows that can exacerbate fuel loads; (3) thin tree plantations to reduce ladder fuels and accelerate the development of fire-resistant trees; and (4) treat thinned plantations with prescribed fire where appropriate. Plantation management should include seasonal road closures.

• **Develop fire management plans for all public lands.** Most national forests, including the Siskiyou National Forest, have yet to complete a comprehensive fire management plan. Fire management therefore has been a knee-jerk reaction, and most fires are quickly snuffed out before they can produce beneficial effects. Fire management plans develop criteria for when to suppress versus when to let nature run the fire show. Without specific criteria, land managers often face urgent decisions that may not be in the best interests of the forest or firefighters.

• **Reintroduce the role of fire through prescribed fire for fire-adapted plant communities.** Prescribed fire, when judiciously applied, can simulate the effects of wildland fire.[53] However, wildland managers must match fire prescriptions to historic conditions (e.g., seasonalities) that have maintained fire-adapted communities. It makes no sense to set prescribed fires in knobcone pine communities or at high elevations since such areas are maintained by high-severity burns that are a natural component of the fire mosaic. Prescribed burning would be best applied to low-elevation areas that historically have burned in low- to moderate-severity regimes but which are more likely to burn hotter now because of fire suppression and logging. In some cases, thinning ladder fuels may be a necessary precursor to the safe introduction of prescribed fire.

• **Conduct fire-safe management in the wildland-urban interface.** Intensive fuel reduction treatments within a narrow band (¼ to ½ mile wide) surrounding homes should be the priority, including creating "defensible space."[54] Evidence from fire studies indicates that the combination of defensible space and homes built of fire-resistant materials (e.g., metal roofing instead of wood) can significantly reduce the risk of fire to homeowners. However, to slow the encroachment of homes into the wildland-urban interface, communities need to plan for zoned or "smart" growth by limiting wildlands development.

Insurance agencies should require homeowners to cover the costs of exurban sprawl through higher insurance premiums and cost adjustments based on defensible space management.

- **Educate the public about fire ecology.** There is a growing gap in the public's perception of fire as the Grim Reaper versus awareness of its ecological benefits.[55] The public's fire phobia is fed by misconceptions and media hype about the "catastrophic" effects of fire. More examples of ecologically sound fire management are needed to assuage the public's fear and build trust in the Forest Service's ability to include conservation planning with fire risk reduction.

- **Educate policymakers and land managers about fire.** It is unfortunate that fire has become the trump card for reversing many landmark environmental laws. While the science of fire ecology is countering some of the fire-phobic rhetoric, more scientists need to speak out if we are to ensure that the best science is used to guide policy decisions. As it stands now, the amount of misinformation about fires presented at congressional hearings and underlying most agency fire policies is quickly outpacing fire ecology research, which is losing ground in the public arena.

- **Design treatments specific to the root causes of fire problems.** Few if any decision makers or land managers deal with the complex array of root causes of the current fire crisis. Most approaches center on treating fuels (a symptom rather than a cause) with more logging and fire suppression (causal agents), and fail to acknowledge the full suite of factors that can contribute to fire-proneness, including livestock grazing, logging of fire-resistant trees, plantations, road building, suppression, and climate change. Treating fuels as the primary target in fire prevention will fail to solve the fire crisis, particularly as climate takes on a bigger role and as more fire-resilient forests are replaced with firebomb plantations.

- **Design roads to manage ignitions.** Transportation planning on federal lands needs, once and for all, to stop building new roads and to manage existing roads through risk reduction measures that strategically and seasonally close roads during fire season,

decommission and obliterate those that are sediment traps
(e.g., those on steep grades), include road closure and obliteration for weed abatement, and restrict off-highway-vehicle
access in the backcountry, especially in high-risk areas and
extreme fire periods.

The appropriate role of management with respect to fire is a decision best made in the context of national, regional, and site-specific
priorities informed by the best available science. Applying the principles of conservation biology, restoration ecology, and sustainable economics, land managers can prioritize pre- and postfire landscapes for
appropriate treatments by identifying places where recovery should
proceed unimpeded as well as areas where nature could use a booster
shot.[56] This means letting natural recovery processes proceed unim-
paired in the backcountry—such as in wilderness, roadless areas, old-
growth reserves, and ecologically sensitive lands—while conducting
active management based on ecological need in degraded lands (plantations) and areas near human settlements. Proper active management
may be warranted even in some protected areas where maintenance of
fire resiliency is a concern, through, for example, light-touch thinning
and prescribed fire.[57] Outside reserves, judiciously applied thinning
could be compatible with economic and ecological values if used in
conjunction with pre- and postfire safeguards. Such restorative actions
can produce jobs through thinning small fire-prone trees and obliterating ecologically risky roads. A landscape as rich and fragile as the
Siskiyous could benefit from a combination of treatments: no touch in
the backcountry; light touch in areas damaged by firefighting activities; aggressive thinning in flammable tree plantations and along the
wildland-urban interface; and sound restorative actions that include
road obliterations, exotic weed abatement, and well-managed prescribed fire.[58]

Humanity is at a historic crossroads over fire and federal fire management policy. If we continue on our current fire-phobic path, forests
of the West will be less natural and healthy, and few areas will remain
that have not been greatly engineered. We must instead forge a new
relationship with fire whereby humans and fire coexist safely and ben-
eficially, as they did historically. While we can never turn back the

clock to the days when indigenous cultures used fire in the primordial landscapes of the West, humanity must now work with nature if we are going to have both landscapes as diverse as the Siskiyous and fire-safe communities. But to live in the company of fire-resistant giants created by the fire mosaic, we must also realize nature's remarkable capacity to renew itself through fire's many contributions.[59]

FIRE IN THE SOUTHWEST

A Historical Context

TOM RIBE

THE SOUTHWEST IS A NATIVE HOME OF FIRE, *a place long dependent on and welcoming of this natural force. A century and a half of intensive land uses such as grazing, logging, and fire suppression have changed the personality of fire on the land and left society and its land managers caught between choosing expensive and difficult ecological restoration or expensive and potentially deadly superfires.*

▼

On June 18, 2002, an underemployed wildland firefighter started a fire in the convoluted ponderosa pine landscape of the White Mountains in eastern Arizona, perhaps to generate work for his idle fire crew. The fire quickly got out of control and began to eat through significant acreage on the White Mountain Apache Reservation. Fifty miles away, on June 20, a lost delivery driver started a signal fire that ignited another forest fire. Over the next two weeks, the two fires grew together and nearly sterilized 468,000 acres of forestland, burning 400 homes along the way. The Rodeo-Chediski Fire became the largest and hottest fire in southwestern history.

Forest fires have been burning for centuries in the Southwest, but a steady ratcheting up of their size and ferocity has alarmed land managers. People are helpless to stop most of these large blazes, for they pop up unpredictably from a variety of human and natural causes.

The Southwest's growing fire problem gained major media attention starting with the 1977 La Mesa Fire near Los Alamos, New Mexico, which scorched 15,000 acres of dog-hair (very dense) ponderosa pine thickets and other forest types, and nearly burned down part of a nuclear weapons research complex. In 2000, the Cerro Grande Fire in the same area burned as a ferocious, wind-driven crown fire over 43,000 acres, including some containing high-explosive storage areas. That fire cost taxpayers $480 million in compensation to its property-loss victims and reconstruction costs at government facilities. The fire seasons of 2002 and 2003 set new records with big, untamable blazes across Arizona, New Mexico, Colorado, and Utah. In 2003 the Aspen Fire burned 85,000 acres and 333 structures, showering ash on nearby Tucson for two weeks. Over the last decade, large fires have burned over most of Mesa Verde National Park in southwestern Colorado, reducing fire-suppressed juniper and Douglas-fir forests to open scrub fields and exposing thousands of previously hidden archaeological sites (though such stand-replacement fires may be natural events in the Mesa Verde ecosystem).

Something has changed in the Southwest. Fire is as native to this region as roadrunners and ponderosa pine. Yet the fierceness of the blazes that have occurred over the last two decades is unprecedented. Some fire seasons in the future promise more of the same as land managers and politicians struggle with the scale and depth of the problem. What happened to natural fire in the Southwest to change it from a positive, natural element to a sometimes-negative force menacing people and forests alike?

PREHISTORIC FIRE IN THE SOUTHWEST

The story of fire in the Southwest is a story of lost wilderness. Perhaps nowhere in North America is fire more an integral part of wildland health than in the Four Corners states of the American Southwest— Colorado, Utah, New Mexico, and Arizona—and the northern mountains of Mexico. In this dry, mountainous region, fire is a keystone element. All native species here have evolved with fire, either directly or indirectly. As important as any other physical element, prehistoric fire in the Southwest nurtured the base of the ecosystem and allowed plant and animal life to flourish. As the ecology of the region has altered from the post-Pleistocene wilderness that persisted until the 1870s, we have seen fire change from an integral evolutionary force to an unruly and often destructive agent of radical environmental change. Unquestionably the most important ecological and environmental force in the prehistoric Southwest was fire. (In the Southwest, "prehistory" can be considered to end with the arrival of Spanish explorers in

1540.) In a region where the rainfall averages less than 15 inches (38.1 centimeters) over the majority of the landscape and relative humidity stays below 20 percent most of the year, decay by biological means is slow. The dryness of the atmosphere, the region's topography, and the dynamics of the region's atmospheric moisture lead to frequent lightning storms, which jab at the landscape from cumulus clouds, starting wildfires as soon as significant convection begins in the summer.

Despite the presence of agrarian human settlements over much of the Southwest beginning around 1,200 years ago, it was a wild region where wolves and grizzly bears topped a food chain based primarily on perennial fire-stimulated grasses. From prolific bird life to small mammals that thrived on grasses, the region supported large grazers and browsers such as Rocky Mountain elk, desert bighorn, mule deer, antelope, and a few bison. Wolves kept these large animals moving and allowed woody deciduous plants like aspen to thrive, even while the wolves lived primarily on mice and other small mammals amid the grasses. Fire, not grazing, was the primary nurturing disturbance from the low valleys to the high mixed-conifer ecosystems, and fire was the primary force of decay and nutrient release for dead vegetation.

In the high-desert environment, upper-atmosphere moisture circulates up from the Gulf of Mexico and the South Pacific and condenses in huge cumulus clouds over the mountains with their summer updrafts. Lightning forks down, hitting trees on the ridges or midslope, often starting wildfires. (Between 1985 and 1994, for example, there were 160,000 lightning strikes in northern New Mexico's Jemez Mountains.)[1] A tree burning at its top would shower coals down into the grasses below, where fire would spread at low temperature through the grass, singeing the bark of the old trees and moving on. Before 1900 such fires would burn up into the high country until the higher fuel moistures above 9,000 feet would snuff out the flames. Meanwhile, the lower edge of the fire could extend out into the river valley grasslands, flashing quickly and coolly through the grass. If the grasses were wet at the onset, fire spread would be limited. If the grasses were dry, the fires would continue burning until rain or snow put them out or until they hit barriers such as cliffs, streams, or riparian areas that were minimally flammable. Grasses not only survived such fires, they were stimulated and nurtured by them.

The Southwest is a landscape of mountains and valleys, ranging from the over-14,000-feet-high Sangre de Cristo Mountains of northern New Mexico and southern Colorado, to southern mountains such as the Dragoon and Gila mountains, which rise to 8,000 feet above desert valleys, to the valleys themselves at around 5,000 feet in elevation. This island geography encompasses the San Francisco Peaks of northern Arizona, the Abajo and La Sal mountains of southern Utah, and on down through New Mexico and Arizona to the fringes of the Chihuahua, Sonoran, and Mojave deserts to the south and west, where vegetation shifts and fire regimes change with decreasing elevation. Fire ecology similar to the high-desert Southwest exists in the Great Basin deserts to the north and west.

In prehistoric times, the Southwest's valleys were filled with perennial grasslands, blended with sparse stands of desert scrub like pinyon pine and juniper in the higher valleys and deciduous desert scrub like catclaw in the more southern valleys. Pinyon and juniper woodlands merged to ponderosa pine forests at middle elevations (7,000–9,000 feet) and thence into mixed-conifer highlands, depending on the latitude of the mountains. Ponderosa pine forests were open parklands of mostly older (100- to 600-year-old) trees, with thick grama and bunch grasses at their bases. Those grasses prohibited most pine seeds from taking root, and they carried frequent, widespread low-intensity fires that would kill most tree seedlings that did get past their grassy competitors. Streams flowed from mountains in relative abundance to the valleys below to join larger rivers like the Gila, Rio Puerco, Rio Grande, Pecos, San Pedro, and San Juan. Those streams and rivers were sheltered by willow and cottonwood riparian forests, where beaver created wetlands critical to subsurface hydrology, and wolves and grizzly bears lurked among the flood-nurtured trees.

Prehistoric fires burned the needles cast from conifers, freeing nutrients and opening the ground for grasses and forbs. Fire prevented the pinyon and juniper from invading the ponderosa pine forests and largely kept the white fir and Douglas-fir from moving down into the ponderosa pine zone. Spreading ground fires kept the prolifically seeding ponderosa pine from creating thickets, and an abundance of wildlife from large predators to birds of all sizes thrived on the grass seed and the small mammals that proliferated in this grass-rich environment. In the valleys and foothills, larger pinyon pine and juniper would survive surface fires, but many of their offspring would not. Thus fire protected and encouraged old-growth forests.

In 1826, James Pattie traversed the Gila River drainage and wrote that after one day of travel, "we were fatigued by the difficulty of getting through the high grass which covered the heavily timbered bottom."[2] Joseph Rothrock of the 1873 Wheeler survey described the "luxuriant bunchgrasses covering the ground as thickly as it could stand."[3] Clearly, grass cover with all its benefits for erosion control, wildlife, and maintenance of forest structure was intact, in parts of the region, up to the end of the 1800s.

In the fire-dependent ponderosa pine forests that were common in the Southwest, prehistoric fires would typically stay on the forest floor, occasionally flaring into treetops, "torching" patches of trees or perhaps running with the wind in crowns of middle-aged trees in times of coincidental drought and high wind. Even so, running crown fires were rare, and there is no reason to believe that crown fires of the scale we see today ever occurred in prehistoric times.

Fire ranged over the entire region, and tree-ring research shows that fires burned every 5 to 20 years in most middle-elevation forest areas of the Southwest. These ground fires would get more active in the periodic droughts that have challenged the Southwest since major climate change at the end of the last Pleistocene ice extension 10,000 years ago. Tree-ring studies reveal "regional fire years" in which large fires would burn here and there over the entire region at the same time. Ecologists Craig Allen and Thomas Swetnam found that there were 122 regional fire years between 1480 and 1900, according to fire scar data gathered across the Southwest.[4] It is highly likely that many areas of today's Four Corners states had fire epidemics in those same dry, regional fire years. Further, Craig Allen's research shows that before 1877, watershed-wide fires occurred in the Jemez Mountains approximately every 16 years.[5]

This prehistoric fire world of semiregular ground fires over most acres in the Southwest went on until industrial-scale land exploitation came to the region around 1880.[6] And while the Pueblo, Ute, Apache, and Navajo had lived in the region for varying lengths of time, any fire they started on the landscape would have largely blended in with naturally started fires and would not have had appreciable ecological effect outside of the natural fire cycle, given the frequency of lightning fires and the fuel regimes that resulted.[7] Further, these native peoples had no domestic livestock before the arrival of the Spanish in the 16th century, and their main impact on the landscape was predation on mammals and removal of woody fuels for firewood over large areas near their villages.

THE CONTEMPORARY WORLD OF SOUTHWEST FIRE

Today, the Southwest is a land of relatively barren, deeply eroded (often urbanized) valleys and overly thick upland forests. The wolf and the grizzly bear are gone, the beaver is all but gone, exotic vegetation competes with native vegetation in key environments, and fire has a radically different place in the current landscape. Deep human misperceptions about nature have forced dramatic change on the regional ecology.

By far the most profound element of change in the Southwest has been livestock grazing.[8] Spanish explorers brought livestock to the Southwest for the first time in the mid-1500s. They introduced cows, sheep, and horses to the region as a portable food supply, as transportation, and for breeding. Francisco Vásquez de Coronado brought 5,000 sheep with him in 1540, and Juan de Oñate had 7,000 head of livestock of various breeds with his conquest party in 1598.[9]

Those livestock began to strip out the native grasses in New Mexico and later throughout the region. Not only was grazing concentrated and persistent, no native animals had impacted grasses in the same way that cows and sheep did.[10] Spanish settlers who followed the conquistadores expanded livestock grazing. In colonial New Mexico (the 17th and 18th centuries), 20 families had 3 million sheep. The sheep industry expanded further in the early 1900s, when sheep raising exploded as an export business. Yet Apache attacks kept stockmen out of most mountains in the Southwest, forcing settlers to pasture their sheep and cows in the valleys close to their villages. Even there, sheep were often stolen, and herders were attacked. Not until 1860, when the Apache and Navajo were finally subdued by the U.S. Army in northern New Mexico and northern Arizona, were the region's northern mountains opened to livestock grazing.[11]

In 1880, the railroads threaded into the Southwest, and an aggressively capitalistic economy previously unknown to the region came with them. Livestock numbers soared, particularly in New Mexico, which became the largest sheep-producing area of the United States. According to some accounts, by 1884 there were 5.5 million sheep in New Mexico.[12] The Navajo built sheep flocks by borrowing animals from the abundant northern Rio Grande Valley flocks as soon as sheep ranching began in earnest in the Southwest, thus beginning the desertification of northern Arizona's Colorado Plateau. By 1850 the Navajo had 500,000 sheep.[13]

By 1890 the sheep industry began to give way to the cattle industry because of economic pressures, including the fencing of the once-open range, declining demand for wool and mutton, increasing demand for beef, and growing political control of the public domain by cattlemen.[14] Cattle became a permanent part of the landscape where no ecologically analogous beast had lived before.[15] Meanwhile, large herds of feral horses could be seen across the Southwest. By 1900 the height and density of most native grasses had been greatly reduced by livestock grazing regionally, while major erosion and vegetation changes set in as livestock consumed native vegetation.[16] At the same time, beaver, which had facilitated water infiltration into soils and aquifers by creating millions of acres of high- and low-elevation wetlands, were trapped out by mountain men for pelt sales to Europe and killed by ranchers, beginning the desiccation of canyons and forests. Many streams stopped flowing from the mountains to the larger rivers, springs dried up, and riparian forests vanished, replaced by barren arroyos (gullies) that further contributed to dropping water tables.

Because livestock grazing had devastated grasses in both the valleys and the mountains, spreading surface fires, which had been the root of ecological balance in the region, all but ceased by 1877.[17] Though forest fires still occurred in the mountains, their fuels had changed from grasslands to pine duff and tree thickets, and the ecological role of forest fire began to shift.[18]

In 1891, the federal government began to set up forest reserves in the Southwest to control lawless grazing and logging, which had been precipitating violence and decimating natural resources on the public domain.[19] In 1903, federal rangers began to fight forest fires, believing that fire was harmful to timber and livestock interests. Early forest reserve employees took particular note of how fire killed tree seedlings and used this issue to justify aggressive fire control. As fire suppression took hold, extremely flammable fuel accumulations developed. Meanwhile, people blithely transferred their fear of structural fires to forests, which, however, had long depended upon fire as part of the natural ecology. Around 1915 a wet decade began, causing a burst of tree seedling growth in the nearly barren soils of southwestern ponderosa pine and mixed-conifer forests. The ensuing excessive and unnatural crop of seedlings would grow into dog-hair tree thickets that would fuel superfires 60 years later and beyond.

Logging of the large old trees that had been nurtured by fire began in earnest with the coming of the railroads in 1880. Loggers built temporary railroads into the Zuni and Jemez mountains of New Mexico and hauled out ponderosa pine and Douglas-fir trees up to 600 years old. Demand for rail ties swept the region as the railroads were being built, and people living in rural areas stripped out trees of all sizes to meet the demand. The federal government regulated logging only minimally.

Logging was the third blow (following livestock grazing and fire suppression) to the Southwest's ecosystems. Cutting out big trees opened the ground to increased sunlight, stimulating the growth of seedlings and brush and drying the soil. Removal of logs and fire changed delicate nutrient cycling that had persisted for centuries. As soil ecology deteriorated, soil erosion increased, with tons of soil washing off mountainsides, filling stream and rivers and reducing grass and forb cover over once-verdant areas.[20]

By 1930 the grasslands of the Southwest were all but gone, and federal efforts to destroy grizzly bears and wolves, which had turned to preying on livestock following the loss of their native food sources, finally succeeded. The region's hydrology shifted as water infiltration to aquifers both shallow and deep declined following major changes to streams and grasslands and the loss of beaver. Many of the region's animal populations went into freefall, and its wilderness ecology collapsed.[21]

Briefly, in the 1920s, a debate had flared between those who would suppress all fires on the forest reserves and those, like Gila Forest Reserve's Aldo Leopold, who suspected fire may belong in forests.[22] However, Wisconsin's Peshtigo Fire in 1871 (3,780,000 acres burned and at least 1,200 humans dead)[23] and the 1910 Big Blowup in western Montana and northern Idaho (more than 3 million acres burned, 85 firefighters dead)[24] had been too traumatic for the nation. Any talk of truce or treaty with wildland fire would have to wait, and public land agencies set about putting out fire with a determination that would not be dissipated by contrary evidence, or by the increasing futility of their efforts.

THE MODERN ERA: SUPERFIRES AND THE WAR ON NATURE

In the 1950s, policymakers and foresters in the Southwest were being pressed between two opposing fire-activity graph lines. On the one hand, the number of fires overall had begun to decline precipitously after fine fuels were decimated by livestock grazing around the turn of the century. Yet the size and severity of fires was trending in the opposite direction, increasing most dramatically with the severe drought of the early 1950s and continuing still today.[25]

Big-fire years happened in 1971 and 1974, and again in 1977, when another drought and regional fire year came around, and the phenomenon of the superfire was firmly established in the Southwest. Convection-driven fires like the 1977 La Mesa Fire in northern New Mexico defied control and ate through thickets of ponderosa pine and Douglas-fir at such extreme temperatures that the land was virtually sterilized in their wake. In 1977, all of Arizona's national forests had "project-level" fires like the La Mesa Fire—ones that required large suppression organizations. Firefighters found old control techniques wanting. Though they were hesitant to admit it publicly, firefighters were essentially helpless against these blazes. These large fires shocked the public though they were small relative to many of today's fires.

The era of Smokey Bear successfully dousing all smokes in the Southwest mountains was passing. Wildland firefighting, long an almost-private art within the land agencies, was becoming a public performance as air tankers skimmed close over Southwest cities and towns and members of the public looked at columns of smoke near their homes with justified foreboding.

The 1980s were a relatively wet period in the Southwest, and public alarm over the big fires of the 1970s seem to calm. With a century of ecological damage from livestock grazing, logging, and fire suppression, fires were finding heavy fuels in forests with up to 3,000 stems per acre as opposed to the 20 to 50 stems per acre in historic forests on the same location with a natural fire regime.[26]

The two major forest managing agencies in the Southwest, the U.S. Forest Service and the National Park Service, have responded to the growing fire crisis in different ways. With rare exceptions (the Gila National Forest being the most notable), the Forest Service continues to fight most fires on the majority of southwestern national forests, viewing fire as a commodity-damaging nuisance similar to insect infestation. Although since the 1990s the Forest Service has gradually eased away from its tree-cropping focus toward a more scientifically oriented land management philosophy and has begun greater use of prescribed fire, the acreage treated relative to that overloaded with fuels is still far out of balance. Today, many in the Forest Service recognize the need to allow low-intensity fire back into southwestern national forests, but funding for prescribed burning continues to fall far short of what is needed. For its part, since the 1980s the National Park Service has worked consistently to reestablish natural fire cycles in the national parks and monuments of the Southwest, with aggressive prescribed and wildland fire use programs (allowing lightning-started fires to burn within acceptable conditions and boundaries) and a cautious approach to firefighting that focuses on protecting natural and cultural elements (such as ruins of prehistoric settlements) on the landscape. Based on a fire research program, prescribed fires in parks such as Bandelier, Grand Canyon, and El Malpais have been geared toward reintroducing fire at natural intervals on almost all acres of NPS lands in these parks and in parks elsewhere in the region.[27]

The NPS prescribed-fire program attained national notoriety and was dealt a severe setback in May 2000, when the 1,000-acre Cerro Grande prescribed burn at Bandelier National Monument escaped onto adjacent Forest Service land and burned 42,000 acres, including 250 homes in Los Alamos, New Mexico. In the same week, and because of the same wind event, Grand Canyon National Park employees lost control of the Outlet prescribed burn on the North Rim, drawing more criticism to NPS prescribed-fire programs. Ironically, the Cerro Grande wildfire started from a fuel reduction program on national park land, but the vast majority of it burned over fuel-choked national forestland close to Los Alamos, where very little fuel reduction work had been done over the preceding decades. In the few places where the Forest Service had done thinning work, the fire dropped from the forest crowns to the ground. The park service took the brunt of blame for the fire, though its ferocity resulted from heavy fuels on poorly managed national forestlands.

As the new century unfolds, the Southwest continues its age-old drought cycles, which lead to periodically increased fire activity, overlaid now by the problem of heavy fuel loading and unnatural forest structure. On top of these intractable problems, global climate change may be intensifying drought by changing moisture distribution patterns over the North American continent. Rising summer temperatures (2003 brought record highs across the region), drying fuels, faster spring runoff, and increasing summer atmospheric instability all fit some models of what global warming could be bringing to the region.

Global climate changes likely will have other unpredictable effects on fire in the Southwest. Given that southwestern drought and wet cycles are driven by ocean temperature changes in the South Pacific that set in motion the El Niño wetting cycles and La Niña drying cycles, global warming's effect on sea temperature and currents could profoundly change weather in the Southwest. As ocean temperature changes, major air currents, such as the jet stream, that move marine moisture onshore shift as well. Such air current shifts can cause seasonal storm patterns to change and make areas like the Southwest fall into drought during key parts of the year.[28]

With heavy fuel loading, dense forest structure, and long-term drought, the potential increases for wind- or convection-driven crown fires, even at high altitudes. Such fires release pent-up carbon into the atmosphere, exacerbating the global warming problem while converting forests to brushlands, with heavy soil erosion across millions of acres of public lands. Even with the scientific uncertainty over the anticipated effects of global climate change, actual changes in southwestern climate over the last decade have contributed to the intensity of forest fires.

The Southwest fire landscape is fraught with dilemma. Firefighting controls large fires only on the margins, despite billions of dollars spent. Controlling large fires almost always depends on weather changes such as rain or snowfall, major wind shifts, or rises in relative humidity that calm or extinguish blazes. Often firefighting methods do considerable damage to the landscape, and a large percentage of fire growth can be attributed to backfires rather than to organic spread of the wildfire itself.[29] In some cases, such as the Cerro Grande (Los Alamos) Fire, backfires contribute to fire escape rather than controlling blazes as intended.

With two of its largest programmatic sources of congressional appropriation—national forest commercial timber sales and livestock grazing—declining, the Forest Service continues to get substantial funding for fire suppression efforts from Congress. Thus the agency has a large incentive to keep up business as usual with firefighting, even as its long-term effects on forests prove paradoxical.

At the same time, the scale of the ecological restoration problem in the Southwest may be beyond the budgets or the manpower of the Forest Service, which finds itself with about 22 million acres of ecologically distorted land in the region.[30] Mechanical thinning costs $800 per acre and is difficult in remote areas. Even with prescribed-fire costs running only about $100 per acre, funds for prescribed fire or for wildland fire use (which is gaining more favor in Washington) are scarce, reflecting confusion in Washington about the problem, its scale, and realistic solutions. Southwestern forests are relatively unproductive, and the idea of using thinned wood material for commercial purposes is problematic. In northeastern New Mexico, the idea of burning forest debris from thinning to generate electricity is being developed. Congress has provided funding for fuel reduction projects through the National Fire Plan, but some of these funds have been diverted to remote timber sale activity. The Forest Service is working to protect communities such as Flagstaff and Santa Fe with thinning projects. These projects and others on the San Juan National Forest in Colorado have not been without controversy.

With public land livestock ranching costing taxpayers many times more than it returns,[31] and southwestern timber sales coming in well below cost, the costs of firefighting far exceed the commercial value of the resources being "protected." Firefighting could be scaled back if communities were protected by effective fire barriers. Fuel breaks built on federal land around rural communities, combined with education programs for rural homeowners, provide the best hope of saving those communities from inevitable wildfires, yet even these programs remain mired in funding shortfalls.

▼

Returning fire to its historic healthy place in southwestern ecosystems may require abandoning the very land use practices that have contributed to ecological collapse in the first place. However, there is little political will to do so with the livestock industry continuing to dominate federal land use across the region.[32] As detailed above, ongoing fire suppression and fuel reduction efforts are among the many indirect costs of a century of livestock grazing and logging, but elected officials do not recognize this fact.

As superfires spring up with regularity in the Southwest and elsewhere, the sense that land managers have control of the fire situation is slipping away. Nature is self-correcting, and the damage done to watersheds and forests by logging, livestock grazing, and fire suppression in the Southwest is being compensated for by large fires that release pent-up energy from natural systems. The default ecological endgame in the Southwest is now intense wildfire, particularly in the ponderosa pine forests, and it is inevitable that vast areas of forestland will be "treated" with such fire, whether or not humans approve.

In the Southwest, the day of reckoning for fire managers has arrived. With Washington largely misunderstanding the fire problem, federal land agencies face a collision of natural and historical forces that promise unstoppable fires, even as urban growth spreads deeper into once-remote forest areas. The time for radically rethinking fire management is overdue. The Southwest is locked into an era of superfires, the latest chapter in a century of ecological deterioration and ecological self-correction.

FIRE IN THE EAST

Welcoming Back a Native Son

GEORGE WUERTHNER

BECAUSE OF THE MOIST YEAR-ROUND CLIMATE *of the East, fire plays a less ubiquitous role in shaping the landscape than in the West. In some eastern ecosystems, however—for example, southern pine, pitch pine–Virginia pine, red pine–jack pine, eastern white pine, and oak-hickory—fire has been, and continues to be, a dominant ecological force. Elsewhere in the East, fire is rare to nonexistent on the landscape.*

▼

Most of the eastern United States has a humid climate and year-round precipitation. Whereas in the western United States wildfire is a major factor in the decomposition of dead litter and woody debris, the warm, humid climate that is common across the eastern United States speeds the natural decomposition of plant material by bacteria and fungi. Abundant rainfall; a long growing season characterized by hot, humid summers; and mild winters support rapid tree growth. A nighttime humidity of 100 percent is not uncommon during the summer months, a factor that tends to quench fires and limit their spread. To simplify, in the West, things burn; in the East, things rot.

Despite the abundant moisture that is common throughout the East, multiyear droughts do occur. Drought conditions quickly dry out vegetation, producing flammable conditions. Unlike the West, where fire season is primarily a summer phenomenon, in much of the eastern United States, fires are most likely to occur in winter (in the more southern states) or spring (in the more northern states). Fires typically occur after hardwood trees have shed their leaves and prior to summer green-up. A secondary fire season occurs in the fall after leaf drop but before snowfall, or during ensuing winter droughts.

Although lightning is common in many parts of the eastern United States, most of the East's electric storms occur in the height of summer, when moist conditions limit ignitions. Nevertheless, lightning can and does spark some blazes—for example, 12 percent of all fires in the southern Appalachians (the other 88 percent are human caused).[1]

Historical records indicate that Native Americans regularly burned eastern woods to facilitate hunting and to clear land for farming, and even as a weapon of warfare (hoping to burn out the enemy).[2] Some historians have used these common cultural practices to suggest that nearly all of the pre-European landscape of the United States was influenced by native peoples.[3] Other scholars counter that the Native American influence was concentrated near major settlements, and that the effect of humans beyond those small areas was minimal, or at least varied considerably across the continent.[4]

Studying the past fire history of eastern fire-influenced land-scapes is difficult because of the massive human disruption of the native plant communities following European settlement. Except for the most rugged, swampy, or inhospitable terrain, eastern settlers generally cleared the land for fields, removing much of the native forest community. Reconstruction of presettlement fire regimes from fire scars on older trees is therefore difficult, if not impossible.

There are, however, well-known regional landscapes for which almost everyone agrees that fire, whether because of natural or human ignitions, has been and continues to be a major ecological influence. Some of the better-known fire landscapes found east of the Mississippi include the southern pine forests that dominate the low, sandy Piedmont of the Southeast; the pitch pine–Virginia pine barrens of New Jersey, Massachusetts, and the Adirondacks; the red pine–jack pine forests of the Great Lakes states; the widespread eastern white pine forests; and the oak-hickory forests of the central Appalachians and Ozarks.

However, I caution readers to avoid the conclusion that fire was a ubiquitous force throughout the East. Recent research suggests that disturbance from fire was exceedingly rare, or even nonexistent, in some parts of the eastern United States, particularly in the high-elevation spruce-fir forests along the spine of the Appalachians, the cove hardwood forests of the southern Appalachians, and the northern hardwood forests of New England. For instance, one study found that the Green and White mountains are "among the least burnable in the northern hardwood region." On average, only 7 to 10 acres per million acres burn annually.[5] A study of northern hardwoods in Maine found the fire rotation to be in excess of 900 years.[6] Because of the general resistance of these hardwoods to burning, even human ignitions had little influence over regional fire regimes. Researchers David Foster and Tim Parshall concluded that "Native Americans likely influenced the local occurrence of fire, but their impact on regional fire regimes in New England is not apparent from this or other studies."[7]

I give here a brief overview of the most fire-influenced eastern landscapes.

SOUTHERN PINE FORESTS

Southern pine forests—including longleaf pine (*Pinus palustris*), shortleaf pine (*Pinus echinata*), loblolly pine (*Pinus taeda*), pond pine (*Pinus serotina*), and slash pine (*Pinus elliottii*)—occur on sandy soils across the South. These pine forests are often open savannahs with a two-story structure consisting of mature old-growth pine and an understory of grasses. The U.S. Fish and Wildlife Service estimates that these pine woodlands may have totaled as much as 200 million acres at the time of European settlement. The most abundant species was longleaf pine, covering an estimated 60 to 92 million acres. Today, in part owing to fire suppression, as well as logging and development, longleaf pine is found on less than 3 million acres, and little of this remaining pine forest has old-growth characteristics.[8]

Drought conditions quickly dry out vegetation, producing flammable conditions. Lightning is a ready and abundant source of ignition. Indeed, Florida and nearby states have the highest rates of lightning strikes in the United States. Historically, added to this naturally high lightning pattern were human-caused ignitions. Prior to the Civil War, a large percentage of southern white residents had livestock, including hogs, and regularly burned the woods to allow growth of new forage for their animals. Indeed, in 1731, burning of the woods in North Carolina was even mandated by law.[9] However, by the time the U.S. Forest Service was established in 1905, active fire suppression was being instituted throughout the region.

Prior to the introduction of widespread fire suppression, southern pines experienced high-frequency/low-intensity blazes. Longleaf pine sites burned on average every 1 to 4 years, while shortleaf pine had a fire return interval of 2 to 15 years, depending on the productivity of the site. Even cypress ponds would dry out sufficiently to burn on average every 20 to 30 years, with the wettest areas sometimes being fire-free for 50 to 150 years. Longer fire intervals favored slash and loblolly pine.

Longleaf pine exhibits many of the fire-adapted traits typical of southern pines. After it is established, longleaf bolts, growing rapidly to rise above the typical flame length found in the high-frequency/low-intensity fire regime. Its bark grows thick with age, providing protection from low-intensity burns. Self-pruning of lower branches creates long, straight boles topped by leafy crowns of needles. Shortleaf pine, another "fire pine," sprouts from top-killed boles. Such adaptations make these pines remarkably adept at surviving frequent low-intensity fires.

As a consequence of fire suppression, the historical two-layered structure of these forests—a canopy of mature, old-growth trees with an understory of grasses—has been altered to a multilayered midstory characterized by hardwoods and little or no ground cover. Logging has also changed the structure of these pine communities, to the detriment of species such as the red-cockaded woodpecker, which is dependent on old-growth forest characteristics.[10]

In efforts to reintroduce fire into these landscapes, private individuals, timber companies, and public land management agencies burn an estimated 8 million acres per year.[11] Nevertheless, wildfire now influences only a small percentage of southern pine ecosystems, in part because so many of today's pine forests are commercial tree farms, where fire is generally excluded, or are increasingly fragmented by exurban development.

Today the southern longleaf pine/wiregrass community is imperiled and stands as an example of how fire suppression combined with habitat destruction has reduced the Southeast's fire-dependent vegetation types to small remnants.

PITCH PINE—VIRGINIA PINE FORESTS

Pitch pine makes up the famous Atlantic Coastal Pine Barrens, which cover the coastal plain of New Jersey, much of the southern half of

Long Island, and Cape Cod, Massachusetts.[12] Smaller, inland pine barrens are found near Albany, New York,[13] and in New York's Adirondack Park.[14] The species, however, ranges from Maine to Georgia, growing on sandy or gravelly well-drained soils.[15] Another fire pine with similar habitat requirements is the Virginia pine. The major center of its range lies in Virginia and the Carolinas, but it is found north as far as New Jersey and west to Indiana.

Pitch pine has thick bark and serotinous cones that open upon heating. It can also sprout from a basal crook just below the soil, where it is protected from the heat of all but the most intense blazes. Another fire adaptation of the pitch pine is precocious (early) cone development. Trees 3 to 10 years old can produce viable seed cones, allowing the pine to rapidly recolonize a burned site.

Historically, understory burning was common in pitch pine–Virginia pine forests, with frequent low-intensity blazes occurring every 2 to 10 years—often due to burning by Native Americans as well as lightning.[16] Such forests likely had scattered larger trees, with few small trees. Even-aged stands established after a large blaze are now more common.

RED PINE–JACK PINE FORESTS

Red pine dominates fire landscapes throughout the Great Lakes states. Jack pine is often an associate but ranges farther north and west in Canada, all the way to the Rockies. Both red and jack pine are favored by fire. Because the cones do not mature and produce seeds for at least 25 years, red pine stands tend to do best where fire intervals are greater than 25 years. Red pines are also susceptible to crown fires. As a consequence, historically the average fire return interval in red pine forests is between 14 and 50 years. Where fire is more frequent, the more precocious jack pine tends to dominate because its cones can produce seeds in 3 to10 years.[17] Furthermore, jack pine cones are serotinous—that is, they require heat to open and shed seeds—and thus they can remain viable on the tree for up to 25 years.

Jack pine is favored by stand-replacement blazes, while red pine does better with low-intensity understory burns. Mature red pine is adept at surviving fire, in part because it possesses branch-free lower boles. Once the mature red pine reaches 60 feet tall, its bark is so thick that it can survive all but the most serious burns. Crown fires occur when the fire interval is longer and fuels build up, or with extreme drought and high winds.

EASTERN WHITE PINE FORESTS

Eastern white pine is one of the most majestic trees in the eastern forest. It ranges from southern Georgia north throughout New England and the Great Lakes states. White pine can reach heights of more than 200 feet, and at least a few specimens have exceeded 600 years of age. Because it can grow on a wide variety of soils and also survive in the shade of hardwoods, the white pine is one of the most widely distributed eastern pine species, growing in pure stands as well as scattered individuals in hardwood forests. Though white pine is not dependent on fire for successful regeneration, fire appears to help sustain the species on sites, since white pine abundance increases as soil moisture decreases, and as light intensity at the forest floor and fire frequency increase.[18]

The thick bark and branch-free lower bole of large white pine have allowed it to survive moderate surface fires.[19] Historically, non-lethal fires burned through white pine stands every 5 to 50 years, while stand-replacement blazes occurred less frequently. On the wettest sites, white pine may experience a fire only once every 150 to 350 years. Though large blazes tend to kill most mature white pines, large blazes also produce excellent ash and mineral soil conditions for white pine regeneration.

OAK-HICKORY FORESTS

Prior to fire suppression, oak-hickory forests dominated the central Appalachian region along the Ohio River and its tributaries in what is today West Virginia, Kentucky, Tennessee, southern Indiana, southern Ohio, western Virginia, and western North Carolina. These forests also dominated the Ozarks of Arkansas and Missouri.

Low-intensity/high-frequency blazes maintained open old-growth stands of oak-hickory with an understory of grasses and forbs. Thick bark on the mature trees helped protect the individual boles from fire. Oak and hickory tend to develop extensive root systems, and many species are root sprouters; even if top-killed by fire, these species will immediately send up new shoots.

Before European settlement, oak-hickory forests burned every 7 to14 years on average. Because most lightning occurs during the moist growing season, when blazes tend to be extinguished by rain, it is believed that Native American ignitions played a strong role in maintaining these forests.[20] And even after the Indians were vanquished, the European settlers who followed continued to burn the woods to maintain feed for livestock.

However, once fire suppression became the norm after 1900, species like white pine, American beech, red maple, and sugar maple began to develop a dense understory beneath the oaks and hickory. Over time these species shaded out the oak and hickory forests on many sites.

▼

Fire is an important component of many eastern forest ecosystems, particularly southern pine, pitch pine, red and jack pine, and oak-hickory. These ecosystems depend on fire to maintain their ecological dominance on sites and to eliminate competing forest species. With the advent of fire suppression and other associated human activities (e.g., logging), many of these ecosystems—such as the longleaf pine/wire-grass community of the South—are now endangered. Restoration of fire—a Native Son of the East—to these forests is crucial if we are going to maintain some semblance of ecosystem health across the landscape.

Part Four

(UN)HEALTHY
FOREST POLICY

SUPPRESSION, SALVAGE, AND SCURRILOUS SOLUTIONS

INTRODUCTION

Vested Interests as Purveyors of Forest Health

The old quip "follow the money" applies to fire policy as much as to anything else. Not surprisingly, exploitative industries like timber and livestock try to define fire issues in such a way that their interests—logging or grazing—become the "solution" to problems they have largely helped to define. Arguing that they can "regenerate" forests after a burn, timber interests lobby for widespread salvage logging, while the livestock industry fosters a perspective that grazing can reduce or prevent wildfires. In many cases there is no problem that needs fixing, and even if in some places there is a problem, the proposed cure may be worse than the disease. All commercial exploitation solutions have many unintended ecological consequences—consequences that may not immediately be apparent, and that certainly are not readily revealed by these industries, which are intent on duping the public into accepting more commercial exploitation of our forests and rangelands.

Ironically, many of these industries have had a major role in degrading the ecological health of our public lands to start with. We have, in a sense, a national "unhealthy" public lands policy that includes fire suppression, logging, livestock grazing, and disease and insect control. By trying to control or eliminate natural processes such as fire, windstorms, insect infestation, disease, or drought, we ultimately create conditions that lead to greater susceptibility to these very same elements. Nature acts to balance resource supply with demand by removing and naturally thinning dense stands of trees and shrubs.

During the recent extensive severe drought in the Southwest, for instance, huge swaths of juniper and ponderosa pine died as a result of water stress and insect attack. In northern Idaho and western Montana, fire suppression, which resulted in dense stands of Douglas-fir, enabled mistletoe, a parasitic plant, to colonize and kill mature trees. From an ecological perspective, these diseases and infestations are part of nature's way of restoring healthy forest ecosystems and are not a forest health problem, as often portrayed by some federal and state agencies as well as timber and grazing industry proponents. Whether thinned by fire, disease, or insects, the resulting forest is healthier as a consequence.

A fundamental assumption held by many resource industry representatives is that all fires are harmful, and that all big fires are especially harmful. In the first essay in this section, I question this assumption and in particular argue that even large blazes are not always "catastrophic," as often portrayed, but rather fill an important and natural role in fire regimes throughout the West. Depending on the circumstances and location, large blazes may be completely within the natural range of variability for a site.

I also consider a second flawed assumption—the notion that cutting trees is a benign means of reducing fuels. Timber industry proponents promote logging forests to reduce stand density, fuel buildup, and insect and disease occurrence—suggesting that logging is a viable alternative to fire. There are, however, significant ecological differences between fire and logging, as well as unintended costs that can cause significant long-term ecological harm, such as the introduction of weeds or tree pathogens into sites by logging operations. To adopt a program of widespread forest thinning across the landscape is fraught with unknown and unintended consequences.

As dubious as widespread logging across the landscape in the name of forest health is, salvage logging—the cutting of burnt trees after a blaze, in the name of forest regeneration and health—is a totally bankrupt concept. Conservation biologist James Strittholt explains why large-scale salvage logging, such as that proposed for the Biscuit Fire recovery project in Oregon, has serious ecological consequences that are frequently brushed aside in the haste to get the trees out of the woods.

Forest ecologist Chris Maser describes in detail the intertwined relationships of the forest ecosystem, showing why dead and dying trees are essential for the recovery of the forest and the long-term ecological stability of the entire ecosystem.

Finally, I examine how livestock grazing has altered fire regimes throughout the West and why the use of livestock grazing for fire suppression is a questionable "solution" to ill-perceived problems.

Before any national or even local plan for "forest health" is adopted, it would be wise to see if the proposal will really lead to "healthy" forests or just to healthy bank accounts for extractive industries. In far too many instances, the second consequence is the usual outcome.

LOGGING AND WILDFIRE

Ecological Differences and the Need to Preserve Large Fires

GEORGE WUERTHNER

THOUGH MANY MAY PERCEIVE THERE TO BE NO *difference between a tree killed by a fire or a tree killed by a chain saw as part of a logging operation, there are vast ecological differences. Furthermore, logging based on the presumption that reduction in fuels will reduce or eliminate large blazes is based on flawed premises. We need big fires.*

▼

Across many landscapes, intensive timber cutting has replaced fire in ecological significance, but not in ecological effect. Because of some commonalities between effects of logging and fire, many people assume that logging emulates natural disturbances like wildfire. There are, however, substantial ecological differences between logging and wildfire.

A second assumption, inherent in many assertions made by timber industry proponents, is that logging can reduce large blazes. As a corollary to this assumption, most proponents of fire control believe suppression of large blazes is desirable. Such assertions are self-serving and play on ecological ignorance and nuances in the ecological literature to create what appears on first review to be a plausible argument in favor of logging—an argument, however, that ignores many ecological realities.

Wildfire, whether from natural sources like lightning or a result of human ignition, has been a major influence on many ecosystems around the world.[1] One mapping of presettlement fire patterns found that more than half of the United States burned on a fire return interval of between 1 and 12 years.[2] In the native plant communities of the western United States, fires have probably played a more critical role in shaping ecosystems than any other disturbance factor. However, as a result of human activities—including logging, road building, fire suppression, and livestock grazing—the ecological influence of fires has been significantly altered from historic regimes.

How a tree dies and is ultimately utilized is critically important to the long-term health of a forest. A tree removed by logging has a different effect on soils, watersheds, wildlife habitat, and, ultimately, biodiversity than one killed by fire and left on-site. The manner of a tree's death affects the structural makeup of the forest, which in turn affects the biological and chemical regimes of the ecosystem. Fire affects both forest structure and ecosystem processes. Tree density per acre, average tree age, species composition of the forest, and related factors can be considered the fire-influenced structural components of a forest. Ecosystem processes have more to do with ecosystem energy flow and maintenance of diversity. Process affects variables such as nutrient cycling, randomness and patchiness of fire events, and the multiple ways in which a fire can burn—whether as intense stand-replacement conflagrations or as light, "cool" ground-creeping burns.

Superficially, logging and wildfire have some gross similarities. Seeds of many western tree species germinate best on bare mineral soil, an outcome of both logging and wildfire. Both remove the trees, exposing the soil to sunshine and allowing sun-tolerant species like Douglas-fir and lodgepole pine to reestablish themselves. Cosmetically, clearcutting shares some similarities with stand-replacement fire, and selective logging may appear comparable to low-intensity burns that kill only an occasional tree. However, exposed soil is just one aspect of the ecological needs of fire-adapted tree species.

Although much more research is needed comparing the impacts of fire and logging on forest ecosystems, a comprehensive overview by Canadian Forest Service fire researcher Douglas McRae and other studies that have looked at various parts of this issue suggest substantial ecological differences between their effects.[3]

Fire differs from logging in many ways. For one, fires vary in intensity and thus create many small, and occasionally very large, burn patches in a mosaic pattern that shifts across time as the vegetation experiences regrowth and reburns.[4] For instance, in Yellowstone National Park, 83 percent of all natural fires are less than 1.2 acres in size, and 94 percent of all natural fires burn less than 100 acres, but the occasional large blazes—such as those in 1988—burn hundreds of thousands of acres.[5] For this reason, fires tend to have a landscape-scale diversifying influence. Logging tends to create more evenly spaced, more evenly sized habitat patches, particularly on sites dominated by commercial forest species.

Fire alters an ecosystem by chemical processes; logging, by the mechanical process of tree removal. Fire rapidly cycles nutrients, kills pathogens, and selectively favors fire-adapted species. Logging leads to the loss of soil nutrients and organic matter[6] and increases soil compaction,[7] thereby reducing water infiltration.[8] Fires that are allowed to burn naturally do not create large road networks. Logging, on the other hand, creates roads that fragment habitat and generally increase human access, both of which affect the use of the land by wildlife. Moreover, roads and logging equipment can become vectors for the dispersal of noxious weeds.[9] It is widely recognized in the scientific community that past commercial logging, road building, livestock grazing, and aggressive firefighting are the sources of many "forest health" problems, including unnaturally severe wildfires.[10]

According to the final report of Sierra Nevada Ecosystem Project, an assessment of the entire Sierra Nevada ecoregion requested by Congress and funded by Congress and the U.S. Forest Service, "Timber harvest, through its effects on forest structure, local microclimate, and fuels accumulation, has increased fire severity more than any other recent human activity."[11]

IMPACTS ASSOCIATED WITH LOGGING

Logging is more than the removal of trees. It typically involves an extensive road network, which has a significant and diverse array of impacts on the land.[12] Since most areas are not logged all at one time and are repeatedly cut over a century, logging has many additional effects, including periodic human invasion and disturbance from human activities. Soil erosion from logging roads is a major impact, particularly on aquatic ecosystems. Logging also significantly increases debris slides.[13] One northern California study, for example, found that 61 percent of the soil displacement (erosion) on the study site resulted from logging roads.[14]

Structural changes in the forest are obvious effects of logging, particularly with clearcutting.[15] Timber harvest tends to leave few or no snags (standing dead trees). Even when it does, the usual prescription is only one or two snags per acre—considerably fewer than needed for cavity-nesting animals. In addition, snags as they rot provide the forest with a long-term nutrient supply; their removal thus short-circuits nutrient cycling on the site. Even selective cutting can radically alter forest stand dynamics, since most commercial logging selects for larger-diameter trees—the very individuals that under a natural fire regime are most likely to survive a blaze and persist on the site.

Commercial logging tends to remove the larger trees—exactly the ones most resistant to fire. By contrast, fires tend to kill the smaller trees, reducing competition for water and light among the remaining trees. In addition, the process of logging takes away the least flammable portion of trees—their main stems—and leaves behind the most flammable parts, the limbs and needles. Partially and totally buried wood debris—especially the tree stems (the boles)—can make up as much as 50 percent of all surface organic matter in old-growth forests and may remain for centuries.[16] Logging eliminates this potential.

The activities associated with logging—including the building of roads that fragment habitat, and the coming and going of workers and vehicles—can displace wildlife sensitive to human presence and reduce the effectiveness of remaining habitat patches.[17] This disturbance may be semipermanent, since logging roads often remain open for subsequent timber harvest or public access. Human activity along roads has been shown to reduce habitat use by elk for up to half a mile on either side,[18] and a study by the Montana Department of Fish, Wildlife and Parks found that grizzly bears avoid roaded areas, often for years after timber activities have ceased.[19] A severe loss of suitable habitat may occur even if the amount of land that is directly disturbed is quite small. Increased access for human trappers and hunters also changes or reduces population structure in species sought, and poaching may increase. Road closures can mitigate some, but usually not all, of these impacts. Research has demonstrated that having no road to start with is better than a closed road.

The physical impact of logging on site topography and soil profile is another difference between timber harvest and fires. Heavy logging equipment compacts soils.[20] Forest Service studies have demonstrated that compaction inhibits forest regeneration and slows growth of tree seedlings that do manage to emerge.[21] Fires, on the other hand, often provide ideal seedbeds for the reestablishment of plant cover.

Weed invasion is another problem often associated with timber harvest, particularly because roads serve as vectors for weed dispersal.[22] Seeds of spotted knapweed and many other invasive exotic species are carried on the chassis of logging trucks to new locations. If logging roads are left open for public access after a logging operation, other vehicles may also disperse weed seed. And the disturbed soils along bulldozed roads provide ideal habitat for the proliferation of weed species.

Wildfire mosaics maintain natural curves and lines, while logging introduces abrupt edges and scars from logging roads and skid trails that take decades to heal. Edge effects are generally more severe with logging than with fire.

The timing of stand-destroying fires differs substantially from the timing of stand-destroying clearcuts. In many managed forests, the goal is to eliminate older trees to favor faster-growing younger ones. The loss of old-growth structural features in a managed forest has many ecological ramifications, including changes in nutrient flows and storage, and in wildlife habitat parameters. Though fires do occasionally burn up substantial acreages of old growth, in many ecosystems the old-growth stands are relatively fireproof except under extreme conditions, such as severe drought. Since standard forestry management practice is to cut trees at or shortly after they reach peak wood production efficiency, most managed timber stands will never possess old-growth features.

Some of the above negative features associated with logging can perhaps be mitigated or reduced by changing timber harvest methods, but one factor that almost certainly cannot be emulated by foresters is the randomness of fire disturbance. Though fire ecologists make predictions about fire frequency and "average" size, wildfires are essentially unpredictable. Logging does not emulate this randomness, and we do know how important it may be to ecosystem integrity and function.[23]

Finally, fire performs many of the above ecological services at no economic cost—unless, of course, it threatens human life or habitation. Foresters claim that timber harvest can achieve the same ends, but frequently it costs far more to taxpayers per treated acre than can be recouped from timber sales.[24] In contrast, a prescribed natural burn policy, particularly if there are no fire suppression costs, is very cost-effective—no more than pennies per acre burned in monitoring costs.

FIRE ECOLOGY PRINCIPLES

Most western forest ecosystems evolved under regimes of periodic forest fires.[25] It's important to note that healthy forests do burn. This is partly a result of the summer drought conditions that characterize many portions of the West. Even the Pacific Northwest, where precipitation is an almost daily occurrence in winter, tends to have dry, nearly rainless summers that favor the spread of wildfires. Indeed, the old-growth Douglas-fir temperate "rainforests" get their start during fires that develop after the region experiences prolonged and severe drought years. For instance, major fires occurred in the Olympic Mountains of Washington in 1309, 1442, 1497, and 1668—all linked to global climatic conditions. Such stand-replacement fires may occur only a couple of times a millennium, but that is frequent enough to maintain the dominance of the long-lived Douglas-fir on a site.[26]

In much of the West, temperatures tend to be warmest when conditions are driest. These factors are unfavorable for biological decomposition by bacteria, fungi, and other decomposers. As a result, decomposition is often extremely slow. Nutrients are "locked up," and unavailable for further growth. Litter that falls to the forest floor gradually builds up. In the West, fire, more than any other factor, is responsible for recycling the nutrients in this dead plant material. Deprived of periodic fires, most western ecosystems gradually decline in productivity for lack of available soil nutrients. In contrast, under natural conditions, net nutrient levels often increase after a fire.[27]

The periodicity between fires varies from ecosystem to ecosystem. For instance, in dry, low-elevation ponderosa pine forests of the Southwest, before the era of fire suppression, fires once burned every 3 to 20 years.[28] Sometimes the higher frequency was a consequence of human ignitions. Native Americans often purposely set fires to reduce brush encroachment and to favor grasses and other forage that attracted large herbivores like elk and deer.[29] The fire regimes in these forests were altered significantly by fire suppression and livestock grazing. However, not all ponderosa pine forests were altered to the same degree.[30] And some researchers caution about the broad application of fire scar research as the primary method of understanding past fire regimes.[31]

On the other hand, in high, cold, snowy places like the Yellowstone Plateau, human ignitions and subsequent attempts at fire suppression may not have had any significant effect, in part because the normally deep snowpack ensures that wet conditions persist well into summer. Conditions favorable to burns are restricted here to a tiny window of opportunity that typically occurs in late summer. In many summers, the window does not open at all.[32]

Litter accumulates much more slowly at these higher elevations because of the limited growth of all plants imposed by the severe climatic conditions. As a result, the normal fire interval in Yellowstone's higher elevations is on the order of 200 to 400 years or longer.[33] Similarly long intervals are characteristic of some more arid landscapes, such as pinyon-juniper.[34] High-elevation subalpine forests throughout the West, as well as the wetter forest belts of the Pacific Northwest coast also experience long intervals between burns.[35] Fires in this higher-elevation forest tend to be episodic, stand-replacement fires, which often burn hundreds of thousands of acres. Because of the long time intervals between major burns in these ecosystems, fire suppression may not yet have substantially influenced normal fire frequency or fuel loading.

There can even be substantial differences in fire frequency within the same range. For instance, historically, the lower to mid elevations of the Sierra Nevada burned on a frequent basis, often every 10 or 20 years, thus maintaining open, parklike forest stands. On the other hand, the higher, subalpine forests of the Sierra Nevada experienced infrequent fires because of the extensive amounts of bare rock, which acted as a fuel break, along with the wet conditions that typically extended well into summer.[36]

The vast majority of acreage burned in any one year, and in any region over time, occurs in a few very large fires. For instance, in Yellowstone National Park, about 83 percent of naturally ignited fires never reach more than 1.2 acres in size, and some 94 percent of fires never burn more than 100 acres. If you add up the total acres burned by all the small blazes, they affect only a fraction of the land burned in one large fire.[37]

Long before fire suppression had any influence on fuel loading, there were huge forest fires in the West. In 1910, for example, more than 3 million acres burned in northern Idaho and western Montana, including many low-elevation areas characterized by frequent low-intensity fires.[38]

The conditions for a major burn often have more to do with drought, wind, and ignition sources than with fuels.[39] Indeed, young regrowing conifer forests that characterize recently reforested clearcuts, or even regrowth after a burn, may be the most flammable fuels under conditions of extreme drought, since green trees, with their flammable resins, burn hotter than dead trees. Also, since young trees have poorly developed root systems, and because the sites where they predominate tend to be hotter and more droughty because of the lack of canopy shade, young trees are among the first to experience drought stress and are extremely flammable. Thus activities like "salvage" logging may actually increase the likelihood of major fires, rather than reduce it, by increasing the amount of young forest regrowth.

WHY LARGE FIRES ARE NECESSARY

There is an inherent assumption by many people, including those who support wildfires in general, that large blazes are somehow abnormal or destructive. Yet it is large fires, not the ordinary small blazes, that set the ecological parameters of western ecosystems. Large blazes are usually weather driven—favored by drought and wind. Furthermore, since fuels are not the driving force behind large blazes, small prescribed burns, and even "salvage" logging and/or mechanical thinning to reduce fuel loading, generally do not have an effect on large fires, nor would this be desirable. In most ecosystems, we should be encouraging, not discouraging, large fires. Current forestry policies of fire suppression, road building to facilitate suppression, fuel reduction, and so on, all contribute to the fragmentation of fire habitat, distorting natural fire regimes. Big fires are as ecologically important to functioning and healthy ecosystems as large predators are to wildlife populations.

Just as large predators are "top-down" regulators of other species, fire serves a similar function for ecosystems.

This is why we need large, protected nature sanctuaries such as large national parks, wilderness areas, and other preserves. *Large natural areas are necessary so that big blazes can "roam" freely across the landscape, just as preserving habitat for wide-ranging species like grizzlies and wolves is important to sustaining natural biodiversity.*

ECOSYSTEM FUNCTIONS PERFORMED BY FIRES

Most fires perform a variety of ecosystem services that are not normally associated with logging. For example, fires cleanse a forest. Heat from fires can kill forest pathogens in the soil, including root rots, as well as pathogenic insects and fungi that may be found in fallen trees or snags.[40]

Heating and subsequent rapid cooling of rocks and boulders cracks and breaks them apart. Repeated numerous times over the centuries, this is an important soil-building process. Logging, of course, provides no such benefits.

The influence of fires often extends beyond the blaze perimeter. Laboratory studies have demonstrated that smoke from fires will kill certain arboreal forest pathogens, reducing, for a time, the influence of some tree diseases. Smoke also aids the germination of some plant species.[41]

Fires also change nutrient flows. Dead litter burns and turns to ash. The heat and combustion change the chemical composition of soils. Depending on how hot they burn,[42] fires can volatilize certain nutrients, like nitrogen, that are lost as gases into the atmosphere. However, the nitrogen pool available to plants is large relative to most fire-induced losses, and nitrogen is quickly replaced in the soil through nitrogen-fixing bacteria, which usually increase significantly after a burn in most western U.S. ecosystems.[43] Studies have shown that bacteria and other nitrogen fixers typically make up all the nitrogen losses to volatilization within two years of a burn. Other important plant nutrients, including phosphorus and calcium, are released from litter by fires and leached into the top layers of the soil. Despite some losses to waterways and the atmosphere, the overall effect of all but the most intense fires is the redistribution of nutrients from the forest canopy and floor into the soil, thus increasing soil fertility. For instance, one study in a southwestern ponderosa pine forest found that ammonium nitrogen levels were 80 times greater after a recent burn than before.[44] In some forests, more than a third of the nitrogen-fixing capacity is provided by microorganisms responsible for decaying wood on the soil surface and in the soil itself, again emphasizing the importance of retaining wood debris even after a fire.[45]

Nutrients may also wind up in waterways by directly washing into a stream or lake, or by settling as ash from the air. Periodic nutrient enrichment from fires may be necessary for the maintenance of aquatic ecosystems, particularly those at higher elevations, which tend to be low in nutrient inputs.[46]

By contrast, timber harvest removes nutrients from the ecosystem, since trees are transported out of the area. The severity of this removal depends on logging practices. In conifers, most nutrients are stored in the branches and needles; thus, the more slash left on-site, the less actual nutrient removal. Nevertheless, to replace the nutrients lost, even when only the boles are extracted, takes longer than the timber rotation period (the time between logging episodes) on many sites. As a result, over time, repeated timber harvest may gradually deplete a site of important nutrients.

By removing forest canopies and increasing sunlight, logging may stimulate the growth of nitrogen-fixing plants, but usually not enough to match the quantities that grow after a fire. Furthermore, foresters usually attempt to truncate such early successional stages in order to hasten the restocking of forests with commercial species. For instance, in the Pacific Northwest, where red alder is an important nitrogen-fixing species that colonizes burned or logged areas, it is standard practice to treat such sites with herbicides to kill off the hardwoods like alder so that commercially preferred conifers can quickly regenerate.

In many forests, another important source of nitrogen input is arboreal lichens. Nitrogen-fixing lichen species are common on the branches and bark of older, larger trees. Rainwater percolating through these lichen-covered branches leaches and transports nitrogen to the soil.[47] Since the rotational age of trees in managed forests (the age at which the trees are large enough to cut profitably) is usually far shorter than the age at which they might otherwise burn, the amount of old growth in managed forests is usually substantially less than in wild, natural forests, reducing the potential input of nitrogen from lichens. How important such contributions may be to forest productivity and health is unknown.

Logging may provide a temporary flush of nutrients, but this is often accompanied by a flush of sediment as well. True, fire-bared slopes will at times wash high sediment loads into river systems, particularly if heavy rains occur immediately after a burn. However, on most sites, within a year or two of a fire, vegetation covers the ground, since fires typically do not kill underground tubers or seeds that may be lodged in the soil. However, logging roads are seldom removed or decommissioned, and thus they are a long-term and unending source of sedimentation. Also, the snags that are left on a burn site often fall across the slope, creating "check dams"—barriers that slow erosion and reduce sediment yield to streams. Again logging, particularly "salvage" logging, removes such snags, hence increasing sedimentation and its many negative effects.

In addition, the soil disturbance caused by logging and heavy equipment strips away soil and the buried seeds and roots that might otherwise sprout and quickly cover a slope. Logging roads are notorious for generating high sediment loads, even higher than typically found on the logged or burned slopes themselves.

Of course, the amount of sedimentation, whether because of fire or because of logging, is largely determined by soil type, gradient, seasonality of runoff, and timing between periodic natural floods. Logging nearly always increases sedimentation over natural levels associated with most, but not all, burns. High sedimentation kills aquatic insects and fish, and changes stream channel patterns.

Fires may temporarily reduce the amount of organic matter in aquatic ecosystems, to the detriment of aquatic invertebrates, particularly in smaller streams. However, within a few years, the flush of new vegetation begins to compensate for these losses.[48]

Unless the blaze is extremely hot, fires do not totally consume a forest. Typically, hundreds of standing fire-killed trees (snags) per acre remain. These snags serve a number of important ecological functions. Woodpeckers carve cavities that provide an abundance of homes for many birds and mammal species, including bluebirds, nuthatches, and flying squirrels.[49] Snags offer perching sites for flycatchers, swallows, and raptors.

Furthermore, many of these snags are invaded by wood-eating beetles and other insects. These in turn provide an abundant food source for woodpeckers and other insect feeders. Some species, like the black-backed woodpecker, show tremendous increases for three or four years after a fire, then decline. The woodpecker is one of several species that may depend on fire-shaped landscapes to maintain adequate population levels. Populations of black-backed woodpeckers do not increase on logged sites since few standing dead trees are left after harvest.

Dead trees continue to play important ecological roles, even after they fall over. On the ground they provide habitat and hiding cover for a mostly different group of invertebrates, as well as rabbits, voles, shrews, and other small mammals.[50] These animals in turn provide a food source for predators like pine marten and lynx. In addition, as these fallen snags molder and rot, they gradually add organic matter to the soil, which increases its fertility and water-holding capacity.

Trees that fall into waterways are important to aquatic ecosystems. Fallen logs create pools and riffles, which provide habitat for aquatic invertebrates and fish. Logs also help to stabilize stream banks, deflecting or reducing the erosive force of water. Furthermore, since submerged logs rot slowly, they are important long-term sources of nutrients for aquatic ecosystems.[51]

Finally, though naturally a live forest provides more cover than the snags left after a blaze, dead tree boles still provide some thermal and hiding cover—much more than found in a clearcut. A burned area thus has far more value as security cover to big game and other hunted species than a logged area. Since snags typically remain for 50 to 100 years after a blaze, they commonly survive until the new forest has a chance to mature sufficiently to provide new hiding and thermal cover.

▼

In sum, wildfire is an important ecological *process* not emulated by logging practices. Some kinds of timber harvest, such as selective cutting of young, small-diameter trees, may superficially mimic the structural influence of fire—creating, for example, open stands of large-diameter trees—but they fail to emulate the ecosystem processes associated with fires. Forest structure is just an outward manifestation of ecosystem processes. If we must husband anything, it should be ecosystem processes, not preconceived notions of "proper" structural appearance.

Maintaining fire as an ecosystem process is still an option. Acknowledging that many people have inappropriately built towns and homes in what is the fire equivalent of a floodplain does not necessarily lead to the conclusion that we have no choice but to suppress wildfires. Indeed, a wise course of action is to make a few areas defensible against wildfire by frequent prescribed burning and limited, selective timber harvest. These management activities should be concentrated along existing roads, around towns, and around other structures deemed worthy of protection. In the rest of forested areas, wildfires should be permitted to burn unsuppressed. Our goal should be ecosystem maintenance, not ecosystem management.

Large wildfires have many of the same characteristics as large carnivores. They range widely, occur in relatively small numbers, are often in conflict with human exploitation schemes, and thus can only exist in large wildlands. They contribute to the ecological processes that maintain ecosystems. A western wilderness without large, episodic wildfires is as ecologically bankrupt as one without grizzlies and wolves. Without them all, our wildlands are no longer truly wild, no longer ecologically intact.

AFTER THE SMOKE CLEARS

Ecological Impacts of Salvage Logging

JAMES R. STRITTHOLT, PH.D.

SALVAGE LOGGING HAS GENERATED MUCH CONTROVERSY *over its effectiveness to achieve desired outcomes and its ecological impacts. Before carrying out salvage and other postfire management operations, we must carefully consider the ecology of fire-prone forests. As long as wildfire is viewed as a force that destroys timber, we will fail to recognize the vital role fire has always played in forming and maintaining native forests and the many ecosystem services they provide.*

▼

After a wildfire is extinguished or burns itself out on public lands, land managers are faced with the aftermath. Postfire management may include a broad array of actions, such as repair to existing roads and road structures, erosion control, and repair or reconstruction of buildings. Site restoration may include control of invasive species, seeding of erosion-prone areas, and planting of disease-resistant seedlings. All of these actions have ecological consequences, but by far the most contentious postfire management activity is the removal of dead or damaged trees—salvage logging.

SALVAGE LOGGING

In general, salvage logging is the harvest of dead or dying trees damaged by fire, wind, flood, insects, or disease; however, salvage logging has never been specifically defined in legal terms.[1] Operating definitions of salvage logging as stated in the National Forest Management Act of 1976 (NFMA) and the Emergency Supplemental Appropriations and Rescissions Act of 1995 allow for the removal of dead, dying, and sometimes associated live trees after fire. In this essay, the emphasis is on dead and dying trees, with the recognition that removal of associated live trees sometimes takes place. Regardless, not all trees impacted by fire are salvageable. Some trees deteriorate rapidly and have no economic value. Some locations are inaccessible because of legal restrictions (e.g., congressionally withdrawn lands such as wilderness areas) or because of prohibitive costs (e.g., new road construction costs or extensive environmental damage control measures).[2] Thus, owing to administrative and operational constraints, only a portion of dead and dying trees can be salvaged.

In most ways, salvage sales do not differ much from other timber sales except that they can be expedited (sometimes bypassing proper administrative and judicial review) because burned timber quickly loses its economic value as it remains in place.[3] However, because of the lack of careful planning and review, and the potential of exposing large areas to rapid mechanical manipulation, salvage logging may have greater environmental impacts than routine timber sales.

Just as wildfires are often improperly referred to as "natural catastrophes" or "ecological disasters," salvage logging is often incorrectly presented as a management imperative to "restore the fire-damaged landscape." Although this misperception is widespread,[4] there is no scientific evidence supporting the position that salvage logging benefits forest ecosystem health or promotes late-successional forest characteristics. In the most extensive review of postfire salvage logging effects to date, a U.S. Forest Service technical report found only 21 scientific papers worldwide that pertain to this topic experimentally.[5] Of these, the salvage logging studies that examined the direct effects from logging operations primarily emphasized the potential negative effects, such as soil disturbance, erosion, sediment yield to streams, and changes in water yield. The few studies on indirect effects (effects due to removal of merchantable timber) focused almost exclusively on the impacts on bird species assemblages. The Forest Service review concludes that "postfire logging is certain to have a wide variety of effects, from subtle to significant, depending on where the site lies in relation to other postfire sites of various ages, site characteristics, logging methods, and intensity of fire." Nowhere in this review—or anywhere in the scientific literature— is salvage logging reported as ecologically beneficial to native forests.

While the number of experimental studies on the effects of salvage logging is quite limited, an abundant scientific literature reports negative impacts from salvage logging and associated management activities on a wide range of biological elements and ecological processes. These studies describe significant ecological degradation to both the terrestrial and aquatic components of natural forests as the result of postfire management as it is currently conducted.[6] The overwhelming body of scientific evidence thus supports a very cautious approach to any postfire management—especially salvage logging—and clearly refutes claims that intensive postfire management is necessary to restore health and vitality to our forestlands.

That is not to say there would never be cause for postfire management based on ecological grounds. There are instances in which "active restoration" is warranted, such as replacing faulty drainage structures and planting native species depleted by fire.[7] The main objectives of any postfire management should be to repair environmental damage caused by fighting the fire and to avoid additional environmental damage; to repair damage to existing human infrastructure, such as roads, that could continue to degrade natural systems if left unrepaired; and to enhance the revegetation of native species.[8] Repairing the environmental damage caused by firefighting alone can be a major and expensive effort. The final cost of fighting the large Biscuit Fire that burned in southern Oregon and northern California during the summer and fall of 2002 was $153 million and included the construction of many miles of fire lines and extensive high-intensity backburning.[9] The ecological damage caused by trying to contain and extinguish this large fire warrants active management attention.

It is clear that scientists need to learn much more about how to carry out postfire management in a way that enhances overall ecological integrity while at the same time allowing for some economic gain where that is possible. Economic gains in postfire salvage logging are possible in some circumstances, but dead and dying trees should not be thought of as black diamonds sprinkled across the landscape just waiting to be collected.[10] As economic studies have shown, there are costs associated with any kind of logging (including salvage), and these costs are frequently greater than the perceived economic gain.[11] It is the United States taxpayer who ultimately pays for economic shortfalls from both green and salvage timber sales, placing into question the rationale for salvage timber sales in the first place.

The greatest cost, however—rarely mentioned by salvage logging proponents—is the cost to the ecological integrity of native forest ecosystems, for salvage logging and its associated activities compromise or degrade fundamentally important ecosystem services, such as the production of clean water, maintenance of healthy soils, and propagation of native biodiversity. Unfortunately, it is difficult to quantify these costs, and they are therefore summarily dismissed as unimportant or, at best, as far less important than the timber values, whether the timber values in a given situation are real or imagined. Any attempt made to defend salvage logging and other postfire management actions (i.e., herbicide treatment and nonnative tree planting) on ecological grounds is unfounded scientifically. One can only conclude that the motivation for such a position is the belief that timber values supersede all other considerations, forming an ideology that leaves little room for broader understanding.

WASTE OR WEALTH?

When most people see a burned forest, they see a great waste and feel a great loss. Their views on wildfire are influenced by television news, with its images of charred trees, barren soil, and burned animal remains. A reporter describes the carnage in a somber voice, leaving doubt in the mind of the viewer that the once-beautiful forest will ever recover. The land management agencies begin formulating a postfire management plan, while logging interests advocate for extensive and immediate salvage—making the best of a terrible tragedy. The news reports and timber interest assertions work hand in hand, perhaps unwittingly, to paint a distorted picture of a type of event that has been taking place for millennia, creating and shaping the very forest we are now told is potentially lost forever and in need of immediate restoration (including salvage logging).

Not surprisingly, the majority of people see fire as bad, and dead and dying trees as having little or no value. By this view, civil society should do its best to clean up nature's mess, and if there is some economic gain as a bonus, so be it. After all, wouldn't you rather see logging of fire-killed trees than of live ones?

Let's face it: live trees appeal to our sense of health far more than charred stems. But to a forest, trees actually have two ecological lives—one when they are alive and another when they are dead. To forest ecologists these dead trees are known as "biological legacies," and they are disproportionately important in maintaining the biodiversity of a natural forest. Biological legacies are organisms, organically derived structures, and organically produced patterns that persist after a major disturbance event.[12] They include standing dead trees (snags), downed logs, intact thickets, and large living trees, and they have been described as keystone habitat elements benefiting many organisms.[13] Biological legacies have a wide range of functions, including:

- Surviving, persisting, and regenerating, becoming incorporated into the recovering stand
- Assisting other species to survive changes to the physical and biological community (lifeboating)—for example, by providing temporary nesting and feeding habitat
- Providing refugia for species that can then recolonize nearby recovering disturbed sites
- Influencing patterns of recolonization in the neighboring disturbed area
- Providing a source of energy and nutrients for other organisms
- Modifying and stabilizing environmental conditions in the recovering stand[14]

Snags and downed logs often persist after fire and serve important ecological functions. Snags provide nesting and denning habitat for many species of birds and mammals.[15] Downed logs return much-needed organic matter to the soil; help to stabilize soil loss from erosion; and aid in the establishment of early successional species (including herbaceous plants and fungi) that condition soil for the natural reestablishment of conifers. In short, the retention of biological legacies is imperative in maintaining productive soils and healthy forests.[16]

POSTFIRE SALVAGE AND FIRE FUELS

One of the most common assertions made by salvage logging proponents is that the removal of the dead and dying trees after fire is "necessary" to reduce fuel loads for the next fire. The fear being promulgated is that by leaving the dead and dying trees on the landscape, we are setting up conditions for another catastrophic fire over the short term, thus risking loss of human life and property. On the surface, this logic may sound reasonable, but closer consideration leads to a very different conclusion. The only known scientific literature on the topic of salvage and fuels reduction concludes there is no scientific evidence that salvage logging decreases the intensity of future fires on burned sites.[17] Claims that removal of dead and dying trees are the main opportunity to reduce risk of recurring fires are unsubstantiated. Fire intensity and behavior—both of which have been empirically studied[18] and modeled[19]—are driven by three main factors: weather, terrain, and fuels, with weather playing the most important role. Under most terrain and fuels situations, if it is hot, dry, and windy enough, wildfires will burn with great intensity. Fuels that are consumed in a fire and contribute most to the burn severity are primarily the fine fuels. The contribution from large trees (greater than 15 inches in diameter at breast height) is almost negligible,[20] since they burn only when finer fuels are sufficient to ignite and sustain the flames. Large wood also burns mainly by smoldering combustion, which does not figure prominently into fire intensity calculations.[21]

After fire, the remaining dead trees begin to decay. Standing trees eventually fall, with smaller-diameter trees falling sooner than larger ones. Regardless of their size, by the time most standing trees fall, they have already lost their fine-fuel component, made up of needles, twigs, and small limbs.[22] Larger trees can remain standing for as much as 30 to 80 years, depending on the species, and are not likely to burn intensely in future events. However, these larger trees are highly prized for salvage logging. If reducing future fire intensity and severity is the desired management outcome for a region, fire management needs to concentrate on reducing fine fuels rather than on the removal of large wood through salvage logging. Removing the most important fire-resistant structures in these forests[23] would actually have the reverse effect. Salvage logging has not been shown to reduce the incidence or severity of wildfires, but it has been shown to do the opposite. For example, the treetops and branches left on the ground after logging (slash) can lead to increased fire severity.[24] Combustible fine fuels were reported to increase between 3 to 13 tons per hectare in Oregon following salvage logging without slash treatment.[25] Heavy logging slash is particularly problematic for potential future fires since it has been shown to generate the highest fire line intensity of any wildland fuel type when the weather is dry and windy.[26] The usual treatment of excessive salvage slash (burning) is not without its own ecological costs. For example, one study reported significant changes in future plant succession as the result of broadcast or slash burning.[27]

POSTFIRE NATURAL SUCCESSION VERSUS TREE PLANTATIONS

Proponents of aggressive salvage logging argue that follow-up silvicultural treatments of herbicide application and conifer planting are necessary to prevent future high-intensity fires and to reestablish conifer forests. Considerable scientific evidence runs counter to both arguments.

Widespread conifer planting after any disturbance results in even-aged stands of trees that are usually closely spaced. This array of same-age trees makes the stands prone to higher fire intensity and severity compared with natural forests because fuels are available in combustible form over a wide area.[28] Examination of the spatial pattern of the 1987 fires in Klamath National Forest showed that tree plantations had twice as much crown fire as closed natural forest.[29] In further support of this finding, analysis of patterns of severity after the 1994 Dillon Creek Fire in the Klamath National Forest found that plantations and adjacent vegetation burned more severely than unlogged forests.[30]

Natural conifer establishment requires favorable soil conditions, available nutrients, and a seed source. Seedlings depend on the natural heterogeneity of the forest landscape, which provides "safe sites" (sites relatively safe from high-intensity fire over the short term) where seedlings can survive future fires when they are young and vulnerable.[31] Plantations lack landscape heterogeneity and safe sites, and once a threshold proportion of even-aged plantations is established, there is potential for a self-reinforcing cycle of stand-replacing fire over a broader landscape area.[32]

Salvage logging proponents state that planting is required to recover forest in a timely fashion, in part because potential seed trees are so far removed from the burn areas where mortality was heavy. However, research on the aftermath of the Yellowstone fires of 1988 showed the majority of severely burned areas to be within 164 to 656 feet of unburned or lightly burned areas, suggesting that few severely burned sites were very distant from potential sources of propagules.[33] In the Yellowstone region, fires also played an unexpected role in the establishment of new aspen clones, a function that would never have been recognized had the area been quickly salvaged.[34]

For the Biscuit Fire in southern Oregon and northern California, a similar analysis yielded similar results.[35] Over 63 percent of the area burned at high severity was within 328 feet of a potential conifer seed source, and approximately 84 percent was within 656 feet. If two of the largest fires in the western United States over the past 20 years are any indication, claims for the need for widespread planting to recover conifer forests after fire are simply not consistent with the data.

SALVAGE AND FOREST SUCCESSION

Another assertion by salvage proponents is that salvage logging and subsequent silvicultural management can significantly reduce the establishment of native shrubs and hardwoods, which they consider a significant threat to the more highly prized conifer forests. However, natural forests have evolved recovery mechanisms after major disturbances, including the rapid resprout and regeneration of shrubs, hardwoods, and herbaceous plants. Natural recovery after fire requires the establishment of many different species that interact over space and time, shaping the forest landscape until the next fire event. These plants serve many important ecological functions. Rapid regrowth of these species stabilizes soils, preventing erosion; protects the soil from direct solar radiation; increases soil moisture; generates needed organic matter; and provides important habitat for many native species of vertebrates and invertebrates. Some shrub species, such as ceanothus spp., relying on seed survival after fire, fix nitrogen that helps restore soil productivity.[36] Other shrub species, like *Arctostaphylos*, facilitate the maintenance of soil mycorrhizae, which are fundamentally important for conifer growth.[37]

Initially after fire, shrubs and hardwoods are generally better competitors than regenerating conifers.[38] This is why foresters often advocate for human intervention with the use of herbicides and mass conifer seeding or planting, which can result in short-term gains in conifer growth, but often at considerable ecological and economic costs. In bypassing the natural early successional stage of a postfire environment, managers reduce species richness and risk sacrificing long-term soil quality. Research has shown that despite slower initial conifer growth when in competition with shrubs, over time higher conifer growth rates often result in these situations.[39] Controlling shrubs and hardwoods to speed up conifer regeneration is therefore not only ecologically unwise but also unnecessary for old-growth habitat restoration. It makes little sense to spend time and money to do something nature will do better than humans and at no cost. However, managers whose goal is to maximize merchantable timber as quickly as possible continue to engineer forests for this purpose, frequently ignoring valuable ecological principles.

Furthermore, the removal of downed logs and snags through salvage logging can actually increase the density of many early successional shrubs and hardwoods because the ground is exposed to more sunlight. By creating large patches of disturbed soil, salvage logging also encourages the establishment of invasive exotic species.[40] A study on the Winema National Forest showed salvage logging to reduce overall vegetation biomass, increase invasive exotics, increase graminoid cover, and reduce overall plant species richness relative to postfire unlogged sites.[41]

These effects are ecologically important, since natural postfire habitat and regenerative processes that occurred previously in evolutionary history are now becoming rare.[42] Moreover, some areas are far more difficult to work in and far more susceptible to damage than others. For example, in southwestern Oregon (location of the Biscuit Fire), forest practitioners understand that much of the region is extremely difficult to engineer silviculturally. In such environments, the widespread application of salvage logging, herbicide treatment, and planting is fraught with even greater ecological risk and substantial economic investment. Total failure to achieve the "desired outcome" is likely, and considerable damage is visited upon the native forests.

SALVAGE LOGGING AND WILDLIFE

Any natural disturbance event or management action (including salvage logging) favors some species at the expense of others. Populations of some species will increase dramatically, some will be suppressed for a time, and others will remain relatively unchanged.

Salvage logging often leads to changes in species composition.[43] Species that prefer even-aged conifer stands (a common habitat type throughout much of the western United States) will undoubtedly benefit, but species that capitalize on a postfire environment or are sensitive to further structural changes will be harmed. Downed logs and standing dead wood are important to a wide range of vertebrate and invertebrate species,[44] many of which are negatively impacted, some significantly, by the removal of these structures (or biological legacies). For example, species such as salamanders, which are sensitive to maintenance of moist microsites, are severely affected by the increased solar radiation and further drying of soils from the removal of standing dead and downed logs. Removal of snags negatively impacts forest predators like marten and fisher since the associated removal of the remaining vegetation structure reduces the numbers of their prey.

Four independent studies in the Intermountain West have shown that salvage logging also significantly reduces the abundance and nest density of cavity-nesting birds.[45] Most cavity-nesting bird species showed consistent patterns of decline after salvage logging, while only one species, Lewis's woodpecker (*Melanerpes lewis*), increased after logging. Most cavity-nesting birds are insectivorous, so the removal of nesting and foraging habitat through salvage logging reduces the natural regulation of postfire insect outbreaks by cavity-nesting birds.[46]

At the landscape level, wildfire creates a spatial heterogeneity that is attractive to many species.[47] To maintain healthy metapopulations of these organisms, it is important to manage postfire patches with great care.[48] Widespread salvage logging simplifies the landscape and biota in a way similar to green tree clearcutting.

SOIL EROSION

High-severity wildfire causes predictable changes in soil characteristics and vegetation structure that can lead to serious erosion problems.[49] In extreme cases, water infiltration of the soils can be slowed by fire-induced effects and decreased uptake and evapotranspiration of water because of the extensive vegetation kill.[50] Conventional ground-based salvage logging (including road construction and reconstruction), especially in stands having steep slopes or unstable soils, will likely exacerbate the erosional problems routinely observed in burn areas.[51] Logging slash can help decrease erosion by impeding overland flows,[52] but leaving slash has the undesirable side effect of increasing fine surface fuels. Soil productivity is irreplaceable in human timescales. Damage done by improper management can result in negative impacts that last centuries; postfire management actions must therefore proceed with great caution to avoid increasing erosion or damaging the soils.[53]

These effects are particularly important with regard to aquatic integrity since some aquatic organisms are sensitive to high sedimentation levels. All riparian areas are important, and those that sustain high burn severities should be protected as much as possible from any further damage. While ground-based salvage logging can take some effective actions to mitigate erosion under certain conditions, it is more likely that salvage logging will increase sedimentation.[54] As the authors of one review in the salvage logging literature conclude, "More importantly, we do not know how site-specific effects accumulate over watersheds, and this knowledge is essential if forest management is to be linked to aquatic integrity."[55]

▼

In summary, there is no scientific evidence that supports the notion that salvage logging is sound on ecological grounds, and any assertion that logging is "required" to restore forests after wildfire is absolutely false. Salvage logging may have economic value under some circumstances, but policymakers and land managers must be careful to weigh the ecological costs of any postfire management plan. Postfire landscapes are fragile but by no means dead. Ecologically responsible management of postfire landscapes should avoid any action that causes additional ecological stress or prevents the natural reestablishment of native species and ecosystem processes.[56] If some salvage logging is permitted on economic grounds, it should be carried out with the greatest of care, and any final management decisions should be governed by the precautionary approach. If there is reasonable concern

that a particular postfire salvage timber sale will cause significant ecological damage, it should not go forward. Sensitive ecological areas not
already congressionally withdrawn from postfire management—such
as inventoried roadless areas and botanic areas, steep slopes on unstable soils, and riparian zones—should be avoided altogether. Other
areas selected for treatment should be managed carefully, paying particular attention to (1) leaving a substantial proportion of biological
legacies, such as large standing dead trees; (2) promoting natural
recovery wherever possible; (3) protecting soils; (4) banning the introduction of exotic species; (5) avoiding the conversion of native forests
to conifer plantations; and (6) prohibiting new road construction.

None of these stated precautions were used in developing the Final
Environmental Impact Statement (FEIS) for the postfire management
plan for the Biscuit Fire. In this plan, over 370 million board feet of
timber are allocated for salvage in a national forest that routinely harvested approximately 25 million board feet of timber per year.[57] This
final management decision—as of 2005 still being challenged in the
courts—allows logging of many sensitive sites, including inventoried
roadless areas and late successional reserves, without proper site
restrictions to assure natural recovery.

Until society and land-managing agencies can see forests as more
than a collection of merchantable trees, we will continue to make
improper ecological decisions regarding postfire management of our
public forests, contributing to the degradation of native forests and
denying present and future generations the many ecosystem services
intact native forests provide.

CONVENTIONAL SALVAGE LOGGING

The Loss of Ecological Reason and Economic Restraint

CHRIS MASER

"ECOLOGY" AND "ECONOMY" HAVE THE SAME GREEK *root*, oikos— *meaning "house." Ecology is the knowledge or understanding of the house, economy the management of the house—and it's the same house. However, any forest product not promptly converted into a usable commodity for human benefit is considered an economic "waste," which forms the philosophical underpinnings of conventional "salvage logging."*

▼

Conventional forestry, but especially conventional "salvage logging," focuses primarily on the greatest economic efficiency in getting merchantable timber from the forest to the mill. Stated differently, while there is no such thing as biological waste in a forest, the economic concept of waste discounts social values and all biophysical values. The economic practice of discounting the aforementioned values as externalities has given rise to the convention of "salvage logging," which usually occurs in the form of clearcutting. Clearcutting, a consummate economic expedient whereby all trees are cut and removed, emulates nothing in nature. As such, clearcut logging has *no biological justification* because it progressively mines the organic material that acts as a reinvestment of biological capital in the health of forest soils, which form the organic foundation of every forest.[1] Moreover, the economic notion of "waste" poses long-term social and environmental problems for all generations—problems that will prove increasingly unaffordable and difficult to remedy. This being the case, we humans must learn to reinvest in a forest as we already do in a business.

REINVESTING BIOLOGICAL CAPITAL

In a business, one makes money (economic capital) and then takes a percentage of those earnings and reinvests it, puts it back as a cost into the maintenance of buildings and equipment in order to continue making a profit by protecting the integrity of the initial investment over time. It is, after all, much easier and less expensive to maintain the infrastructure of a business in good repair than to replace it. In a business, one reinvests economic capital after the fact, after the profits have been earned.

Unlike business reinvestments, biological capital, which is generated from within the biological system and equates to its long-term sustainability, must be reinvested *before* the fact, before the profits are earned. In a forest, one reinvests biological capital by leaving some proportion of the largest merchantable trees—both alive and dead—in the forest to rot (compost, if you will) and recycle themselves into the soil, thereby maintaining nature's biophysical processes, through which available nutrients are replenished within the living system. Given this circumstance, the question that needs to be asked is, *How much of the forest must be left intact to protect its functional integrity so it can continue producing the products and services for which we valued it in the first place?* The question is *not*, How much wood can be taken out of the forest to promote short-term economic profitability?[2]

The latter question is the premise of most industrial forestry, and conventional salvage logging in particular. Therefore, most people think of the timber industry as encompassing nothing more than getting trees from the forest to the mill. But society in the United States is founded largely on an interdependent suite of *forest-dependent* industries that individually and collectively rely much more heavily on the abundant clean water that flows from forests than they do on the growing and harvesting of wood fiber. What is true in the United States is true throughout most of the world.

A forest-dependent industry is any industry that uses raw materials from the forest, including amenities and services like oxygen, water, electricity, and recreation, as well as perceived commodities like migratory animals such as salmon and steelhead. A forest-dependent industry also includes any industry that uses extractive goods like minerals, wood fiber, forage for livestock, resident fish and game animals, and pelts from fur-bearing mammals. Finally, forest-dependent industries are all interconnected, because each industry uses one or more of the others' products, such as water, electricity, wood fiber, red meat, and vegetables irrigated on farms with water from the forest.[3]

Because we, the lay public, are taught about forests largely through commercial advertising, we tend to see only the commercial "product"—that is, the "conversion potential" of a tree for being turned into lumber, lumber into houses that are remodeled and/or resold, and so forth. The rationale for converting trees into money came from the classic liberal 19th-century economic theory of "soil rent"—that is, "renting" or using a piece of land for a crop that would maximize profits while minimizing costs.[4] Since adoption of the soil-rent theory by early foresters, maximum profit at minimum cost has become the overriding objective for conventional exploitive "forestry" worldwide.

This economic theory, however, is based on six greatly flawed assumptions, all of which presume "constants" in nature: (1) that the depth and fertility of the soil in which the forest grows is nondegradable; (2) that the quality and quantity of precipitation reaching the forest is unchanging; (3) that pure, unpolluted air infuses the forest; (4) that diversity (biological, genetic, and functional) is unimportant; (5) that the amount and quality of solar energy available to the forest are constants; and (6) that climate is unchanging.

Erroneously assuming that biophysical variables can be considered economic constants leads to the further false assumption that nature recognizes the economic notion of an "independent variable"—in the case of forestry, the tree. That is to say, that a single desired economic entity—the tree—can be manipulated without affecting other components of the forest ecosystem, such as soil, water, air, biodiversity, and so forth. *If* there were such a thing as an independent variable, then—and only then—could biological sustainability for any tree species be calculated using only two considerations, a tree's rate of growth and the age at which it must be cut in order to gain the highest rate of economic return in the shortest time for the least investment.

A forest, however, is an interdependent, living system in which everything is defined by its relationship to everything else; every relationship fits perfectly into every other relationship and is constantly changing. So, the question becomes, *What will we really lose if we practice conventional salvage logging?*[5]

In answering this question, we must first understand that each component of a forest has intrinsic value, be it a microscopic bacterium or a towering 800-year-old tree. Each component develops its natural structure, carries out its natural function, and interacts with other components of the forest through natural, interdependent processes. No component is more or less valuable than another. Each may differ in form, but all are complementary in the functioning of the whole as a living system forever in the throes of evolution.

The spatial and temporal connectivity of landscape patterns is an important consideration in dealing with a forest. I say this because the timber industry slogan "We plant ten trees for every one we cut" is ecologically misleading. It implies that the number of trees can somehow replace the relationship among trees in time and space as they constitute a forest. However, it is not the number of trees planted that confers stability on ecosystems but rather the biophysical pattern of their relationship across the land.

PATTERNS ACROSS THE LANDSCAPE

In the case of landscapes (including forests), spatial patterns result from complex interactions among physical, biological, and social forces. Most landscapes have been influenced by the cultural patterns created by human use, such as farm fields intermixed with the patches of forest that surround a small town or large city. The resulting landscape is an ever-changing mosaic of nonmanipulated and manipulated patches of habitat that vary in size, shape, and arrangement.[6]

Important biophysical processes in shaping landscapes include such ecological disturbance regimes as fires, floods, windstorms, and insect outbreaks—coupled with such disturbances of human society as habitat fragmentation, urbanization, and pollution. The ecological outcome of these disturbances is influenced by the diversity of the existing landscape pattern. Disturbances vary in character and are often controlled by physical features, such as mountain ranges, and the established patterns of vegetation, such as meadows on thin, rocky soil. The variability of each disturbance, along with the area's previous history and its particular soil, leads to the existing vegetation mosaic.

The greatest single disturbance to an ecosystem is usually human manipulation, often in the form of our continual and systematic attempts to control the size—to minimize the scale—of the various cycles of natural disturbance with which the ecosystem has evolved and to which it has become adapted. Among the most obvious are the suppression of fire and clearcut logging, which have greatly altered the distribution of old forests across North America.

As we humans struggle to minimize the scale of nature's visible disturbances, we alter an ecosystem's ability to resist or to cope with a multitude of invisible stresses.[7] We, on the other hand, attempt to control the existence and dynamics of the very cycles of disturbance to which ecosystems are adapted—often with long-term, catastrophic results. For example, our attempt to minimize forest fires has caused today's fires to be more intense and more extensive since the 1950s because of the buildup of fuels since the onset of fire suppression in the first decade of the last century.[8] Many forested areas once "fire-proofed" by forest maintenance fires have, since the onset of fire suppression, become primed for forest-replacing fires.[9]

Given enough time, virtually all forest ecosystems evolve toward a critical state in which a minor event sooner or later leads to a major event, one that alters the ecosystem in some fundamental way.[10] To illustrate, as a young forest grows, it converts energy from the sun into living tissue that ultimately dies and accumulates as organic debris on the forest floor. There, through decomposition, the organic debris releases the energy stored in its dead tissue. In this sense, a forest is a dissipative system in that energy acquired from the sun is dissipated gradually through decomposition or rapidly through fire.[11]

Of course, rates of decomposition vary. A leaf rots quickly and releases its stored energy rapidly. Wood, on the other hand, generally rots more slowly, often over centuries in moist environments.[12] As wood accumulates, so does the energy stored in its fibers. Before suppression, fires burned frequently enough to generally control the amount of energy stored in accumulating dead wood by burning it up, and thus protected a forest for decades, even centuries, from a "catastrophic" forest-replacing fire. (Keep in mind, however, that the notion of a "catastrophic" fire is an economic concept—not an ecological one.)

Regardless, a forest eventually builds up enough dead wood to fuel a forest-replacing fire. Once available, the dead wood needs only one or two very dry, hot years with lightning storms to ignite such a fire, which kills *parts* of a forest and sets them back to the forest's earliest developmental stage, the herbaceous stage of grasses and herbs. (This is a critical point, because fire rarely kills an entire forest, but rather creates a diversity of habitats by how intensely it burns in a particular area.[13]) From this early stage, a new forest again evolves toward old age, again accumulating stored energy in dead wood, again organizing itself toward the next critical state, a forest-replacing fire that starts the cycle over.

In this way, a 700-year-old forest that burned could be replaced by another, albeit different, 700-year-old forest on the same acreage. In this way, despite a series of "catastrophic fires" over the millennia, a forest ecosystem could remain a forest ecosystem. And that's why the centuries-old forests of western North America, with their incredible biophysical diversity, have been evolving from one major fire to the next, from one critical state to the next for generations.

The precise mechanisms that allow ecosystems to cope with stresses accompanying biophysical disturbances vary, but one mechanism is closely tied to the genetic plasticity of the species inhabiting the ecosystem. That is, as an ecosystem changes and is influenced by increasing magnitudes of stresses, genetic plasticity allows the replacement of a stress-sensitive species with a functionally similar but more stress-resistant species. These more stress-resistant species function as nature's ecological "backups."

While there may be two or three separate species with successive levels of stress resistance, each acting as a backup in maintaining the ecosystem's overall productivity, they must exist concurrently within the biological community. Although species that comprise nature's backups must be protected and encouraged, human-introduced disturbances (especially fragmentation of habitat) impose stresses that ecosystems are ill adapted to cope with, such as fire suppression and clearcut logging.

Not surprisingly, "connectivity" of habitats within a landscape is of prime importance to the persistence of plants and animals in viable numbers within their respective habitats—again, a matter of biophysical diversity. In this sense, the landscape must be considered a mosaic of interconnected patches of habitats that, in the collective, act as corridors or routes of travel between and among specific patches of suitable habitats.[14]

Consider, for example, the coniferous forests of the Pacific Northwest, in which Douglas-fir and western hemlock predominate in the old-growth canopy. Herein lives the northern spotted owl, which preys on the northern flying squirrel as its stable diet. The flying squirrel, in turn, depends on truffles, the belowground fruiting bodies of certain mycorrhizal fungi. (The term *mycorrhizal*, meaning "fungus-root," denotes the obligatory, symbiotic relationship between various fungi and plant roots.) Flying squirrels, having eaten truffles, defecate live fungal spores onto the forest floor, which, upon being washed into the soil by rain, inoculate the roots of the forest trees.

These fungi depend for survival on the live trees, whose roots they inoculate, to feed them carbohydrates, which the trees produce in their green crowns. In turn, the fungi form extensions of the trees' root systems by collecting minerals, other nutrients, and water vital to the trees' survival. Mycorrhizal fungi also depend on large rotting trees lying on and buried in the forest floor as reservoirs of water and for the creation of humus in the soil. Further, nitrogen-fixing bacteria associated with the mycorrhizae convert atmospheric nitrogen into a form that is usable by both the fungus and the tree. Such mycorrhizal–small mammal–tree relationships have been documented throughout the coniferous forests of the United States (including Alaska) and Canada.[15] They are also known from Argentina, Europe, and Australia.[16]

To add to the overall complexity of nature's forest, a live old-growth tree eventually becomes injured and/or sickened with disease and begins to die. How a tree dies determines how it decomposes, thereby reinvesting its biological capital (organic material, chemical elements, and functional processes) back into the soil and eventually into another forest.[17]

An old tree may die standing as a large snag, eventually to crumble and fall piecemeal to the forest floor over decades. Or, it may fall directly to the forest floor as a whole tree. Regardless of how it dies, the large snag and large fallen tree are only altered states of the live, old tree. Ergo, the live old tree must exist before there can be a large snag or large fallen tree.[18]

How a tree dies is important to the health of the forest because its manner of death determines the structure of its body (i.e., crumbled snag or whole tree) as habitat. Structure, in turn, determines the kind of biophysical diversity hidden within the tree's decomposing body as ecological processes incorporate the dead tree into the soil from which the next forest must grow. That trees become injured and diseased and die is therefore critical to the long-term biophysical health of the forest. This in turn influences the long-term socioeconomic health of humanity, which depends on healthy soils to grow sustainable forests for all generations. Yet what goes on inside the decomposing body of a dying or dead tree is the hidden biological and functional diversity that is totally ignored by economic valuation.[19]

Every forest is an interdependent, organic whole defined not by the pieces of its body, but rather by the functional relationships of those pieces in creating the whole—the intrinsic value of each piece and its complementary function. These functional relationships are totally ignored in salvage logging.

THE ECOLOGICAL FOLLY OF CONVENTIONAL SALVAGE LOGGING

Let's return for a moment to the Pacific Northwest and consider that the spotted owl preys on the flying squirrel, which depends on truffles for its diet. The fungus, of which the truffle is a part, is closely associated with large, rotting wood on and in the forest floor. The squirrel, the owl, the fungus, and the live tree all depend on the same, large, decomposing wood.

Conventional salvage logging, which is still practiced, disrupts this interdependent relationship by removing all merchantable dying and dead trees. The danger of such logging lies primarily in its philosophical underpinnings, which justify immediate economic considerations to the exclusion of all else. Conventional salvage logging has these immediate consequences:

- Areas in which logging has heretofore been prohibited—i.e., roadless areas—will likely be opened to roads, thus destroying forever their integrity as roadless areas.
- Arson fires will probably increase to stimulate salvage sales as a means of logging as much of the remaining old-growth forest as possible.
- Timber will most likely be salvaged through clearcutting, which

is a drastic biological simplification of a complex forest ecosystem.
- Conventional salvage logging emulates clearcutting—and clearcutting emulates nothing in nature.
- Conventional exploitive logging is designed to make money, but within some minimal ecological constraints—those imposed by nature. Conventional salvage logging is *reactive*, to keep from losing possible monetary gains, and is thus unplanned, opportunistic, without ecological constraints.
- Conventional exploitive logging compacts soil and removes a preestablished volume of timber, theoretically within some ecological constraints. Conventional salvage logging involves either the reentry of logged sites, which further compacts the soil, or the penetration of heretofore unentered sites, both of which nullify any previous ecological constraints.
- Conventional logging is most often based on what is and is not to be cut. Conventional salvage logging, on the other hand, inevitably opens the possibility of individual on-site interpretation and economic rationalization of what to cut—including such things as live "risk trees" or live "associated trees."[20]

Conventional salvage logging epitomizes exploitive forestry, which is the myopic, economic exploitation of trees at the supreme cost of the biophysical health of the forest as a living system. Exploitive forestry focuses on growing and cutting trees as rapidly as possible to maximize short-term profits while minimizing financial investments.

Exploitive forestry practices, now outmoded because we have improved social-environmental knowledge, began with the idea that forests (considered only as collections of trees) were perpetual economic producers of wood. With such thinking, it was necessary to convert a tree into an economic commodity before it could be assigned a value.

WHAT LEGACY SHALL WE LEAVE THE CHILDREN?

The potential for converting trees and other resources ("conversion potential") into money counts so heavily because the effective horizon in most economic planning is only about five years away. Thus, in linear economic thinking, any merchantable tree that reinvests its biophysical capital into the soil is considered an economic waste because it has not immediately been converted into money through human use.

Forests are being decimated the world over because "conversion potential" dignifies, with a name, the erroneous notion that non-harvested resources have no intrinsic value and must be converted into money before any value can be assigned. This notion assumes that anything without monetary value has no value, and anything with immediate monetary value is wasted if not used by humans. Unfortunately, the long-term biophysical price for this simplistic, economic view and the economic expedient of clearcut logging will be paid for by the generations of the future. The choice is ours as adults. To the children we bequeath equally the consequences of our wisdom and of our folly. How shall we choose?

PYRO COWS

The Role of Livestock Grazing in Worsening Fire Severity

GEORGE WUERTHNER

LIVESTOCK PRODUCTION HAS ALTERED FIRE REGIMES *in many parts of the West. Range fires are suppressed to reduce loss of livestock forage. Reduction of fine fuels by grazing has interrupted low-intensity/high-frequency fires. Livestock, by removing grass, free tree seedlings from competition for nutrients, leading to denser, more fire-prone forest stands. In some instances, livestock actually increase fire frequency by assisting the spread of highly flammable exotics like cheatgrass.*

▼

In recent years, large blazes have scorched various regions of the West, prompting a national debate about fire polices. Congress directed federal agencies to create a National Fire Plan to address the factors contributing to rising firefighting costs. Included in the plan are funds for increased firefighting and suppression, homeowner education, and prescribed burning to reduce fuels, but nowhere in this plan is there anything about reducing one of the most pervasive causative factors contributing to increased flammability of many western landscapes—livestock grazing.

Frequently overlooked, livestock production is a major factor contributing to fire hazard.[1] While climatic and weather conditions, such as extreme drought and high winds, are the key ingredients in any large blaze,[2] past management practices—including logging, fire suppression, and livestock grazing—have exacerbated the situation by creating densely stocked timber stands that in some instances are more vulnerable to high-intensity fires.[3] Depending on the ecosystem, and how long livestock have utilized an area, livestock grazing can either increase fire intensity or reduce fire frequency. In either case, livestock production is responsible for altering fire regimes from prelivestock conditions. Historically, throughout the lower-elevation forest and grass ecosystems of the West, fires frequently blazed across the landscape, consuming grasses and litter and killing smaller trees, but typically only scarring larger-diameter trees.[4] However, before this generalization is applied too widely, it should be noted that high-intensity fires always occurred in some ecosystems,[5] even at lower elevations, though at much lower frequency than light, low-intensity blazes.[6] In addition, there is some concern that climatic changes make it impossible to tease out the effects of fire suppression from changes in fire frequency due to climatic conditions.[7]

Despite these qualifiers, it is well accepted that the frequent low-intensity fires that characterized low-elevation areas of the West prior to the advent of livestock prevented the invasion of meadows and grasslands by trees and reduced the stocking rates (number of trees per acre) within forest stands. Young seedlings and saplings of common tree species like juniper and ponderosa pine are extremely vulnerable to even moderate levels of heat. As a consequence, low-intensity blazes carried by grasses tend to thin forest stands, resulting in open, parklike stands dominated by a few widely spaced large trees.[8]

Livestock grazing is frequently overlooked by agencies, the media, and the public as a factor in changing forest stand condition and fire regimes. Nevertheless, a substantial body of scientific literature identifies livestock grazing as a major factor in the alteration of historic fire regimes and as a contributor to fire hazard.[9] Relentless overgrazing in the late 19th century contributed to the near-elimination of grasslands and severe erosion in many parts of the West, but particularly in the Southwest. As a consequence, the role of livestock grazing in the alteration of southwestern ecosystems is better documented than in any other part of the West.[10]

Livestock production disrupts natural fire regimes in several ways. First, the need for animal forage can be a motivation to suppress wildfires in grasslands and other areas where livestock graze.

Second, livestock, by removing grass, free tree seedlings from competition for water and nutrients. Ultimately this cycle leads to denser tree stands and the loss of historic parklike conditions. Studies of ungrazed sites in several ponderosa pine–dominated ecosystems have found that in the absence of livestock grazing, and without any fires at all, stands of ponderosa pine were open, with a minimum of under-story pine seedling establishment.[11] For instance, one study found pon-derosa pine stands on the ungrazed Meeks Table in eastern Washington to be open and parklike, with only 85 small trees per acre. In contrast, more than 3,291 small trees per acre were counted on nearby grazed Devil's Table. This difference was observed even though neither mesa had burned in over 125 years.[12]

Third, fire frequency in sites ungrazed by livestock remained unchanged throughout the 19th and 20th centuries, while similar grazed sites experienced a steep decline in fire frequency as a result of livestock removal of fine fuels like grasses,[13] suggesting that livestock grazing was a factor in forest stand and fire frequency changes.

Fourth, many western tree species require bare soil for successful germination. Heavy livestock grazing, by removing the grassy under-story of many forest sites and creating the bare disturbed soil sites that favor tree establishment, leads to greater tree-stocking density.[14] Though removal of fine litter by livestock can lead to fewer low-intensity fires, higher tree density can lead to less frequent but ultimately more intense and more severe blazes.

Livestock grazing is also partially responsible for the presumed "invasion" of juniper in some parts of the West because of grazing-induced fuel reduction and fire suppression,[15] which allows young saplings and trees to become established in the forest, leading to much higher stand density.[16] Furthermore, it has been suggested that trails and trampling of fuels by livestock also create fire breaks that limit the spread of fires.[17]

Fifth, as livestock grazing permits a large number of small saplings to become established, competition for water among existing living trees is increased, making trees more vulnerable to insects and other pathogens, particularly during drought.[18] Such vulnerability, in turn, sometimes creates greater fuel loads of dead or dying trees, which then help to carry blazes.

Sixth, in a seeming paradox, livestock can actually increase fire hazard in some areas by facilitating the spread and persistence of fire-prone and highly flammable exotic (alien) weedy species like cheatgrass.[19]

ARE LIVESTOCK A TOOL TO CONTROL FUELS?

Some livestock advocates assert that livestock grazing can be used as a tool to reduce fuels, particularly the highly flammable cheatgrass, and thus presumably to reduce fire hazard.[20] However, unless cheatgrass is grazed to the ground, grazing alone is not likely to reduce the long-term presence of this exotic.[21] And grazing rangelands to this degree has other serious detrimental consequences, including loss of hiding cover for wildlife, trampling of soil crusts, and even the further spread of weedy species by livestock. Rangeland management specialist Steven Smith, while asserting that "livestock grazing is an important tool for controlling wildfire," cautions that "livestock can have and has had a very detrimental effect on western ecosystems." What's more, the idea that livestock can reduce flashy fuels like cheatgrass is not supported by the evidence. A review by researchers John Vallentine and Allan Stevens reported that "grazing is concluded not to be an effective general tool for cheatgrass control."[22]

Grazing also tends to increase the very fire-prone species it is supposedly eliminating, for cattle still prefer to consume native perennials over exotic annuals like cheatgrass. Over time, continued livestock grazing weakens and/or harms native perennials, making it difficult for them to outcompete exotics. In a recent *Conservation Biology* article, ecologists Sarah Kimball and Paula Schiffman note that alien annual species in California can compensate for herbivory and regrow after being clipped, while the native species are harmed by clipping. They concluded, "In the grassland we studied, the strategy of livestock grazing for restoration is counterproductive. It harms native species and promotes alien plant growth."[23]

In another California study, researchers of grasslands found that native species are better competitors than annuals in the absence of livestock grazing.[24] In other words, if native perennials are not stressed, limited by livestock grazing, or otherwise harmed by livestock, they can sustain themselves on restored California grasslands.

A study of burned grazed and ungrazed plots in Utah found that while annuals like cheatgrass may increase immediately after a fire, on ungrazed sites perennial grasses were eventually able to dominate plant cover.[25] Thus, at least on some sites, continued livestock grazing tends to favor the continued existence of the highly flammable cheat-grass on sites, thus increasing fire hazard and frequency.

Finally, anecdotal evidence suggests that livestock grazing is not likely to make a substantial reduction in the occurrence of large blazes, as proponents assert. Most of the larger blazes in the West occur in drought years. Drought also reduces the growth of grasses and other fuels.[26] And since forage is less abundant but livestock numbers are seldom reduced during drought years, livestock grazing tends to remove a greater percentage of the aboveground biomass in drought years. If livestock grazing were as effective in reducing fire hazard as grazing advocates assert, we would expect to see fewer large blazes and less acreage burned in drought years. But, in fact, quite the opposite is the case: there is a direct correlation between drought and big-fire years.[27]

Despite the contribution of livestock grazing to the growing fire hazard in the West, livestock grazing on public lands continues unabated and is seldom altered to reduce the incidence or intensity of fires. The role of livestock grazing in changing vegetative communities' response to fires is just one more uncounted cost of livestock production in the West.

Given the major ecological and evolutionary influence of fire in most western ecosystems, and the undisputed negative impacts on natural fire regimes from livestock grazing, it may be time to terminate livestock production on public lands. It makes no sense to continue creating conditions that increase fire hazards while we spend billions annually in fighting fires or dealing with the consequences of an ecologically bankrupt policy.

Part Five

THE NEW
GRAVY TRAIN

THE EMERGENCE OF THE
FIRE-MILITARY-INDUSTRIAL COMPLEX

INTRODUCTION

The Flawed Economics of Fire Suppression

Wildfire has become the new gravy train for federal agencies and the many private contractors who increasingly supply the equipment and human resources needed to suppress a blaze. Many agencies and companies have a financial stake in maintaining the public's fear of fire, and in creating policies that support a fire-military-industrial complex to fight wildfires. Other interest groups support the gravy train indirectly through loopholes and poor planning practices. For example, when a land developer subdivides rural land and allows the construction of homes in the midst of fire-prone landscapes, then turns around and requests redevelopment aid from the government after a fire, the developer is in effect sitting on the gravy train as well—benefiting from the public funds that are used to support and protect a poorly situated development.

No matter who is involved, many benefit from the rising cost of fire suppression. However, as with a real war, it is seen as unpatriotic to question expenditures on the troops, and few politicians are going to tell agencies to save money and to stop fighting fires. The problem is, fires are often uncontrollable unless the weather changes. One might as well be throwing money out the window for all the good fire suppression efforts have on the final outcome. Yet it is easy to understand why so few question these expenditures. How do you explain to a homeowner whose house is about to be engulfed in flames that trying to stop the blaze is pointless? Many in the firefighting community know their puny efforts are meaningless, but it is perceived as important to make the attempt, no matter how futile. Less money would be spent, by land use planners and firefighting agencies alike, by avoiding construction in fire-prone areas and by teaching homeowners about defending their homes from a fire. There needs to be a shift in how we live with fire, and this section explains the many ways in which we can save costs and risk fewer lives by challenging the system of the fire-military-industrial complex.

Thomas Power takes on the economic rationalizations often cited by proponents of commercial logging and firefighting agencies to justify their actions. A common retort from these interest groups is that we will "lose" valuable timber to fires or that we will "lose" forest industry jobs if trees are allowed to burn or to go uncut. Power argues that nearly all proposals related to firefighting, thinning, or postfire salvage logging on public lands make little commercial sense. Furthermore, if the environmental costs were also given some validity and consideration, the true economic price of these activities would make them impractical and economically unsustainable.

Randal O'Toole provides an account of the perverse incentives that drive federal agencies like the Forest Service. Because of shifts in public priorities—a decline in logging and grazing due to ecological concerns—agencies have had to seek other missions and funding opportunities. As O'Toole points out, fire has become the new gravy train for these agencies. Conversely, he argues that while money for fire suppression is nearly unlimited, activities that would reduce fire hazards, such as prescribed burning, are woefully underfunded.

Many vested interests that provide the food, showers, clothes, and equipment it takes to run a fire campaign often make more money than the firefighters on the front lines who are taking the risks. As Timothy Ingalsbee writes in his essay, fire suppression is analogous to a military invasion, with its "army" of firefighters, supporting equipment, and infrastructure. As in a war, no one questions spending money like a drunken sailor when there's an emergency. There are many costs that go beyond paying the wages of those on the "front lines." Fire camps must be set up to lay siege, and all sorts of people are hired, from the cooks and purchasing agents who buy supplies, to the nurses who run on-site clinics, to the erection and maintenance of electrical generation and communication centers. Ingalsbee exposes the philosophical/economic/policy motivations that have created a fire-military-industrial complex and how these incentives have spawned a class of fire-dependent agencies and private contractors who exploit fires to maintain budgets and profits.

As with many other environmental issues, if the actual cost of manipulation and control were fully accounted for, learning to live safely with nature rather than fighting against nature would prove to be the most economical approach, and the least environmentally destructive one as well. Until fire policy is changed to remove the incentives that support the fire-military-industrial complex, we will continue to see the gravy train chugging along toward the next fire.

AVOIDING A NEW
"CONSPIRACY OF OPTIMISM"

The Economics of Forest Fuel Reduction Strategies

THOMAS MICHAEL POWER, PH.D.

BETWEEN 1945 AND 1990, FEDERAL TIMBER *harvests quadrupled, supported by a "conspiracy of optimism" built around a faith that harvests were good for the forests and economically profitable. Instead we got widespread ecological disruption and massive economic losses. As a result, federal timber harvests fell back to 1945 levels. Are new proposals for massive, landscape-scale removal of wood fiber from our national forests in the name of "hazardous forest fuel reduction" and "forest health" a new "conspiracy of optimism"?*

▼

For at least 30 years, citizens, academics, and environmental groups have struggled to get the full range of values associated with our public lands reflected in land management decisions. Many people perceived that since the 1950s, commercial values had come to dominate public land management priorities and decisions. Wildlife, watersheds, fisheries, biological diversity, recreation, and scenic beauty were being seriously damaged by commercial timber harvests and livestock grazing, which often lost money when all of the costs associated with them were taken into account.[1]

To an economist these broad-ranging environmental losses in the pursuit of money-losing commercial ventures appeared to be a classic case of the misallocation of scarce resources. Low-value resources were favored by agency management at the expense of uses with much higher economic and social value. In short, the existing pattern of public land use represented pure economic waste: many, if not most, timber sales and grazing leases could not be justified even in commercial terms because their costs exceeded the value of the raw materials harvested. In addition to that out-of-pocket net loss there were also the costs of the massive environmental damage associated with logging and livestock grazing.[2]

As the economies of the communities adjacent to national forests shifted away from dependence on timber harvests and livestock production toward the natural amenities associated with those natural landscapes and the recreation they supported, the political pressure on federal land management agencies to change their priorities increased. A coalition of fiscal conservatives and environmentally concerned citizens pressured Congress to end money-losing commercial uses of public lands that were damaging the environment. As a result of these economic and political changes, national forest timber harvests, which had reached peak levels in 1988–1989, declined dramatically in the 1990s. Authorized grazing levels on public lands also began to decline.

Critics of the reduction of timber harvests in our national forests have used the extensive wildfires of the late 1990s and early 2000s to argue that commercial timber harvests are necessary to control fuels in our public forests and to prevent catastrophic wildfires. They argue that the "environmental" policies now dominating forest management are naive since they are built around the concept of a "natural forest" that will take care of itself if only humans would leave it alone. Those who support very active timber management of our public forests insist that active human intervention is now necessary, both because of past policies such as fire suppression and because of the values our citizens expect forests to produce, including residential homesites, recreation, and big-game hunting, as well as wood fiber production. They assert that passive management allowing "natural forests" to slowly emerge will lead to catastrophic wildfires that will do permanent damage to almost all forest values and render large parts of the western United States unsafe for human habitation.

Similar arguments have been made about the "need" to have livestock continue to graze on public lands. Without livestock use, we are told, those rangelands will deteriorate in ways that threaten the natural environment and the habitability of the West.[3] These claims about the need for intensive human uses of natural landscapes represent a powerful counterattack on the direction that public forestland and grassland management had been taking throughout the 1990s and on significant elements of the foundation of modern environmentalism.

CONTROLLING WILDFIRE:
THE CASE FOR FUEL REDUCTION STRATEGIES

Beginning in the late 1990s, the extent of wildfires across the United States appears to have increased significantly as compared with the previous 40 years. Although there had been earlier peak fire years, such as 1988, the frequency of heavy wildfire years appeared to increase at the end of the 1990s and in the early part of the first decade of the 21st century.

In addition, wildfires began to receive much more public attention, largely because more and more people were living within or adjacent to forestlands. Residential settlement patterns in the 1990s often involved homesites in "wild" or "natural" settings. Entire subdivisions were built in forest, scrub, or desert landscapes. With the outbreak of wildfire, these residents, homes, and communities were at risk. In 2003, for instance, numerous wildfires burned on the outskirts of Missoula, Montana, an urban area of about 100,000 people. That same year, Kelowna, British Columbia, a city of similar size, was also threatened for two weeks by wildfire burning on its periphery. The heroic efforts of firefighters across the nation to protect people, homes, and communities captured the attention of the news media.

Other concerns are also driving efforts to reduce the fuels that feed wildfires. During the 1990s, the commercial harvest of timber from national forestlands declined by three-quarters, from 10.5 to 2.5 billion board feet.[4] The forest products industry and communities that had previously depended on these federal timber harvests have objected strenuously to their loss of access to this federal source of wood fiber. Considerable political pressure has been placed on the U.S. Forest Service to boost its commercial timber harvests back toward previous levels. In the public debate over commercial timber harvest on public lands, wildfire control and fuel reduction issues have been mixed in. Some believe that timber harvest reduces the flammability of forests. Others see commercial timber harvest as a way of funding the removal of noncommercial forest fuels such as brush and small trees. Still others simply believe that allowing commercially valuable trees to burn in wildfires is a terrible economic waste and that those large trees should be harvested before they burn.

The more sophisticated case for widespread forest fuel reduction programs on public lands is built around the idea that these public forestlands are ecologically "unhealthy" in the sense of having developed much higher volumes of flammable vegetation than naturally would have been the case. The contrast is often made between the parklike forests of the past, with widely spaced, very large trees, and the tangled mix of brush and tightly spaced small-diameter trees that we now have.

Human safety, economic, and ecological arguments have all been mobilized to justify extensive vegetative manipulation of federal forest- and rangelands to reduce the risk of catastrophic wildfire. The economic logic of such a widespread modification of our public lands to control wildfire is, however, anything but clear.

THE POTENTIAL SCALE
OF FUEL REDUCTION STRATEGIES

From a coarse review of the vegetative fuel buildup across much of the nation's natural landscapes, federal land management officials estimated in 2004 that 190 million acres of federal land were at increased risk for "extreme" wildfires.[5] For federal forestland, about two-thirds, or 139 million acres, were said to be at moderate to high risk of catastrophic fire. Figures such as these are based on an estimation of how many cycles of natural wildfire have been missed on any particular type of natural landscape because of fire suppression or other unnatural circumstances.

If private lands are included, estimates of acreages of fire-prone lands are much larger. Roughly 622 million acres of private and public grasslands, scrublands, and forestlands are at "moderate" or "high" risk of catastrophic fire. Almost 400 million acres of private and public forestland fall into these risk categories.[6] These figures represent huge areas of the nation. The 622 million acres of private and public land represent almost half of the entire natural landscape in the United States. The 400 million acres of private and public forestland represent almost 60 percent of all of the nation's forestlands. Public programs to reduce the threat of catastrophic wildfire on these lands to the "low" category would require human manipulation of vegetation across much of the nation's natural landscapes.

A fuel reduction effort of this scale would represent a dramatic expansion in such activities. In 2000–2003, the federal government financed fuel reduction activities on 2 to 3 million acres of federal land.[7] At that rate, it would take a century or two to treat all of the 622 million acres of public and private acres said to be at risk. Alternatively, fuel control efforts would have to be expanded 10- to 20-fold to treat all of these lands within the next two decades. Such landscapewide vegetative manipulation over such a brief period would represent one of the most ambitious environmental modifications ever undertaken by humanity. The cost of such an effort, both environmental and economic, and the expected benefits certainly should be considered before such a heroic effort is undertaken.

REASONS TO BE CAUTIOUS ABOUT AMBITIOUS FOREST MANAGEMENT PLANS

The management of our federal forestlands has been guided by shifting public policies. For the first half-century following the establishment of the Forest Service in 1905, the role of the agency was largely custodial, protecting the national forests from illegal commercial uses, controlling wildfires and insect infestations, and maintaining some of the more important environmental services provided by those forests, such as watersheds, wildlife, and fisheries. After World War II, the Forest Service shifted to a more aggressive commercial timber harvest program. One of the objectives of this program was to help meet the pent-up demand for housing following the deprivations of the Great Depression and the war. A substantial flow of commercial timber from the national forests would help to keep the cost of housing low and affordable to a broader cross-section of Americans.

Commercial harvests on federal lands rose dramatically, peaking amid considerable environmental controversy in the late 1960s. That controversy led to some declines in timber harvest during the 1970s as new environmental laws and regulations were put in place. High interest rates and back-to-back recessions in the late 1970s and early 1980s led to a sharp decline in the demand for federal timber. By the late 1980s, however, federal timber harvest had reached a peak that was again surrounded by considerable environmental controversy.

Since then, however, federal timber harvests have fallen to a quarter of their 1988 peak as federal land management agencies have wrestled with an increasingly complex set of environmental constraints.

The explosive growth and then collapse of federal timber harvest programs were energized by what environmental historian Paul Hirt has called a "conspiracy of optimism."[8] Despite being constrained by federal laws requiring that national forests be managed for a variety of "multiple uses"—including commercial and noncommercial environmental objectives—the Forest Service acted on the assumption that none of these multiple objectives were in conflict with each other. This led to what forest economist Randal O'Toole has labeled the "multiple-use clearcut"—huge swaths of stripped forestland that the Forest Service and its timber industry allies insisted not only supported a profitable commercial forest products industry but also stabilized local communities, improved wildlife habitat, increased water production, expanded recreational opportunities, and increased biodiversity.[9] All of these multiple uses were imagined to be compatible with one another so that no trade-offs need be considered. This mentality led to the implementation of forest plans that involved extremely ambitious timber harvest programs.

Of course, there were very real trade-offs that optimism could not make go away. The courts and the American public became increasingly critical of the damage being done to these public forestlands, and that backlash led to the near-complete abandonment of commercial timber harvest on federal lands in the 1990s and first half of the first decade of the 21st century.

Interestingly, after being forced to abandon one aggressive landscapewide vegetative management plan—i.e., managing public lands primarily for commercial timber harvest—the U.S. Forest Service is now enthusiastically embracing a new landscapewide vegetative management plan under a variety of rubrics: "hazardous fuels management," "healthy forests," and "ecosystem management." We are again being told that timber harvest is compatible with pursuing or protecting most of the other important forest values: fire reduction, community stability, conserving valuable natural resources such as community watersheds and commercially valuable trees, restoring forests to natural conditions, avoiding environmental damage, and so forth.

In evaluating today's confident assertions about why aggressive human manipulation of natural systems is necessary, we should recall how the forest problems that forest thinning is supposed to solve originally developed. It was not "natural forest gone wild" that caused present abnormal forest fuel buildups. Conscious forest management decisions, supposedly supported by careful science, led to current anomalies. Initiating the problems, commercial timber harvest removed the overstory of trees, opening the canopy to allow the understory of vegetation to "bloom," including dense regrowth of trees. In addition, the timber harvest produced large quantities of highly combustible waste woody material. With the land open to sun and wind, forest fuels could dry out rapidly and become highly flammable.

Commercial livestock grazing also played a role, for the livestock consumed the grasses and forbs that had previously provided light fuels for frequent ground fires.[10] The grasses and forbs were then replaced by woody plants that provide ladder fuels, thus increasing the potential for ground fires to burn hotter and quickly move into the forest canopy. Finally, in some lower-elevation forests, fire suppression policies to protect commercially valuable timber have also contributed to changes from historical conditions. The frequent light ground fires that eliminated fuel buildup were eliminated as a matter of policy, making those forests more vulnerable to hot, stand-replacing fires.

The point is that it was human intervention and vegetative manipulation, supposedly backed by "the best science," that got us into the current "forest health crisis." Now the same agency that created the problem is confidently promoting a solution that again involves massive vegetative manipulation and widespread harvest of trees. This new program is also said to be supported by the "best science." If some observers have a feeling of déjà vu and see a new "conspiracy of optimism," it may be understandable. Unfortunately, instead of being comforted by a cautiousness born of past forest management errors, we now find primarily a renewed enthusiasm for grand landscapewide experiments.

THE LIMITS OF ENTHUSIASM AND
THE LACK OF EMPIRICAL DATA

While it is easy to show that some lower-elevation forests currently have tree densities that are way beyond historical conditions,[11] the parklike model of the "ideal forest" has limited applicability. Many forested landscapes never were open forests that experienced frequent light fires. Instead, much of the forested landscape experienced either fires of mixed intensity that left a complex mosaic of heavily burned and lightly burned areas, or infrequent intense fires that killed most of the trees. Much of the latter type of landscape burned only once every 100 to 300 years. Because of the historical infrequency of such intense burns, these lands have not been pushed out of their historical range of conditions. These lands are densely stocked, and fires will burn very hot, killing all of the trees at some point in the future, but that is the natural pattern. Forest health is not synonymous with preventing wildfires. Healthy forests burn, sometimes catastrophically. Thus natural forest restoration efforts must be distinguished from forest fuel reduction and fire prevention efforts. The two are not at all the same and should not be run together. It is still more of an error to treat commercial timber harvest as a hazardous fuel reduction strategy.

These distinctions are being made by the Forest Service as it sets its priorities for the expenditure of forest fuel reduction funds, but there has been intense political pressure to ignore these distinctions and to use fuel reduction objectives to justify timber harvest in remote roadless areas. For instance, in each of the congressional debates over funding of forest fuel reduction, one of the most contentious issues has been the allocation of those dollars between the wildland-urban interface and relatively remote forestlands.

We actually know very little about how changes in forest structure in particular settings affect fire behavior and fire damage. In a report to the federal Joint Fire Science Program, two of the nation's leading fire scientists put it this way: "Evidence of fuel treatment efficacy for reducing wildfire damages is largely restricted to anecdotal observations and simulations, and easily dismissed by skeptics. The lack of empirical assessment of fuel treatment performance has become conspicuous."[12] The lack of empirical data is not surprising, since it is hard to conduct laboratory experiments with full-blown forest fires. Most of the current proposals for hazardous fuel reduction are tied to computer modeling rather than to empirical analysis of how actual wildfires responded to different fuel treatments. The computer models, like all such models, whether in macroeconomics or weather analysis or other complex systems, are calibrated on the basis of a variety of previous research and informed assumptions. But this type of analysis is still modeling and simulation. Just as economic and weather forecasters rarely get it right, we cannot act as if these wildfire fuel management models represent entirely reliable "scientific fact."

Forest fire scientists are just beginning to build an empirical base derived from actual wildfire response to fuel management prescriptions. It will take many years of empirical analysis and hypothesis testing in a wide variety of different habitats and different weather conditions before we will be able to confidently predict what type of fuels treatment will actually have the desired effect in any particular location. That is not to say that we do not know anything. But the range of uncertainty about what is appropriate from a historical point of view, what is necessary from the point of view of the fire control level we seek, and what the impacts of those treatments will be on other natural system values is so great at this point that we have an obligation to proceed cautiously with a profound sense of humility. We must recognize that there will be significant costs, both monetary and environmental, associated with the steps we take and that we will often be wrong in our judgments. That is not an excuse for inaction, simply a commonsense warning to not get lured into another wave of destructive enthusiasm and naive optimism.

PROTECTING PEOPLE AND PROPERTY

The federal government's top priority for wildfire control is protecting people and communities. This priority is the source of the drama that plays itself out in the media each fire season: firefighters heroically trying to turn fires away from homes and towns, people being evacuated as walls of flames and smoke move toward their homes, distraught residents returning to find their homes and most of their belongings destroyed, and the trauma of young people losing their lives trying to control an overwhelming natural force. The enormous resources that go into protecting individual homes and subdivisions on flammable natural landscapes reflect the high priority placed on people and property by the government agencies directing the fire control efforts.

A rational public policy aimed at pursuing our highest-priority wildfire objectives should begin with the landscapes that people currently inhabit. Beginning fire control efforts here has several advantages.

First, a strategic focus on the highest-priority areas can keep resources from being diverted to questionable objectives.

Second, in these largely human-dominated landscapes, heavy human presence and the human activities associated with it have significantly changed the natural systems. Actions to reduce the threat of wildfire damage here are unlikely to raise the same environmental issues that would be raised in the wild backcountry, where the preservation of wilderness qualities is important. Agreement on appropriate actions should be easier to reach in the human-dominated landscapes we inhabit.

Third, in these areas it is clear who the direct beneficiaries of wildfire protection are. We can expect (even demand) cooperation from those immediately at risk in protecting their own lives and property rather than simply dipping into the federal government's deep pockets.

In focusing our initial efforts on the wildland-urban interface, the following points should be kept in mind:

- Homes and communities cannot be protected by thinning distant forests.
- Public policy should encourage homeowners to take responsibility for their own location decisions.
- Public officials should work with insurance companies to get homeowner incentives right.

Why Thinning Distant Forests Cannot Protect Homes

When a home is lost as wildfire moves through forests and grasslands, it is not surprising that we blame that loss on the fire. After all, wildfires usually originate at sites far removed from our homes, and it is the forests and grasslands that bring the fire to our homes. But home loss to wildfire is not some random act of God or simply the result of inappropriate forest management policy. Not all homes confronted by wildfire burn; only some do. It is important to understand what it is about homes and homesites that leads to these disparate outcomes. In addition, forest fires cannot burn homes that are not built in fire-prone forests.

The issues here are similar to those associated with homes built on a river's floodplain or in earthquake-prone areas. Since it is the home-owner who decides where to build the home, how to construct it, and how to maintain it in a way that minimizes the damage from such expected and natural events, those private decisions have to be considered in setting public policy. Public policy that ignores the importance of the private decisions that often determine the human consequences of natural events risks reinforcing irrational private decisions and creating a perverse incentive system. The expected outcome from such an arrangement is much higher total costs associated with preparing for, coping with, and recovering from natural "disasters."

Fire scientists have been studying how wildfires lead to home ignition for quite some time. They experiment with the flammability of home structural components immediately adjacent to burning forests. They also analyze why some homes burn while adjacent structures do not. Finally, they study in detail just how homes ignite in flames. The results of this fire science research are important in designing policies to minimize the damage done by wildfire.

Stated bluntly, forest fires by themselves rarely burn homes. The intense radiant heat from wildfire flames is not usually the source of home ignition. Instead, wildfire reaches homes by traveling along the ground—using fuels that the homeowner has either planted or allowed to accumulate there—or is carried by firebrands to flammable roofs, pine needles in rain gutters, or even through open windows.[13] If homes are constructed with appropriate materials, if dense tree stands are not immediately adjacent to the home, if the grounds and home are maintained to reduce ground and ladder fuels, and if there is water available to keep the home and surroundings moist, the wildfire will pass the house by, leaving it relatively undamaged.

At Los Alamos, New Mexico, for instance, during the 2000 fire season, the tragic home loss was not due to flaming trees adjacent to homes torching those homes. Although forests surrounding Los Alamos did burn, as the fire hit the residential areas, in general, it became a ground fire, following surface fuels, when available, to the homes and then igniting them when there were flammable materials immediately adjacent to or on the homes.[14] In residential neighborhoods that forest fires supposedly destroyed, it is startling to see burned-out homes surrounded by healthy green conifer trees.

An important forest policy implication follows from these fire science results. Efforts to protect homes and communities from wildfire by mechanically removing fuels from surrounding forests are likely to be ineffective. If the forests are thinned but homeowners do not manage their homesites and homes to reduce the chance of ignition, the homes will still be at risk. Winds can carry firebrands even from relatively light wildfires for very long distances, literally miles. When they fall on fuel-loaded homesites, homes will ignite even though the wildfires in the surrounding forest are not threatening the trees. On the other hand, if homeowners do build and maintain their homes and homesites to reduce the threat from ground fires and firebrands, the surrounding forest does not need to be thinned except in the immediate vicinity of the home (e.g., 30 to 120 feet). There may be other reasons besides home safety to thin forests extensively, such as allowing the remaining trees to grow larger or providing more wildlife habitat, but extensive thinning is not necessary for home safety.[15]

The Responsibility of Homeowners for Location Decisions

During the 2000 fire season, frustrated by all of the resources dedicated to saving homes that otherwise could have been deployed to reduce the damage to public natural resources, Montana governor Marc Racicot raised the question of homeowner responsibility for choosing to live in harm's way. He admitted, of course, that trying to regulate home location and characteristics that influence the likelihood of home ignition raised difficult property rights questions, especially for a Republican like himself.[16] But these are not new questions. Almost all of us build our homes subject to local and state building codes that enforce certain fire and safety standards. People may or may not be able to build on a floodplain; if they can, the house and sewage system have to meet certain standards. All buildings in earthquake-prone areas have to meet earthquake codes. Coastal states have hurricane construction standards.

Several states have adopted regulations aimed at requiring homeowners in areas at high risk for wildfire to take responsibility to reduce the likelihood that a wildfire will ignite their homes or travel across their homesites to neighboring residential areas. California and Oregon, for instance, have adopted statewide regulations for at-risk areas that require firebreaks to be constructed around homes and maintained so that wildfire cannot move through trees or along the ground to reach the home. In addition, roofs, gutters, decks, and areas under decks and houses must be kept free of flammable materials. In Oregon, these requirements are being phased in over several years, beginning with counties deemed to be at highest risk for wildfires.[17]

Counties and cities in wildfire-prone areas are beginning to adopt similar codes to increase the survivability of homes. Some local governments in California, Colorado, Florida, Idaho, Montana, New Mexico, Utah, and Washington have acted to hold homeowners responsible for making their homes and homesites more resistant to wildfire. In Summit County, Colorado, for instance, those who wish to build in forested areas must use fire-resistant materials, install sprinklers, cut back trees, and keep enough water on hand in large cisterns to douse an out-of-control blaze. In Orange County in southern California and in the Sun Valley area of Idaho, similar codes to protect homes against wildfire damage have been adopted. In subdivisions, wider streets are required as firebreaks and to allow easier escape for residents and easier access for fire equipment. The greater the wildfire risk because of the character of the surrounding vegetation or the steepness of slope, the more stringent are the requirements. On some locations—for instance, on very steep slopes where fire can spread very rapidly—building is simply banned.

In other local areas, fire departments, supported by state and local regulations, have imposed fire standards, especially for new developments in areas at high risk of wildfire. Several states have developed model ordinances for local governments to incorporate into their zoning and land use ordinances. The general idea is to get those who choose to live in areas where wildfire is a regular part of the natural environment to take on a major share of the costs of effectively coping with that danger rather than shifting that cost to others at the time of an emergency.

Homeowner Insurance Incentives for Reducing Wildfire Hazard

Insurance companies and local firefighting units have roles to play in improving the rationality of private decisions that have significant social consequences. If insurance companies required regular certification by local fire departments that residential structures were in fact defensible in the event of wildfires, mortgage holders would automatically apply considerable pressure on homeowners to appropriately maintain their property for the forest, scrublands, or grasslands location they inhabit. Insurance companies, mortgage lenders, and local fire departments can also contribute significantly in terms of education and enforcement. Regular inspections of homes in fire-prone areas by local fire officials would alert homeowners, firefighters, insurance companies, and mortgage holders to growing fuel problems at the homesite or home maintenance problems that increase the likelihood of a home's igniting when a wildfire is near. Homeowners, of course, would be responsible for paying for such inspections and certification, either directly through their fire protection taxes or indirectly through their insurance rates.

Insurance companies have already begun to do exactly this. State Farm Insurance Company has begun implementing a new program to reduce the potential for future financial losses in some areas of the West with high wildfire hazard. Policy owners in the states of Arizona, Nevada, New Mexico, Utah, Colorado, and Wyoming are affected. State Farm will begin inspecting homes in high-risk areas to identify steps that need to be taken to reduce wildfire hazard and has hired a private firm to work with state forestry and fire control agencies in training workers to carry out these inspections.

After the inspections, State Farm will inform homeowners of the steps that need to be taken to reduce the wildfire hazard, provide a specified time period within which corrective measures must be taken, and then reinspect the homesite. For homesites with very serious wildfire hazard problems, the homeowner will be required to work with local fire control agencies to develop a correction strategy. If homeowners choose not to adopt the recommended measures, their insurance is likely to be canceled.

The state of California has acted to encourage all insurance companies to distinguish homesites whose character and maintenance increase the wildfire hazard. The requirements for lower insurance rates in higher-risk areas include creating and maintaining defensible spaces around structures, such as the removal of brush and other flammable vegetation to a minimum of 200 to 300 feet. In addition, homes must be maintained to reduce the risk of ignition from wildfire. Homeowners who do not follow these requirements face significantly higher insurance rates.[18] Basing insurance rates on actual risk provides homeowners with an incentive to choose their homesites more responsibly and then to maintain them to reduce wildfire hazards.

▼

None of these new requirements will sit well with many rural residents. They are used to doing things as they please and to being left alone. But when the fires rage, they are not left alone. Firefighting personnel with equipment camp out at their doorsteps, waiting to risk their lives to protect those homes. In addition, huge expenditures are made to try to guide the fire away from areas of human habitation. Federal and state taxpayers pick up the tab. Similarly, the federal government and its taxpayers would have to pick up the tab if the proposals to "fireproof" most of the forested landscape were pursued. Because there are public costs incurred partially because of private decisions, those decisions cannot be treated as entirely a private matter.

Some change in federal law may be required to encourage responsible behavior by individual homeowners. In the past, the federal government has taken on the responsibility of keeping wildfires that originate on federal land from crossing onto and damaging nonfederal land. Wildfires originating on federal land have implicitly been made the responsibility of federal land managers.

This assumption of responsibility for all home losses that can be associated with fires that originate on federal land is unreasonable and encourages passive and irresponsible behavior by other landowners. Congress needs to indicate clearly that wildfires are natural events like floods or hurricanes. Wildfires serve natural functions that are important to maintaining healthy forests, scrublands, and grasslands. For that reason, federal agencies should not be required to extinguish all wildfires, even wildfires that may cross onto nonfederal property. Just as upstream landowners cannot be held responsible for floods that partially develop upstream and then travel downstream, the same is true of wildfire. All landowners who choose to inhabit natural areas must individually shoulder responsibility for protecting themselves from the natural dangers inherent in their location decisions.

THE ECONOMIC COSTS AND BENEFITS
OF FOREST FUEL MANAGEMENT

It may be physically possible to manage our forestlands to minimize the possibility of large, hot, stand-replacing wildfires. A key question, however, is, What would such wildfire control cost—in terms of money and in terms of other forest values that might have to be sacrificed— and how would those costs compare with the benefits of such an effort?

The Dollar Costs of Forest Fuel Reduction

As discussed above, federal agencies estimate that 190 million acres of federal forestlands and rangelands are threatened with "unnaturally extreme fires" because of the levels of fuels that have accumulated on them.[19] If the 430 million acres of private lands threatened in the same way are included, more than three times that amount—622 million acres—would be similarly classified.[20] In 2001–2004, the Forest Service and the Bureau of Land Management engaged in fuel reduction activities on an average of about 2.5 million acres a year.[21] The Healthy Forest Restoration Act of 2003 authorized fuel reduction treatment on a cumulative total of 20 million acres of federal land. It appropriated $760 million for the first year of that effort in 2004.

Clearly the current level of forest fuels reduction will not be sufficient to "treat" all of the lands judged to have hazardous fuel accumulations. At 2.5 million acres a year, it would take 76 years to treat all 190 million federal acres at moderate or high risk of extreme forest fires. Well before the end of that period, previously treated acres would again be at risk. Then there are the other 430 million acres of nonfederal, largely private, lands at moderate to high risk. If all lands with hazardous accumulations of fuels are to be treated in the near future, a dramatically expanded effort will be necessary. The question is, What would that cost?

We cannot use the recent fuel reduction expenditures per acre to estimate that cost, for several reasons. First, half or more of recent fuel control expenditures have been associated with maintenance programs carried out in the southeastern United States. These decades-old programs aim at keeping hazardous fuel levels from developing by treating each acre every three to five years. Because hazardous fuel levels have not been allowed to develop, the costs of annual treatment are quite low, although these lands must be regularly treated because the warm, moist climate of the Southeast causes rapid regrowth of fuels.[22] In addition, as the General Accounting Office, the investigative arm of Congress, has repeatedly pointed out, federal land managers have as their fuel reduction objective to treat as many acres as possible.[23] As a result, their focus is not on treating the highest-risk areas or the high-est-priority areas. Instead, low-cost areas are pursued to allow a larger number of acres to be reported as treated. If hazardous fuel reduction efforts were focused on high-priority areas, the costs would likely be quite different.

U.S. Forest Service researchers have made several attempts to estimate that cost by using a combination of forest and fire modeling and past fuel reduction costs. Although the results have to be considered preliminary until cost data associated with actual implementation have accumulated, this research indicates that the cost of landscapewide hazardous fuel reduction would be very high. One study of a 28-million-acre swath of forestland stretching from the Columbia River across central Oregon into northern California estimated that a fuel reduction program that attempted to maximize the amount of forest fuels removed from lands at high risk to catastrophic wildfire would cost about $1,700 per acre. In contrast, $1,300 per acre in net revenue would be generated if the focus were on commercial logging. That is a $3,000-per-acre difference in the net cost of these two different "treatments."[24]

In a more detailed analysis of Oregon's 4.6-million-acre Klamath ecoregion portion of the larger study area, the cost results were similar, but little of the total acreage could be treated without incurring very high costs. If fuel reduction measures had to pay for themselves, only 3 to 4 percent of the acres could be treated. If net revenues from some acres could cover the costs of more costly acres, 10 to 20 percent of the acres open to treatment could have fuels reduced. If the objective were to maximize the volume of fuels removed, the costs would be $1,800 per acre, and 59 percent of the land would be treated. If the objective were to maximize the number of acres treated, the cost would be about $1,000 per acre, and 65 percent of the acres would be treated. If the objective were to maximize net revenues by removing the commercially valuable materials, 10 percent of the area would be "treated," generating $1,300 in net revenue per acre.[25]

These results suggest that a commitment to reducing forest fuels across much of the landscape could be enormously expensive. Even at $1,000 per acre, treating 190 million federal acres would cost $190 billion; treating all 622 million acres of private and public land with dangerous fuel accumulations would cost $622 billion. In contrast, the 2004 annual appropriation for hazardous fuel reduction associated with the Healthy Forest Restoration Act was $760 million.

An Economically Rational Response to Hazardous Fuels Buildup

Of course, these high costs simply demonstrate that the nation cannot afford to treat all lands having accumulations of fuel that could feed wildfires. Such a blanket landscapewide policy makes neither economic nor ecological sense. Fortunately, when we look in more detail at what we are trying to accomplish and what the economic and ecological opportunities are, we see considerable opportunity to protect both our communities and our forests and rangelands.

First, all acres of land with accumulations of fuels are not equally threatening to communities and property. The focus should be on the wildland-urban interface. Second, all lands with fuel accumulations are not in an ecologically unhealthy condition. Fuel accumulations and wildfires are a natural and productive part of forest and rangeland environments. Third, the net costs of hazardous fuel reduction vary from one site to another depending on a host of conditions: the mix of merchantable and nonmerchantable material, the steepness and remoteness of the terrain, the fluctuating value of wood fiber, and available technologies and facilities that could make use of the hazardous fuels removed.

Given this complex of considerations, the rational approach to hazardous fuels and the wildfire threat is to be selective about where fuel reduction efforts are focused, choosing initially those areas of greatest immediate threat to people and communities, those areas with lower economic costs, and those areas where past human activities have most damaged natural processes, reducing the ecosystems' abilities to adapt productively themselves.

While careful analysis and selection of areas to treat to reduce hazardous fuel buildup is clearly the rational path to take, the focus should not be primarily on the out-of-pocket costs associated with fuel treatment. This is an important point, because there are potentially conflicting motivations behind the drive to "treat" areas with hazardous fuel accumulations. Some interests are primarily concerned about the threat to people and property from wildfire. Other interests are concerned with "restoring" forests and rangelands where human activities have pushed these ecosystems beyond their ability to productively adapt and recover. Still other interests have their eyes on gaining cheap access to the commercially valuable timber these lands contain.

While at any given site all three of these interests might be pursued simultaneously to a certain extent, their objectives are not the same and are certain to be in conflict in many situations. In some settings, infrequent, hot, stand-replacing fires are part of the natural process. Adjacent to communities, however, they may be unacceptable. In that situation, fire control may trump, preventing fire from proceeding as a natural process. It is possible, however, that after homes and forestlands have been modified to reduce the likelihood of home- and forest-threatening fires, light ground fires could be used to maintain that low-risk forested landscape while pursuing the fire control objective.

More important, commercial timber harvest is not a wildfire control strategy. From a commercial timber point of view, the largest and most fire-resistant trees are the biomass to be removed. In the process of extracting those large trees, efforts would be made to minimize the associated costs, including those associated with the disposal of the very flammable noncommercial wood fiber waste, the slash. If the area is replanted or allowed to regenerate, the commercially optimal spacing of the new trees is likely to be much closer than fire control advocates would recommend.

Fuel management, on the other hand, is likely to focus on removing densely packed smaller trees and the brush and very young trees that provide ladder fuels allowing wildfire to reach the crowns of the older trees. Most of the older, more commercially valuable trees would be left. However, much of the fuel that needs to be removed has no commercial value. In addition, removing noncommercial fiber must be repeated regularly to control brush and young trees. Thus, whether the removal is done mechanically or with controlled burns, it will not be profitable.

If we are to avoid a new "conspiracy of optimism" that damages our forests while not protecting our communities, we must face the fact that the several legitimate objectives for managing our forests and rangelands do not, in general, coincide. Pursuing one usually means that we cannot pursue the other as far as we would like. There are trade-offs. As we set public policy, we must make difficult choices.

Trade-offs Between Commercial Timber Harvest, Hazardous Fuel Reduction, and Ecosystem Restoration

Removal of forest biomass guided only by commercial considerations will do nothing to reduce wildfire danger. A modeling analysis of fuel reduction strategies in south-central Oregon's Fremont National Forest used as one of its reference points a prescription that removed all trees 12 inches or more in diameter, but nothing smaller. The study focused on the third of the forest area that was already at high risk for unnaturally intense wildfire. Removal of only the commercially valuable vegetation left 80 percent of the treated area still in the high-risk category and moved none of it into the low-risk category, although the projected strategy was a commercial success, yielding $1,244 per acre. Only treatments that removed substantial amounts of the smaller-diameter vegetation had significant impacts on the high-risk stands.[26] Alternatives that removed substantial amounts of noncommercial fuel material, however, were projected to have considerable net costs unless relatively low treatment costs were assumed. Similar modeling results were obtained on the Okanogan and Wenatchee national forests.

Removing merchantable trees, of course, increases the revenue generated by a fuel reduction treatment. It is therefore tempting to solve the problem of the high cost of removing noncommercial vegetation by purposely harvesting more of the larger, high-value trees. That approach, however, raises questions about whether forest health and fire control objectives are seriously compromised by applying commercially oriented criteria to the design of the forest treatment.

As a practical matter, in some areas, because there is not much commercially valuable fiber or because of the high costs of accessing and removing the trees, including more commercially valuable trees in the treatment will have little impact in lowering the net costs of fuel reduction. For instance, in modeling of Oregon's Blue Mountains, removal of just the smaller trees was shown to significantly reduce wildfire danger, but at a substantial net cost. If merchantable trees could also be removed without constraint, only 6 percent of the stands were projected to generate positive net revenues because of the limited density of merchantable trees. The vast majority of the stands still could be treated only at a net cost.[27]

In other areas, removal of larger trees may be necessary simply to get the density of trees down to a level where crown fires are not easily propagated from tree to tree. That was the conclusion drawn from the modeling study of central Oregon and northern California discussed above. In that modeling, if trees in the 9- to 21-inch-diameter range were harvested when doing so would reduce the risk of crown fire propagation, the revenues from those commercially valuable trees allowed additional treatment in stands that had net costs associated with them, effectively tripling the total number of acres that could be treated. As a result, almost a third of the forest that was open to treatment could be treated on a break-even basis. Of course, two-thirds of the lands judged to need treatment still could be treated only at substantial cost, more than $1,000 an acre.[28] In addition, the subsidization of the treatment of many acres with the net revenues from other acres simply obscures the high costs associated with treating those acres too.

To the extent that a "healthy" forest is defined as one that has very widely spaced trees and there also is no prohibition on the removal of large commercially valuable trees, even more hazardous fuel reduction can be funded through the sale of the commercially valuable trees.

The density of trees in a forested area is usually measured in terms of the "basal area," the sum of the cross-sectional area of all trees at "breast height" (4.5 feet) across that forested area, expressed as square feet per acre. The central Oregon–northern California modeling analysis used a target tree density of 80–125 square feet of remaining trees per acre (basal area). A limit was also placed on harvesting any trees greater than 21 inches in diameter. Other modeling studies have assumed that the appropriate target density is 40–50 square feet of remaining trees per acre. When forests are thinned to this level, much of the commercially valuable wood fiber is removed, and many more acres can be thinned without incurring a net cost. Modeling studies of Montana and New Mexico national forests that assumed it was appropriate to reduce tree density to levels this low found that the economics of hazardous fuel reduction were greatly improved and that there was a long-term reduction in fire danger. In Montana, these studies projected that about half of the forestlands in the moderate- to high-fuel-hazard categories could be treated at no net cost. Those forests with higher numbers of large trees generated commercial sales revenues that covered the removal of the noncommercial vegetation. As a result, 60 percent of western Montana's high- and moderate-hazard forestlands could be treated, but only 40 percent of the lands in those categories in eastern Montana could break even.[29] The modeling analysis in New Mexico, which has even more limited commercial forestland, found that even when there were few limits on the removal of larger commercially valuable trees, only 25 percent of the moderate- and high-risk forestlands could be treated at no net cost.[30]

When planning hazardous fuel reduction programs, it is hard not to be aware of the high cost of eliminating fuels that have no commercial value. It is also nearly impossible to ignore the budget constraints on the Forest Service. These factors are likely to lead narrow economic concerns to influence the designation of what "the forest needs." Federal land managers and the public need to openly discuss the trade-offs between conflicting objectives and to make an explicit policy decision rather than letting the financial constraints corrupt the biological or fire control analysis. It is important to weigh explicitly what is gained (if anything) in terms of the reduction in the risk of catastrophic wildfire and what is lost (and/or, possibly, gained) in terms of the broad range of natural forest values for which our public lands are supposed to be managed. These are important public choices that should not be hidden in broad assertions about "healthy forests" or fearful descriptions about the assumed damage caused by wildfire.

The Environmental Costs of Forest Fuel Reduction

Besides the out-of-pocket costs associated with managing forest fuel loads, there are environmental costs arising from other forest values—such as wildlife habitat, biodiversity, water quality, and wildland characteristics—that may be compromised. Whatever its benefits for fire control, a continuous parklike setting of widely spaced trees with minimal ground cover is not, in general, a natural forest. Analysis of site-specific historical forest characteristics and their range of natural variability can provide objective guidance as to where such a parklike end result is appropriate and where it is not. Such analysis indicates that, in general, natural forests are patchworks of different tree densities, tree species, ground cover, nonforested grasslands or shrublands, and so forth. Each patch serves a different ecological function in the larger forest "quilt." To take one obvious example, big game requires the cover provided by dense thickets of trees. If, in the pursuit of fire control, such thickets are systematically eliminated, substantial big-game habitat would be lost. It would not be much of an ecological improvement to jump from primarily managing our forests for commercial timber to primarily managing them for fire control under the guise of "forest health." Single-focus management is likely to always be environmentally damaging no matter what the single objective happens to be. True forest restoration efforts match the complexities of forest ecosystems, pursuing multiple objectives in an adaptive way over time and across landscapes.

Finally, wildfire control is being pursued because of its perceived benefits. Implicit is the assumption that wildfire causes damage. Although that clearly can be the case in some important and prevalent settings, in general wildfire is a productive part of forest and grassland ecosystems. Just as periodic floods are important in renewing rivers and riparian areas, fires play an important role in keeping our forests productive and healthy. In that context, wildfire provides important benefits rather than imposing costs. The Yellowstone fires of 1988, as catastrophic as they seemed at the time, have provided a case study of how resilient forest systems can be to even very hot fires that appear to be so destructive that they literally sterilize local natural systems. Given our increasing knowledge of the importance, even necessity, of retaining fire as an active part of our western forests, the first judgment that must be made is whether any fire control is appropriate in each particular forest setting.

The Net Costs of Backcountry Forest Fuel Reduction

In evaluating the economic rationality of proposals to manage forest fuels mechanically, we must distinguish between (1) lower-elevation forests that are already roaded and that have been managed for timber in the past and (2) less-accessible mountainous backcountry, much of which is not currently roaded and is not scheduled for timber harvest. In rough, steep, unroaded terrain, significant timber harvests to drastically thin the forests and repeated entry to remove slash, brush, and young trees would be extremely costly. The costs would almost certainly exceed the value of the commercial products extracted and the discounted future harvest values on these high, isolated sites with slow-growing trees. It was precisely their low net commercial timber value that kept these areas from being roaded and logged in the past.

In these forest types, it is not clear that there is any justification for fuel management by mechanical means. Costly mechanical manipulation of these forests is inappropriate in ecological terms because many of these higher-elevation forests have not been changed by human logging, livestock grazing, or fire suppression to the extent that their fuel loads and forest conditions lie outside of historical norms. Fuel management efforts there do not promote human safety because of these forests' remote locations far from human habitation. Fire control cannot be justified in terms of saving a commercial resource because the value of the standing inventory of trees is below the cost of extracting them. If these naturally dense forests were to be mechanically thinned to very wide spacing, other forest values—watershed, fishery, wildlife, recreation, scenery, and so forth—would be sacrificed. In short, there are few or no benefits of extensive backcountry thinning, and the costs—financial and ecological—are high. Fuel management policy should focus elsewhere.

A RATIONAL RESPONSE TO
THE DANGERS OF WILDFIRE

What, then, is an appropriate public policy response to the dangers posed by wildfire? On the basis of the above discussion and analysis, I offer the following recommendations.

Because concerns over community and human health and safety will remain a top priority of wildfire management, mechanical treatments to reduce forest fuels should be focused on areas in the immediate vicinity of human habitation. Because of their proximity to human settlement, these areas already tend to be human-dominated land-scapes. Roads, past logging, livestock grazing, home construction, pets, fencing, clearing, irrigation structures, fire suppression, and the like have already significantly modified local ecosystems. It may be possible to manipulate the character of those forests to reduce wildfire threats to human life and property while still protecting many of the forest values that attracted people to the area: a "natural" setting, scenic beauty, wildlife habitat, and open space. Heavy-handed management of the landscape that disregards the damage being done to natural systems, however, would be foolish. Cautious, adaptive management is what is called for.

No attempt should be made to "fireproof" the forested landscape. We should allow wildfires to burn in our forests. The focus should be on reducing the possible damage caused by those fires. Homeowners should be fireproofing their homes and homesites. Forest ecosystems should not be harmed because homeowners have not taken the necessary safety measures needed where fire is a common and natural occurrence. Education, incentives from insurance companies, and local building codes and land use regulations should be used to shift home protection costs from the public and the surrounding natural forests to the homeowners themselves.

No attempt should be made to impose a single model of a "healthy" or "fire-safe" forest on all forested landscapes. In some forested settings, infrequent stand-replacing fires are as natural as frequent light ground fires at other sites that threaten no mature trees. Not all forests should be open and parklike. Complex patchworks or mosaics of diverse forest conditions are what make up a natural forested landscape.

Commercial timber harvest is obviously a legitimate activity in some forested landscapes. Commercial timber harvest, however, is not a form of hazardous fuel management. The two should not be confused. One should not be a cover or excuse for the other. The pursuit of commercial timber values usually comes at the expense of wildfire control and forest health.

Hazardous fuel management has significant costs—both out-of-pocket costs and the opportunity costs associated with the loss of other forest values. Fuel management should be subjected to the same economic scrutiny of its costs and benefits as any other natural resource use. In our eagerness to reduce the threat of wildfire, we should not ignore the ecological costs of our fire control efforts nor the long-term maintenance costs that may be associated with particular mechanical treatments of the forest.

We are just beginning to develop the scientific knowledge base to support our efforts at fire control and ecosystem restoration. We have very limited on-the-ground experience with the effectiveness and consequences of different hazardous fuel treatment regimes. Most of the literature is based on complex computer simulation models or anecdotal evidence. Before we spend billions of dollars on landscapewide vegetative manipulation, we should rigorously test these modeling and intuitive results on the ground. It is a time for creative but careful experimentation to see what works and what does not. It is not a time for a new "conspiracy of optimism."

Ultimately, humility is called for in the face of powerful natural forces that we only partially understand and often will not be able to control. We should learn from our experiences with river systems and the painful management reevaluations we have had to undergo with respect to flood control. We have learned that we cannot and should not try to eliminate all floods and ultimately cannot manage large floods. The same is true of wildfire. We need wildfire. Even if we did not need it, we often would not be able to contain or control it. At those times, all we can do is what other animals who inhabit our forests, scrublands, and grasslands do: get out of the way until the fire passes and then take advantage of the changes and opportunities that wildfire brings in its wake.

MONEY TO BURN

Wildfire and the Budget

RANDAL O'TOOLE

CONGRESS HAS HISTORICALLY GIVEN THE FOREST SERVICE *a blank check for suppressing fires but has been stingy with funds for preventing fires. The incentives created by this budgetary reality have strongly influenced Forest Service research, national forest management, and federal wildfire programs. Any attempts to improve or reform national forest management or fire programs that do not take these incentives into account are doomed to fail.*

▼

Forest Service histories of wildfire often begin with the great Idaho-Montana fires of 1910. But the real history began two years before, when Congress created an emergency fire suppression fund. Under the Forest Fires Emergency Act of 1908, in the event of a fire emergency, the Forest Service could use any available funds to put out the fire, and Congress would reimburse those expenses. In effect, Congress gave the Forest Service a blank check, which was absolutely unique for a peacetime agency. When the 1910 fires were over, the Forest Service had spent $1.1 million trying to put them out—nearly 25 percent of its entire budget for the year. Congress dutifully reimbursed these funds, thus assuring the Forest Service that it indeed had a blank check.[1]

Early Forest Service leaders such as Gifford Pinchot, Henry S. Graves, and William B. Greeley were urbanites with typical urban attitudes toward fire. As fire historian Stephen Pyne observes, rural landowners have always treated fire as a tool to be used to kill weeds and harmful insects and to promote desirable plants and forage for domestic livestock. But urban residents knew fire only as something that could destroy the cities in which they lived.[2] "As urbanites' personal experience of fire waned, so did their tolerance of its consequences," says Pyne. "They saw fire as social horror. . . . If they could banish it, they would."[3] Led by urbanites, the Forest Service set a goal of banishing fire from the forests. "The first measure necessary for the successful practice of forestry is protection from fire," said Chief Graves in 1914.[4] When asked in 1923 to summarize the main problem with forests, Chief Greeley's answer was: "Stop the fires."[5]

For nearly 40 years, fire exclusion was the chief goal of the Forest Service. "Sanctified by an administrative theory granting zealous technocrats broad latitude for action," observes historian Ashley Schiff, "purpose was transmuted into mission, a campaign into a crusade."[6] Yet the fire exclusion crusade was not a foregone conclusion, as people both in and out of the Forest Service supported light burning—the term used at that time for what would now be called prescribed burning—of pine forests. What tipped the balance to the fire exclusionists was the blank check. The blank check not only rewarded the Forest Service for putting out fires, it rewarded the Forest Service for spending a lot of money putting out fires. No other national forest activity was so rewarding until timber became prominent, owing to another set of budgetary incentives, in the 1950s.[7]

The Forest Service was not simply recalcitrant. When other Forest Service policies conflicted with its incentives, it changed the policies. Gifford Pinchot (chief, 1905–1910) believed national forest timber should be sold only to family-owned sawmills, not large corporations. William B. Greeley (chief, 1920–1928) overturned that policy in the 1920s because he wanted both the political support and the revenue large companies could provide. Pinchot also opposed clearcutting. When clearcutting proved to augment national forest budgets better than other forms of cutting, however, it quickly became the agency's dominant cutting method.[8] The blank check, however, allowed and encouraged the Forest Service to steadfastly maintain its fire exclusion policy for many decades. Even today, after Congress has supposedly repealed the blank-check law and the Forest Service in public supports increased fire in the forest, a de facto blank check still rules much of wildfire policy and operations.

Initially, says Pyne, the blank-check fund "produced a profound ambivalence among professional foresters," some of whom believed that drawing upon that check was an admission of failure.[9] But in the long run, "of course, the money was irresistible," adds Pyne. "Whatever

else the fire establishment did or wanted to do, actual firefighting paid
the freight." As a result, "fire agencies will follow the money."[10]

By the 1930s, writes Pyne, "federal fire control became increasingly dominated by emergency funding programs existing outside regular, budgeted appropriations"—in other words, by the blank check.[11]
The blank check was reinforced in 1935 when the Forest Service
adopted the well-known "10 a.m." policy stipulating that a fire was to
be contained and controlled by 10 a.m. following its detection.[12] Less
well known was another change in policy adopted at the same time:
instead of being limited to fire suppression, the blank check could now
be spent on presuppression—that is, things needed to get ready for fire
season, such as equipment purchases—during periods of extreme fire
danger.[13] This opened the floodgates to additional spending on fire. All
a forest supervisor had to do was declare that a drought existed, and he
could spend unlimited amounts of money on fire crews and materials.

THE BLANK CHECK VERSUS LIGHT BURNING

In 1908, the same year Congress gave the Forest Service a blank check
for fire suppression, Yale forestry professor H. H. Chapman published
research showing that fire was necessary to regenerate southern longleaf pine forests. Chapman suggested that landowners who wanted to
regenerate longleaf pine should burn in the fall. Then, after two years,
seedlings could survive another controlled burn, which would eliminate competition and burn the duff that, if allowed to accumulate,
would provide the fuel for a catastrophic fire. Later research also
found that loblolly pine needed frequent burns.[14]

As described in Ashley Schiff's classic study *Fire and Water*, the
Forest Service not only ridiculed Chapman and other light burning supporters, it suppressed research done by its own scientists that reached
the same conclusions.[15] For example, the Forest Service burned a stand
of longleaf pine seedlings and then published a report showing that fire
had killed some of the seedlings, whereas an unburned plot had more
seedlings per acre. But when later remeasurements found that the fire-
thinned seedlings had grown faster than the unburned ones, the Forest
Service refused to publish the data.[16] It also used its muscle to prevent
other federal agencies from publishing reports favoring fire.[17]

Excluding fire from national forests was one thing. But in 1924, Congress passed the Clarke-McNary Act to encourage the states to control fires on private lands. The act gave the Forest Service power to hand out money to state and local fire protection districts. The agency used that power to promote its fire-exclusion crusade by refusing to give any money to districts that allowed landowners to use prescribed burning.[18] The blank check and Clarke-McNary Act gave the Forest Service power, and as Stephen Pyne notes, "as that power grew, the Service found itself subtly corrupted in spirit and imagination."[19]

Greeley and other Forest Service leaders of the 1920s and 1930s had gained their fire experience in the 1910 Idaho and Montana fires, and the Forest Service had no national forests in the South at that time. But in 1911, Congress passed the Weeks Act, giving the Forest Service money and authority to buy forests in the East and South. National forest managers in the South soon learned that Chapman was right: if they didn't do prescribed burning, catastrophic fire would result. By the 1930s, many southern national forests were doing prescribed burning on thousands of acres each year. The Washington office of the Forest Service tolerated controlled burning on southern national forests, provided it was kept secret. Yet agency leaders still tried to prevent, through the denial of Clarke-McNary funds, similar burning on private lands.[20] As late as 1939, the Forest Service hired a psychologist to find out why "our pappies burned the woods." He concluded it was "the defense beliefs of a disadvantaged cultural group"— in other words, that people who burned were ignorant.[21]

In 1939, the Forest Service did finally allow its own researchers to publish studies supporting the use of fire.[22] Catastrophic fires in the South in the early 1940s helped convince the agency to let forest protection districts allow prescribed burning in longleaf pine stands in 1943—but it refused to make its decision public for fear it would encourage people to light fires.[23] Nor did it allow prescribed burning in southern loblolly pine until 1954.[24]

One curious result of the Forest Service's denial of Clarke-McNary funds to protection districts that allowed burning is a severe distortion of the record of acres burned in the 20th century. Data published in several places indicate that wildfires burned 39 million acres a year during the 1930s, falling to 9.4 million acres a year in the 1950s, 4.6

million in the 1960s and 3.2 million in the 1970s.[25] "By the late 1950s, as a result of increasingly sophisticated fire protection," bragged one Forest Service report, "both the area burned and the size of fires had been substantially reduced."[26] In fact, most of the reduction was not from fire protection but from the Forest Service's admitting that many fires it had once called "wildfires" were in fact prescribed burns.

A close look at the data reveals that, through the early 1950s, the vast majority of the acres burned were on "unprotected" lands—that is, lands outside of Clarke-McNary fire protection districts.[27] A footnote included in some of the Forest Service fire reports in those early years says, "Figures for unprotected acres are based on partial information from incomplete reports. Reliable data are not obtainable."[28] From 1931 through 1956, Forest Service reports say that 10 to 20 percent of all the unprotected acres burned each year, almost all in the South. By comparison, only 0.5 to 2.2 percent of private protected acres and 0.1 to 0.5 percent of federal forest acres burned each year.[29]

It seems certain that, until lands were included in fire protection districts, the Forest Service counted light burning as wildfires. Since it did not accept fire protection districts that allowed wildfires until the late 1940s, most of the acres supposedly burned in wildfires in the 1920s, 1930s, 1940s, and early 1950s were actually controlled burns. Agency officials may also have exaggerated the number of acres burned outside of protection districts to prove to Congress the value of forest protection or to apply pressure to states to accept the Forest Service's fire exclusion policies. The amount of unprotected land fell from more than 140 million acres prior to 1942 to under 40 million after 1956.[30] This huge decrease, almost all of which was in the South, was attributable mainly to the Forest Service's acceptance of light burning in southern pine forests, which led southern forest landowners to join Forest Service–funded fire protection districts.

It took nearly 50 years to go from Chapman's 1908 paper about the need for fire in longleaf pines to the Forest Service's complete acceptance of such fire in longleaf and loblolly pines.[31] As much as anything else, this delay was caused by the fire suppression mentality created by the blank-check law and the Forest Service's hunger for power, whetted by the Clarke-McNary Act. Even then, the Forest Service continued for at least another two decades to resist prescribed fire in the West except as a way of disposing of debris after timber cutting.

CONGRESS REPEALS THE BLANK CHECK

After World War II, the Forest Service acquired all sorts of aerial means of detecting and fighting forest fires. Initially, it didn't cost much to drop water from an obsolete bomber onto a fire. But costs quickly rose as WWII–vintage planes were replaced by newer models and water was replaced by fire retardant. Rising fire suppression and aircraft costs led the Office of Management and Budget (OMB) in 1975 "to wonder what kind of return we were getting for our money."[32] The Forest Service chief ordered a review of fire planning methods, which concluded that they were "basically sound and rational."[33] That didn't satisfy either the OMB or Congress, so in 1977 the Forest Service ended the 10 a.m. policy and endorsed more prescribed burning in the West.[34]

In 1978, in what appeared to be the most dramatic change in fire policy in 70 years, Congress repealed the blank-check law. Starting in the 1980s, Congress tried to appropriate fire suppression funds like any other line item. It gave the Forest Service a fixed budget for suppression, usually around $110 to $125 million a year. If costs in one year exceeded that amount, the Forest Service was expected to pay for them out of other funds. For this purposes, the agency turned to the Knutson-Vandenberg (K-V) reforestation fund and then repaid the K-V fund in later years when costs were lower than $125 million. The K-V fund was originally created by the Knutson-Vandenberg Act of 1930, which authorized the agency to keep a portion of timber receipts for reforestation and—after 1976—wildlife, recreation, and other forest improvements. This fund typically had hundreds of millions of dollars at any given time, making it the perfect source of emergency suppression funds.

These policy shifts led to subtle yet significant changes on the ground. Rather than try to minimize the number of acres burned at any cost, Forest Service fire managers focused suppression strategies on containment within natural boundaries. This led to more acres of fire but supposedly lower costs and greater firefighter safety. Some forest managers eagerly began experimenting with letting fires burn—mainly in wilderness areas—but because of various restrictions the Forest Service continued to aggressively suppress more than 99 percent of all fires. As late as the year 2000, for example, the Forest Service allowed only 60, or 0.5 percent, of the 11,729 fires detected on national forests to burn.[35]

With help from mild weather, these actions succeeded in reducing Forest Service fire suppression costs. Actual suppression costs fell from an average of $125 million a year (adjusted for inflation to match the dollar in 2002) in the mid-1970s to an average of just $61 million from 1977 to 1984. Costs reached $167 million in 1985, which wouldn't have been a problem since costs dropped to $115 million in 1986.[36] If costs had remained below $125 million for a couple of years more, the Forest Service would have quickly repaid the deficit from 1985. But they did not: the great California fires of 1987 and the Yellowstone and Alaska fires of 1988 cost the Forest Service a total of $722 million, which was $472 million more than the $250 million Congress had given the agency for fire suppression in those two years.[37]

It is well known that the 1988 Yellowstone fires dealt a setback to the Forest Service's hesitant let-burn policy, as the secretaries of agriculture and the interior directed federal agencies to suppress all fires until after they had completed fire management plans that carefully described the conditions under which fires would be allowed to burn. What is less well known is that the 1987 and 1988 fires dealt an even more severe setback to efforts to control fire suppression costs.

CONGRESS LOSES ITS NERVE

If the 1910 fires tested Congress's willingness to sign a blank check, the 1987 and 1988 fires tested Congress's willingness to resist returning to the blank check. After paying the $472 million deficit out of the Knutson-Vandenberg fund, the Forest Service pleaded with Congress to restore the fund so that the agency would not run out of money for reforestation and other K-V activities. Congress responded by tripling the Forest Service's annual firefighting appropriation to $375 million in 1989. But no end was in sight: 1989 costs were $335 million, and 1990 costs were $254 million. The Forest Service publicly fretted that it would run out of reforestation dollars, so Congress finally gave the agency a supplemental appropriation of nearly $280 million in 1990 to repay the K-V fund.[38]

In losing its nerve and failing this test, Congress effectively restored the blank check. Even though the blank-check law was no longer on the books, the Forest Service now knew that Congress would reimburse fire suppression costs when they exceeded budgeted levels. Money was abundant once again, and forest managers no longer felt pressured to constrain costs. Technically, Congress still gives the Forest Service a fixed amount of money for firefighting. But if costs exceed that amount, the president can let the Forest Service spend more out of an emergency contingency fund. The president rarely, if ever, says no to the Forest Service, which has drawn on this contingency fund every year since 1993. In the decade ending in 2001, Congress gave the Forest Service $3 billion for presuppression, $2.3 billion for suppression, and $2.4 billion in contingency funds—nearly two-and-one-half times the amount provided for the same activities in the previous decade.[39]

Between 1950 and 1990, the Forest Service's fire program was eclipsed in size and prestige by the agency's timber program. Driven at least in part by incentives created by the Knutson-Vandenberg Act of 1930 and other laws that allowed forest managers to keep an unlimited share of timber receipts, timber sales grew from around 3 billion board feet in 1950 to 11 billion in 1980. But after 1990, timber sales quickly declined to 4.5 billion board feet in 1993, and to less than 2 billion board feet per year in the first decade of the 21st century.[40] Some people began to question whether the Forest Service had a future.

It did have a future, and that future was once again fire. Large fires in the late 1990s, in particular the Los Alamos fire in 2000, led Congress to begin a firestorm of spending. This included increasing the Forest Service budget for reducing fuels in the national forests ("fuels treatment") from less than $10 million a year in the early 1990s to well over $200 million a year a decade later, and presuppression budgets from $175 million a year in the early 1990s to more than $600 million a year a decade later.[41]

THE BLANK CHECK ON THE GROUND

The blank check still governs much of what the agency does. Under a policy adopted after the Yellowstone fires, federal land managers are not allowed to let fires burn until they have written a fire management plan. Yet as late as 2001, the General Accounting Office criticized the Forest Service and Department of the Interior for not having written fire management plans for most of the lands in their jurisdiction.[42] Thanks to the blank check, the agency has plenty of money to put out fires, but it claims it lacks the appropriations needed to write fire management plans.

Few, if any, fire management plans allow fires to burn outside of the large wilderness areas that cover less than 18 percent of national forestlands. Forest Service policy also only allows fires to burn in wilderness areas if they have natural causes; human-caused fires need not apply. Since only about 12 percent of fires have natural causes, something less than 2.2 percent (a little less than 18 percent times 12 percent) of fires on national forestlands are likely to qualify. So it is not surprising that, in 2003, the Forest Service allowed only 1.8 percent of the fires detected on national forests to burn.[43]

Even if a fire qualifies for "wildland fire use" (Forest Service terminology for letting fires burn), managers may decide to suppress it anyway. The paperwork required to let a fire burn is more formidable than that for suppressing fires. "Stricter planning and documentation requirements exist for management of wildland fires where resource benefits are a primary objective," says a Forest Service fire guide.[44] Managers who decide to let a fire burn must prepare a short-term risk assessment, a complexity analysis, a needs assessment, fire behavior predictions, and a long-term risk assessment. This makes it a lot easier to simply suppress fires than to let them burn. The Forest Service probably did not put barriers in the way of managers who want to let fires burn just so that it could maximize emergency suppression funds. But without the blank check, the agency would be much more eager to consider letting fires burn if it would save money.

When the Forest Service decides not to let a fire burn, the initial suppression effort is paid for out of presuppression funds. If that effort fails, emergency funds can kick in. Then fire commanders may decide to pour enormous resources on the fire. Firefighter Peter Leschak tells of "Mr. Mud," the nickname of an air attack supervisor who "had a well-deserved reputation for initiating and sustaining extremely aggressive air assaults." Leschak adds that "his personal record was 22,000 gallons of fire retardant dumped on a five-acre fire," which is about a gallon every 10 square feet or (as Leschak puts it) a 12-ounce bottle of beer on every square foot.[45]

Firefighters such as Leschak all tell stories of profligate spending on fires. "The Forest Service tries to put out fires by dumping money on them," firefighters commonly say. One Forest Service employee confided to me that his district had enough funds to pay its staff only 11 to 11.5 months of the year—and relied on fires to fill in the two- to four-week gap. Firefighters don't mind spending money on fires, since that is the source of their pay; Leschak notes that firefighters call smoke clouds "money bubbles" because they are "ensuring more paychecks for somebody."[46]

SOLUTIONS

What are some alternatives to a blank fire-suppression check that wastes taxpayers' money and leads to bad forest management? To be successful, any solution has to somehow persuade Congress that it is no longer responsible for saving people from fire. It is not enough to argue that the Forest Service should follow a particular prescription, such as putting firebreaks around homes and other structures. As long as members of Congress are tempted to "be heroes" by spending more money on fire suppression, federal agencies will face incentives to manage land poorly.

University of Maryland professor Robert Nelson thinks the only solution is to turn federal lands over to the states.[47] This would get Congress out of the picture, but, aside from the political infeasibility, there is little evidence that the states do much better at land management than the federal government.[48]

My own preference is to fund each national forest, park, or BLM district out of its own receipts. Centralized bureaucracies would be replaced by boards of directors elected by "friends of the forest/park/ district" whose membership would be open to anyone interested in paying a nominal fee. The boards would have a trust obligation to manage the lands in their care for the public good and would fund that management out of user fees, which—in most cases—would come mainly from recreationists.[49] Each board would find the best fire solution for their situation, whether by joining local forest protection districts, buying fire insurance, or simply letting fires burn. Of course, this alternative faces only a little less opposition than Nelson's.

A less radical idea is to purchase insurance to cover costs during especially severe fire years. Appropriations could be based on spending during an average fire year. Congress would allow agencies to carry over unspent funds from mild fire years. The insurance companies would have an incentive to work with the agencies to make sure their costs were as low as possible. The problem is that the insurance industry may not be able to handle this much coverage. Until recently, Oregon was the only state whose fire protection districts bought insurance for severe fire years, but their coverage was canceled after the 2002 season.

Another solution is to dismantle federal fire programs and turn fire suppression on federal lands over to state and local fire protection districts. Some Bureau of Land Management districts already rely on fire protection districts to do their fire suppression. As with private landowners, federal agencies would pay annual fees to the fire protection districts—typically based on the number of acres of land each manages—which would be used for fire suppression. Since the fees would be paid out of appropriations, it is not clear that this would give the agencies much incentive to reduce fire risks.

Given the uncertainties about all these ideas, the best policy for now would be to try each of them on two or three forests, parks, or districts. A pilot program could be evaluated after five years to see which worked best, which might lead to improved policies for all federal lands. A group of timber industry leaders, environmentalists, and Forest Service officials known as the Forest Options Group has made a similar proposal for national forests, which shows that such an idea might receive support from a broad range of interests.[50]

The default solution is to continue with the de facto blank check. This policy will cost taxpayers billions of dollars a year, allow the continued destruction of homes and other structures, and discourage sound management of many federal lands. The blank check will probably prevail as long as Congress has the money and as long as environmentalists and the resource industry remain polarized. But if the interest groups can find an incentive to get together, or if Congress is motivated by a major fiscal crisis, some reform will probably be adopted.

To be successful, any reforms must recognize that the Forest Service is not a machine that automatically carries out the will and intent of Congress. Instead, it is a very human institution made up of people who respond to political pressures, fads, and—most important—to budgetary incentives. The people who manage the national forests and other federal lands may have the best of intentions, but if those intentions conflict with their incentives, the incentives all too often prevail.

This is not to imply that public land managers are venal or corrupt. As in the case of the debate over light burning versus complete suppression, land managers will always have disagreements among themselves over the best policies and techniques. Given a level playing field, such disagreements would be resolved through experience and research. But when agencies face such powerful incentives as the blank check, experience is ignored and research suppressed in favor of the policy that most benefits from the incentive.

In adopting reforms, then, Congress must take care that the incentives created by those reforms, and the budgetary process as a whole, are aligned with Congress's goals for the public lands. Incentives should not favor one resource over another or one policy over another but instead provide a level playing field for land managers and land users to work together to find the best mix of resources and policies. Such incentives must encourage solutions that respond to local conditions, not one-size-fits-all policies. Incentives should reward efficiency, not waste; the sustained production of multiple uses, not a single dominant use; and a fire policy that effectively minimizes the long-run costs of fire damage and suppression, not one that maximizes short-term budgets. This is a tall order, but one that can be met if Congress applies the right combination of policies and budgetary programs.

THE WAR ON WILDFIRE

Firefighting and the Militarization of Forest Fire Management

TIMOTHY INGALSBEE, PH.D.

THE FEDERAL GOVERNMENT CONDUCTS WILDLAND FIRE *suppression through a militaristic paradigm—as fire "fighting" in a "war on wildfire." This war enjoys strong public support because most people are kept unaware of the social and environmental impacts, or "collateral damage," of aggressive firefighting. The endless and escalating war against wildfire represents an increasing militarization of forest management—to the detriment of democracy as well as ecology.*

▼

The year 2005 marked the 100th anniversary of the creation of the U.S. Forest Service and, along with that, a century-long war against wildland fire. Every summer for a hundred years running, the U.S. government has made war in America's wildlands under the pretense of "fighting" fires. Under the command of the Forest Service and other federal land management agencies, tens of thousands of young people are sent into the forests of the West to suppress wildfires at a cost to taxpayers of more than a billion dollars a year.[1] Organized with military structure and discipline, and supplemented with an armada of firefighting vehicles, heavy equipment, and aircraft, Uncle Sam's firefighting army is unrivaled in size and expense in the world.

Helping to perpetuate this annual seasonal conflict are powerful political and economic interests with vested stakes in the perpetuation of warfare. A new "fire-dependent" class of government agencies and private corporations has accumulated enormous power and profits from firefighting. Indeed, a new "fire-industrial complex" is rapidly developing. If not for the deepening fiscal crisis of the federal government—due to tax reductions for the wealthy elite, and foreign military adventures—the war on wildfire would have provided the perfect patriotic instrument for big government and big business to siphon surplus dollars from the taxpayers' till.

Unlike other wars the U.S. government has waged, the war on wildfire faces very few voices of dissent. The mainstream news media enthusiastically cheer on the war effort with as much hype and hysteria as they can muster within a hackneyed story frame: "catastrophic wildfire" is a hellish force, homeowners are its helpless victims, and wildland firefighters are our stoic heroes defending civilization against destructive chaos. Considering that most of what people know about wildfires comes from a comic book (*Smokey Bear*), a cartoon movie (*Bambi*), and the corporate press, it is no wonder that firefighting enjoys widespread popularity with the public. There is no hint of protest emanating from peace activists, religious leaders, concerned taxpayers, or frightened parents. Wildland firefighting is regarded as the "moral equivalent of war."[2]

Wildland firefighting strikes a resonant chord in the American people because it epitomizes the Western Enlightenment's crusade to control and exploit nature, and it continually reenacts the uniquely American experience of conquering the western frontier and all the wild forces of nature, from American Indians to grizzly bears to wildfires. But in this great modern crusade to conquer one of the most powerful forces of nature, even though we may win all the battles against blazes, society has embarked on a war it cannot hope to win. Indeed, each successfully contained and controlled fire offers only a fleeting victory over an "enemy" that returns year after year with escalating power and fury.

As a youthful firefighter, I relished the hard work, the adventure, the income, and esprit de corps of firefighting. I truly believed back then that I was protecting the environment, and defending public forests against primal forces of destruction. I eagerly carried out my orders with a gung-ho attitude and few gripes, and I look back at those years of service as a ground-pounding grunt on the fire line with great pride. But over time my youthful idealism waned. I directly witnessed or participated in suppression actions that were sometimes more damaging to the land than the fire itself. Many times our crew's actions were grossly inefficient or completely ineffective given the prevailing weather, terrain, and fuel conditions and became huge wastes of taxpayer dollars and resources. Occasionally we were ordered to do extremely hazardous things that put our health and safety at greater risk for no apparent reason. Later, after learning through the science of fire ecology that our efforts to contain and control all wildfires did not protect the land, but actually degraded many of the natural values I cherish and, ironically, made the landscape more prone to future severe wildfires, I developed in hindsight a critical perspective of wildland firefighting.

I have the utmost respect and affinity for the women and men who continue to serve as wildland firefighters, for there will always be a need for some kind of suppression actions to protect specific places from unwanted fire behavior or fire effects. But my conscience compels me to challenge the militaristic paradigm that frames fire suppression practices and dominates federal fire management programs. Current and future generations of fire crews and the public they serve must come to realize that there are alternatives to "fighting" fires and making warfare on wildfire. Unfortunately, decades of flawed forest fire prevention education have induced a collective amnesia in American society, making people forget our species' vital relationship to fire on the land since time immemorial and inhibiting the public from envisioning alternatives. A vision of human communities that can live safely and sustainably with wildland fire seems to most people more like a remote fantasy than a historical fact or a future possibility. Hence, it seems entirely normal, natural, almost "instinctual" in modern American culture that humans always fear and "fight" wildland fires.

Before any alternative vision can emerge, there must first be a realization that a problem exists, and then a recognition that there needs to be change. Certainly there is the popular perception that a wildfire "crisis" exists, but most people believe that aggressive firefighting is the solution rather than one of the problems fueling the crisis. Remarkably, despite all the billions of tax dollars consumed, millions of acres scorched, and thousands of firefighters toiling in the federal fire suppression program each year, the public is kept largely ignorant about the strategies and tactics, methods and motives of firefighting. I therefore want to describe some of the standard techniques of firefighting and explain the environmental damage and ecological degradation—the "collateral damage," if you will—firefighting inflicts upon natural resources, specific wild places, and society at large. As billions upon billions of tax dollars continue to pour into the coffers of the fire-industrial complex under the edicts of the National Fire Plan, I fear that this recent escalation of the war on wildfire signals an ever-increasing militarization of forest management that portends dangerous consequences for both native ecosystems and democratic society.

TRENCH WARFARE TACTICS: FIRE LINE CONSTRUCTION

Fire management is currently in the midst of a minor technological revolution with the aid of satellite- and computer-based mapping and modeling systems. Yet when it comes to controlling forest fires, the same basic technique has endured relatively unchanged for the last century: A containment line is cut around the perimeter of the fire to stop its spread. Once the fire is encircled by this fire line, steps are taken to "mop up" or extinguish all remaining burning material within a couple hundred feet of the perimeter. It then becomes a waiting game for a change in weather or the simple passage of time before the fire eventually dies.

Constructing a fire containment line, or "fire line," involves removing all live and dead vegetation to create a relatively narrow strip of bare mineral soil that cannot ignite or burn. Consequently, fire line construction causes a number of adverse environmental impacts: it kills and removes vegetation; displaces, compacts, and erodes soil; degrades water quality; fragments forest stands; and leaves unsightly scars on the landscape. There are two basic kinds of fire line: hand lines cut by crews on foot using hand tools, and dozer lines cut by bulldozers and other heavy equipment. Generally, hand lines are shallow trenches approximately 4 feet wide, bordered on the outside by 15-foot-wide swaths from which all small trees and brush have been cleared. Dozer lines can be 18 feet wide, or even as wide as an interstate highway. Perhaps the most recent technological "advance" in fire line construction involves the use of explosives. Devices like "blaster cord" (an electric detonating wire wrapped with explosive material) are used to blast soil and brush for fire lines, especially on very steep, rocky ground that would be too hazardous for crews working with hand tools. Using explosives on erosive ground is a clear example of the military mindset at work in fire suppression—literally blasting away the earth to stop a fire.

Although hand lines are narrow, they are also built on steeper, more rugged terrain where bulldozers cannot maneuver. Steeper slope gradients increase the erosive power of water, causing many hand lines to become instant gullies, sluicing soil right down into forest streams and fouling fish habitat. Dozer lines have a qualitatively more severe impact from the steel blades ripping up the ground, followed by the huge tank treads alternately chewing and crushing the exposed soil. The berms caused by dozer lines tearing up mountainsides create canals that can alter the hydrological flow, channeling water and silt directly into streams.

The destructive impacts of logging roads on water quality and fish habitat are well documented, but the impacts of suppression dozer lines are arguably worse. Logging roads are engineered and constructed with at least some attempt to minimize erosion, but not so dozer lines, for they are quickly carved into the landscape with little foresight or planning—literally by the seat of the pants of the dozer operators. When dozer lines are cut into roadless areas, they also create long-term visual scars that can ruin the wilderness experience of roadless area recreationists, and in many cases they become new, unmapped "ghost" roads that enable unauthorized or illegal off-road-vehicle users to invade unroaded wildlands. Along with ORVs come a host of other impacts such as invasive weeds, wildlife harassment and poaching, and arson fires.[3]

Hikers encountering fire lines, especially dozer lines, are hit with the unmistakable impression of entering a scarred battlefield. The ground surface is torn up and lifeless. The carcasses of large trees line the berm of soil and boulders left by the dozer's blade, literally heaved over at their roots by the earth-gouging machines. Fire lines essentially represent trench warfare tactics: stop the "enemy" from advancing and wait until its ammunition and fuel are spent, then subdue the few surviving embers. On some of the recent siegelike "superfires" (greater than 50,000 acres in size), fire lines have been hundreds of miles in length. In addition to primary fire lines—which during "indirect attack" strategies are often cut miles away from the fire's edge—there are also often secondary or "contingency" fire lines that are built at an even greater distance. Most of these contingency lines will never be touched by fire but leave the earth scarred by the instruments of fire combat.

After the fire has been declared contained and controlled, some modest mitigation actions are taken to reduce the negative environmental effects of fire lines; for example, a few shallow "water bars" are dug into the line to help reduce erosion. But usually only the final perimeter lines are "rehabbed," while all the burned-over interior fire lines are left for nature to deal with. Given enough time, natural recovery processes can almost erase the effects of low-intensity fires—but not the effects of firefighting. Eroded soil from fire lines is essentially a permanent loss, and the fragmentation of forest cover caused by fire lines leaves wounds that may fester for decades after the battle was fought.

CHEMICAL WEAPONS: FIRE RETARDANTS

Some of the most dramatic scenes of firefighting incidents are those of World War II–vintage air tankers swooping down over mountain ridges to bomb the forest canopy with red-colored fire retardant chemicals. If dumped in the right places at the right times under the right conditions, retardant can temporarily delay ignition in vegetation. But firefighters must be positioned on the ground ready to take advantage of retardant drops, for the chemicals slow down but do not stop fires from spreading. If retardant is dumped at the wrong place or time, or in the wrong conditions, or if there are no firefighters at the ready, the drops are basically expensive but futile attempts at controlling fire, and are routinely scoffed at by firefighters as "political shows" and "photo-drops" meant to impress the public on the evening news.

Although the effects of retardant chemicals on fire behavior last only a few hours, their toxic effects on vegetation and wildlife can endure for weeks.[4] A host of different chemicals are used during fire suppression operations. One of the most popular retardants degrades into cyanide at levels highly toxic to fish and frogs, but all retardants can be harmful to the aquatic environment.[5] The federal government tries to assure firefighters and the public that retardant chemicals are benign to humans and function merely as fertilizer that will help get new plants growing inside a burned forest. But the seemingly beneficial fertilizer is deadly to aquatic wildlife when it is dumped or washes into streams. Toxic plumes of nitrogen, phosphorus, and ammonia instantly kill fish and insects in streams, and initiate algae blooms (sudden growth in algae) in ponds, lakes, and reservoirs that kill fish more slowly by consuming all the oxygen in water. When dumped on the ground, the fertilizer in retardant can stimulate the growth of invasive weeds, which often enter remote sites from seeds inadvertently transported by firefighters and their equipment.[6] In spring 2000, the U.S. Forest Service briefly suspended the use of cyanide-leaching retardants because of their adverse effects on aquatic species—effects known by laboratory scientists since the 1950s[7]—but within a few weeks, the agency lost its nerve and reversed policy.[8] Millions of gallons of retardant chemicals have spewed from bombers in the last five years, and will continue to flow under the assumption that the toxic effects of the chemicals are less harmful than the effects of wildfire. Indeed, the Environmental Protection Agency exempts fire retardant from the Clean Water Act because its use is considered a "cataclysmic release" intended to prevent assumed greater destruction to the environment by wildfire.[9] Yet in the case of aquatic wildlife, this assumption is invalid: it is doubtful that many frogs, for example, are fried by fires, but who knows how many have "croaked" from cyanide coursing through their veins? In essence, fire retardant is a chemical weapon, and the deliberate dumping of hundreds of millions of gallons of fire retardants every year on forests constitutes chemical warfare.

FELLED BY FRIENDLY FIRE: OLD-GROWTH TREE CUTTING

Backcountry hikers are often stunned to see giant blackened stumps deep in the interior of wilderness and roadless areas where logging is restricted. These stumps mark the sites of former battlefields in the war on wildfire. Most people believe that firefighting "saves trees," but another component of fire line construction involves tree cutting. Both large overstory and small understory trees are felled during suppression incidents. Routinely, teams of professional loggers are hired as contract firefighters to sweep through the forest on search-and-destroy missions to drop all large dead trees ("snags") in areas where fire-fighters might be working. Burning snags are the most hazardous kind of trees to firefighters: they can fall across fire lines and allow the fire to escape containment, or worse, they can fall onto firefighters with deadly consequences. But these snags are also the most valuable trees to certain rare or endangered wildlife species that use dead, dying, or "defective" trees for food or shelter. Indeed, if Mother Nature could choose which of the trees were most precious and in need of protection from wildfire, it would likely be snags. Perversely, these are the very trees most likely to be felled during suppression.

Firefighting in the Forest Service is fundamentally interlinked with logging—before, during, and after a wildfire. In fact, the agency's primary motivation for fighting fires is not to save trees for the sake of habitat or scenery, but to save them for the sawmills. Over the last 30 years, the Forest Service has responded to growing public opposition to its timber sale program, in which logging companies are allowed to clearcut old-growth stands for private profit on public lands, by con-cocting new excuses for logging native forests. Beginning in the early 1990s, the federal government announced a "forest health crisis," claiming that insects, disease, and fires were running rampant through the public's forests and that "dead and dying" trees needed to be logged to prevent "catastrophic wildfires." After numerous scandals— including the notorious "Salvage Rider" of 1995, in which the nation's environmental protection laws were suspended to allow logging corpo-rations to cut live, intact ancient forests in the name of "forest health"—federal officials constructed a new rationale for logging.

Beginning in 2000, the forest health crisis morphed into what could be called "fire hazard hysteria." Logging proponents argued that millions of acres of public lands needed "mechanical fuels reduction" and "thinning" (that is, commercial logging) to remove trees before they could burn. A related form of prefire logging involves the con-struction of "fuel breaks" designed to function as potential fire lines to combat future wildfires. California, for example, has a long history of grandiose fuel-break programs going back to the 1930s. From the 1950s through the 1970s, during the height of the Cold War with the former Soviet Union, nearly 2,000 linear miles of fuel breaks were

carved into national forests in California to prepare for conflagrations
in the event of thermonuclear war.[10] Apparently no one in either the
Forest Service or the Department of Civil Defense dared to ask
whether anyone would be willing or able to fight forest fires after Los
Angeles and San Francisco were incinerated. Regardless, this "Dr.
Strangelovian" fuel-break program provides one of the clearest historical examples of the fusion of firefighting and logging with military
objectives.

While prefire fuel-break projects are gaining popularity in the
Forest Service, the most common form of fuel-break timber sale comes
in the guise of postfire "salvage" logging. There are numerous examples throughout the Pacific Northwest of "salvage" timber sales
designed to create clearcut corridors as fuel breaks, lessen what the
agency calls "resistance to control," and provide sites for allegedly
"safe, efficient" firefighting. For example, in the Biscuit Fire Recovery
Project in southern Oregon, the largest Forest Service timber sale proposal in modern history, the agency intends to construct 309 linear
miles of fuel breaks throughout the Siskiyou National Forest.[11] Much
of this fuel-break system will permanently maintain the fire lines left
from the 2002 Biscuit Fire suppression operations.

The problem with these fuel-break "Maginot Lines" is that, like
the German army in World War II, under the right weather conditions
wildfire is highly mobile and is able to outflank or fly over these fixed
fire line positions. Moreover, historically the Forest Service has failed
to properly maintain or even map extensive fuel-break systems. Once
the commercial timber has been extracted, the agency has had little
financial incentive to return to these sites. Consequently, in the wake of
these cut-and-run logging projects, soil disturbance and increased sunlight enable grasses and brush to grow prolifically in the place of trees,
making these sites vastly more flammable than the original forest
cover. Far from being sites for safe, efficient firefighting, as the Forest
Service claims they will be, these fuel breaks will become extremely
hazardous fuel beds that would be death traps for any firefighters
seeking sanctuary in them.[12]

Tree felling occurs during a wildfire, too. Increasingly popular are
"feller bunchers," big logging machines that mimic Dr. Seuss's "Super-
Axe-Hacker" machine,[13] as they have the ability to simultaneously cut,

delimb, and deck trees ready for commercial log truck removal. Put to work cutting fire lines in dense tree stands, feller bunchers create long, linear clearcuts that resemble power line paths minus the towers and cable. A recent Forest Service trend is to offer postfire timber sales of trees cut alongside fire lines. For example, in the Siskiyou National Forest, the agency quickly sold nearly half a million board feet of mature and old-growth trees that were felled during the Biscuit Fire. For the cash-hungry Forest Service, this sale sets up a perverse incentive to cut excessive fire lines in order to generate timber sales soon after the smoke has cleared.

Opportunistically using the public's socially conditioned fear of forest fires, the Forest Service raises the specter of "catastrophic wildfire" as a justification to log old-growth trees before, during, and after fire. Essentially the same arguments are used for prefire thinning, postfire salvage, and fuel-break timber sales: to reduce fuels, prevent fires, and prepare for firefighting. In so doing, the Forest Service has apparently reversed means and ends: whereas the agency formerly fought fires in order to log trees, nowadays it is logging trees in order to fight fires. But it seems that the same logic that fueled the American war in Vietnam is justifying these logging-for-firefighting schemes: we have to destroy the forest in order to save it.

SCORCHED-EARTH TACTICS: SUPPRESSION FIRING OPERATIONS

Although fire suppression is a key factor in the exclusion of fire across the landscape, one of the many paradoxes of firefighting is that it involves a considerable amount of fire *lighting*. The old adage "Fight fire with fire" is routine procedure: firefighters are ordered to ignite many fires while suppressing wildfires. In the most routine kind of suppression firing operation, called "burnout," firefighters ignite low-intensity fires adjacent to the fire line in order to consume all surface fuels and "blacken" the fire line, thereby strengthening and securing it. Nearly every linear foot of perimeter fire line cut on each large wildfire is burned out by firefighters, a practice that can add up to a lot of acreage, depending on the total amount of fire line cut. In another kind of firing operation, called "backfiring," firefighters ignite a high-intensity fire near a wildfire's flaming edge, with or without a secured containment line, in order to consume fuels and change the direction or force of a spreading wildfire. Together, burnouts and backfires can add up to more than a third of the total burned acreage on large wild-fires.[14]

Large unburned "green islands" in the interior of wildfires are often deliberately burned out to eliminate any pockets of unburned fuels within wildfire perimeters. Such burns tend to shorten the time period needed to declare a wildfire under control, but creating large, contiguous blocks of blackened soil and vegetation can homogenize fire effects, reducing the beneficial landscape diversity of fire patterns, commonly called the "fire mosaic." As well, pockets of unburned soil and vegetation offer critical refugia for native flora and fauna, espe-cially soil microfauna, which provide vital sources of biological activ-ity needed for natural postfire recovery processes. Thus, although burnouts tend to be lower-intensity underburns, uniformly applied to the land they can greatly reduce the beneficial effects of natural fires as agents in creating landscape, structural, and biological diversity.

Backfires represent classic scorched-earth tactics, aiming to starve a wildfire of any burnable fuel by creating a solid swath of charred vegetation. When the timing and conditions are right, a backfire is effectively pulled into the main fire and can lower its rate of spread and intensity. But in the "kill zone" between the backfire and wildfire, radiant heat can reach peak levels, causing extreme fire line intensity and high mortality of vegetation and wildlife entrapped between the two flame fronts. When the timing or conditions are wrong, backfires can literally *backfire* and burn in the wrong direction or never meet up with a wildfire. In 2000, 113 families in Montana's Bitterroot Valley sued the Forest Service over an errant backfire that destroyed their homes and businesses.[15] Less known is the fact that the fire that raged through Los Alamos, New Mexico, in 2000 and destroyed over 200 homes was the result of a backfire ignited on the Cerro Grande Fire at Bandelier National Monument.[16] In 2004, a firefighter for the California Department of Forestry was killed when a backfire unex-pectedly changed direction and overran her crew.[17]

The two kinds of suppression firing operations are now fusing into a hybrid of backfiring/burnout that for the sake of brevity has been dubbed "backburning." Large-scale backburns are increasingly being ignited on wildfires during extreme weather conditions or in rugged, steep terrain with limited road access, such as wilderness and roadless areas. These conditions eliminate any pretense of these being "controlled" fires. Backburning is also commonly used on fire "complexes" (clusters of small fires, usually ignited by several lightning strikes in a given area) to merge the small fires together into a single large fire perimeter. It is generally more efficient to cut fire line around a single large area than around many small areas. But backburns designed to merge fire complexes also greatly add to the total acreage of wildfires and are a key factor in the recent phenomenon of what that media have dubbed "megafires" (wildfires several hundreds of thousands of acres in size). The news media are typically obsessed with reporting the size of fires but rarely question fire managers about the role backburns are playing in the increasing size and severity of wildfires.

The federal government deploys a wide arsenal of incendiary devices to ignite burnouts and backfires: handheld drip torches and fusees (similar to road flares); flares launched by special pistols and mortars; truck-mounted flamethrowers called "terratorches"; helicopters with suspended barrels of flaming diesel fuel called "helitorches"; and aircraft-delivered incendiary bomblets called "ping-pong balls." In some cases, ordnance is delivered to ground crews who are ordered not to return to fire camp with any of it unused. Ironically, after igniting burnouts, firefighters must "mop up" the area closest to the fire line to extinguish all visible smokes. The working mantra of firefighters is "First we light it, then we fight it." The experience of firing out forests and torching up whole mountainsides in the dark rivals the adrenaline rush of military combat, with one exception: there is no enemy firing back.

The irony of fighting fire with fire is that, with the right motives and methodology, these suppression fires could be the most natural and least damaging way to manipulate fire spread and mitigate fire severity. Indeed, using natural ignitions as trigger points for the times and places to burn, firefighters could utilize burnouts and backfires to steer flames into areas that planners have previously identified as needing to burn for various ecological restoration reasons, and to stop fire from spreading into areas that for social reasons should not burn, such as near towns. Unfortunately, suppression firing operations are usually implemented without any concern for ecological effects or restoration objectives; instead, they are part of a single-minded focus on containing and controlling wildfire at any cost. Consequently, managers often order firefighters to ignite backburns during severe fire weather conditions, or to light fires at the base of steep, densely vegetated slopes, and these methods tend to maximize mortality of big trees and to minimize any semblance of human control over the spread or intensity of the backburn.

The most perverse aspect of suppression firing operations involves their relationship to postfire salvage logging. Given the knee-jerk institutional response of the Forest Service to try to "salvage-log" all the commercially valuable scorched trees it can, the larger the wildfire, the larger the salvage sale. This issue first came to light after the arson-ignited 1991 Warner Creek Fire in Oregon, where many of the units proposed for postfire salvage logging were in the same areas deliberately burned out or backfired during suppression operations. Worse, many of these areas were designated habitat conservation areas in an inventoried roadless area that had strict prohibitions against commercial logging, but these restrictions were eliminated by the Forest Service simply because the stands had burned.[18] More recently, in the 1999 Big Bar Fire in northern California and the 2002 Biscuit Fire— both of them extensively backburned and coincidentally the largest wildfires in the country those years—the Forest Service proposed salvage timber sales in old-growth reserves and roadless areas that were backburned.[19]

Some forest conservationists are highly suspicious: the supposed coincidence that large-scale backburns become large-scale salvage timber sales they see as a matter of conspiracy. In my opinion, large-scale backburns are ignited not with future salvage logging in mind, but with the myopic obsession to stop wildfires from spreading even if they do not threaten any human communities or are having beneficial ecological effects on the land. Regardless of the intentions of fire managers, the objective effects are clear: high-severity suppression firing operations provide Forest Service timber managers with an opportunistic excuse to log areas that otherwise would be prohibited or restricted from further commercial logging. The agency has thus

revised the firefighter's mantra to "Light it, fight it, *and log it.*" The
close relationship of suppression firing to "salvage" logging raises the
question, Are firefighters being used as de facto timber sale marking
crews, using fusees and drip torches instead of paint cans and plastic
ribbons?

THE WAR AGAINST THE WILD SISKIYOUS:
BISCUIT FIREFIGHTING ACTIONS AND EFFECTS

The Klamath-Siskiyou bioregion in northern California and southern
Oregon is world renowned for its complex geology, rushing wild rivers,
fire-sculpted forests, and rich diversity of endemic plants. Comprised
of fire-adapted ecosystems in the largest wilderness and roadless area
complex on the Pacific coast, this rugged, remote landscape is truly the
realm of Sasquatch. It is the last place on earth that should have been
the target of a military-style suppression siege, which happened during
the 2002 Biscuit Fire. Adding further insult to injury, the Forest
Service followed up with a proposed half-billion-board-foot salvage
timber sale in the Biscuit burn—the largest Forest Service timber sale
proposal in modern history.[20]

On the Biscuit Fire, approximately 405 miles of fire line were constructed in the course of two months. This compares to the 500 miles
of logging roads in the entire Siskiyou National Forest that were plotted and put in over the course of 60 years. Many fire lines used existing logging roads, hiking trails, primitive jeep trails, or even old fire
lines from the 1987 Silver Fire—which were easy to locate since they
had not revegetated after 15 years' time—and "improved" them with
bulldozers.[21] Other fire lines were plotted through virgin forest stands
in unroaded areas.

Fire lines were carved into steep and highly erosive slopes comprised of serpentine soils. These sensitive soils are especially prone to
erosion and landslides, and are slow to revegetate. Out of approximately 160 total miles of dozer lines, over 57 linear miles were carved
into serpentine soils. Moreover, at least 9 miles were constructed within
fish-bearing riparian zones, and dozers plowed straight across streams
nearly 200 times.[22] During certain periods of the fire, 30 bulldozers
were running 24 hours a day.

In this area with world-class wild rivers, Biscuit Fire suppression records reveal that in just one management zone of the fire, half a million gallons of fire retardant were used, at a cost of nearly $600,000. On one day alone (August 14), nearly 105,000 gallons were used. It was further documented that fire retardant was dropped within some riparian areas, including heavy direct applications into tributaries of the lower Illinois Wild and Scenic River.[23] Retardant dumped onto serpentine soils poses the danger of fundamentally altering the soil chemistry, to the detriment of the endemic plants that have evolved with the ability to grow on these naturally nutrient-poor soils, and to the benefit of invasive weeds, which take advantage of the fertilizer in the retardants.

Countless big old trees were felled during fire line construction, mop-up, and hazard-tree removal. There were several near-miss accidents and reports of falling crews engaging in "recreational" tree falling. Fire lines constructed in the northern portions of the Biscuit were located in areas of mature conifer forest, and many old-growth trees were felled with dozers and feller bunchers. Even before the wildfire had been contained, fire line logs were limbed, bucked into 40-foot lengths, and then decked for ease of commercial removal. At the time of this writing (August 2005) the Siskiyou National Forest managers have authorized the commercial extraction of approximately 10 million board feet of so-called "hazard" trees alongside roads and fire lines, nearly all of which had been burned out during the fire. Another 372 million board feet of trees are planned for "economic recovery" in salvage timber sales.

An issue gaining much attention from local conservationists is the scale and severity of suppression firing operations: a historically unprecedented amount of backburning occurred during the 2002 Biscuit Fire. The press and politicians made a lot of noise about the 500,000-acre size of the fire—the largest wildfire in Oregon in over 100 years. Yet, according to independent analysis conducted by this author, approximately 107,000 acres were burned from suppression firing operations in just one of four total incident management zones of the fire, covering roughly one-third of the total wildfire area. (I was not able to examine records for the other three zones, but anecdotally it is known that extensive backburning occurred in these areas, too.)

For several locations, suppression records reveal that the backburns were the major source of active burning or fire spread. In some areas, burnouts were ignited along fire lines that were located as much as 8 miles away from the main fire. For some of the backburns, aerial ignition was used even though the ignition sites were located on steep slopes with heavy fuels that managers predicted would cause extreme fire behavior. Some backburns lasted several days, burning strips for over 30 miles and encompassing 30,000 acres in a single firing operation.[24] In fact, some of the Biscuit backburns were larger than most of the other wildfires burning elsewhere in Oregon during the 2002 fire season.

The firing operations are credited by the Forest Service with helping to successfully contain the wildfire, stopping its spread toward the communities located in the Illinois Valley. However, during the episodes of major fire spread, winds were actually pushing the wildfire westward away from the communities, thereby facilitating the successful control of the large-scale burnouts. Ironically, the closest the Biscuit Fire ever came to the rural communities in the Illinois Valley was the result of the backburns, not the wildfire itself.

The backburns ran the full range from low-severity underburns to high-severity crown fires. In terms of the environmental effects of the backburns, the *Biscuit Fire Recovery Project Environmental Impact Statement* presents some stark figures: in two old-growth reserves that were extensively backburned, 40,536 acres of late-successional habitat and 37,244 acres of suitable spotted owl habitat were severely burned. Arguably, the starkest indication of the severity of the suppression firing operations is their association with proposed salvage logging units: approximately 11,275 acres of the Forest Service's proposed salvage logging units are located in areas that were backburned.[25]

Vexing questions remain as to whether the wildfire would have naturally spread to the areas that were backburned, and if it had, would it have burned with the same intensity or severity as the backburns? A more troubling issue from an ethical standpoint is the Forest Service's intention to salvage-log areas that were previously protected from commercial logging (for example, wildlife habitat reserves and inventoried roadless areas) because they were intentionally burned by suppression firing operations. One thing is clear, though: even if the Forest Service's salvage timber sale is stopped and the logging industry does not pluck another blackened tree from the burn, the war on wildfire has claimed another victim, for some of the worst "war crimes" occurred in one of the best wild places left in the continental United States.

DECLARING MARTIAL LAW: PUBLIC CLOSURES AND FOREST MANAGEMENT BY GOVERNMENT DECREE

The war on wildfire not only is devastating to native ecosystems, it also has dangerous consequences for democratic society. Every large fire suppression incident is declared a "state of emergency" in which the normal rules of government behavior do not fully apply. First, citing concerns for "public safety," the local Forest Service supervisor declares a federal closure around a wildfire area. Federal closures prohibit citizens from entering public land a manager declares off-limits. Armed Forest Service guards enforce closures, and citizens can be arrested for trespassing on their own land if they trek past a closure boundary. Some of these closures can be sweeping in size; for example, the entire Siskiyou National Forest—over 1,700 square miles—was closed to the public during the Biscuit Fire. Citizens could not set foot anywhere on the forest, even on areas several miles away from the wildfire or any suppression activities.

Second, the nation's environmental protection laws, as well as Forest Service standards and guidelines, conservation strategies, and general forest plans, are all essentially unenforced, if not suspended, for the duration of the "state of emergency." Bedrock conservation laws such as the National Environmental Policy Act, the National Forest Management Act, the Endangered Species Act, and the Clean Water and Clean Air acts are not applicable to the actions of the federal government while it is engaged in emergency fire suppression. In this situation, forest management is totally at the discretion of Forest Service managers unencumbered by the normal inconvenience of complying with federal laws, agency regulations, or public involvement.

The federal government does not engage in environmental analysis or citizen input in fire suppression operations, and the Forest Service believes there really is no law or regulation that constrains it from doing anything anywhere it chooses to fight a fire—it is a virtual state of martial law. Suppression plans are drafted by incident commanders who hand them down the military-style chain of command to fire crews who must carry out orders without question. Funded with nearly unlimited tax dollars at their disposal from the Emergency Fire Fighting Fund, "nameless, faceless bureaucrats" working as fire incident commanders are truly all-powerful technocrats. But managing public forests by government decree is fundamentally antidemocratic, and suppressing and excluding fires that burn in fire-dependent ecosystems is fundamentally antiscientific and antiecological.

It is time for the American people to force federal land management agencies such as the Forest Service and Bureau of Land Management to include scientists, conservationists, local communities, and other concerned citizens as fully informed partners collaborating in forest fire planning and management. One important first step in this process is to subject the fire suppression program to a rigorous scientific analysis using the provisions of the National Environmental Policy Act (NEPA). The direct, indirect, and cumulative environmental effects of firefighting are inflicting a serious toll of damage and destruction on some of America's most precious wildlands. The time to do NEPA analysis is not after a fire ignites, but long before. Prefire NEPA studies should perform trade-off analyses comparing the social and environmental effects of suppression actions versus prescribed fire, managed wildland fire use, and wildfire without any management actions.

The federal government will never voluntarily take the initiative to do such suppression studies; thus it is going to require a national educational campaign, litigation, and legislation to compel the federal land management agencies to utilize and comply with NEPA regulations in planning fire management programs. Federal land managers must fully disclose to the American people the safety risks to firefighters, economic costs to taxpayers, and environmental impacts to fire-adapted ecosystems from aggressive fire suppression. Federal fire management must become less technocratic and more democratic if it is to succeed in fulfilling the Forest Service's motto of "caring for the land and serving people."

STOPPING THE WAR ON WILDFIRE

Formerly perceived as the forester's worst foe, wildfire has paradoxically become the federal government's best friend. Fire allows federal agencies such as the Forest Service access to money, lands, and power inconceivable in any other circumstance. As American society at large marches steadily toward a more militarized culture with the war against terrorism, the ongoing and escalating war against wildfire promises to militarize forest management—to the detriment of democracy as well as ecology. It is quite likely that in the near future, the equivalent of the Department of Homeland Security will be created for fire management: a superbureaucracy combining all the fire programs of all the federal land management agencies. Fire management will be put on a permanent war footing; citizen rights to information and access to their own lands will be highly restricted; laws will be changed to exclude court oversight; and government actions will be less politically or legally accountable.

The recent "100 Years' War" against wildland fire promises to become a millennial crusade, since there will be no final victory; indeed, as long as the sun shines, the rain falls, vegetation grows and dies, and lightning strikes, there will be fires. It is a given that wildfires will continue to ignite and burn in America's wildlands, but it is not a necessity that we should react to them in a militaristic manner, "fighting" all fires and battling all blazes with no regard for the risks, costs, and impacts of suppression. The warlike approach to wildfire suppression and fire management will go on racking up untold social and ecological costs until an informed citizenry forces the government to end its warmongering. For numerous ecological and social reasons, a new, peaceful coexistence with wildlands and wildfires must be established, based on a renewed respect for the wildness of nature.

To stop making warfare on wildfire does not mean that society should stop all fire suppression. As long as there are human communities and natural resource values at risk of unwanted damage from wildland fires, there will always be a need for some suppression activities. But the very meaning and definition of suppression must change on the level of a paradigm shift to reflect a new, emerging restorationist ethos, and to conform to some system of democratic citizen involvement and government accountability. Suppression should no longer be practiced as the myopic attempt to aggressively contain and control fires to the least possible size or duration. Rather, suppression should be redefined to mean reducing unnatural severity of fires while per-

mitting them to burn as much acreage as safely possible to meet ecological restoration objectives.

One suggestion for putting this new suppression philosophy into
practice is to stop doing "perimeter control" to corral every wildfire
within a containment line, and thereby avoid all the resource damage
associated with fire lines, especially when conditions are ideal for ecologically beneficial burning. Instead, firefighters should switch to a system of "point protection" to keep flames away from specific sites of
high social or ecological value that cannot tolerate burning. This way,
more acreage can burn under appropriate environmental conditions
for desired fire behavior and fire effects while our limited suppression
forces are focused on those places where they will have the maximum
need and effectiveness. In effect, suppression will involve strategic
management actions to try to slow or steer fires rather than simply stop
them. Ultimately, what is most needed is a deep, long-range vision of
ecological integrity coupled with a restoration ethos to ensure that
every fire management action, including suppression, meets carefully
planned socioecological objectives.

To fully actualize the social, cultural, and ecological changes necessary to enjoy a peaceful coexistence with wildland fire will require
the creation of new language, for the discourse of fire management is
thoroughly tainted with war metaphors. From terms such as "initial
attack" to the foundational concept of "fire*fighting*," this language is
not only flawed, it is inaccurate. The bottom line is that although we
call it *fire*fighting, we are not really fighting fires; we are fighting
forests. We are not making war on wildfire; we are making war on
wildlands. Perhaps someday in the future the label *firefighter* will
become anachronistic and obsolete, to be replaced by terms more representative of the fire restoration mission ahead, such as *fire guider* or
pyrotechnician. Such efforts to change social consciousness through
altering common language will require, as renowned fire historian
Stephen Pyne suggests, a "new narrative" crafted by novelists, artists,
philosophers, pundits, and poets.[26]

Wildland firefighters are widely regarded as heroes by the public,
and it will indeed take some heroic firefighters to stand up and speak
out for fundamental change in fire management programs, policies,
and practices. Other fire professionals—including scientists, man-

agers, and educators—will also need to articulate a vision for progressive change. Rural homeowners preparing their properties for wildfire will also need to serve as model citizens showing their neighbors how to live with fire. It will require something similar to a "peace movement" to end the current militaristic style of fire suppression. The vanguard of this movement will most likely be ground-level wildland firefighters who can speak truth to power as "veterans for peace" with unrivaled moral authority. It is time for this war to end, to declare "victory" and go home, and to invest the "peace dividend" from the billions of dollars wasted in futile fire suppression in long-term projects to prepare fire-adapted communities and restore fire-adapted ecosystems. Engaging in ecological restoration promises not only to heal the land but also to heal our (dis)connections with the land, and to reconnect us with our species' long-forgotten ecological legacy as torchbearers of terrestrial fire.

Part Six

ELIMINATING THE SMOKESCREEN

TOWARD AN INTELLIGENT FIRE POLICY

INTRODUCTION

Learning to Live with Fire-Dependent Ecosystems

The public fears fire. In general, this is a rational response. None of us want to see our homes set ablaze or our lives threatened by flames. Yet protecting homes from a fire caused by a wood stove or bad wiring should not be put in the same category as protecting homes from a wildlands fire. Wildlands are, by definition, influenced by natural processes, and fire is one of the most important in shaping landscape features and values. Not only is it undesirable to control fires across most of the landscape, it isn't working. Wildfires are larger than ever. More homes and lives are being put at risk or lost each year.

We possess a war mentality toward fire because we view fire as an enemy. What we need is a change of perspective to see fire as a creative and life-sustaining process—a force we live with, rather than fight. An important part of this transformation is to make our communities safe, so people feel comfortable with wildfires, while at the same time restoring fire to the landscape. Each of the following essays tries to address these issues.

Timothy Ingalsbee looks at prescribed burning and prescribed natural wildfire use as a fire management tool. While not necessarily the only method, or the most effective in certain areas, prescribed burning is an ideal tool for reducing fuels and fire severity near buildings and communities, and for this reason I have chosen to highlight this technique in this book. Although prescribed fire is commonly used by land management agencies, its role needs to be greatly expanded. As Ingalsbee points out, a fraction of the money now used to fight fires is allotted to prescribed burning. If we put the same resources currently expended on fighting fires toward restoring fire to the landscape and fireproofing homes, our communities would be far safer, our forests and rangelands far healthier, and the risk of catastrophic blazes far less.

While prescribed burning is a useful tool, it should not replace good community and land use planning. Crystal Stanionis and Dennis Glick explore how uncontrolled sprawl contributes to the ever-increasing costs of fire suppression. Building a house in an isolated canyon or perched upon some mountaintop may seem romantic, but such homes are infinitely more difficult to defend against flames than homes constructed in a compact city or town. The authors argue that firefighting and fire suppression costs are one of the uncounted expenses of sprawl not currently considered in land use debates.

John Krist suggests in his essay that taxpayers and politicians who respond to fire losses with public funds for rebuilding in the same fire-prone landscapes are exacerbating the conflicts between humans and fire. Rather than discouraging such unwise decisions, the current system insulates people from the costs as well as the consequences of their choices by spending millions or billions of dollars in trying to keep these structures from burning up—and by reconstructing them with disaster relief funds in the aftermath of a blaze.

Finally, Brian Nowicki and Todd Schulke round out this section by describing the many ways in which individual homeowners and communities can reduce the risk from wildfire, and thus the presumed "need" for fire suppression. Simple measures such as removing trees near homes and using nonflammable roofing materials can greatly diminish wildfire hazard. Placing more responsibility on homeowners and communities for their own fire protection would redirect the war on wildfire toward learning to live with wildfire.

KEEP THE GREENFIRE BURNING

Deep Ecology and Prescribed Fire

TIMOTHY INGALSBEE, PH.D.

SINCE TIME IMMEMORIAL, HUMANS HAVE INTENTIONALLY *applied fire to the land for a multitude of sociocultural, ecological, and resource benefits. There is a vital need for prescribed burning to help restore fire processes in fire-excluded ecosystems; however, gaining public support for increased prescribed and wildland fire use presents a number of challenges. Deep ecology and ecocentric consciousness can help promote prescribed burning for both ecological and cultural restoration.*

▼

Twenty-five years ago I participated in my first forest fire, and it has never let go of my imagination since. It sparked a whole new education and career path for me, fueled by the passion of that first encounter with flames in the forest.

Ironically, the forest fire came from my own hands and those of my coworkers in the U.S. Forest Service. I was but a teenager then, hired to be a wildland firefighter. Much to my astonishment, my first field assignment was not to go chase a smoke or stop a wildfire, but, instead, to start a fire! I was not told anything by my superiors as to the reasons why we were burning, other than it was a "prescribed fire ecology burn." Whatever the heck that meant, I did not have time to ask, for they put a lit drip torch in my hands and sent me trooping into the forest to burn it up. It was at that moment, though, that the two concepts of prescribed fire and fire ecology first became linked in my mind.

Over the course of the week-long burn operation in a mature ponderosa pine stand, my initial horror at our actions was quickly replaced with fascination at the process of ignition and combustion. I soon learned how to regulate my firing technique and modify the speed and direction of fire spread. I was bewitched by the mystery and beauty of forest fire from that moment on. This love of fire has only deepened when I occasionally return to the site of my initial "baptism by fire" and observe the most wonderful parklike grove of big, old ponderosa pine trees standing amid a verdant green carpet of bunchgrasses and wildflowers.

THE HISTORY OF PRESCRIBED BURNING

The vast majority of people living in modern urban-industrial society have no experience whatsoever with prescribed burning and are almost completely ignorant of its history, purposes, and benefits to society and forest ecology. The prehistory of prescribed burning goes back to the dawn of the earliest hominids, who were the original "smokechasers." At first, early humans were opportunistically drawn to lightning-caused fires and learned how to scavenge food in the wake of fires. Eventually, they learned how to sustain fires by sheltering them from the elements, to steer fires by variously adding or subtracting fuel, and to ignite fires in new places by carrying torches or burning embers overland.[1]

More recently, Native Americans were the most expert practitioners of intentional human-caused ignitions, doing what is called "light burning" and "spot burning" of specific sites for practical purposes.[2] Indian fires stimulated natural regeneration processes in ways that enhanced the bounty of their harvests and hunts while also sustaining the habitat needs of a number of other species and communities. Over the span of hundreds of human generations, many vegetation communities composed of fire-dependent species evolved with fire regimes that were highly influenced by the unique frequency, timing, pattern, or intensity of Indian burning, which either supplemented or in a few cases superseded lightning-caused fires.[3] Thus, for example, the grassy "prairies" in coastal redwood communities were maintained by regular Indian burning in an ecosystem that otherwise would not have received sufficient lightning ignitions to maintain that specific fire-dependent community.[4]

The westward expansion of Euro-Americans brought a new kind of intentional burning that could hardly be described as "light." Trailblazers, miners, and settlers all set highly destructive fires in order to remove vegetation for the passage of wagon trains, expose surface mineral veins for prospecting, and convert forest stands into farmsteads.[5] Ironically, while many forested areas back East were converted to farms through the use of these land-clearing fires, many prairies in the Midwest converted back to forestlands from the lack of fire following the genocide and forced removal of the indigenous inhabitants who had been lighting prairie fires. With the closing of the frontier toward the end of the 19th century, Euro-Americans' indiscriminate burning ceased, but the rise of cut-and-run industrial logging caused enormous wildfires—some of the deadliest wildfires in U.S. history—as railroads spewed sparks onto vast stumpfields strewn with logging slash and flammable brush.[6]

When the U.S. Forest Service was created at the beginning of the 20th century, it disdained the legacy of light burning, deriding it in racist terms as "Paiute" forestry. Considering light burning as contrary to "modern scientific forestry" because fire killed conifer saplings and thus threatened its goal of maximizing timber yields, the agency sought to exclude all human-caused fires from the landscape.[7] Suddenly, by government decree, the age-old practice of light burning was outlawed, and the few Native American fire practitioners who continued their craft were subject to arrest as alleged "arsonists." However, in California the federal agency had to contend with private timber owners and ranchers who strongly advocated for the continued use of light burning. Loggers argued that light burning kept hazardous surface fuels low, and thus prevented more severe wildfires from destroying the big trees. Ranchers argued that annual burning maintained pastures and stimulated healthier forage for grazing livestock. A contentious public debate between the Forest Service's policy of fire exclusion versus the proponents of prescribed fire use raged up until the 1930s, when the agency won out over its critics and fire exclusion became the law of the land.[8]

Fortunately, the Forest Service's attempted fire exclusion was never absolutely successful. Natural lightning and accidental human-caused ignitions provided a regular supply of burning in the West. More significantly, private foresters continued to use light burning in the piney woods of the Southeast. Even though it was conducted for agricultural rather than ecological reasons, this use of fire in forestry was treated almost like an official state secret by the Forest Service. The agency was concerned that "mixed messages" about fire use in the East would confuse the public and undermine the campaign for fire exclusion in the West. The Forest Service literally censored any public disclosure about controlled burning from its own scientific literature.[9] To this day, the majority of people living outside the Southeast are almost completely ignorant of that region's successful program, which annually burns hundreds of thousands of acres of public and private land.

The practice of "prescribed" burning finally migrated out West thanks to the tireless efforts of two pioneering fire ecologists, Harold Weaver and Harold Biswell. Weaver, working for the Bureau of Indian Affairs, and Biswell, a professor at the University of California, Berkeley, conducted several successful field experiments from the 1940s to the 1960s using broadcast underburning to thin "dog-hair" thickets of trees. Biswell, from his position in the university, helped to educate and inspire many of today's most esteemed fire scientists and managers, who continue his work promoting prescribed burning. For much of their careers, both Harolds were seen as heretics by their peers in forestry, but the empirical evidence of their successful burns eventually won over their professional critics. Prescribed burning finally became part of accepted federal policy when it was adopted by the National Park Service in 1968 and authorized by the U.S. Forest Service in 1978.[10]

THE ECOLOGICAL BENEFITS
OF PRESCRIBED BURNING

There can be huge differences in the intentions and outcomes of prescribed burns depending on whether they are intended for industrial, agricultural, or ecological objectives. For example, there are "conversion" burns (which change the vegetation from one type to another— for example, from a forest to pasture); "entry" burns (the first of a series of planned burns on a site from which fire has been excluded for a significant time); and "maintenance" burns (regularly scheduled burns to maintain a desired vegetation community or fuel load level). Depending on these different purposes and the site-specific environmental conditions of vegetation, terrain, and weather, prescribed burns can use several different ignition devices and patterns. Although prescribed burning is touted as a science, fuels managers understand that it is as much a craft skill and a landscape art. The ecological effects of prescribed fires are thus highly dependent on the social objectives, management techniques, and environmental conditions of the specific sites where the fires are ignited.

Some of the many ecological benefits of fire on vegetation include helping to prepare seedbeds by recycling downed woody debris into available nutrients and removing litter to create bare soil; stimulating the flowering, fruiting, and seeding of understory vegetation; and reducing thickets of trees, thus limiting the competition for moisture, nutrients, and sunlight.[11] On a landscape scale, prescribed fire can help restore and maintain the "fire mosaic" of patches of various ages of trees, and supply a vital disturbance process that helps regulate the structure, function, and species composition of specific sites. Although most prescribed burns aim for low to moderate severity, fires of varying intensities are necessary depending on the type of ecosystem; in general, "pyrodiversity promotes biodiversity."[12]

THE RESOURCE BENEFITS
OF PRESCRIBED BURNING

In fire-dependent communities, ecosystems, and landscapes that have been adversely altered by past fire exclusion policies, prescribed burning has obvious benefits by restoring a vital ecological process. But advocating for a program of prescribed burning from a biocentric position will be extremely difficult given the ideological dominance of anthropocentrism in mass culture and especially land management agencies. An emphasis on the resource management benefits of burning could help to increase support for the program and lead to more ecological objectives in the future. The effects of prescribed burning in reducing wildfire risks and hazards to lives and property are the most cited: by reducing the number of small-diameter trees, brush, downed limbs, and needles, prescribed burning can reduce the size, rate of spread, intensity, and severity of wildfires by reducing the kinds of fuel that carry flames.[13]

But there are several other resourcist arguments to tout—for example, prescribed fire is a superb silvicultural tool for reducing logging debris (i.e., "slash") and preparing logged sites for tree planting (a.k.a. "reforestation").[14] It has great potential as a thinning and pruning tool that stimulates faster tree growth.[15] Prescribed fire is also a superior range management tool for stimulating production of grassy forage for livestock, and for eliminating tree encroachment into grazing sites.[16] Burns also produce brushy browse for game species like deer and elk, and create habitat structures like snags and logs for nongame wildlife species.[17] All of the above arguments can be used to help build popular support for prescribed fire use from erstwhile opponents of fire and other natural ecosystem processes.

The beneficial thermal effects derived from low- to moderate-severity fires cannot be fully replicated by other chemical or mechanical or biological methods.[18] Indeed, there simply is no technological substitute for fire in reducing hazardous fuel loads and at the same time restoring the health and biodiversity of fire-adapted ecosystems and fire-dependent vegetation. For a variety of industrial, agricultural, and ecological objectives, then, prescribed burning should be a prime management tool widely accepted by the public. Unfortunately, prescribed burning has vastly more skeptics than supporters among the public, politicians, and the press.

THE SOCIOCULTURAL BENEFITS OF PRESCRIBED BURNING

Prescribed fire operations offer excellent opportunities for educating citizens about a whole array of fire management issues. Agencies such as the National Park Service are increasingly publicizing their prescribed fire programs in their educational literature and interpretive displays, but the day must come when all agencies allow burn operations to become public events open to on-site citizen observers and news reporters. A few "public participation" prescribed burns like this could have a huge impact on changing people's perceptions and attitudes about prescribed and wildland fires. This is a real necessity, for all those homes and communities located in fire-prone places or fire-dependent ecosystems will eventually have to rely on some form of prescribed burning for any hope of securing their property and rediscovering a long-term, sustainable relationship with the land.

The social benefits of prescribed fire are more direct within certain Native American communities, for prescribed burning often restores or maintains plant and animal habitats desired for traditional foods, medicines, and crafts. Fire also helps to maintain certain historic landscape conditions on sacred sites needed for religious ceremonies and spiritual practices. And prescribed fire can help expose Native American artifacts and enhance archaeological research. But fire can also destroy some archaeological objects and make others vulnerable to looters, so there is a trade-off in burning cultural heritage sites. Least mentioned but most important, prescribed burning restores an indigenous cultural tradition that has long been suppressed.[19]

THE PROBLEMATICS OF PRESCRIBED BURNING

In spite of its many social and ecological benefits, prescribed burning also has many practical and philosophical challenges that limit its use, effectiveness, and acceptance. First, prescribed burning can be difficult and potentially dangerous to implement. In many but not all areas, the adverse effects resulting from past fire suppression, commercial logging, and livestock grazing have greatly increased hazardous fuel loads and thus made forests more flammable and less resilient to fire.[20] In some places, terrain and fuel conditions make it almost impossible to ignite and control fires without some kind of manual or mechanical pretreatment to prepare sites for the safe reintroduction of fire. Even with careful planning and preparation, there is always the possibility that weather conditions will suddenly change, causing a fire to burn out of control. At the onset of an ecological restoration program to reintroduce fire, accidental wildfire will be a risk, but gradually, as ecosystems are restored, this risk—while never completely disappearing—will greatly diminish.

Second, prescribed burning can be expensive to plan and implement. Compared with other fuels reduction methods, prescribed burning is generally the least expensive, but it is still not cheap to burn places the right way. Proponents of commercial logging often tout that commodity timber outputs will offset the costs of using heavy equipment for "mechanical" fuels reduction, but very rarely do these timber receipts match the administrative costs of implementing these projects, and the inevitable environmental damage from commercial timber extraction is counterproductive to wider ecosystem restoration goals. Still, with prescribed burning projects, all expenses must be paid from appropriated budgets, with no potential sources of revenue.

Relatedly, in an odd twist of conservationist logic, some people think that burning fuels rather than using them for wood products is "wasteful."[21] The true calculation of waste must consider the net environmental impact of operations, for when felling trees and dragging logs across steep slopes results in soil erosion that silts up streams, this too creates waste. Additionally, most of the fuels that prescribed fires target are small-diameter surface fuels that have no market value. These fuels accumulate in ecosystems where summers are too dry and winters are too cold to support other decomposition processes besides fire. This biomass should rightly be recycled into soil nutrients, not extracted as "commodity outputs."

Despite the numerous ecological and sociocultural benefits of prescribed burning, some people will still be opposed to burning because they think it is ugly and unhealthy. In my opinion, to stand inside a giant sequoia grove where repeated fires have carved out immense charred "caverns" in tree trunks holding up towering green canopies is an awe-inspiring experience. Millions of tourists flocking to the sequoia groves seem to agree that burned trees can be beautiful. In low-severity fire regimes, the thinning effects of prescribed fires can help maintain beautiful parklike stands of widely spaced big, old trees with grassy, flower-carpeted understories; in ecosystems with mixed-severity fire regimes, fire creates a landscape mosaic of diverse age classes and vegetation types that is also visually appealing. With some modest amount of fire ecology interpretation to explain the goals and effects of prescribed burning programs, burned forests can actually become a scenic and recreational attraction.

Smoke is perhaps the Achilles heel of prescribed fire, doing more to constrain its use than any other philosophical or practical obstacle. Research has shown that in order to restore historic fire regimes on remaining wildlands in the lower 48 states, four to eight times more biomass must be burned, producing up to six to nine times more emissions than at present.[22] Even small amounts of woodsmoke can be unhealthy or intolerable to some people, especially individuals with respiratory ailments or allergic sensitivities to air pollution. In fire-dependent ecosystems like the giant sequoia groves of the Sierra Nevada, the poor air quality of California's Central Valley imposes serious restrictions on the ability of fire managers to light prescribed fires. For example, fuels managers in Yosemite National Park have been forced to prematurely put out prescribed burns when local residents complained about the smoke.

There are actually some ecological arguments justifying production of smoke from prescribed fires for the sake of biodiversity and forest health. For example, some species of tree lichens can absorb vital nutrients from woodsmoke, and smoke can help reduce some tree pathogens. But the most compelling argument is that the inevitable smoke produced from prescribed burning pales in comparison to the amount spewed by high-intensity wildfires burning in places where fuel loads are high because fires have been excluded. By using certain ignition techniques and setting fires under prescribed fuel and weather conditions, fire managers can control the amount, duration, and dispersion of smoke—they can "play the wind" to steer it away from communities. In contrast, high-intensity wildfires generate more total tonnage of smoke in larger particulate sizes, and it blows uncontrollably wherever the winds take it.[23]

A public education campaign must be developed to convey the message that fire-dependent forest ecosystems will inevitably burn, one way or the other, and that a smoke-free solution to managing forest fuels is therefore not available. The choice is between some control over smoke emissions in a prescribed fire versus no control in a wildfire. One must assume that the public would prefer to have less smoke coming from a series of carefully managed low-intensity prescribed burns rather than a lot of smoke all at once from a high-intensity wildfire. And in some places, people are simply going to have to learn to live with flames and smoke of one sort or another if they are to dwell sustainably within fire-prone landscapes.[24]

ALTERNATIVES TO PRESCRIBED BURNING?

The various technical, social, and ecological challenges to increasing the use of prescribed burning provide plenty of excuses for seeking other methods to manage forest fuels, but there really is no functional

alternative for the array of beneficial ecological functions performed
by fire. While pro-industry politicians push for increased logging,
spraying, and grazing projects to prevent "catastrophic" wildfires,
claiming that prescribed fire is socially unacceptable to use, the incredible irony is that under the smokescreen of wildfire suppression, we are
actually reintroducing management-ignited fires on a scale unimagin-
able by even the most ambitious fire advocate.

Using the logic of "fighting fire with fire," the Forest Service is
igniting huge backfires to suppress wildfires, especially in roadless and
wilderness areas. Backfires have been a significant source of burning on
large wildfires, influencing their size, shape, and severity, ever since the
"Big Blowup" of 1910.[25] But a major factor in the recent rise of
"megafires" is the increasing use of backfires and large-scale burnouts
during wildfire suppression operations; for example, on the half-mil-
lion-acre Biscuit Fire in 2002, over 100,000 acres burned from backfires that were ignited several miles away from the edge of the wildfire.[26]

Backfires are a reactive, emergency form of "prescribed" burning
conducted with the least planning and preparation, and often ignited
under the worst possible weather or fuel conditions that almost guarantee extreme fire behavior and severe fire effects. In contrast, proactive prescribed burns are carefully planned to occur under the best of
weather and fuel conditions for managing fire behavior and achieving
desired ecological effects. Yet a terrible double standard exists that
allows nearly all reactive backfires to escape public scrutiny and legal
accountability, while proactive prescribed fires are subjected to the
utmost regulatory restrictions and political opposition. There is unlimited funding for backfires, since the money comes from fire suppression budgets, but dollars for prescribed fires come from fixed fuels-
reduction budgets, which are often skewed toward "mechanical
thinning" or commercial logging projects. Worst of all, uncontrollable
backfires are celebrated as heroic acts by the news media, while
restorative prescribed fires that accidentally escape control are con-
demned as incompetent, almost criminal acts by demagogic politicians
playing to the news media.

Under the current insidious system of "controlled" backburning
for wildfire suppression, firefighters actually put in far more fire than
they put out. When backfires cause uncharacteristically large blocks of

severely burned land, they fail to "protect" the forest and further degrade, rather than restore, fire-dependent ecosystems. This paradox—starting backfires in order to stop wildfires—exacerbates what the renowned fire historian Stephen Pyne calls the "maldistribution of fire": In short, we have too much of the wrong kinds of fire occurring at the wrong places, times, and conditions, and not enough of the right kinds of fire occurring in the right places, times, and conditions.[27] It is time for elected officials and land managers to publicly acknowledge that the choice we face in managing fuels is not between fire and no fire, nor even between prescribed fire and wildfire, but rather between prescribed fire and backfire.

A DEEP ECOLOGICAL CRITIQUE OF PRESCRIBED FIRE

Deep ecologists and others who reject the use of wildlands for commodity resource extraction generally prefer prescribed burning—if they agree to any active fuel management at all—because it comes the closest to mimicking natural processes. But in addition to several practical and political challenges, there are also a few philosophical issues that can generate opposition to prescribed burning from a deep ecology standpoint. For one thing, the term "prescribed fire" is flawed since it utilizes the discourse of modern medicine and implies a paternalistic relationship between humans and nature. In essence, managers play the role of good doctors prescribing "treatments" to restore forest "health." This mentality compounds another discursive error in the concept of "controlled" burning. Like the quixotic quest to control nature, the attempt to exert absolute fire control is illusory and ultimately futile. Human ability to ignite or extinguish flames can delude us with a self-perceived Promethean power we do not really have, for humans cannot directly control fire itself, only influence its behavior indirectly through manipulation of the elements of the combustion process—heat, oxygen, or fuel. The numerous environmental variables of the wildland fire environment and their inherent dynamism further complicate and ultimately prevent humans from exerting direct or absolute control over fire. Thus, every prescribed fire is at best a tenuously "controlled" burn, but the labels affixed to the practice do not lend themselves to the appropriate level of humility that deep ecologists would argue is needed by managers manipulating natural habitats with fire.[28]

Finally, the most prevalent criticism of prescribed burning presented by deep ecologists is that it is an unnatural intrusion into wild nature. This is especially the case in regard to proposed burn projects in designated wilderness areas. The perception that prescribed burning is "interventionist," however, denies the cultural and ecological legacy of human fire use since time immemorial. Native Americans actively used fire on the land for a variety of reasons. Light burning was a routine, naturalized human activity, and over the span of hundreds of human generations where light burning was practiced, various species, communities, and landscapes coevolved with Indian fires. Though Native Americans did not indiscriminately burn the entire landscape, it is clear that in many places, including some current designated wilderness areas, the natural fire regime was significantly influenced by the cultural fire regimen.[29]

Given the overwhelming evidence of the adverse effects of fire exclusion on biodiversity and ecological integrity, and the subsequent dire need for fire *inclusion* to restore fire-dependent species and habitats, prescribed fire is an effective "minimum tool" for restoring protected natural areas such as designated wilderness.[30] Importantly, the development of a deep ecological restorationist ethic must guide efforts to apply the torch in wilderness and other sensitive wildlands.[31] If deep ecologists cannot support management-ignited prescribed fires in wildlands, the next best thing is "wildland fire use" (WFU), formerly called "prescribed natural fires." WFU involves careful planning for the eventuality of a natural lightning ignition during weather and fuel conditions that would achieve desired ecological effects and then, instead of aggressively suppressing the fire, allowing the fire to burn.[32] In most cases, WFU would require simple monitoring of the fire, but should a fire threaten to burn outside the prescribed area or set of environmental conditions, certain management techniques could be applied to keep the fire burning for ecosystem benefits. These management techniques would essentially steer the fire rather than stop it, and would apply minimum-impact suppression tactics to limit the intensity or severity of the flames rather than the size or duration of the blaze.[33]

Deep ecologists should strongly advocate for an increase in WFU at the same time as they actively oppose firefighting in wilderness and roadless areas.

DEEP ECOLOGICAL PATHWAYS
TO SUPPORT PRESCRIBED FIRE

Deep ecologists have a knack of making a virtue out of ecological necessity, but convincing the public of the need to do less firefighting and instead to do much more fire lighting will be a tough task. How can we possibly overcome the effects of the Forest Service's antifire Smokey Bear propaganda, the news media's hyped and hysterical coverage of wildfires, and the dominant social paradigm that makes it seem "natural" for humans to attempt to control wild nature and make warfare on wildfire? Fire ecologists have plenty of scientific research and empirical evidence to demonstrate the wisdom of restoring wildland fire, but to stimulate a gestalt shift in the way people relate to prescribed and wildland fire will require more than appeals to reason and facts.

Deep ecologists can begin by drawing upon the many positive metaphoric uses of fire in language, music, and art to inspire in themselves and others an awareness of our ecological selves as fire-dependent beings. As every wilderness campfire attests, people are naturally drawn to fire, are fascinated by its spectacle, and are acutely aware of its life-giving powers to provide light, warmth, food, security. And professional wildland firefighters will admit that they are drawn to the job not because they hate fire, but because they *love* it, and there are few jobs with as much joy and adventure as "dancing with flames" in the wilderness. The word for this innate, natural attraction and love of fire is *pyrophilia*. A product of our evolutionary development and rooted in our psychological and biological structure, it is a far more powerful motive force than our socially conditioned fear and hatred of fire, or *pyrophobia*.

An ambitious reeducation campaign via the arts and sciences is a necessary but insufficient process to nurture an ecocentric change in consciousness and rediscover our vital interconnectedness with fire. People must not only know it or believe it, they must *feel* it. A visceral

sense of ourselves as fire beings can be gained only by actually participating in prescribed burning and all the related tasks to plan, prepare,
ignite, manage, and monitor fires. People must experience for themselves the transformational powers of fire as a constructive, not merely
destructive, force in nature and society. With direct participation in
burning, a newfound respect will develop, with new metaphors created
to describe fire as a vital force, a virtual being, a welcomed ally in nurturing the health and diversity of life on Earth. The Native American
belief that it is a human duty to help Mother Earth renew and regenerate herself must be resurrected in the modern practice of prescribed
burning. Indeed, along with ecological restoration, cultural restoration
is a needed objective and outcome of burning. Deep ecology philosophy should help frame the changes in consciousness and culture
needed for broad public support of biocentric burning.

It has been too many years since I last used a drip torch to light-
burn the land, but that experience and connection have never left me.
I now confess to being a hopeless, incurable pyromantic. There is no
contradiction between deep ecology and the greenfire of ecological prescribed burning—it is a mission our species has been called to perform
for many millennia. I see the great promise of returning fire to the forest, restoring fire-dependent ecosystems, and ending our misguided,
ultimately self-destructive war against wildland fire. I yearn to see the
day my children will have the opportunity to participate in restorative
light burning, and thereby fulfill their own ecocentric duty to the land
with a loving torch in hand.

SPRAWLING INTO DISASTER

The Growing Impact of Rural Residential Development on Wildland Fire Management in the Greater Yellowstone Area

CRYSTAL STANIONIS AND DENNIS GLICK

THE GREATER YELLOWSTONE AREA IS ARGUABLY *the wildest place in the lower 48. It's a place where grizzlies roam, geysers erupt, and fires burn. In a time of increasing residential development, many individuals are working to ensure Yellowstone's grizzlies, wolves, and geysers remain. Yet very few lament how development affects wildfire—an ecological process common and native to Greater Yellowstone. Even fewer speak about what can be done.*

▼

Peruse any brochure featuring real estate in the Greater Yellowstone Area and you are apt to read glowing descriptions of rural homes that promise "a national forest right outside your door." That may be good news for the back-to-nature crowd, but it's bad news for the well-being of wildlife and wilderness, and particularly for ecological processes like wildfire—a keystone phenomenon that sustains the ecological integrity of Greater Yellowstone and many wildlands across the American West. But what's the connection between real estate and wildfire? The connection is this: residential development in Greater Yellowstone's fire-prone areas—its wildland-urban interface—leads to the suppression of wildfire—a process that has shaped Greater Yellowstone's landscapes for thousands of years.

For the most part, public land agencies, local governments, and even the conservation community have shied away from advocating limits to development in fire-prone areas. But for the health of our western wildlands, and the safety of people living at the wildland-urban interface, we need to view fire-prone areas in the same manner that we view areas subject to natural hazards like flooding, landslides, or seismic events: growth should be well managed, and in some cases prohibited. Although it has taken decades for the public to accept restrictions on growth in hazardous places like floodplains, we need to foster a similar attitude regarding our "fire plains." And we must recognize that while such an approach makes good sense, implementing growth management strategies at the wildland-urban interface will be a challenge.

BUILDING IN THE TINDERBOX

The Greater Yellowstone Area comprises approximately 19 million acres and includes portions of Montana, Idaho, and Wyoming.[1] At its core are the Yellowstone and Grand Teton national parks. Surrounding these parks are six national forests, three national wildlife refuges, Bureau of Land Management lands, and lands managed by individual states and landowners. It is a place known for its wilderness attributes: clean water, clean air, abundant wildlife, and eons-old ecological processes like wildfire.

Like many regions in the western United States, Greater Yellowstone is experiencing high population growth. From 1970 to 2000, the population increase of Greater Yellowstone was 61 percent, while that of the nation was 38 percent.[2] However, more alarming than the rate of growth is the pattern of growth: much of it occurs in rural areas,[3] a pattern that is predicted to continue if the character of current development remains unchanged.[4] Because of various environmental, socioeconomic, and political reasons, a good portion of the developed land in Greater Yellowstone is located in valleys, but increasingly, new development is springing up in forested foothills, and adjacent to forested public lands—rural places that are often far from community infrastructure and services. In light of the important role that wildfire plays in Greater Yellowstone's forests, the occurrence of this type of development—sprawl, which is creating a wildland-urban interface—is concerning.

Sprawl is concerning because scientists and public land managers agree that fire is an important ecological process and in many ways a hallmark of Greater Yellowstone.[5] Increasingly, however, development at the wildland-urban interface (WUI, pronounced *WOO-ee*) is dictating fire management actions throughout the region. Even in areas where land managers have the flexibility to allow lightning-caused fires to burn, aggressive suppression is pursued because of the risk to the WUI. Protecting the WUI is analogous to protecting human life and property, which is given the utmost consideration when deciding how to manage a fire. Protecting the WUI also allows land managers to justify fuel manipulation both at the interface and beyond, a tactic that is being used more and more in Greater Yellowstone. But are these actions justified? Who do they benefit? Who and/or what do they hurt? And are these actions based on long-term or short-term goals?

Ecological Disadvantages of Development in the Wildland-Urban Interface

From an ecological standpoint, a major disadvantage of development in the WUI is the inevitable suppression of the natural process of wildfire (not to mention facilitation of habitat fragmentation, bioinvasion, and human-wildlife conflicts). In Greater Yellowstone—*one of the last essentially intact temperate-zone ecosystems in the country*[6]—the suppression of a dominant ecological process such as wildfire runs counter to the notion that the area is being managed for its wild character or being managed for long-term ecological integrity (a notion that is critical and appropriate in a large portion of the public lands of Greater Yellowstone). Within Greater Yellowstone—in places like Grand Teton and Yellowstone national parks and the Absaroka-Beartooth Wilderness—management policy does recognize the powerful, positive force of wildfire, and allows lightning-caused wildfires to burn in order to maintain functional, thriving landscapes.

Nevertheless, as development in areas adjoining forested public lands increases, lightning-caused wildfires on these lands are being suppressed with increasing frequency, even in areas where wildfire has been tolerated, such as in the backcountry of Yellowstone. For example, managers can allow lightning-caused wildfires to burn "for resource benefit" (known as "wildland fire use") in the Jedediah Smith Wilderness in the Caribou-Targhee National Forest. However, if even one of a list of specific fire management criteria is not met, such a fire could be suppressed—for example, if adequate funding is not available to manage the fire; if acceptable air quality is not assured; if protection of property outside of the wilderness is not certain; or if social/political/economic assessments indicate that there would be significant impact to neighboring communities and residents.[7] These criteria are similar to those found elsewhere in other Greater Yellowstone administrative units with individual fire management plans. Using such criteria, managers can suppress fires that threaten development (i.e., property) in the WUI, as has been the case with numerous fires over the past few years (e.g., the Arthur Fire in east-central Yellowstone National Park in 2001).

Similarly, the WUI remains an obstacle for Greater Yellowstone managers who want to use, or expand their use of, wildfire as a management tool. For example, the Gallatin National Forest in northern Greater Yellowstone is considering allowing lightning-caused wildfires to burn "for resource benefit" outside of designated wilderness areas (currently the only areas where managers can allow such fires). While managers can foresee changing the general forest management plan to accommodate this management change (as other Greater Yellowstone national forests have done), they express skepticism over whether they would actually have the option of allowing a fire to burn anywhere outside of wilderness, because of the enormous WUI issues throughout the forest. Even the Gallatin's fire management plan makes several references to the WUI, explicitly mentioning development near the forest as a problem. The plan notes that development stems from rapid population growth in and around Gallatin County, with seemingly little attention given to potential wildfire risk.[8]

In conversations with federal fire managers in Greater Yellowstone, a common, undeniable theme emerges: development in the WUI leads to the suppression of lightning-caused wildfires in places they would otherwise be allowed to burn. Many are concerned about this issue, mostly for ecological and safety reasons. But they feel there is only so much they, in their federal capacities, can do to address the problem.

Getting at the Root of the Problem: Socioeconomic Disadvantages of Development in the Wildland-Urban Interface

The root of the problem of sprawl in fire-prone areas is the array of subsidies in both the public and private sector that promote development and lead to costly efforts to protect homes. For example, fighting wildfires at the WUI generally costs significantly more than fighting wildfires where there is no development. A review of the firefighting costs associated with wildfires in developed versus undeveloped areas in Greater Yellowstone is revealing. In the year 2000, costs associated with the 598-acre Hechtman Fire in the Jedediah Smith Wilderness within the Caribou-Targhee National Forest totaled $10,250.[9] In contrast, the 262-acre Siddoway Fire in the same year on the Caribou-Targhee National Forest near Wilson, Wyoming, cost over $229,000 for fire suppression efforts.[10] The dramatic difference in costs associated with these two fires is directly related to the proximity of human development. Similarly, the 4,470-acre Green Knoll Fire in the Bridger-Teton National Forest in 2001, also near Wilson, ended up costing over $13 million because of the extraordinary efforts necessary to protect expensive real estate at the edge of the forest.[11] In contrast, the 4,500-acre Boulder Creek Fire of 2000—in the same forest but in an area without wildland-urban growth issues (the Gros Ventre Wilderness)—cost $750,000.[12]

The fact that firefighting agencies pay more to fight fires when a WUI component is present gives people living in the WUI a firefighting subsidy; after all, they do not pay for firefighting directly out of their own pockets. While federal and state agencies are not to blame for individual decisions or for society's general lack of efforts to control growth, wildfire suppression by firefighting agencies sets the stage for even more development in fire-prone areas. Some charge that firefighting agencies have no incentive to change aggressive fire suppression efforts. Firefighting, like rural subdivisions, has become big business. In 2000 and 2002, firefighting totaled $1.3 and $1.6 billion, respectively,[13] and the National Fire Plan, established in 2000, ensures that firefighting budgets will remain high. With agency budgets dependent on fire suppression and prevention efforts, and with development pressure mounting in fire-prone areas, reversing this trend will be a challenge.

Another subsidy for sprawl in fire-prone areas is homeowner's insurance: many insurance companies still do not mandate higher rates of insurance for those living in the WUI, unlike the higher rates often faced by those living in floodplains. However, after recent "catastrophic" fires in southern California, and increasingly in the Rocky Mountains, insurance companies are threatening to raise rates, or to not provide coverage at all.[14] The communities of Greater Yellowstone and of the West in general further add to these subsidies through local taxpayer dollars that provide expensive services to far-flung developments in fire-prone areas. Such services range from police and fire protection to roads and road maintenance, schools and school busing, and other services whose costs would be considerably lower if the developments were located near existing services and infrastructure.

While it is true that rural development adds considerable revenue to the tax base, that revenue rarely covers the associated expenses. For example, economists Roger Coupal of the University of Wyoming and Andy Seidl of Colorado State University found that for every $1 in revenue received from dispersed rural residential housing in Colorado, county governments and schools expended $1.65.[15] Dozens of other similar "cost of community service" studies have also shown similar trends: dispersed rural development costs significantly more to service than agricultural/open-space lands.[16] Local governments subsidize this rural development, and the Forest Service subsidizes its fire protection.

Growing public awareness of the financial and human costs of defending fire-prone homesites from wildfire and a growing public recognition of the ecological importance of wildfire in many western ecosystems are slowly beginning to galvanize support for reforms in both fire and land use policies. As the Institute for Business and Home Safety, an initiative of the insurance industry, stated in 1998, "If we don't want to lose entire communities to a hurricane, if we don't want homes turned to ashes in a wildfire, let's stop putting them in harm's way, or at least manage development with natural hazards in mind."[17]

Shifting the cost of firefighting, insurance, and services from the public to individual property owners living in, or at, the forest edge is a necessary component of any strategy to reverse these development trends. For their own well-being, it is not a good idea to allow people to build in fire-prone areas. It is even less wise to subsidize that choice.

KEEPING PEOPLE OUT OF HARM'S WAY

Long-term solutions to problems associated with WUI development will require collaborative actions between public land managers, rural landowners, and local governments. Solutions must expand beyond oft-promoted efforts to "fireproof" forests and homes to include the notions of limiting development in hazardous areas in order to protect public health and safety; minimizing overall costs; and sustaining ecological processes.

A number of issues related to fire management are really problems associated with growth management. After horrendous loss of life and property from natural phenomena such as floods and earthquakes, many communities and the nation as a whole have taken steps to significantly limit or modify development in these hazardous areas. Fire is analogous to floods and earthquakes, but local governments have few incentives to take the often-unpopular regulatory actions needed to limit growth at the WUI. Additionally, why limit growth at the local level when the federal government seems willing to continue paying for most fire-prevention and suppression measures?

Another obstacle to meaningful efforts to manage growth is the deep-seated western belief that private property rights are sacrosanct, regardless of how one individual's land use affects others. This attitude is shared not only by many landowners but also by many government officials, and is sometimes reflected in public land management policies. However, as western landscapes fill up with homes, and as land use activities negatively affect adjoining property values, this attitude is beginning to change. As stated by University of Montana economist Thomas Power:

> We are used to doing things as we please and being left alone. Firefighting personnel and equipment camp out at our doorstep waiting to risk their lives to protect our homes. In addition, huge expenditures are made to try to guide the fire away from areas of human habitation. The federal and state governments pick up the tab. Some of us even demand that the entire forested landscape be fireproofed—as plausible a concept as stopping a hurricane or earthquake, at a cost of billions of taxpayers' dollars and untold environmental costs. Because of the public costs incurred partially because of private decisions, those decisions cannot be treated as entirely a private matter.[18]

In the Greater Yellowstone Area, counties vary in their recognition of wildfire as a natural hazard in their land use planning documents. When land use documents do address wildfire, language emphasizes hazard mitigation (building codes, construction materials) and public education. The concept of "defensible space" is readily advertised to homeowners as the responsible action to take if they live in the WUI. However, while defensible space can facilitate a safer environment for firefighters to fight wildfires, it can also create a false sense of security for homeowners. It also does nothing to address the inevitable loss of wildfire as an ecological process. Even if residents in the WUI make their homes "defensible," land mangers will not allow a wildfire to burn through a developed area. While we need to continue to apply fire mitigation at existing homesites, we also need to embark on a more regional approach to growth management efforts in landscapes prone to wildfire.

MANAGING GROWTH AS WELL AS WILDFIRE

Growth in Greater Yellowstone is inevitable, but a sprawl pattern of growth in the WUI is not. A variety of growth management tools—some regulatory, some voluntary; some incentive based, some market based—can be used to direct growth away from hazardous areas like the fire plain. Despite resistance to the use of these tools, local governments and private landowners have initiated efforts to limit or prohibit development in hazardous areas or in landscapes critical to wildlife. For example, several Montana communities have enacted building setbacks along floodplains, such as the 500-foot setbacks along the Madison River in Southwest Montana, and proposed subdivisions have been denied or significantly conditioned to reduce impacts on wildlife, as is the case with conditions imposed on the Canyon Club development in Teton County, Wyoming. These efforts need to be replicated on a broader scale, and the importance of maintaining ecological processes like wildfire needs to be viewed in the same way we recognize the importance of critical wildlife habitats.

A number of planning principles and tools could be utilized to manage growth in a manner that meets local development needs without sacrificing ecosystem functions that maintain our wildlife and wildlands. Developing and using community conservation plans and critical land protection tools are two ways in which we can achieve this goal.

Community Conservation Plans

Communities in ecologically important settings, such as those at the edge of national parks, should develop conservation plans that identify and prioritize important natural resources, including keystone ecological processes and critical wild habitats. These documents should identify for protection or special treatment hazardous areas such as the fire-prone WUI, floodplains, steep slopes, and so forth. Such conservation plans should become an important part of all planning efforts, including efforts pertaining to land use, transportation, and capital improvement (infrastructure). Development projects should be integrated into these conservation plans, avoiding construction in hazardous or ecologically important areas.

Critical Land Protection Tools

Once conservation values are identified, steps should be taken to limit land uses that degrade conservation values or put people in harm's way by allowing growth in hazardous areas. Land use planning tools— some regulatory, some voluntary, some incentive driven, and some market based—can create patterns of growth that are lighter on the land, fiscally responsible, and conducive to public safety and welfare. The most effective strategies for managing growth combine these different approaches.

Regulations, though not politically popular, have proven to be necessary both because of their direct impact on land use and because they encourage broader use of incentive- and market-based tools. Regulations may include zoning and subdivision regulations, which identify what can be built and where it can be sited on a landscape or subdivision scale; permitting standards, which provide specific guidance on how a development should be designed; and transfer of development rights, which serves as a mechanism for moving proposed development out of fragile or hazardous areas and into more suitable landscapes, among others.

Incentive-based approaches include purchase of development rights, in which willing sellers are paid to forego development options in areas that are important for their natural values; conservation easements, in which landowners voluntarily give up certain development rights and often receive significant tax benefits; density bonuses for clustering housing away from critical areas, in which developers are allowed to build more houses than existing zoning allows if they avoid building in critical areas; and other government-funded open-space and land conservation programs, such as the Conservation Reserve

Program and land exchanges, in which public lands are swapped for important private lands in order to bring those private lands into public ownership and protection. Market-based approaches—for example, the purchase of key private parcels by conservation buyers who do not want to develop and who may be more tolerant of natural processes such as wildfire—also show promise for conserving open lands.

NEEDED: SOCIETAL AND POLITICAL WILL

While the ecological role of fire is now recognized by many land use managers and scientists as important and worth defending, few individuals seem to be willing to address one of the principal reasons why this keystone ecological function is being suppressed: people living in fire-prone areas. The authors of this essay believe that vegetative management, creation of defensible space, and the use of less flammable building materials are, in many instances, appropriate and necessary steps for the protection of life and property in the current WUI. But these measures also facilitate continued building in fire-prone areas, which is ecologically destructive, fiscally draining, and ultimately hazardous for people.

A more commonsense approach is needed that will direct rural sprawl away from places that are inappropriate for development. Planning and growth management tools exist that could facilitate this process. Political will at the state and national policy levels is needed to implement these mechanisms. Incentives ranging from federal funding for firefighting to homeowner's insurance rates that do not take the threat of wildfire into account militate against the application of planning and growth management tools.

Additionally, a major paradigm shift is needed among public and private firefighting and land management agencies, as well as among local government officials, rural landowners, and insurance companies. We need to recognize that what we view as a natural disaster is, in actuality, a natural process. We need to begin living sustainably with such processes when and where this is possible. A more enlightened approach to land use has been adopted by many communities in the management of their floodplains. A similar approach to land use in our "fire plains" would benefit the people, the wildlife, and the wildlands of many areas, including Greater Yellowstone.

BURNING DOWN THE HOUSE

The Role of Disaster Aid in Subsidizing Catastrophe

JOHN KRIST

IN THE AFTERMATH OF WILDFIRES AND OTHER DISASTERS, *public agencies and private insurers spring into action, offering a smorgasbord of grants, loans, fee waivers, and insurance payments to help victims rebuild their lives and reconstruct or replace their property. Too often, such aid serves merely to guarantee another disaster by encouraging people to remain in harm's way.*

▼

As the last flames flickered out in the fall of 2003 and the pall of choking smoke dissipated, southern California's most recent confrontation with incendiary disaster lost its dramatic pulse. The migrant media horde decamped, seeking some fresh nightmare to plumb, and politicians began seeking new images to replace smoldering homes as backdrops for press conferences.

In some ways, however, that enervated pause after the inferno passed (and before the inevitable mudslides began) was the most important phase in the wildfire cycle. Typically, this phase is referred to as "disaster recovery." What it ought to be called is "disaster facilitation," for in seeking to soothe the pain of one catastrophe, institutions of public aid all but guarantee its repetition by rewarding the bad decisions that helped to make it possible in the first place. In the immediate aftermath of one disaster, the seeds of the next often are sown.

In October 2003, 15 large fires scorched more than 750,000 acres and destroyed more than 3,600 homes over a broad swath of southern California, from Ventura County to Mexico. As the weary firefighters who battled those blazes departed, they were replaced by insurance claims adjusters, charity workers, and representatives of the Small Business Administration, the Federal Emergency Management Agency

(FEMA), the California Department of Social Services, and local planning and tax authorities. Together, these institutional Samaritans offered a multibillion-dollar smorgasbord of grants, loans, fee waivers, and insurance payments to help those who lived in the path of the flames rebuild their lives and reconstruct or replace incinerated property.

By year's end, FEMA reported that more than $135 million in such aid had been extended to 21,000 southern California residents, including $110.7 million in low-interest disaster loans for homeowners, renters, and businesses; $5.7 million in grants to help with temporary housing and essential home repairs; and $16 million in payments to replace personal property and cover medical, dental, funeral, transportation, moving, and storage expenses.

A similar outpouring of publicly subsidized assistance has followed countless other disasters in the nation's recent history: hurricanes that periodically turn coastal cities along the Gulf of Mexico and the southern Atlantic seaboard into heaps of soggy matchsticks; tornadoes that annually rearrange the urban furniture of the Midwest and Great Plains; floods of nearly biblical scale that repeatedly submerge towns in the ancestral pathways of the Mississippi and Missouri rivers; earthquakes that rip open California as if its golden landscape lay atop a giant geological zipper. In the aftermath of each fresh nightmare, special assistance centers have been set up, websites created, toll-free hotlines established, and the vast machinery of recovery has rumbled and clanked into gear.

The urge to help others in need is an admirable trait, reflecting a truth written in DNA: human beings are social creatures whose biologically improbable dominance as a species owes as much to their cooperative instinct as to their big brains and tool-making ability. Public aid programs are the institutional embodiment of this trait.

It seems churlish to question the appropriateness of such aid, especially when the recipients are so deserving of sympathy; homeless, bereft, often injured, and sometimes mourning the deaths of friends, neighbors, and family members, they touch all but the hardest of hearts. Nevertheless, critical examination of the aid process is needed, because much of the help offered to burned-out homeowners in the aftermath of the southern California infernos—like the assistance extended to many suffering the effects of flood, fire, and similar events nationwide—will merely ensure future suffering. From a public policy perspective, it is money ill spent.

▼

Strictly speaking, there is no such thing as a "natural disaster." The term refers to what happens when human beings put themselves in the way of natural phenomena such as earthquakes, landslides, volcanoes, floods, and wildfires. These are predictable events, in the sense that they inevitably recur in the places they have occurred before, and thus are avoidable. They inflict no permanent damage on natural systems adapted to them; it is only when people move into their path that such events become "disasters."

There is no better illustration of this than southern California's 2003 wildfires. The Piru Fire, for example, which burned 64,000 acres west of Lake Piru in Ventura County, destroyed only a single home. The slightly smaller Grand Prix Fire in San Bernardino County, which charred 60,000 acres, destroyed 135 homes and damaged 71 more. The difference between the two was the presence of large suburban housing tracts in the fire-prone San Bernardino Mountains, and the absence of such development in the path of the Piru blaze.

The recent litany of similar events throughout the dry and fire-prone West is long and dismayingly familiar: in 2000, a prescribed burn roared out of control and destroyed more than 200 homes in Los Alamos, New Mexico, and fires in Montana's Bitterroot Valley burned 70 homes; in 2002, Arizona's 460,000-acre Rodeo-Chediski Fire destroyed 465 homes, and Colorado's 137,000-acre Hayman Fire burned 132 homes; in 2003, the Aspen Fire near Tucson, Arizona, destroyed 323 homes. For the most part, the homes that burned during these attention-grabbing fires were in vulnerable places, either deep within flammable forests and brush, or in that friction zone where suburbia gnaws at neighboring wildlands.

There is no such thing as a perfectly safe place to live, for the earth is a restive landlord engaged almost continuously in a vast and chaotic remodeling project that frequently inconveniences and occasionally kills its tenants; its tools are blunt and elemental: wind, fire, water, tectonism. Yet clearly the risks are higher in some areas than in others, and those risks are statistically quantifiable. To put it simply, really bad (from a narrow human perspective) things will happen in the future where they have happened before, and prudence would dictate that the most dangerous of such places be avoided when erecting permanent structures.

Absent government prohibition against such construction through zoning and other laws, home builders who insist on living in harm's way ought to at least be forced to bear the burden of their stubborn folly alone, without help in the form of publicly financed protection services—firefighting crews, flood control structures, seawalls, and the like—and without public underwriting of their recovery after the inevitable destruction. To do otherwise is to squander public resources that might better be devoted to other urgent needs.

Seldom, however, has there been a deliberate effort to remove this least obvious contributing factor—reconstruction aid—from the disaster equation.

Federal authorities have provided some evidence that they might, under extraordinary circumstances, be willing to confront the issue. In the wake of the devastating 1993 floods that struck the Missouri and Mississippi river drainages, for example, federal agencies moved entire towns to higher ground and bought out floodplain farmers rather than simply pay again to rebuild communities in places that had been repeatedly inundated and to reimburse growers for yet another episode of crop destruction. Some farmers, it turned out, were making more money from disaster relief than from selling crops.

Sometimes, the federal agencies reluctantly admitted, even billions of dollars in protective structures cannot stop the forces of nature, and simply getting out of the way is the best strategy.

"Floods are repetitive natural phenomena," a presidential task force concluded in the aftermath of the 1993 floods, belaboring the obvious in way that could serve as inspirational text for disaster planners confronting a wide range of natural phenomena. "Considering the nation's short history of hydrologic record-keeping as well as the limited knowledge of long-term weather patterns, flood recurrence intervals are hard to predict. Activities in the floodplain, even with levee protection, continue to remain at risk."[1]

That lesson has not been widely embraced even by flood control agencies, and it has made no inroads whatsoever into management of the wildfire zones of southern California and the rest of the combustible West. Despite the evident risk of fire in the areas that have recently burned, and the statistical certainty that they will burn again, vast sums of money have been poured over the past few years into reconstruction of homes in the danger zone. Although well meaning, this assistance amounts to the public subsidy of recurring disaster.

Malibu is a celebrity poster child for the phenomenon of recurring catastrophe. Although spared from the 2003 wildfires that scorched the region, the wealthy coastal enclave on the edge of southern California's fire-prone Santa Monica Mountains has burned so many times over the past century that its flammability has become a dark regional joke.

In his 1998 book *Ecology of Fear: Los Angeles and the Imagination of Disaster*, urban historian Mike Davis catalogs 13 blazes of 10,000 acres or more in that slender strip of dreamland since 1930: "Since 1970 five such holocausts have destroyed more than one thousand luxury residences and inflicted more than $1 billion in property damage," he wrote in a chapter provocatively titled "The Case for Letting Malibu Burn." "Some unhappy homeowners have been burnt out twice in a generation, and there are individual patches of coastline or mountain, especially between Point Dume and Tuna Canyon, that have been incinerated as many as eight times since 1930."[2]

Davis also noted the role of public and private aid in abetting Malibu's recurrent incineration: "Defended in 1993 (when fires destroyed 350 homes) by the largest army of firefighters in American history, wealthy Malibu homeowners benefited as well from an extraordinary range of insurance, land-use and disaster relief subsidies."[3]

And subsidies they are. The difference in price between FEMA's low-interest loans and the commercial lending rate represents a cost borne by U.S. taxpayers. Building and permit fees waived to expedite reconstruction of fire-ruined homes are a financial drain on local government and, by extension, all the local residents who rely on its services.

Insurance companies cover repeated losses to wildfire and other disasters by raising premiums for all their customers, even those who have chosen to live far from danger. And then there is the several millions of dollars a day in taxpayer money—not to mention the blood—federal, state, and local firefighting agencies may expend to protect private homes built in a combustible landscape.

Many strategies have been employed to reduce the destructive capacity of wildfires in southern California: brush-clearance laws, purchase of expensive firefighting equipment, nonflammable building material codes. Many of these progressive strategies could serve as models for other fire-prone areas. Yet the damage toll rises year after year.

More could be done, certainly. As long ago as 1930, in a report analyzing opportunities for parks and recreation in Los Angeles, the urban design firm Olmstead Brothers (founded by famed landscape architect Frederick Law Olmstead, designer of New York's Central Park) recommended that local governments prevent speculative development of the region's unstable and flammable canyons and hillsides by imposing a system of hazard zoning, outlawing construction in the most dangerous places. "[The] burden of wrong development does not fall on the purchaser alone, and scarcely ever on the vendor" they wrote prophetically, "but most heavily on the community at large."[4]

Tougher zoning restrictions—often fought energetically by developers and real estate speculators, who share the blame for the sprawl of homes into predictably dangerous landscapes—would help in those areas of the fire-threatened West that have not yet been subdivided. For those who regard such restrictions as an unacceptable violation of property owners' rights, a compromise might be in order: allow landowners to build in harm's way, but deny them insurance, taxpayer-provided firefighting services, and reconstruction aid. Why should the risk that attends their choice in housing be shared with everyone, when the rewards—private enjoyment of a home in the woods or commanding a view of the Pacific—are not?

In those areas of extremely high risk where homes already have been built, public and private relief agencies should offer relocation assistance after the inevitable fire, rather than helping burned-out residents stubbornly rebuild in the same vulnerable places. This might seem heartless now, but in the long run it may be the most compassionate thing to do, for it will spare future generations from suffering the same pain as today's fire casualties.

THE COMMUNITY PROTECTION ZONE

Defending Homes and Communities
from the Threat of Forest Fire

BRIAN NOWICKI AND TODD SCHULKE

FOCUSED TREATMENT OF THE WILDLAND-URBAN INTERFACE *can pro-vide homes and communities with effective protection from wildfire. Treatment of the home ignition zone—the house itself and the sur-rounding area up to 200 feet—can provide direct protection from ignition sources. Creation of a community protection zone can pro-vide an additional safety zone in which firefighters can defend a community from forest fires.*

▼

The protection of homes and communities from the threat of forest fire depends on the proper treatment of the wildland-urban inter-face, the area directly adjacent to homes and communities. However, current efforts to protect communities from the threat of forest fire are often planned without consideration for what is actually effective at protecting homes and communities from forest fires. Projects that reduce forest fuels are often implemented far away from communities, in areas where treatment will do the least good. Considering the cur-rent risks and the limited resources available for the implementation of fuels reduction projects, individual projects and strategic plans need to utilize the best available science to develop the most effective and effi-cient methods for protecting homes and communities. At the same time, focused fuels reduction in the wildland-urban interface is neces-sary to avoid damaging adjacent forest ecosystems and wildlife habi-tat with poorly planned and ineffective logging projects.

To determine what is actually necessary and effective at protecting homes and communities from the threat of forest fire, we reviewed all the available scientific literature addressing home and community fire protection. We found from this research that wildland-urban interface treatments providing effective protection of homes from forest fires can be implemented relatively quickly in and around the home ignition zone (the house itself plus the area within 200 feet of the house), and with a minimum of impact on the wildland forest. In addition, fuels reduction treatments up to ¼ mile from structures can create a "community protection zone" that provides a safe zone for firefighters engaged in home protection.

PROTECTING THE HOUSE

Effective fire protection eliminates opportunities for ignition of the house: a structure that does not ignite does not burn, regardless of what occurs around it. Forest fires can ignite houses in three ways: (1) flames of the burning forest can provide enough radiant heat, without reaching the house directly, to ignite the surface of the house; (2) flames of the burning forest can reach the surface of the house through surrounding vegetation; and (3) firebrands (burning embers from a fire) can be carried by wind to fall on or near the house. The first of these threats can be effectively treated by breaking up forest fuel continuity for a maximum of 200 feet from the house; the second requires removal of vegetation immediately adjacent to the house; and the third is addressed by treating the house itself.

For a forest fire to ignite a house without reaching it directly, the fire must provide sufficient radiant heat for a long enough time to raise the temperature of the surface of the house to its ignition point. Experimental studies and modeling have shown that partial removal of trees within 132 feet of a house protects it against radiant ignition from the flames of a forest fire that is torching and crowning (burning in the tops of trees intermittently or continuously).[1] These studies assumed severe conditions, so lesser distances may suffice. Another study found a precipitous drop in structural ignition with a distance of only 66 feet between the house and forest vegetation.[2] A treatment extending 200 feet from the house therefore provides a margin of safety allowing for particularly steep slopes or tall trees and protects against scorching of exterior walls.

The number of trees that must be removed is a function of site-specific factors such as slope and tree species. The goal of the treatment is to break up any flame front to such an extent that radiant heat is not great enough to ignite the surface of the house over the duration of the exposure to the flame front. Removal of all vegetation within the home ignition zone is not necessary. In fact, trees that are adequately spaced from the house and the surrounding forest can provide heat protection by blocking the radiating heat of the forest fire. Vegetation with the potential to produce smaller flames can safely be located relatively close to the house.[3]

Even when a house is protected from the intense heat of the flame front, there is a serious threat of its igniting from direct contact with flames from nearby shrubs, firewood, or even dried grass and needle litter. In fact, most of the houses that burn during forest fires do not ignite from intense crown fire, but rather from relatively low-intensity surface fire.[4] Surface fire can burn grass and needle litter right up to the house, or ignite a tree, shrub, or structure (such as a deck or shed) near the house. A minimal break in the continuous surface fuels, such as a simple rake line around the perimeter of the house, can be effective in preventing direct ignition.[5] For this reason, homesite protection must include eliminating continuous ground fuels that lead from the forest to the house. Rock landscaping, cement sidewalks, green grass, or raking away needles and dried vegetation can eliminate such fuels.

The most dispersed source of home ignition is firebrands, the burning embers generated by a forest fire. Firebrands can be lifted high into the air and carried by wind to ignite fires miles ahead of the forest fire. They can be blown onto the roof of a house or into any exposed flammable area, causing fires that can ignite the house even if the forest fire is miles away. Firebrands are thus an extremely dangerous source of ignition on and adjacent to houses.[6] Even highly effective fire prevention or suppression miles from the homesite cannot adequately protect houses from this threat of ignition. Similarly, wildland-urban fuels treatments that neglect to treat the home ignition zone will be dangerously ineffective at protecting homes and communities from firebrand ignitions.

Because of the threat of firebrand ignitions, reducing the flammability of the house itself is absolutely necessary, regardless of the vegetation treatment in the surrounding forest, and regardless of the distance between the house and the adjacent forest. In general, treating the house against firebrands involves using fire-resistant materials in the building of the house and adjacent structures, especially roofs and wooden decks; covering or removing flammable materials from corners and nooks where firebrands can accumulate; and clearing roofs and gutters of dead branches, leaves, and needles.[7] These basic treatments are essential elements in any home or community protection plan.

THE COMMUNITY PROTECTION ZONE

Additional thinning of fuels beyond the home ignition zone may enhance the ability of firefighters to safely defend community space. Creating an area of reduced fuels immediately adjacent to the community can provide options for firefighters to control fire in this space, and also provide a safety zone in which firefighters are "free from danger, risk, or injury."[8] Such a community protection zone requires breaking up fuel continuity at greater distances from houses than necessary to protect the homes themselves, because injury to humans can occur with a small fraction of the heat and time required to ignite wood.[9]

Experimental studies and modeling have shown that the width requirements of a firefighter safety zone are related to the average sustained flame length of the forest fire flame front at the edge of the safety zone.[10] The sustained flame length is significantly different from the maximum observed flame length; the latter includes tall flame bursts that do not produce heat of the same magnitude as do sustained flames. This same modeling approximated the maximum potential sustained flame length as twice (2×) the height of the average overstory tree at the site (not to be confused with the maximum tree height).

The great majority of wildland-urban interface communities in the West are surrounded by trees between 33 and 165 feet tall. Using the 2× factor, we calculated the maximum sustained flame length for a tree 165 feet tall to be 330 feet. A calculation of four times (4×) the sustained flame length was used in the modeling to determine the minimum distance required for a community protection zone to effectively act as a safety zone under these assumptions of maximum conditions.[11] Using this 4× factor, we can calculate that a forest fire with a sustained flame length of 330 feet requires a community protection zone 1,312 feet, or approximately ¼ mile, wide.

Very few communities are surrounded by forests consisting of trees with an average height greater than 165 feet, and it is highly unlikely that trees of any height can produce sustained flame lengths greater than 330 feet. However, we determined the maximum possible treatment distance needed to create a community protection zone by assuming a hypothetical average overstory tree height of 200 feet. A community protection zone in such a forest could conceivably require a treatment area 1,600 feet wide under these unlikely conditions. We also incorporated a large safety factor in our calculations by using maximum values for every possible variable (such as the range of high winds and steep slopes), whether or not such conditions are present or physically possible.

Creation of a community protection zone does not require removal of all trees within the zone. Rather, it involves thinning the forest to create breaks in the continuity of tree crowns and removing ladder fuels and small-diameter understory trees. In addition, community protection zone treatment is dependent on site conditions such as forest type, average tree height, and slope. Rules of thumb recommend reducing crown cover to less than 35 percent, with a minimum of 10 feet of open space between crowns; pruning branches up to 10 feet high; and removing small-diameter understory trees or spacing them the same distance as the overstory trees.[12] Trees—particularly large, fire-resistant trees—should be retained in the community protection zone, because trees suppress the growth of highly flammable brush, thus limiting the amount of vegetative maintenance needed, as well as reducing wind speeds and blocking heat from the forest fire.

A properly implemented community protection zone treatment can reduce the area required for home ignition zone treatment. The distance requirement for home ignition zone treatment is based on the assumption of a continuous, uninterrupted flame front. Community protection zone treatment breaks up forest fuels facing the house, thus decreasing the ability of the flame front to provide enough heat to ignite the house. However, the community protection zone is not a replacement for treatment in the home ignition zone. Treatment of the home ignition zone is an integral and critical component of an effective community protection zone. That is, the community protection zone will not be effective without adequate homesite treatment as well.

BEYOND THE COMMUNITY PROTECTION ZONE

Studies have shown that vegetation management beyond the structure's immediate vicinity has little effect on house ignitions.[13] Jack Cohen, a leading fire researcher at the U.S. Forest Service Fire Sciences Lab, states: "The evidence suggests that wildland fuel reduction for reducing home losses may be inefficient and ineffective. Inefficient because wildland fuel reduction for several hundred meters or more around homes is greater than necessary for reducing ignitions from flames. Ineffective because it does not sufficiently reduce firebrand ignitions."[14] In short, a properly implemented homesite treatment provides protection for the house; the community protection zone offers additional protection against encroaching ground fires that can ignite houses if home ignition zone treatment is not properly implemented; and treating the forest beyond the community protection zone provides no additional protection for houses or communities. In some cases there may be reasons to treat forests outside the wildland-urban interface, but such forest restoration projects should be based entirely on ecological objectives, such as restoring the forest ecosystem and reducing the risk of crown fires.

MAINTAINING THE WILDLAND-URBAN INTERFACE

The more that tree thinning is used to treat the wildland-urban interface, the greater the need for near-term precautions against fire hazard and for long-term maintenance of the treated area. Thinning greatly increases the immediate fire hazard because it creates a large amount of highly flammable slash and debris, and the open forest structure produces conditions conducive to drier and warmer surface fuels and higher wind speeds. The increased fire hazard must be mitigated as soon as possible following the thinning operation, by reducing surface fuels and debris. The most efficient and effective fuel reduction methods may be prescribed burning, or chipping followed by removal of the remaining fuel. Some sites may require an initial piling and burning of flammable branches and debris followed by a low-intensity burn of the area to maintain low fuel loads. Others may require an incremental approach, in which a series of prescribed burns is used to remove fuels.

Subsequent prescribed broadcast burns may also be the most efficient and effective for maintaining the wildland-urban interface treatment over time. Such burns would maintain lower fuel loads within the forest, as well as reduce the growth of highly flammable shrubs and understory trees. Regular (possibly annual) maintenance is critical for maintaining the community protection zone.

SETTING PRIORITIES

Wildland-urban interface communities can be categorized as (1) interface (neighborhoods extending into the forest), (2) intermix (groups of houses within the forest), and (3) individual properties (isolated inholdings) within the forest. The U.S. Departments of Agriculture and the Interior have defined the interface community as having a population density of 250 or more people per square mile, and the intermix community as having 28 to 250 people per square mile.[15] While these population densities should not be taken as hard definitions, they do serve as a guideline for the prioritization of fuels reduction and community protection projects. Projects can be prioritized in this order by relative risk to life and property, and by the relative amount of protection gained from each project.

Within the wildland-urban interface (WUI), interface communities contain the greatest number of houses and people per square mile. Furthermore, because of the relatively dense development and extensive road systems in interface communities, WUI treatment projects involve a relatively small area per house and are relatively easy to implement. WUI treatment projects for interface communities can therefore provide the greatest protection for the greatest resources (houses and people) with the smallest amount of time and effort, and thus may be considered as the highest-priority locations for concentrating fire reduction resources such as funding and planning. Of course, all WUI communities and houses should be protected from the threat of forest fire. Thus homesite treatments should be implemented as soon as possible on all WUI communities and houses, thereby providing immediate protection for the homes until the site can be assessed for the implementation of a community protection zone treatment.

Part Seven

TIME TO RETIRE SMOKEY BEAR

AFTERWORD

As I have tried to convey throughout this book, fire is an important ecological force that plays a key role in many ecosystems. That alone is reason enough to restore wildfire to the landscape. It can reasonably be asserted that fire suppression ultimately does not work. Fire eventually seeks expression across the landscape, and, sooner or later, if fuels build and conditions exist that favor fire, you will eventually have a blaze. Suppressing fires today generally leads to larger fires later.

In envisioning the future, I would like to see fire restored to all ecosystems in which it plays a dominant functional role. To make an analogy, I see wildfire as similar to the natural flooding of rivers. Flooding is a normal and necessary process that shapes river channels, dissipates energy, and creates fresh new habitat that sustains many plants and animals. Hydrologists say the way to think about a river is to include not only the water and channel where a waterway may flow in a normal year, but also the 100-year and even the 500-year floodplain, for the floodplain is as much a part of the river as the area underwater at any particular time. Similarly, we need to think about the "fire plain" — the area that normally burns at some point in time as part of an ecosystem's normal processes.

In the book's final essay, Andy Kerr uses wit to challenge the fire-industrial complex. In order to save the forests, we must "kill Smokey Bear"—that is, the old ways of thinking about forest fires. Such a shift will require educating the public on the ecological and spiritual values of wildfire. We must stop talking about fire as "destructive" or even as a "disturbance," for the way we speak about fire affects our perception of fire. We need to encourage the media to change the way they report on wildfires, and land management agencies also to change the way they portray fire. At the very least, we should be thinking critically about how these entities present fire.

Kerr asks us to challenge the military-industrial firefighting complex that seeks to perpetuate current fire policies—including the timber industry, which sees fire as a new excuse for logging America's public lands, either in the name of fuel reduction or under the aegis of salvage logging in the aftermath of a blaze.

Adopting strong private lands policies that limit sprawl, particularly sprawl into fire-prone areas, could and should be justified, not only because such policies save taxpayer money but also because they save lives. In some places—chiefly around existing communities—we need to reduce fuels and to create firebreaks so that the inevitable fire does not burn down dozens of homes. But beyond the boundaries and influence of our communities, we need to accept and restore wildfire. On the nation's public lands, such a policy is entirely reasonable.

How do we accomplish such a change in policy? I have sought to show in this book, through the insightful essays of the contributing authors, that nearly all our most prized landscapes—the places we see as some of the most beautiful in the country—are shaped by fire. I have also sought to demonstrate the folly of firefighting. Most of our largest blazes are controlled by the weather. Weather starts fires. Weather puts them out. What we do in between, we call "firefighting"—which is mostly a flamboyant sideshow to convince the public that the government is doing something, even if that something is misguided, in addition to funding the fire-industrial complex.

A greater appreciation of the important ecological function of wildfire would also be a step toward changing human attitudes toward nature in general. For to become comfortable with such a powerful natural force as fire can only lead us toward a greater appreciation and respect for all wild nature. Such a change in our cultural relationship to nature is necessary if we are to survive, much less thrive, on planet Earth over the long haul.

We end with the Smokey the Bear Sutra, in the hopes that we "will enter the age of harmony of man and nature, . . . will always have ripe blackberries to eat and a sunny spot under a pine tree to sit at."

THE ULTIMATE FIREFIGHT

Changing Hearts and Minds

ANDY KERR

PUBLIC ATTITUDES TOWARD WILDFIRE ARE WILDLY *at odds with the best available science. The challenge for the conservation movement is to move the public away from seeing forests and fire through the eyes of Bambi to viewing them through the lenses of science and economics. This means taking on the fire-industrial complex, which is very content to fleece the taxpayer while destroying forests in the name of saving them.*

▼

Conservationists have to kill Smokey Bear. While certainly not a short-term winning public relations strategy, there may be no other way in the long term to actually save and restore forests. Yes, off-ing Smokey Bear would be like ordering a hit on Santa Claus, the Easter Bunny, or the Tooth Fairy. Although all these icons are primarily the domain of children, Smokey Bear is different from them in two important respects.

First, at some point in their lives, most people stop believing in Santa Claus, the Easter Bunny, and the Tooth Fairy—but nearly all American adults still believe in Smokey Bear.

Second, only Smokey preaches a message that, when heeded by others, actually causes harm to the forest. (We shall leave aside concerns about juvenile icons that encourage excessive material consumption, imply that rabbits lay eggs, or condone the selling of human body parts.) Smokey advocates certain policies that damage forests, waste tax dollars, and actually make people less safe.

Smokey's indoctrination has been incredibly effective—98 percent of Americans can finish the sentence that begins: "Only you . . . "

Smokey is a creation of the Ad Council, an entity that seeks to do good for good causes by marshaling advertising industry talent to use their skills—at least once in a while—for a higher purpose than selling unnecessary and/or poorly made crap that wreaks havoc on our individual and collective waistlines, pocketbooks, and/or self-esteem.

Smokey should go back to school and update his message. It's happened before. Smokey's original 1944 message was that all fires in the forest were bad ("Only you can prevent *forest* fires"). In 2001, Smokey changed his tune, then stating that there are both good and bad fires ("Only you can prevent *wild*fires").[1]

Smokey Bear may again be changing his tune. When turning 60 in 2004, he said, "I don't promote the suppression of wildfires or prescribed fires . . . my message is to help prevent *careless* wildfires! Prescribed fires can be beneficial to plants and animals and prevent wildfires if they are done under *supervised* conditions!" (emphasis original).[2] Is Smokey now in favor of *not* suppressing wildfires? Is Mr. Bear okay with *careful* wildfires? This doesn't make any sense to me either (as 60 is quite old for a bear, perhaps he's losing his mind). A fire in the wild started by nature, or by an unauthorized human, is now deemed a "bad" fire, while a fire set in the wild by a duly authorized human is a "good" fire. It's a start.

Advertising theory says that to sell a product, service, or concept, it's best to appeal to the customer's beliefs ("what people think the world is like") and values ("guiding principles of what is moral, desirable or just").[3] Conservationists have learned to appeal to people's belief that excessive exploitation and pollution are bad for humans and the environment and that conservation and stewardship are valuable to protect the land, air, water, and wildlife for this and future generations.

Such marketing strategies are effective for conservation when the public's beliefs and values coincide with those of sound science and good conservation policy. It's simply a matter of motivating the public to act in some way to further its own beliefs and values. However, in the case of wildfire, the beliefs and values of the conservation community (not to mention the overwhelming scientific evidence and the professional opinion of the academic community)[4] are deeply—and at this point, almost totally—at odds with those of the public.

The public generally fears all fire, and generally this is a rational fear. In the wrong place, fire is very bad. We don't want our buildings to burn, especially not with people in them. However, most of the public fail to distinguish between the generally built-up environment ("frontcountry"), where humans can and should control fire, and the generally natural environment ("backcountry"), where humans cannot and should not.

Wildfire is not "prevented," but merely delayed—often incurring later and greater fiscal and ecological costs. More importantly, wildfire is generally beneficial to the forest. Most forests of the American West coevolved with fire. Wildfire sustains and renews these forests.[5]

The behemoth fire-industrial complex profits directly from current firefighting policies. Keeping the public in the dark about the benefits of wildfire rewards this mutual back-scratching collaboration of government bureaucrats, private contractors, timber corporations, and elected officials.

Blissfully ignorant, the overwhelming majority of the public has been misled on the issue of backcountry (wildlands) fire. This vast majority now believes that backcountry fires can and should be fought just as those in the frontcountry (urban, suburban, and rural) areas.

As conservationists, we have no choice but to directly confront the public and challenge its values and beliefs about fighting backcountry fires. However, as a rule, people don't like it when their beliefs and values are questioned.

The tried-and-true method of promoting just causes—"speak truth to power"—is not applicable. Rather than confronting the powerful before the masses, this is a case of needing to challenge the masses directly.

Conservationists must take steps to move the public's beliefs about wildlands fire to be in line with the scientific understanding of wildlands fire. While comprehensive strategy and tactics for each step are not discussed here, techniques and methods that immediately come to mind include litigation, protest, theater, legislation, regulation, ridicule, and education.

1. CHANGE THE PUBLIC'S TIME FRAME AND VIEWPOINT

In 1987, the editor of a local daily newspaper was on the brink of editorializing that much of a nearby national forest in southwest Oregon should be made a national park. He had learned of the extraordinary biodiversity, the pristine watersheds, and the beauty of the area. Then a portion of it burned, as forests have been doing throughout the ages in the Klamath-Siskiyou ecoregion. After the fire, the editor changed his mind. In his view, since the forest had burned, the area was no longer national-park quality. A year later, much of Yellowstone National Park burned. However, this editor never wrote an editorial calling for the park's abolishment.

While a burned forest is not pretty, wildfire is either the birth of the next forest or the continuation of the present one. Before nature reveals her healing powers and rebirth, a burned landscape offends our aesthetics of what a forest should look like. The public needs to think beyond today's video clip of a singed forest and understand that both the forest that was and the forest that will be are dependent on fire. If more of the public saw the rebirth of the Yellowstone forests that burned in 1988, they would better understand this phenomenon.

2. EXPOSE THE FIRE-INDUSTRIAL COMPLEX

The fire-industrial complex must be exposed for the racket it appears to be—an annual raid on the public treasury for enriching private interests, furthering bureaucratic careers, aiding reelections, and providing a feedstock of public timber for private gain. The fire-industrial complex is a "racket" in almost every sense of the word:

> **racket** *n* 1: confused clattering noise: CLAMOR. 2a: social whirl or excitement. b: the strain of exciting or trying experiences. 3a: a fraudulent scheme, enterprise, or activity. b: a usually illegitimate enterprise made workable by bribery or intimidation. c: an easy and lucrative means of livelihood. d: slang: OCCUPATION, BUSINESS.[6]

Staggering sums of money are spent in mostly futile attempts to extinguish wildfires. Taxpayers are being fleeced by an iron quadrangle of government bureaucrats, private contractors, timber corporations, and elected officials.

Government bureaucrats rely on private contractors and timber corporations to lobby elected officials to give the bureaucrats money, much of which is passed through to contractors to supposedly prevent timber from burning, so it can be logged more profitably later by the corporations. This is all done in the name of and under the cover of the public's genuine—though ignorant and misplaced—concern about forests and fire.

Every player in the fire-industrial complex pulls its weight. If it is a slow wildfire season, sometimes someone—usually in the contracting corps, sometimes in the bureaucracy—may well start fires to get the money flowing. Frontcountry firefighters are paid full time whether something is burning or not. Backcountry firefighters and/or fire companies are not paid as much, or at all, unless there is a fire to be fought.

3. HOLD FIRE BUREAUCRATS ACCOUNTABLE

The public needs to understand that the paramilitary effort in generally futile attempts to put out wildfires can cause more environmental harm than is purportedly caused by a wildfire left to burn. Fish-killing fire-retardant chemicals in streams, eroding bulldozed fire lines, felled (and later logged) trees, backburns, and burnouts are far more destructive than natural wildfires, and often result in hotter fires.[7]

Elected officials give government agencies a blank check when it comes to paying bureaucrats and private contractors to fight wildfire. The limitation on spending during fire season is not set by any sort of budget, but by the simple fact that there are no more people or equipment available to be contracted at any price.

4. EMPOWER PYROPHILES

Since the early 1970s, scientists at Oregon State University have urged Forest Service officials to burn the grass balds of Marys Peak on the Siuslaw National Forest. For almost as long, the Forest Service has said that it has plans to do just that. Historically, this highest point in the Oregon Coast Range has not been covered with forest, primarily because of Native American and lightning-caused burning. Besides the cultural and aesthetic reasons to keep the balds, they are also great wildflower habitat. Today, still unchallenged by fire, the noble fir trees continue their ignoble march upon the meadow.

There is probably not a more risk-free management burn than on Marys Peak. The risk of a fire burning out of control is almost nil. The bald is the highest point in the Coast Range and fire usually travels uphill. The surrounding forest is noble fir—not Douglas-fir—an indicator of seasonal snow pack and adequate residual moisture. The Siuslaw National Forest is a rainforest. Northwest Oregon has the lowest incidence of lightning strikes in the lower 48 states. Natural forest in the Oregon Coast Range thus burns only during the most severe dry and windy weather. Such extreme weather conditions are very rare and easy to plan for and manage around.

Yet, in over three decades, no Forest Service official has had the courage to drop the match, even if the first storm after the annual summer drought is predicted in the next 24 hours. Bureaucratic incentives—both positive and negative—need to be changed so professional managers are encouraged to restore natural wildfire to natural ecosystems.

5. RECLASSIFY MOST BAD FIRES AS GOOD FIRES

In the late 1990s, a lightning-caused wildfire erupted in the Hells Canyon Wilderness on the Idaho-Oregon border. The terrain is hellacious, and the sparse timber in the area is off-limits to logging. The management plan said that naturally caused fire in the Hells Canyon Wilderness would be allowed to burn, and indeed the wildfire was left alone to ebb and flow with the day and night and whims of the weather and available fuel. It was a nice, healthy, and necessary fire.

However, the wildfire eventually crossed the line from a "good" fire to a "bad" fire. The line was the Hells Canyon Wilderness boundary. The fire moved from protected "Wilderness" to unprotected wilderness. These wildlands adjacent to the designated Wilderness were just as natural, roadless, and wild (and had as few commercially valuable trees). And though these lands were in a national recreation area, the management prescription in case of wildfire was full and immediate "suppression." As soon as the wildfire crossed the good-bad boundary, the Forest Service fired up its firefighting machine and spent several million dollars over just a few days to try to put out the now-unauthorized fire. The fearless firefighters only abandoned their Herculean expenditure after they awoke one August morning to snow. No problem. There would be another wildfire soon enough to go play with, while the taxpayers pay.

6. DISTINGUISH BETWEEN GOOD AND BAD FIREFIGHTERS

A good firefighter fights bad fires; a bad firefighter fights good fires. Fires in the frontcountry are generally bad; fires in the backcountry are generally good. A firefighter who goes into burning buildings to try to save people is a good and heroic firefighter. A firefighter who goes into the burning backcountry to try to stop nature—or risks his or her life trying to save someone's inappropriately placed third home—is a bad and foolish firefighter.

In this post-9/11 era, when we are tragically short of heroes as it is, frontcountry firefighters are true heroes who don't get paid anywhere near enough for what society asks of them. Their compensation comes more from helping others and occasionally basking in the public gratitude that episodically befalls them after performing a particularly selfless (and usually very dangerous, and sometimes tragic) act.

Backcountry firefighters receive misplaced gratitude, if not adulation. During the 2002 Biscuit Fire on the Siskiyou National Forest in Oregon, handmade and heartfelt signs of appreciation sprouted in the nearby town of Cave Junction for the battalions of firefighters who encamped there for several weeks.

In the case of the Biscuit Fire and many other fires, the hottest and most dangerous burns were those set by the firefighters themselves as backburns and burnouts. These officially sanctioned burns were far more threatening to the town than the naturally burning Biscuit Fire— yet even those backburns were not much of a threat.

Nonetheless, the thick smoke that hung over the town, along with residents being able to see some glowing embers at night and all those firefighters hanging around, meant that most townsfolk were indeed truly scared, even if they had little reason to be.

Eventually, as other fires (actually, even better money) called, the Biscuit Fire settled into an uneasy truce with firefighters (it was extinguished only after the fall rains came).

(N.B.: To this day, most of the homes in and around Cave Junction are not fire-safe. Too many still have flammable roofs and flammable vegetation adjacent to them. At this writing [August 2005], even the Forest Service ranger station fails the guidelines for defensible space around buildings, as posted on its own bulletin board.)

7. CHALLENGE THE MEDIA COVERAGE

While some national media have critically reexamined their reporting of western wildfires, most regional and local media have not.

How many news reports have you heard that say, "The fire has 'destroyed' X thousand acres"? Even at ground zero, an acre is still an acre; it is not destroyed. What they probably meant to say is that "X thousands of acres *of forest* have been destroyed." However, that's not true either. The forest was changed, altered, and renewed—not destroyed. Many news reports speak of "charred" forest, when "singed" is more accurate.

Ironically, many news organizations correctly report that it is weather—not human effort—that finally quashes wildfires. There are countless quotes from the fire boss on scene that state in effect, "We had the fire contained, but then the weather changed," or "We now have the fire controlled, thanks to some help from the weather." Weather ignites most wildfires, and weather extinguishes most wild-fires.

Wildfire media coverage may be divided into three categories: before, during, and after the fire. The best reporting is always after a fire has gone out. The worst reporting is during the fire, while the reporting before a wildfire flares up is mixed.

Fire-industrial-complex public relations flacks keep busy in the off-season. Before the fire, the stories they push are generally of two genera: protecting homes from wildfire or ominous predictions of a coming terrible wildfire season.

The home-protection stories focus on efforts to help wildland-urban interface homeowners take prudent and effective measures to prevent their homes from burning when a wildfire does come.

The coming-terrible-wildfire-season stories are worse. Without exception, the story line is that the next wildfire season could possibly be the worst on record. If the spring was dry, then the fire-industrial-complex mouthpiece forecasts "horribly dry tinderbox conditions" for the coming summer and fall. If it was a notably wet spring, then the public relations line is that the wet weather has "caused so much plant growth that, when it dries out, it will provide more fuel for destructive wildfires!" In any case, the fire-industrial complex—taxpayers willing—is always ready to milk the challenge.

Media coverage during a wildfire is—with very few exceptions—appalling. There are multiple reasons for this.

First, most reporters are generalists—particularly on television, where most people get their news—who don't know much about nature and wildfire, and so they must rely on what they are fed by the fire-industrial-complex public relations flacks. In the course of a week's work, the same reporter might do stories on a wildfire, a house fire, a car wreck, a football game, a city council meeting, a robbery, and the circus coming to town.

Second, wildfire areas are tightly controlled. Reporters are herded by flacks to see only what the fire propaganda machine wants them to see, and are told only what the fire-industrial complex wants them to hear.

Third, television images are selected for the most impact. A typical cool-burning fire on the forest floor won't make CNN. Only atypical hot-burning "crown" fires make it on the news. (Crown fires do occur, but on comparably little acreage.) Dispatching an expensive satellite uplink truck to the scene must be justified with compelling footage.

Fourth, viewers—especially the 98 percent that are Smokey Bear's faithful—want both to see drama and to hear good news. They love viewing people and machines marshaled to fight a wildfire and save homes. If asked, they would say that wildlands firefighting is one of the few things they don't mind paying taxes for.

The coverage after a wildfire is almost uniformly good. The follow-up pieces are not done as "breaking" news and are therefore more thoughtful and better researched. They often focus on the magnificent healing powers of nature. Reporters who specialize in science, the environment, or natural resources usually do these stories. They tend to be print stories, not television.

8. SHOW THE FUTILITY AND COST OF FIGHTING BACKCOUNTRY FIRES

The public must be made to realize that the environmental impacts on air, water, and soil from firefighting can exceed those from the wildfire itself. That the long-term upsides of wildfire outweigh any short-term downsides. That most of the fires that the fire-industrial complex claims to have extinguished would have gone out anyway. That after a wildfire reaches critical mass, it is weather that dictates the course of the fire, not human intervention. That the huge sums spent trying to put out what are in fact beneficial fires at the height of the wildfire season would be better spent: (1) helping people fire-safe buildings; (2) preventing fires in the frontcountry, where most people live; and (3) starting (prescribed) fires in the backcountry the rest of the year to restore natural fire regimes and healthy forests.

9. SHOW THE UTILITY OF MAKING ALL BUILDINGS FIRE-SAFE

The wildland-urban interface (WUI, or *"WOO-ee"*) is where the frontcountry and backcountry collide. Fireproofing WUI structures can reasonably ensure that they will not ignite from nearby fire.[8] It would be much more efficient for the government to require nonflammable roofing material and vegetation management within a few hundred feet of a house or other building than trying to fight WUI fires. Indeed, it would be much cheaper for taxpayers to pay the full cost of fireproofing private property than the cost of our present wildfire strategy. Buildings can and should be defended against wildfire; forests cannot and should not be.

10. PROMOTE A NEW ICON FOR JUVENILES OF ALL AGES

The creation of Forest Service Employees for Environmental Ethics, Reddy Squirrel teaches children (and adults) that the best—and most responsible—way to protect buildings against wildfire is to create and maintain a defensible space around them, and to use flame-resistant construction. Reddy is cute and lovable and wears a hard hat and work boots (but no pants).[9]

11. TRANSFER RESPONSIBILITY FROM THE PUBLIC SECTOR TO THE PRIVATE SECTOR

The contrast between fire regulations in the frontcountry and the backcountry is remarkable. Building codes in cities are full of provisions to prevent structures from burning, or, if they do, from burning others. Firewalls are required between buildings, fire doors for stairwells, fire-resistant building materials, and so on. It is illegal in most jurisdictions to have unmowed fields in summer within city limits. Eccentrics are prevented from filling their homes with old newspapers lest a fire start. Commercial buildings have sprinklers and other fire prevention or fire control devices. Private homes are built to code and must have smoke detectors. Fewer regulations exist for WUI buildings.

In the frontcountry, one's taxes pay for the cost of fire prevention and fire control. In the wildland-urban interface, few fire districts exist. WUI building owners may pay a small fee to a state forestry agency for fire protection, but it nowhere approaches the costs of fire protection. Other taxpayers pick up the remainder of the cost.

Few insurance policies distinguish between highly regulated frontcountry buildings and essentially unregulated buildings in the WUI (or even the backcountry, where no buildings should be); most charge all policyholders the same. Thus most insurance holders end up subsidizing the few that live in the woods. Other kinds of insurance routinely distinguish between good and bad drivers and give discounts to nonsmokers. Most homeowner's insurance makes those who live in flood zones and "tornado alleys" and hurricane country pay more (or have more "Act of God" exclusions), but for some reason the same logic is not applied to people who build in the path of fire.

12. STOP THE CYCLE OF BUILD AND BURN AND BUILD AND BURN AND BUILD AND . . .

A major role of government is to prevent people from doing stupid things, especially things that also have the potential to harm others.

Government sometimes limits people's ability to build in floodplains. It requires life jackets on all watercraft. Building in the path of wildfire is no different than building an unsafe building.

In an example of supply-side ecology, in 1982 President Ronald Reagan signed into law the Coastal Barriers Resources System (CBRS). The law prohibits the expenditure of federal funds in specified low-lying undeveloped areas on the East and Gulf Coasts that are often ravaged by hurricanes. In units of the CBRS, no federal funds are available for highways, sewer systems, flood insurance, disaster relief, and other programs that encourage people to build in harm's way. The federal government does not prevent a local government or private landowner from developing or building anything in a CBRS unit; it just removes the possibility of federal bailouts after the inevitable disaster. It has worked very well.

In another example, after rebuilding entire towns multiple times following Mississippi River floods, the federal government has paid to move entire towns out of the floodplain.

It is time for a policy that puts WUI building owners on notice that government will no longer bail them out during and after the next fire. Such a policy would put WUI building owners on their own. They can assume the risk themselves, they can pay to fire-safe their structures, they can create fire districts and tax themselves for their own fire protection, or they can do nothing. That is the American way.

13. STARVE THE BEAST

The timber industry has long benefited by not having forests burn, so they could be logged at their leisure. However, public attitudes—especially about public forests—have changed. The public no longer views public forests as fountains of timber, but rather as refugia of biodiversity, sources of cold clean water, recreation spots, and scenic vistas. In this case, the public's values and beliefs are correct.

The timber industry has discovered that their best and last hope to continue logging public forests is to convince the public that the only way to save its cherished forests from wildfire is to log them. Increasingly, the timber industry is making its moves on the public's trees after every wildfire. Postwildfire logging cannot be ecologically justified.[10] "Salvage logging" after a wildfire is done only for economic reasons, and—even more than with regular timber sales—the taxpayers subsidize it. Salvage logging does nothing to help replace, restore, or recover a burned forest. Ecologically, logging after a forest fire is akin to mugging a burn victim.

▼

So, what is the conservation movement to do when the masses are so wrong? As Thoreau noted in "Civil Disobedience," "Moreover, any man more right than his neighbors, constitutes a majority of one already."[11]

There have been times in this nation when the vast majority of the public has been wrong on issues. At the time, of course, those in the majority had no clue they were wrong, because nearly everyone around them felt the same way. However, even overwhelming majorities can be changed over time. Thoreau opposed slavery at a time when a majority of Americans favored the practice, or at least did not oppose it (politically, the effect is identical).

Conservationists are not going to convert the public on the wildfire issue by being stealthy, clever, or patient, or by using the perfect sound bite. Merely having better spokespeople (scientists, enlightened firefighters, etc.) will not bring about the necessary changes, and appealing to the public's existing beliefs and values won't conserve forests either. Only by confronting the public—and forcing it to first reexamine and then change its collective beliefs and values—can people coexist with forests and wildfire.

Consider other political issues about which most of the public eventually changed their minds because their beliefs and values were directly challenged—for example, child labor, woman suffrage, segregation, smoking, seatbelts, Pacific Northwest old-growth logging. Sometimes it takes a human generation for the public's collective mind to change on an issue.

Before Smokey Bear brainwashed America, Americans had a more balanced attitude toward fire. Most Americans—particularly rural ones (who are now far fewer in both relative and absolute numbers)—saw fire as a tool and as a part of nature, like the tides, winds, and rains.

Converting the American public back to a balanced view about wildfire cannot be accomplished overnight. It will take decades. There is no way around it. If it were easy, it would have been done already.

SMOKEY THE BEAR SUTRA

Once in the Jurassic, about 150 million years ago,
the Great Sun Buddha in this corner of the Infinite
Void gave a great Discourse to all the assembled elements
and energies: to the standing beings, the walking beings,
the flying beings, and the sitting beings
—even grasses, to the number of thirteen billion, each one born from a
seed, assembled there: a Discourse concerning
Enlightenment on the planet Earth.

"In some future time, there will be a continent called
America. It will have great centers of power called such as
Pyramid Lake, Walden Pond, Mt. Rainier, Big Sur,
Everglades, and so forth; and powerful nerves and channels
such as Columbia River, Mississippi River, and Grand Canyon.
The human race in that era will get into troubles all over
its head, and practically wreck everything in spite of its own strong
    intelligent
Buddha-nature."

"The Twisting strata of the great mountains and the pulsings
of great volcanoes are my love burning deep in the earth.
My obstinate compassion is schist and basalt and
granite, to be mountains, to bring down the rain. In that
future American Era I shall enter a new form: to cure
the world of loveless knowledge that seeks with blind hunger;
and mindless rage eating food that will not fill it."

And he showed himself in his true form of

SMOKEY THE BEAR.

A handsome smokey-colored brown bear standing on his
hind legs, showing that he is aroused and watchful.

Bearing in his right paw the Shovel that digs to the
truth beneath appearances; cuts the root of useless attachments,
and flings damp sand on the fires of greed and war;

His left paw in the Mudra of Comradely Display—indicating
that all creatures
have the full right to live to their limits
and that deer, rabbits, chipmunks, snakes, dandelions,
and lizard all grow in the realm of the Dharma;

Wearing the blue work overalls symbolic of slaves and
laborers, the countless men oppressed by a civilization
that claims to save but only destroys;

Wearing the broad-brimmed hat of the West, symbolic of
the forces that guard the Wilderness, which is the Natural
State of the Dharma and the True Path of man on earth;
all true paths lead through mountains—

With a halo of smoke and flame behind, the forest fires
of the kali-yuga, fires caused by the stupidity of those
who think things can be gained and lost whereas in truth all is
    contained vast and free in the Blue Sky and Green Earth
of One Mind;

Round-bellied to show his kind nature and that the great
earth has food enough for everyone who loves her and trusts
her;

Trampling underfoot wasteful freeways and needless
suburbs; smashing the worms of capitalism and totalitarianism;

Indicating the Task: his followers, becoming free of cars,
houses, canned food, universities, and shoes, master the
Three Mysteries of their own Body, Speech, and Mind; and
fearlessly chop down the rotten trees and prune out the sick limbs of
    this country
America and then burn the leftover
trash.

Wrathful but Calm, Austere but Comic, Smokey the Bear will
Illuminate those who would help him; but for those who would
hinder or slander him,

HE WILL PUT THEM OUT.

Thus his great Mantra:

Namah samanta vajranam chanda maharoshana
Sphataya hum traka ham mam

"I DEDICATE MYSELF TO THE UNIVERSAL DIAMOND
BE THIS RAGING FURY DESTROYED"

And he will protect those who love woods and rivers,
Gods and animals, hobos and madmen, prisoners and sick
people, musicians, playful women, and hopeful children;

And if anyone is threatened by advertising, air pollution,
or the police, they should chant SMOKEY THE BEAR'S WAR SPELL:

DROWN THEIR BUTTS
CRUSH THEIR BUTTS
DROWN THEIR BUTTS
CRUSH THEIR BUTTS

And SMOKEY THE BEAR will surely appear to put the enemy out
with his vajra-shovel.

Now those who recite this Sutra and then try to put it in
practice will accumulate merit as countless as the sands
of Arizona and Nevada,
Will help save the planet Earth from total oil slick,
Will enter the age of harmony of man and nature,
Will win the tender love and caresses of men, women, and
beasts
Will always have ripe blackberries to eat and a sunny spot
under a pine tree to sit at,

AND IN THE END WILL WIN HIGHEST PERFECT
ENLIGHTENMENT.

> thus have we heard.

> *(Yuba River redaction.*
> *May be reproduced free forever.)*

REGARDING THE 'SMOKEY THE BEAR SUTRA'

When the Wild gave the U.S. Forest Service the gift of the Sacred Cub
some years back, the Agency failed to understand the depth of its
responsibility. Instead of seeking to comprehend who this little mes-
senger was, the young bear was simply reduced to a mere anti–forest
fire icon, and manipulated in its one-sided and foolish campaign
against wildfire. Now it is time for the truth to come out. "Smokey
Bear" brought a rich and complex teaching of Non-Dualism that pro-
claimed the power and the truth of the Two Sides of Wildfire. This was
the inevitable resurfacing of our ancient Benefactor as Guide and
Teacher in the new millennium. The Agency never guessed that it was
serving as a vehicle for the magical reemergence of the teachings and
ceremonies of The Great Bear.

As one might expect, The Great Bear's true role of teaching and
enlightening through the practice and examination of both the creative
and destructive sides of Fire was not evident at first. As with so much
else in regard to the Forest Service, it was for the ordinary people, trail
crew workers and fire line firefighters, to expose the deeper truths. On
fire lines and lookouts in the remote mountains, through deep conversations all night among the backcountry men and women workers, it
came to be seen that The Great Bear was no other than that Auspicious
Being described in Archaic Texts as having taught in the unimaginably
distant past, the one referred to as "The Ancient One." This was the
Buddha who only delivered her teachings to mountain and river spir-
its, wild creatures, storm gods, Whale ascetics, bison philosophers, and
a few lost human stragglers.

It will take this sort of Teaching to quell the fires of greed and war and to guide us in how to stave off the biological holocaust that the 21st century may prove to be. The return of the Ancient Wild Teachings! The little Cub that restored our relationship with that Old Inspirer! What marvels!

We can start enacting these newly rediscovered truths by making fires, storms, and floods our friends rather than our enemies, and by choosing for wise restraint and humorous balance on behalf of all.

▼

A sutra is a talk given by a Buddha-teacher. The Smokey the Bear Sutra *first appeared on Turtle Island, North America. Like all sutras, it is anonymous and free.*

A GLOSSARY OF EUPHEMISMS AND SPIN

Many public agencies use euphemisms—the substitution of agreeable or inoffensive expressions for ones that may offend or suggest something unpleasant—to frame their actions in a positive light. The military, for instance, speaks in terms of "collateral damage" when referring to civilian casualties inflicted during the course of war. Use of this more "neutral" term is meant to avert public objections to such costs—to disguise the harm to innocent lives with a euphemism that distances us from the reality of it.

Similarly, the fire-industrial complex and the beneficiaries of that industry, including developers and the timber and livestock industries, use language that deliberately blurs the distinction between ecological restoration, public safety, public benefits, and commercial profiteering. One example is the use of military metaphors. We "fight" fires. We have "firefighters." We seek to stop the "inferno" from "destroying" the forest. We talk about the "advancing front" of the blaze as if it were an enemy army on the march. Firefighters mount a "direct attack" with water or chemicals in an effort to "control" the blaze. If that fails, they resort to an "extended attack incident," in which more firefighting personnel—a "strike team"—are called into action by the "incident commander." The metaphors of war place firefighting and fire suppression in a positive, patriotic light while casting wildfire as the enemy that must be halted.

If, on the other hand, we frame the issue by suggesting that fire is nature's way of "rejuvenating" or "regenerating" the forest rather than "destroying" it, we create a radically different perspective on wildfire. Why, then, do agencies such as the Forest Service or the Bureau of Land Management—agencies that are full of scientists and researchers who have studied wildfire and who repeatedly suggest that society reframe its view of fire as a natural process for healthy ecosystems—continue to use terms that paint fire as "destructive" or "catastrophic," as something that must be "fought" and "controlled"?

A large part of the answer lies in the bias of these agencies toward timber and grass production, compounded by a Washington administration that favors resource exploitation. One need not look far to find examples of this bias in the choice of terminology used in relation to wildfire.

"Salvage Logging"

Logging on public lands is a practice that has been called into question for a host of reasons, including concern about its impact on wildlife, watersheds, fisheries, and scenery. As a consequence, it has become more difficult for agencies to cut trees on public lands. In order to skirt environmental regulations and public opposition to the timber industry, a sympathetic Bush administration and members of Congress have ordered the Forest Service to offer "salvage logging" timber sales, which are exempt from most public scrutiny and most environmental measures. Public opposition to logging burned forests is lessened because people are led to believe that charred trees are a "wasted resource"—an ecologically flawed assumption that our current timber-friendly government does nothing to counter. Given the excuse that there is an "urgent" need to extract burned timber to "help" forest regeneration (another flawed assertion), agencies are directed to circumvent proper environmental review, as well as other environmental restrictions and regulations, in an effort to get the cut out.

The Bush administration has capitalized on the word "salvage" as a euphemism that implies saving something of value—seemingly a beneficial effort. Using the claim of "salvaging" some value from the "destruction" created by the fire, agencies portray salvage logging as a win-win scenario for everyone—the timber industry profits from logging, the public gets wood products, and the forest is "aided in its recovery." The best thing about salvage sales, we are told, is that the forest benefits because salvage logging will hasten forest regeneration—a patently false assertion challenged by numerous postfire studies.

"Catastrophic" Fires/"Restoring" the "Damaged" Forest

Often in government proposals and reports, we find many euphemisms used to frame and justify the cutting of trees in the aftermath of a blaze. We are told about the need to remove burned trees resulting from "catastrophic" fires and the need to "restore" the "damaged" forest. "Catastrophic" is a loaded term meaning disastrous, calamitous, or ruinous. Yet large blazes are completely normal in many ecosystems— for instance, the Yellowstone fires of 1988 are often referred to as "catastrophic" when, in fact, from an ecological perspective, long-interval, but very large stand-replacement fires are the norm for this landscape. Large fires create new, healthy forests and at the same time recycle nutrients, enrich watersheds, and create snags and downed woody debris critical to many wildlife species. To label such blazes as "catastrophic" is pejorative and misleading.

By the same token, the idea that logging "restores" the forest is misleading at best, since the intrusion of logging roads, introduction of weeds on trucks and equipment, soil compaction from heavy equipment, and removal of woody debris and snags harm the forest. Even the planting of trees in the name of "restoration" can short-circuit normal ecological processes. In many instances, a burned landscape is first nourished by a proliferation of nitrogen-fixing plants that enrich the soil, setting the stage for later tree regeneration.

Finally, "damaged" implies that fire harms the forest and that prompt logging will "improve" the forest, again casting a negative and pejorative spin on a creative natural process of combustion.

"Hazard Reduction Logging"

Closely related to salvage logging is "hazard reduction logging," which is—far too often—just another name for commercial logging under the guise of fire prevention. Reduction of fuels by the removal of small-diameter trees and brush will—in some instances—reduce the likelihood of a larger blaze and increase the effectiveness of fire suppression, and is thus a legitimate strategy to implement, say, near a community. However, in many instances, agencies feel compelled through lobbying pressure to make such "hazard reduction logging" lucrative and attractive to private logging companies by offering timber sales that include a substantial amount of large-diameter trees. These large-bole trees are the most fire-resistant and are exactly the kind of tree that we should leave, not cut. Furthermore, the term "hazard reduction" in reference to fire suggests that having the forest burn is somehow "bad," whereas, in many instances, fire is part of the forest's normal ecological process.

"Balanced Forest Management"

We often hear politicians and industry representatives talking about "balanced forest management" in relation to forest fire policy. The implication of such a phrase is that the current policy is out of whack. What "balanced forest management" really means is giving commercial industries unfettered access to public lands and resources. Thus any "balance" is nearly always in favor of commercial interests.

The "Healthy Forests Initiative"

The Bush administration's "Healthy Forests Initiative" is another euphemism, and a cynical attempt at spin, for many of the policies in the initiative actually lead to less forest health, not more. The initiative, passed into law as the Healthy Forest Act in 2003, allows logging of large-bole trees under the guise of thinning forest stands for "fire prevention" and limits public scrutiny and environmental review. It places priority on short-term economic and property considerations rather than on the long-term ecological health of the forest. The initiative was described as a "commonsense" approach, suggesting to an often-unquestioning public that the plan unequivocally makes sense at all levels despite its actually being harmful in practice.

In creating a positive spin for the initiative, one government supporter called loggers "the physicians of the forest." This is a clever use of metaphor, implying that the way to "cure" the presumed forest health problem—even though sometimes there isn't one—is by allowing the "physicians" to cut the trees.

"Clarifying Rules"/"Regulatory Streamlining"

"Clarifying rules" protecting wildlife and "regulatory streamlining" are euphemisms often used by pro-industry administrations to reduce government oversight and monitoring. These terms are usually code for eliminating regulations and public oversight that hinder exploitation of public resources for private profit.

"Controlling" a Blaze

Even the legitimate terms used to describe fires have concealed implications. For instance, we often hear media and government agencies claim that firefighters have a blaze "under control." What does this phrase really mean? In most instances, it means that the weather changed: it rained or snowed. Most small fires go out on their own, without any suppression. Big blazes are most often driven by drought and wind—conditions under which fire suppression efforts usually fail to have any significant impact. Big blazes are extinguished after the weather changes—typically not as a result of firefighting efforts. The next time you hear that a wildfire was "controlled," check to see whether there was an accompanying change in the weather that facilitated the "control." The use of the term "controlled" to describe the natural extinguishment of a blaze blurs the lines of cause and effect. Agencies accept credit for "stopping" a big blaze for obvious reasons—it increases public support and money for future suppression activity. Yet natural events like large blazes are affected by so many variables that the opportunity for human control of these processes is actually minimal.

▼

What all these terms have in common is that they have been twisted to serve logging or fire industry interests, and turned into a matrix of metaphors and euphemisms to support a fire-industrial complex that benefits from fire suppression and fire-related logging. Beware.

A GLOSSARY OF WILDLAND FIRE TERMS

aerial ignition The ignition of fuels by dropping incendiary devices or materials from aircraft.

agency Any federal, state, or county government organization participating with jurisdictional responsibilities.

air tanker A fixed-wing aircraft equipped to drop fire retardants or suppressants.

backburn A blaze deliberately ignited in advance of a fire front to eliminate fuels so as to deflect or stop the spread of the fire.

backfire A fire set along the inner edge of a fire line to consume the fuel in the path of a wildfire and/or change the direction of force of the fire's convection column.

backpack pump A portable sprayer with hand pump, fed from a liquid-filled container fitted with straps.

biodiversity Biological diversity at genetic, population, ecosystem, and landscape scales.

biological legacies Standing dead trees (snags), downed logs, intact thickets, and large living trees that persist after disturbance events, such as a forest fire.

biomass In the context of a forest, downed logs and other biologically derived materials.

blowup A sudden increase in fire intensity or rate of spread.

broadcast burn A fire that is permitted to burn over a large area in order to achieve a preplanned objective.

brush Stands of vegetation dominated by shrubby, woody plants or low-growing trees.

buck To cut up, as in cutting up a log.

buffer zone An area of reduced vegetation that separates wildlands from vulnerable residential or business developments.

burnout A fire set inside a control line to widen the line, or to consume fuel between the edge of the fire and the control line.

canopy The uppermost spreading branchy layer of a forest; may be closed (providing shade) or open (providing light).

cargo chute A smokejumping parachute used to carry supplies.

chaining Ripping trees and shrubs from the ground by means of giant logging chain pulled between two tractors.

chaparral A plant community of low, often evergreen shrubs; primarily found in California.

choker setter The person in a logging operation who wraps a chain (choker) around a log so it can be hauled to a landing.

clearcutting The removal of all standing trees.

cold trailing Inspecting a partly dead fire edge by feeling with the hand for heat, then digging out every live spot and trenching any live edge.

community protection zone An area surrounding a town from which fuels like brush and trees are removed in order to stop advancing fires.

complex Two or more individual fires located in the same general area.

contain a fire To complete a fuel break around a fire.

control a fire To completely extinguish a fire, including spot fires.

conversion burns Burns that change the vegetation from one type to another—for example, from a forest to a pasture.

creeping fire A fire burning with a low flame and spreading slowly.

crown (of a tree) The top of a tree.

crown fire A fire that moves through the crowns of trees or shrubs more or less independently of the surface fire.

defensible space An area in which material capable of causing a fire to spread has been cleared and treated to act as a barrier to an advancing wildland fire.

deployment bag A bag that holds a parachute and keeps its ropes from tangling.

direct attack A method of wildfire control in which firefighting techniques are used directly on the fire perimeter; can only be used safely with slow-moving fires.

dog-hair thickets A dense stand of trees packed like hair on a dog's back.

downed logs Fallen trees on forest floor.

downfall Trees and branches that have fallen to forest floor.

dozer Any tracked vehicle with a front-mounted blade used for exposing mineral soil.

dozer line A fire line constructed by the front blade of a dozer.

drift streamer A piece of flagging dropped from an airplane by smokejumpers to determine the wind direction prior to a jump.

drip torch A handheld device for igniting fires by dripping flaming liquid fuel on the materials to be burned.

drop spot The landing target of smokejumpers.

dry lightning storm A thunderstorm in which negligible precipitation reaches the ground; also called a dry storm.

duff The layer of decomposing organic materials lying below the litter layer of freshly fallen twigs, needles, and leaves and immediately above the mineral soil.

duff hoe A tool, part hoe and part rake, used to remove duff from around trees prior to the prescribed burning of site.

engine A ground vehicle with pumping, water, and hose capacity.

entry burns The first of a series of planned burns on a site from which fire has been excluded for a significant time.

environmental impact statement (EIS) An analysis of the probable effects of proposed actions upon the environment; authorized by the National Environmental Policy Act (NEPA) of 1969.

escaped fire A fire that is no longer under control.

extreme fire behavior Fire behavior that is difficult to control because of a high rate of spread, prolific crowning and/or spotting, presence of fire whirls, and/or strong convection column.

faller A person who fells (cuts down) trees.

feller buncher A tractor used in logging that cuts, stacks, and loads trees.

fine fuels *See* light fuels.

fire barrier A natural (rock outcrop or river) or artificial (road) feature that prevents the spread of a fire.

fire behavior The manner in which a fire reacts to the influences of fuel, weather, and topography.

firebrands Burning embers thrown by the wind in advance of a fire front.

fire break A natural or constructed barrier used to stop or check fires that may occur, or to provide a control line from which to work.

fire crew An organized group of firefighters under the leadership of a designated leader.

fire ecology The study of the influence of fire on natural landscapes.

fire exclusion The exclusion of fire from an area through suppression.

fire front The part of a fire within which continuous flaming combustion is taking place; usually the leading edge of the fire perimeter.

fire intensity A general term relating to the heat energy released by a fire.

fire line A linear fire barrier that is scraped or dug to mineral soil.

fire management plan A strategic plan that defines a program to manage wildland and prescribed fires.

fire mosaic The pattern of burned and unburned patches of vegetation created by fire on the landscape.

fire perimeter The entire outer edge or boundary of a fire.

fire regime The dominant fire pattern for an area, including the normal frequency and intensity of blazes.

fire retardant A chemical used to extinguish flames.

fire rotation The average time between blazes.

fire season The period of the year during which wildland fires are likely to occur.

fire shelter An aluminized tent offering protection to wildland firefighters during a fire entrapment situation.

firestorm Violent convection caused by a large, continuous area of intense fire.

fire suppression All the work of extinguishing or containing a fire, beginning with its discovery.

fire weather Weather conditions that influence fire ignition, behavior, and suppression.

flame front The advancing front of a fire.

flash fuels *See* light fuels.

foehn winds Warm, dry winds that occur where air masses climb over mountains, decompressing rapidly as they descend—e.g., the Santa Anas of southern California.

forb A plant with a soft rather than a permanent woody stem that is not a grass or grasslike plant.

fuel Combustible material that feeds a fire, including vegetation such as grass, leaves, ground litter, plants, shrubs, and trees.

fuel breaks Areas where fuel is removed in advance of a fire front to slow or stop the fire.

fuel load The amount of fuel present, expressed quantitatively in terms of weight of fuel per unit area.

fuel treatment Any method, including prescribed burning or mechanical thinning, that removes or reduces fuels.

fusee A colored flare designed as a railway warning device and widely used to ignite suppression and prescription fires.

g-force The force of gravity.

ground fires Fires that burn on the surface and in belowground parts of plants such as their roots.

ground fuels All combustible materials below the surface litter that normally support a glowing combustion without flame.

hand line A fire line built with hand tools.

heat flux The heat transfer rate per unit of area.

heavy fuels Fuels of large diameter—such as snags, logs, and large-limbed wood—that ignite and are consumed more slowly than flash fuels.

helitorch A torch dragged beneath a helicopter to ignite fires.

historical range of variability The normal frequency pattern of disturbance common to a particular area.

home ignition zone The house and the area within 200 feet of the house.

hotshot crew A highly trained fire crew used mainly to hand-build fire lines.

incident commander The person responsible for managing all operations at a fire site.

indirect attack A method of wildfire control in which the control line is located at a considerable distance from the fire's active edge; necessary with fast-moving or large blazes.

jump spot The selected landing area for smokejumpers.
jump suit A protection suit worn by smokejumpers.

keystone An important species or ecological process (such as fire) that is crucial to the organization and diversity of an ecosystem.

ladder fuels Trees and shrubs that provide a "ladder" of fuels permitting a fire to jump from the surface into the crowns of trees.
large fire A big fire for a particular ecosystem, usually burning hotter and over a greater area than the average blaze for that region.
legacy trees *See* biological legacies.
light burning The burning of litter and other fine fuels that do not normally create hot blazes.
light (fine) fuels Fast-drying fuels, generally less than ¼ inch in diameter, that readily ignite and are rapidly consumed by fire when dry.
litter The top layer of forest floor debris, consisting of recently fallen material that has been little altered by decomposition.
log skidding The dragging of logs across a logging site.

maintenance burns Regularly scheduled burns to maintain a desired vegetation community or fuel load level.
megafires Very large blazes, usually in the hundreds of thousands of acres.
mineral soil Soil layers consisting of dirt without organic matter.
mop-up The patrol of a fire perimeter to extinguish any remaining embers or flames.

National Environmental Policy Act (NEPA) The basic national law for protection of the environment, passed by Congress in 1969.
National Fire Danger Rating System (NFDRS) A uniform fire danger rating system that focuses on the environmental factors that control the moisture content of fuels.
Nomex The trade name for a fire-resistant synthetic material.

Osborne Fire Finder A device used in fire lookouts for pinpointing a fire location.

parachute riser An attachment that connects parachute ropes to the harness of the parachuter.

prescribed fire/prescribed burn A fire ignited by management actions under predetermined conditions to meet objectives related to hazardous fuels or habitat improvement.

prescribed natural burn policies Fire management policies that permit naturally ignited fires to burn under specific prescribed circumstances.

prescription Defined conditions under which a prescribed fire may be ignited.

presuppression activities Activities, such as tree thinning, carried out prior to fire suppression.

project fire A fire of such size or complexity that a large organization and prolonged activity are required to suppress it.

pulaski A combination chopping and trenching tool that combines a single-bitted ax blade with a narrow, adzelike trenching blade fitted to a straight handle.

refugia Sites that provide refuge for species from disturbances such as fire.

relative humidity The ratio of the amount of moisture in the air to the maximum amount of moisture that the air would contain if it were saturated.

retardant A substance or chemical agent that reduces the flammability of combustibles.

rotational age In terms of economic efficiency, the ideal age for cutting a forest.

safety zone An area cleared of flammable materials to allow firefighters to escape in case the fire line is outflanked or becomes unsafe.

salvage logging The postfire removal of dead or damaged trees designed to "salvage" the economic value of the wood.

Santa Ana winds High winds that blow from the California desert toward the Pacific Ocean and often help to sustain large wildfires in southern California.

scrub A stunted tree or shrub.

serotinous cones Cones that remain closed on the tree until opened by heating, whereupon they release their seeds.

sink population A declining part of a larger species population that does not produce enough young to maintain the population.

slash The debris left after logging, pruning, thinning, or brush cutting; includes logs, chips, bark, branches, stumps, and broken understory trees or brush.

slipstream A low-pressure area immediately behind a moving airplane; often encountered by smokejumpers as they leave the plane.

slurry bomber An airplane that drops fire retardant.

smokejumper A firefighter who travels to fires by aircraft and parachute.

smoldering fire A fire burning without flame and barely spreading.

snag A standing dead tree or part of a dead tree from which at least the smaller branches have fallen.

source populations An expanding part of a species population that is exporting members to vacant habitat.

spot fire A fire ignited outside the perimeter of the main fire by flying sparks or embers.

spotter In smokejumping, the person responsible for selecting drop targets and supervising all aspects of dropping smokejumpers.

stand-maintenance fires Fires that maintain forest stands by thinning excess trees.

stand-replacement fires Fires that kill all trees in an area so that the stand can be replaced by younger trees.

static line A line attaching a smokejumper's parachute to a cable within the airplane that jerks open the chute as the jumper exits the plane.

superfire A large blaze, usually covering more than 50,000 acres.

suppressant An agent, such as water or foam, used to extinguish the flaming and glowing phases of combustion when directly applied to burning fuels.

suppression *See* fire suppression.

surface fire Usually, a fire that is limited to burning litter on the surface of the ground.

surface fuels Fallen leaves or needles, twigs, bark, cones, small branches, grasses, and shrubs on the surface of the ground that help to sustain a blaze.

Terra Torch The trade name for a device that throws a stream of flaming liquid; used for rapid ignition during burnout or prescribed fire operations.

timber rotation period The time it takes for a tree to grow large enough to be cut.

torching The ignition and flare-up of a tree or small group of trees, usually from bottom to top.

treatment *See* fuels treatment.

underburn A fire that consumes surface fuels but not trees or shrubs.

water bar A barrier such as a log placed across a slope to slow water flow and thereby reduce erosion.

wildland fire Any nonstructure fire, other than a prescribed fire, that occurs in the wildland.

wildland fire use (WFU) Allowing naturally ignited wildland fires to burn in order to accomplish specific prestated resource management goals.

wildland-urban interface (WUI) The line, area, or zone where structures and other human development meet or intermingle with undeveloped wildland or vegetative fuels.

wise use A human-centered philosophy that promotes exploitation of natural resources, usually for the benefit of corporative interests.

woody debris Downed logs and fallen snags.

CONTRIBUTORS

LES AUCOIN is a frequent Oregon newspaper essayist and public radio commentator. A retired U.S. congressman, he coauthored the 1984 Oregon Wilderness Act and the 1988 Oregon Omnibus Wild and Scenic Rivers Act, wrote the first ban on oil drilling off the Oregon and California coasts, and appropriated funds to purchase Rock Mesa in the Oregon Cascades' Three Sisters Wilderness. A retired professor of political science and environmental studies at Southern Oregon University, Les is a resident of Ashland, Oregon.

DOMINICK A. DELLASALA is director of World Wildlife Fund's Klamath-Siskiyou Program in Ashland, Oregon. An internationally renowned author of over 150 articles and book chapters, he has been instrumental in U.S. and Canadian protected-area campaigns spanning two decades. Dr. DellaSala is on the board of directors of the Society for Conservation Biology, is subject and guest editor for scientific journals, and has received WWF's distinguished World of a Difference award for his outstanding conservation achievements.

CJ FOTHERINGHAM is a doctoral student in the Department of Ecology and Evolutionary Biology at the University of California, Los Angeles. Her research is focused on the evolutionary patterns of species response to fires in Mediterranean-climate shrublands of California and South Africa and in non-Mediterranean-climate shrublands of the Southwest. She has published papers in *Science, Ecology*, the *Journal of Ecology*, and various other international journals. CJ resides in Los Angeles.

JOE FOX was a wildland firefighter for 23 years, including 19 years as a smokejumper. As an aerial initial attack specialist skilled at suppressing emerging wildfires in rugged terrain, he experienced wildfires in western states, including Alaska. Joe received a Ph.D. in forest entomology from the University of California, Berkeley, where he was a Regents Fellow while researching symbiosis among insects and plant pathogens in deteriorating environments. He also holds a J.D. degree from the College of Law, University of Idaho.

DENNIS GLICK earned a B.S. degree from the School of Forestry at Oregon State University, and an M.S. degree from the School of Natural Resources at the University of Michigan. For the past 16 years he has worked on conservation issues in the Yellowstone area, focusing primarily on private land conservation and land use planning.

TIMOTHY INGALSBEE is the executive director of Firefighters United for Safety, Ethics, and Ecology (FUSEE), a nonprofit organization dedicated to public education and policy advocacy to support safe, ethical, and ecological fire management. He is also a research associate and adjunct instructor at the University of Oregon and secretary of the board for the Association for Fire Ecology, a nonprofit organization promoting the application of fire ecology in land management.

JON E. KEELEY is a research scientist with the U.S. Geological Survey and a professor of biology at the University of California, Los Angeles. He has authored over 250 research papers dealing with the ecology, evolution, physiology, and taxonomy of California plants. His current research is on historical patterns of burning and their effect on alien plant invasions. Jon resides near Sequoia National Park in the community of Three Rivers, California.

ANDY KERR is czar of the Larch Company, a for-profit nonmembership conservation organization that advocates for species that cannot talk and for humans not yet born. All profits are dedicated to conservation. Since 1976, Andy has been associated with the Oregon Natural Resources Council, best known for having brought you the northern spotted owl. The author of *Oregon Desert Guide* and *Oregon Wild: Endangered Forest Wilderness*, his main gig is director of the National Public Lands Grazing Campaign.

JOHN KRIST is a senior reporter and opinion-page columnist at the *Ventura County Star*, a southern California daily newspaper where he has worked since 1983. His commentaries on land use policy, natural resources, and environmental issues have been published in newspapers throughout the western United States. A graduate of the University of California at Santa Barbara, he is the author of three books about California's parks and wilderness areas. He lives in Ventura, California.

CHRIS MASER is a vertebrate zoologist who has spent over 25 years as a research scientist in forest, shrub-steppe, subarctic, desert, coastal, and agricultural settings. He has worked and/or lectured in Europe, Asia, Egypt, Canada, and throughout the United States and has written 270 publications, including 26 books. He is also an international lecturer; a facilitator in resolving environmental conflicts, creating vision statements, and developing sustainable communities; and an international consultant in forest ecology and sustainable forestry practices.

MOLLIE MATTESON is a writer, editor, and wilderness activist. She obtained an M.S. degree in wildlife biology from the University of Montana while studying a recovering population of gray wolves. She has worked as a wilderness ranger, wildlife researcher, environmental educator, and teacher and has published two books, along with a variety of essays on environmental philosophy and ethics.

BRIAN NOWICKI is a conservation biologist at the Center for Biological Diversity, based in Tucson, Arizona. He holds an M.S. degree in forestry from Northern Arizona University, with a focus on conservation biology. Since 2000, he has worked on the management of forests and wildlife on public lands in the Southwest.

RANDAL O'TOOLE is a forest economist who has visited most of the national forests, collecting data on timber, recreation, budgets, and other forest issues. Randal works for the Thoreau Institute, a nonprofit organization that finds ways to protect the environment without big government. His 1988 book *Reforming the Forest Service* showed that most national forest controversies stem from incentives built into the Forest Service budget, including incentives to lose money on environmentally destructive activities.

THOMAS MICHAEL POWER is professor of economics and chairman of the Economics Department at the University of Montana. He specializes in natural resource and regional economic development issues and is the author of several books, including *Post-Cowboy Economics: Pay and Prosperity in the New American West* (2001), *Lost Landscapes and Failed Economies: The Search for a Value of Place* (1996), and *Environmental Protection and Economic Well-Being: The Economic Pursuit of Quality* (1996).

STEPHEN J. PYNE's career kindled in 1967 when he joined the North Rim Longshots, a fire crew at Grand Canyon National Park. He returned for 19 seasons in three parks. Currently a professor at Arizona State University, he is the author of 16 books, including a six-volume global suite of fire histories, *Cycle of Fire*, and *Tending Fire: Coping with America's Wildland Fires* (2004). His degrees include a B.A. from Stanford University and an M.A. and Ph.D. from the University of Texas at Austin.

TOM RIBE holds a master's of science degree in environmental studies from the University of Oregon and has worked as an environmental educator for 24 years. A native of northern New Mexico, Tom has served on prescribed-fire teams at Bandelier National Monument and Yosemite National Park and is on the board of directors of FUSEE (Firefighters United for Safety, Ethics, and Ecology). He is currently completing a book on the 2000 Cerro Grande (Los Alamos) Fire.

TODD SCHULKE is the forest program director for the Center for Biological Diversity. He sits on the Western Governors' Forest Health Advisory Committee, Arizona Governor Napolitano's Forest Health Oversight Committee, and Senator Bingaman's Collaborative Forest Restoration Program Advisory Committee. He lives with his wife and two young sons in a fire-prone forest on the Gila National Forest in New Mexico.

CONRAD SMITH is a professor of journalism at the University of Wyoming in Laramie. Before accepting that position in 1996, he taught aspiring journalists at The Ohio State University in Columbus, Colorado State University in Fort Collins, and Idaho State University in Pocatello. In 1988, when the Yellowstone fires became national news, Conrad was in the park's backcountry leading a group of trail work volunteers who watched the Clover and Mist fires burn together into the Clover-Mist Fire.

GARY SNYDER—writer, Buddhist, forest landowner, and bioregionalist—was born in San Francisco in 1930. He has published 16 books of poetry and prose, including the poems of *Turtle Island* (Pulitzer Prize, 1975), *Mountains and Rivers Without End* (Bollingen Prize, 1997), and the paradigm-shifting essays of *The Practice of the Wild* (1990). He has been a logger, a forest firefighter, a lookout, a professor, and a Zen student in Japan. He lives in the Yuba watershed of the northern Sierra.

CRYSTAL STANIONIS graduated from Penn State University with a B.S. degree in geography, a B.A. degree in journalism, and a minor in sociology. She holds an M.S. degree in earth sciences/geography from Montana State University. Her master's thesis explored the prevalence of ecosystem management in the Greater Yellowstone Ecosystem through the use of case studies, including wildfire management.

JAMES R. STRITTHOLT is a conservation biologist with more than 12 years' experience in applying computer mapping technologies to address conservation in the United States and abroad. He founded the Conservation Biology Institute (located in Corvallis, Oregon) in 1997 and currently serves as its executive director. His degrees include a B.S. in botany, zoology, and secondary education; an M.S. in zoology from Miami University, Oxford, Ohio; and a Ph.D. from The Ohio State University in a self-designed program emphasizing landscape ecology and conservation planning.

THOMAS R. VALE has spent more than 30 years in the Department of Geography at the University of Wisconsin, Madison, where he has written about and offered courses in biogeography (especially vegetation dynamics), natural resources (notably nature protection), landscape change, and the American West. He has published more than three dozen professional articles and eight books, including *Fire, Native Peoples, and the Natural Landscape*.

JAN W. VAN WAGTENDONK has spent over three decades in Yosemite investigating the role of fire in Sierra Nevada ecosystems. Summers as a hotshot firefighter and smokejumper in Oregon and Alaska convinced him of the folly of total fire exclusion. Building on this experience, he obtained his Ph.D. at the University of California, Berkeley, studying under Dr. Harold Biswell, the father of California fire ecology. He has published extensively and has served on several federal fire policy reviews.

GEORGE WUERTHNER is an ecologist, longtime wildlands activist, and wilderness visionary with interests in conservation history and conservation biology. He has undergraduate degrees in wildlife biology and botany, and a master's degree in science communications from the University of California at Santa Cruz. He has worked previously as a wilderness ranger, biologist, and range conservationist for the federal government and more recently as a university instructor, photography instructor, consulting biologist, and wildlife policy analyst. His photographs have appeared in hundreds of publications, and he is also the author of more than two dozen books on natural history and other environmental topics. He is currently the ecological projects director for the Foundation for Deep Ecology.

ACKNOWLEDGMENTS

This book came together through the hard work, dedication, and patience of many people. First and foremost, I would like to thank the authors, who unselfishly contributed their valuable time, expertise, and excellent writing.

Next, I would like to thank two people in particular for their work in bringing this book to fruition. Doug Tompkins, founder and president of the Foundation for Deep Ecology, provided the insight, creative ideas, and spirited oversight for the entire project. Without his enthusiastic support, this book would not have materialized. Sharon Donovan, FDE's publishing manager and organizational genius, kept the production flowing while constantly striving for exceptionally high standards on the path to publication.

John Davis and Mollie Matteson offered astute suggestions in their review of the initial manuscript, and Mary Davis lent her assistance in painstakingly pinning down the myriad endnotes in the early stages of the book. In addition, we are grateful to our anonymous peer reviewer, who—often playing the role of devil's advocate—provided the important feedback required during the development of a volume such as this.

We were incredibly fortunate to have Mary Anne Stewart as our developmental editor and copy editor. Beyond strengthening and sharpening the writing of each piece, her tenacity and extraordinary skill with complicated editorial matters helped us to create a better book. Editorial assistant Berwin Song deftly handled some of the last-minute details that needed his eagle-eye attention. As always the wonderful folks at BookMatters created this Reader edition as a companion to the larger, photo-format edition published simultaneously. Proofreader Carrie Pickett did a tremendous job of uncovering and correcting those ever-elusive mistakes before we went to press, and indexer Ellen Sherron masterfully pulled together into a coherent form the various issues and salient points developed by the different authors.

Finally, I would like to thank Island Press, particularly executive editor Barbara Dean and editor-in-chief Todd Baldwin, for their publishing expertise and invaluable assistance in bringing this book to the public.

—The Editor

NOTES

INTRODUCTION

1. G. Wuerthner, "Introduction," in *Unmanaged Landscapes: Voices for Untamed Nature*, ed. W. B. Willers (Washington, D.C.: Island Press, 1999).

2. Central Idaho anti-Wolf Coalition; www.usa4id.com/ciwc.

3. M. E. Soulé, J. A. Estes, B. Miller, and D. L. Honnold, "Strongly Interacting Species: Conservation Policy, Management, and Ethics," *Bioscience* 55, no. 2 (2005): 168–176.

PART TWO

FIRE AND NATIVE PEOPLES

1. S. Budiansky, *Nature's Keepers: The New Science of Nature Management* (New York: Free Press, 1995); A. Chase, *Playing God in Yellowstone* (San Diego: Harcourt Brace Jovanovich, 1987); D. Flores, "The West That Was, and the West That Can Be," *High Country News* 29, no. 15 (1997): 1, 6–7; M. Pollan, *Second Nature: A Gardener's Education* (New York: Dell, 1991); S. Pyne, *Fire in America* (Princeton: Princeton University Press, 1982).

2. W. Denevan, "The Pristine Myth: The Landscape of the Americas in 1492," *Annals of the Association of American Geographers* 82 (1992): 369–385.

3. R. Haydon, "A Look at How We Look at What Is 'Natural,'" *Natural Areas News* 2, no. 1 (1997): 2–5.

4. K. Olwig, "Reinventing Common Nature: Yosemite and Mount Rushmore—A Meandering Tale of a Double Nature," in *Uncommon Ground: Toward Reinventing Nature*, ed. W. Cronon (New York: Norton, 1995).

5. R. Solnit, "Up the River of Mercy," *Sierra* 77, no. 6 (1992), 50–57, 78–84.

6. N. K. Anderson and G. P. Nabhan, "Gardeners in Eden," *Wilderness* 55, no. 194 (1991): 27–30.

7. E. Diringer, "From This Valley," *San Francisco Chronicle*, May 18, 1997, pp. 1, 4–5.

8. Anderson and Nabhan, "Gardeners."

9. J. W. van Wagtendonk, "The Role of Fire in the Yosemite Wilderness," in *Proceedings of the National Wilderness Research Conference: Current Research*, U.S. Forest Service General Technical Report INT-212 (Ogden, Utah: U.S. Forest Service, Intermountain Research Station, 1986).

10. P. W. Rundel, D. J. Parsons, and D. T. Gordon, "Montane and Subalpine Vegetation of the Sierra Nevada and Cascade Ranges," in *Terrestrial Vegetation of California*, ed. M. G. Barbour and J. Major (New York: Wiley, 1977), pp. 559–600; T. W. Swetnam, "Fire History and Climate Change in Giant Sequoia Groves," *Science* 262 (1993): 885–889; van Wagtendonk, "The Role of Fire"; T. E. Warner,

"Fire History in the Yellow Pine Forest of Kings Canyon National Park," in *Proceedings of the Fire History Workshop*, U.S. Forest Service General Technical Report RM-81 (Fort Collins, Colo.: U.S. Forest Service, Intermountain Forest and Range Experiment Station, 1980), pp. 89–92; H. A. Wright and A. W. Bailey, *Fire Ecology* (New York: Wiley, 1982).

11. A. C. Caprio and T. W. Swetnam, "Historic Fire Regimes Along an Elevational Gradient on the West Slope of the Sierra Nevada, California," in *Proceedings: Symposium on Fire in Wilderness and Park Management*, U.S. Forest Service General Technical Report INT-320 (Ogden, Utah: U.S. Forest Service, Intermountain Research Station, 1995), pp. 173–179; Swetnam, "Fire History and Climate Change."

12. van Wagtendonk, "The Role of Fire."

13. U.S. Forest Service, *National Forest Fire Report* (annual) (Washington, D.C.: U.S. Forest Service, 1972–1987).

14. van Wagtendonk, "The Role of Fire."

15. E. W. B. Russell, "Indian-Set Fires in the Forests of the Northeastern United States," *Ecology* 64 (1983): 78–88; G. G. Whitney, *From Coastal Wilderness to Fruited Plain: A History of Environmental Change in Temperate North America from 1500 to the Present* (Cambridge, England: Cambridge University Press, 1994).

16. L. Greene, *Historic Resource Study, Yosemite National Park, California*, vol. 1 (Denver: National Park Service, 1987).

17. J. A. Bennyhoff, *An Appraisal of the Archaeological Resources of Yosemite National Park*, Archaeological Survey Reports (Berkeley: University of California, 1956); Greene, *Historic Resource Study*; K. L. Hull, *The 1985 and 1986 Wawona Archeological Excavations*, Yosemite Research Publications in Anthropology No. 8 (National Park Service, Yosemite National Park, 1989); K. L. Hull and W. J. Mundy, *The 1984 Yosemite Archeological Surveys: The South Entrance, Mariposa Grove, Tioga Road, Crane Flat, and Glacier Point Road Areas*, Yosemite Research Publications in Anthropology No. 1 (National Park Service, Yosemite National Park, 1985).

18. Greene, *Historic Resource Study*.

19. Bennyhoff, *An Appraisal of the Archaeological Resources*.

20. J. Chapman, H. Delcourt, and P. Delcourt, "Strawberry Fields, Almost Forever," *Natural History* 98, no. 9 (1989): 50–58.

21. J. Curtis, *The Vegetation of Wisconsin* (Madison: University of Wisconsin Press, 1959).

22. W. Cronon, *Changes in the Land: Indians, Colonists, and Ecology of New England* (New York: Hill and Wang, 1983); S. Olson, "The Historical Occurrence of Fire in the Central Hardwoods, with Emphasis on Southcentral Indiana," *Natural Areas Journal* 16 (1996): 248–256.

23. G. G. Whitney, *From Coastal Wilderness to Fruited Plain: A History of Environmental Change in Temperate North America from 1500 to the Present* (Cambridge, England: Cambridge University Press, 1994).

24. V. Holliday, "A Reexamination of Late-Pleistocene Boreal Forest Reconstructions for the Southern High Plains," *Quaternary Research* 28 (1987): 238–244.

25. M. Barbour and W. Billings, *North American Terrestrial Vegetation* (Cambridge, England: Cambridge University Press, 1988); T. Vale, *Plants and People: Vegetation Change in North America* (Washington, D.C.: Association of American Geographers, 1982).

26. Flores, "The West That Was."

27. P. Limerick, *The Legacy of Conquest: The Unbroken Past of the American West* (New York: Norton, 1987); R. White, "Introduction: American Indians and the Environment," *Environmental Review* 9 (1985): 101–103.

28. Cronon, *Changes in the Land.*

29. B. J. Morehouse, *A Place Called Grand Canyon: Contested Geographies* (Tucson: University of Arizona Press, 1996).

30. Budiansky, *Nature's Keepers.*

31. J. B. Callicott, "American Indian Land Wisdom? Sorting Out the Issues," *Journal of Forest History* 33 (1989): 35–42.

32. W. Cronon, "The Trouble with Wilderness, or, Getting Back to the Wrong Nature," in *Uncommon Ground*, pp. 69–90.

33. Y.-F. Tuan, "Space and Place: Humanistic Perspective," in *Philosophy in Geography*, ed. S. Gale and G. Olsson (Boston: D. Reidel, 1979), pp. 387–427.

34. A. Shields, *A Yosemite Naturalist's Odyssey: Journals and Drawings by William L. Neeley* (Mariposa, Calif.: Jerseydale Ranch Press, 1994).

35. E. S. O'Neill, *Mountain Sage: The Life Story of Carl Sharsmith, Yosemite's Famous Ranger/Naturalist* (Yosemite National Park: Yosemite Association, 1988).

36. J. Snyder, "Remembering Steve Lyman in Yosemite," *Yosemite* 58, no. 4 (1996): 10–15.

37. H. Weamer, "Winter in the Backcountry," *Yosemite* 58, no. 1 (1996): 2–7.

38. S. Sargent, "Tuolumne Tomboy," *Yosemite* 55, no. 3 (1993): 6–9.

39. B. Sanford, "Putting Some Work in Your Leisure," *Yosemite* 57, no. 4 (1995): 6–9.

40. S. Rabkin, "Portable Magic," *Yosemite* 57, no. 3 (1995): 2–7.

41. D. Brower, *For Earth's Sake: The Life and Times of David Brower* (Salt Lake City: Peregrine Smith, 1990).

42. T. Vale and G. Vale, *Time and the Tuolumne Landscape: Continuity and Change in the Yosemite High Country* (Salt Lake City: University of Utah Press, 1994).

43. Solnit, "Up the River."

HOT NEWS

1. Associated Press, "12 Die, 48 Injured As Forest Burns," *New York Times*, August 23, 1937, p. 8.

2. Ibid., "Forest Fire Fatal to 14 Is Dying Out," *New York Times*, August 23, 1937, p. 23.

3. Ibid., "Fire Traps 50 Firefighters in Colorado, Killing 11," July 7, 1994, p. A14; ibid., "Fatal Wildfire Contained," July 10, 1994, p. A17; J. H. Cushman, "Mountain Fire Pushed Back As 2 More Bodies Are Found," July 9, 1994, p. A9; T. Egan, "Elite Crew Mourns Deaths of 12 in a Wildfire Blast in Colorado," July 8, 1994, p. A1; S. Mydans, "Town of Firefighters Weeps for 9 of Them," July 9, 1994,

p. 1A; R. Perez-Pena, "Decades Later, Echo of Montana Firestorm," July 8, 1994, p. A16. All articles are from the late edition final (Lexis/Nexis).

4. The statement that scientists who study wildfire concluded that about the same order of magnitude would have burned in the park even if all 1988 Yellowstone fires had been fought immediately is based on conversations with wildfire scientists I interviewed in 1989, including Stephen Arno, James Brown, and Richard Rothermel, then with the U.S. Forest Service Intermountain Fire Sciences lab in Missoula, Montana; and James Habeck and Ron Wakimoto of the University of Montana.

5. See, for example, W. H. Romme and D. G. Despain, "The Yellowstone Fires," *Scientific American* 261 (November 1989): 37–46.

6. For the period July 1–December 31, 1989, I looked at all stories in the *New York Times, Washington Post,* and *Los Angeles Times* that contained the words "Yellowstone" and "fire(s)" or "wildfire(s)" via Lexis/Nexis; at all stories in the *Billings (MT) Gazette* identified by that newspaper's librarian as having covered the fires during that time period; at all stories in the library files on the Yellowstone fires at the *Bozeman (MT) Chronicle* and *Casper (WY) Star Tribune;* at all evening network TV stories about the fires listed in the index to the Vanderbilt University television news archive; and at 73 additional stories about the Yellowstone-area wildfires published in 11 other newspapers while those fires burned.

7. P. Matthiessen, "Our National Parks: The Case for Burning," *New York Times Magazine,* December 11, 1988, p. 39.

8. A. S. Leopold, S. A. Cain, C. M. Cottam, et al., "Wildlife Management in the National Parks," in *Transactions of the North American Wildlife and Natural Resources Conference* 28 (1963): 28–45.

9. R. Nash, "Sorry, Bambi, But Man Must Enter the Forest: Perspectives on the Old Wilderness and the New," in *Fire's Effects on Wildlife Habitat: Symposium Proceedings, Missoula, Montana, March 21, 1984,* ed. J. E. Lotan and J. K. Brown (Ogden, Utah: U.S. Forest Service, Intermountain Research Laboratory, 1985).

10. During the fall of 1988, I mailed questionnaires to reporters whose bylines appeared on the Yellowstone fire stories I had then assembled (about 100) and to the named information sources for whom I could find mailing addresses (about 90 percent of those to whom reporters attributed information), asking them how well they thought the fires and their scientific context had been reported.

11. One panel consisted of the following incident commanders who had overall responsibility for suppression efforts on one or more of the major Yellowstone-area fires: Denny Bungarz, Richard Gale, David Liebersbach, David Poncin, and Fred Roach. A second panel was composed of fire policy experts Bruce Kilgore and John Chambers, key fire policy officials in the National Park Service and U.S. Forest Service, respectively, and Ron Wakimoto of the University of Montana. Kilgore and Wakimoto participated in the Fire Management Policy Review requested by the secretaries of interior and agriculture to investigate how the 1988 Yellowstone fires were suppressed. The third panel was made up of fire behavior experts Richard Rothermel of the Intermountain Fire Sciences Lab in Missoula, who pioneered the scientific study of wildfire behavior; Rod Norum of the Interagency Fire Center in Boise; and John Krebs and David Thomas, who were fire behavior specialists assigned to specific fire suppression efforts in Yellowstone. The fourth panel con-

sisted of fire ecologists Stephen Arno and James Brown of the Intermountain Fire Sciences Lab in Missoula and Norman Christensen of Duke University. Members of panel 4 have published numerous scientific papers on fire ecology. Four additional people provided me with informal analyses of these stories: fire historian Stephen Pyne, ABC correspondent Gary Shepard, NBC correspondent Roger O'Neil, and Salt Lake City TV reporter Larry Warren.

12. G. Shepard, telephone interview, March 15, 1989.

13. B. McNamara, telephone interview, March 3, 1989; personal interview, July 1, 1991.

14. R. O'Neil, personal correspondence, March 6, 1989.

15. T. R. Reid, "When the Press Yelled 'Fire!': Reports of Yellowstone's Death Last Year Were Wildly Exaggerated," *Washington Post*, July 23, 1989, p. D5.

16. See, for example, T. Egan, "New Hazard in Fire Zones: Houses of Urban Refugees," *New York Times*, September 16, 1994, p. A1; J. Muller, correspondent, ABC World News Tonight, story about Yellowstone fire policy, August 22, 1994, 5:50:20 (CDT) to 5:52:50 P.M., Vanderbilt TV News Index; M. Obmascik, "Wildfires a Deadly Reminder of Nature's Unforgiving Force," *Denver Post*, July 16, 1994, p. B1.

17. J. Carey, "Why and How: The Dark Continent of American Journalism," in *Reading the News*, ed. R. K. Manhoff and M. Schudson (New York: Pantheon, 1986), pp. 146–196.

18. See, for example, S. C. Borman, "Communication Accuracy in Magazine Science Reporting," *Journalism Quarterly* 55 (1978): 345–346; L. J. Lundburg, "Comprehensiveness of Coverage of Tropical Rain Deforestation," *Journalism Quarterly* 61 (1984): 378–382; and M. Ryan and D. Owen, "An Accuracy Survey of Metropolitan Newspaper Coverage of Social Issues," *Journalism Quarterly* 54 (1977): 27–32.

19. D. L. Altheide, *Creating Reality: How TV News Distorts Events* (Beverly Hills, Calif.: Sage, 1976); C. R. Bantz, S. McCorkle, and R. C. Baade, "The News Factory," *Communication Research* 7 (1980): 45–68; M. Fishman, *Manufacturing the News* (Austin: University of Texas Press, 1980); G. Tuchman, *Making News: A Study in the Construction of Reality* (New York: Free Press, 1978).

20. H. J. Gans, *Deciding What's News: A Study of* CBS Evening News, NBC Nightly News, Newsweek, *and* Time (New York: Vintage, 1980).

21. R. M. Entman, *Democracy Without Citizens: Media and the Decay of American Politics* (New York: Oxford University Press, 1989); H. Molotch and M. Lester, "News as Purposive Behavior: On the Strategic Use of Routine Events, Accidents, and Scandals," *American Sociological Review* 39 (1974): 101–112; ibid., "Accidental News: The Great Oil Spill as Local Occurrence and National Event," *American Journal of Sociology* 81 (1975): 235–260; L. V. Sigal, *Reporters and Officials: The Organization and Politics of Newsmaking* (Lexington, Mass.: Heath, 1973).

22. S. Dunwoody and M. Ryan, "Scientific Barriers to the Popularization of Science in the Mass Media," *Journal of Communication* 35 (1985): 26–42; S. Dunwoody, and B. T. Scott, "Scientists as Mass Media Sources," *Journalism Quarterly* 59 (1982): 52–59; R. B. McCall, "Science and the Press: Like Oil and Water?" *American Psychologist* 43 (1988): 87–94; D. Nelkin, "The Culture of Science Journalism," *Society* (September/October 1987): 17–25.

23. C. Z. Nunn, "Readership and Coverage of Science and Technology in Newspapers," *Journalism Quarterly* 56 (1982): 27–30, cited by Dunwoody and Scott, "Scientists as Mass Media Sources."

24. J. F. Ahearne, "Addressing Public Concerns in Science," *Physics Today* (September 1988): 36–42.

25. C. Smith, *Media and Apocalypse: News Coverage of the Yellowstone Forest Fires, Exxon Valdez Oil Spill, and Loma Prieta Earthquake* (Westport, Conn.: Greenwood, 1992).

26. Ibid.

27. Ibid.

28. C. Smith, "Reporters, News Sources, and Bogus Science: The New Madrid Earthquake Prediction," *Public Understanding of Science* 5 (1996): 205–216.

29. Molotch and Lester, "News as Purposive Behavior."

30. Entman, *Democracy Without Citizens.*

31. Sample Kelso sound bite (at a press conference) as he held up a copy of Alaska oil consortium Alyeska's "Oil Spill Contingency Plan for Prince William Sound," on which he had earlier signed off as Alaska's commissioner of environmental conservation: "This is probably the biggest piece of American maritime fiction since *Moby Dick*"; see M. McQueen, "Alaska Asks to Take Lead in Oil Cleanup," *USA Today*, May 10, 1989, final edition, p. 1A; "Neglect Primed Oil Spill," *St. Louis (MO) Post-Dispatch*, April 9, 1989, late five-star edition, p. 1A.

Admiral Yost, talking about the area where the *Exxon Valdez* ran aground in 1989: "It is not treacherous in the area they went aground. It's 10 miles wide. Your children could drive a tanker up through it"; quoted by D. Hoffman, "Coast Guard Faults Ship's Navigation; Site Not 'Treacherous,'" *Washington Post*, March 31, 1989, final edition, p. A6.

Under President Ronald Reagan, the U.S. Coast Guard was given a major new mission without major new funds: to intercept drug smugglers. Between 1980 and 1990, the proportion of the Coast Guard operating budget allocated to the war on drugs grew from near zero to 25 percent while the portion dedicated to marine safety was reduced from 14.2 percent to 5.9 percent, according to E. Diringer, "The Troubled Coast Guard: Critics Say It Shares Responsibility for the *Valdez* Oil Spill," *San Francisco Chronicle*, final edition, March 23, 1990, p. A1 (Lexis/Nexis). Because of these shifting priorities, the frequency with which oil tankers were inspected and the number of Coast Guard employees monitoring maritime safety were reduced substantially.

The Port Valdez Coast Guard shared the shortfall. The number of radar operators per watch in Valdez, for example, was cut from three in 1977, when the pipeline opened, to one in 1989, according to "Blueprint for Disaster: Empty Promises; Coast Guard Bowed to Industry Pressure," *Anchorage Daily News*, October 15 1989, p. A1 (VU/TEXT). In 1984, the vessel-tracking radar in Prince William Sound was replaced with a cheaper and less powerful unit to save money. The process of plotting tanker locations in Prince William Sound every five minutes as long as the ships were visible on radar, part of the original maritime safety effort, was dropped.

Under pressure from the oil industry, the Coast Guard reduced the minimum required size of tanker crews. The industry argued that newer ships had more sophisticated technology and therefore needed fewer crew members for safe operation. The tanker *Exxon Valdez*, designed in 1986 for a crew of 33, was operating with a crew of 19 when it ran aground on Bligh Reef, according to M. A. Stein and W. Rempel, "Tanker Sailors Say They're Being Pushed to Limits of Safety by Reductions in Crews," *Los Angeles Times*, home edition, April 22, 1989, p. 1:26 (Lexis/Nexis). Maritime unions maintained that smaller crews increased the danger of accidents because of longer hours and less sleep, especially during the demanding hours when a tanker is in port being filled with or emptied of oil. In another decision that saved money for the oil industry, the Coast Guard reduced the experience level required of tanker officers to get an unlimited pilotage endorsement for Prince William Sound. The original rules required experience on large ships before an officer could pilot them, but the new rules accepted experience on smaller ships as good enough.

The Valdez Coast Guard station did not rigorously follow some of the safety precautions that were in place. Outbound tankers were routinely given permission to cross into Prince William Sound's inbound traffic lane, closer to Bligh Reef, to navigate around chunks of glacial ice, despite the fact they could travel safely through the ice by slowing down. According to an internal Coast Guard safety study obtained by the *Seattle Times*, tanker crews transporting Alaskan crude were under considerable pressure to maintain high speeds in order to save money for the companies that owned the ships; see E. Nalder, "Oil-Tanker Regulations: 'Formidable Problems': Coast Guard Releases Full Report on the Risks," *Seattle Times*, final edition, April 17, 1990, p. A1 (Lexis/Nexis). Because of a decline in the availability of seafaring jobs, ship masters who ignored these pressures did so at the peril of their jobs. (According to the *Los Angeles Times*, the number of U.S. seamen declined from 86,000 in 1951 to 10,657 in 1987; Stein and Rempel, "Tanker Sailors Say They're Being Pushed," cited above.)

32. R. Wallace, United States Geological Survey, Menlo Park, Calif., personal interview, June 12, 1990.

33. The assessment that USGS Menlo Park geologists rated news coverage of the 1989 Loma Prieta earthquake much more accurate and complete than did seismic engineers is based on my statistical analysis of evaluations of coverage by geologists and seismic engineers who were named as sources in stories about the 1989 earthquake. For more detail, see Smith, *Media and Apocalypse.*

34. W. Spence, R. B. Herrmann, A. C. Johnston, and G. Reagor, *Responses to Iben Browning's Prediction of a 1990 New Madrid, Missouri, Earthquake*, U.S. Geological Survey Circular 1083 (Washington, D.C.: U.S. Government Printing Office, 1993).

35. C. Smith, "Reporters, News Sources, and Scientific Intervention: The New Madrid Earthquake Prediction," *Public Understanding of Science* 5 (1996): 205–216.

36. A. Malcolm, "In Ashes of Burned Forests, a Rare Chance to Study Nature's Recovery," *New York Times*, September 27, 1988, p. C1; T. H. Maugh II, "Policy Squabble: Forest Fires—The Debate Heats Up," *Los Angeles Times*, October 13, 1988, p. A1.

37. D. Chandler, "Forest Service Plays Down Effects of Fires," *Boston Globe*, January 20, 1989.

38. P. Meyer, *Ethical Journalism* (New York: Longman, 1987).

39. R. Nash, *Wilderness and the American Mind*, 3rd ed. (New Haven: Yale University Press, 1982).

40. ABC World News Sunday, September 18, 1988.

DON'T GET HOSED

1. I served with Congressman Ralph Regula on the House Interior and Related Agencies Appropriations Subcommittee, which has jurisdiction for national parks and forests. His words in the committee session were so striking that I've never forgotten them.

2. Conrad Smith, *Media and Apocalypse: News Coverage of the Yellowstone Forest Fires*, Exxon Valdez *Oil Spill, and Loma Prieta Earthquake* (Westport, Conn.: Greenwood, 1992).

3. U.S. Senator Max Baucus, *Congressional Record*, September 23, 1988.

4. U.S. Senator Malcolm Wallop, *Salt Lake City Tribune*, September 10, 1988.

5. John Varley, Ph.D., director of the Yellowstone Center for Resources, personal interview, June 24, 2004.

6. B. Kauffman, "Death Rides the Forest: Perceptions of Fire, Land Use, and Ecological Restoration of Western Forests," *Conservation Biology* 18, no. 4 (2004): 878–882.

7. John Varley interview, June 24, 2004.

8. M. Hofferber, "Yellowstone Fires Produce New Trees, Not Meadows," *High Country News*, October 17, 2004.

9. Ibid.

10. D. A. DellaSala, J. Williams, C. Deacon-Williams, and J. F. Franklin, "Beyond Smoke and Mirrors: A Synthesis of Fire Policy and Science," *Conservation Biology* 18, no. 4 (2004): 976–986.

11. "Old Growth Reserve Logging Begins at Biscuit," *Oregonian*, March 3, 2005.

12. U.S. Forest Service and Bureau of Land Management, *Biscuit Fire Recovery Project Final Environmental Impact Statement* (Rogue River/Siskiyou National Forest, 2004); www.fs.fed.us/r6/rogue-siskiyou/biscuit-fire/feis.shtml.

13. M. Udall, "Our Publicly Owned Forests Are Being Subverted," *High Country News*, October 17, 2004.

14. Karla Bird, natural resources officer, Umpqua National Forest, as quoted by Michael Milstein, *Oregonian*, September 1, 2002.

15. Interview with Dr. Jack Ward Thomas, March 17, 2005. Dr. Thomas, who would become President Clinton's Forest Service chief, led a group of more than 100 scientists of various disciplines—the Forest Ecosystem Management Assessment Team—in developing the Northwest Forest Plan. The plan was unveiled in July 1993.

16. Judge William Dwyer of the Ninth U.S. Circuit Court enjoined the Forest Service from offering timber sales in Oregon and Washington, for failure to manage forests to ensure that the spotted owl, an "indicator species," would be managed to "maintain viable populations" under the National Forest Management Act.

17. J. E. Franklin, "Comments Submitted to the U.S. Forest Service on Its Draft

Environmental Impact Statement for the Biscuit Recovery Project," January 20, 2004.

18. Ibid.

19. "Speaker Biography: Mark Rey," found on the website of the Ecosystem Management Initiative (School of Natural Resources and Environment, University of Michigan, Ann Arbor); www.snre.umich.edu/ecomgt//events/bios/rey.htm.

20. P. Dobbyn, "Roadless Rule Exemptions Sought," *Anchorage Daily News*, July 10, 2003.

21. Poll, *Los Angeles Times*, March 30, 2001. Results showed that when the environment and the economy are in conflict, by a 50 percent to 36 percent margin Americans believe the environment should be given the priority; 14 percent were "unsure."

22. For the concept of "framing" I am indebted to Thomas Patterson, author of *Out of Order* (New York: Knopf, 1993).

23. Patterson, *Out of Order*, p. 80.

24. "How Americans Get Their News," Gallup survey, December 31, 2002.

25. Brookings Institution, "Hess Report on Campaign Coverage on Nightly Network News," 1988.

26. R. Nash, *Wilderness and the American Mind*, 3rd ed. (New Haven: Yale University Press, 2001).

27. A. de Tocqueville, *Democracy in America*, ed. P. Bradley (1835; reprint, New York: Knopf, 1945), p. 2; as quoted in Nash, *Wilderness and the American Mind*, p. 23.

PART THREE

THE YELLOWSTONE FIRES OF 1988

1. F. C. Noss, C. Carroll, K. Vance-Borland, and G. Wuerthner, "A Multi-Criteria Assessment of the Irreplaceability and Vulnerability of Sites in the Greater Yellowstone Ecosystem," *Conservation Biology* 16, no. 4 (2002): 895–908.

2. R. C. Rothermel, R. A. Hartford, and C. H. Chase, *Fire Growth Maps for the Greater Yellowstone Area Fires*, U.S. Forest Service General Technical Report INT 304 (Ogden, Utah: U.S. Forest Service, Intermountain Research Station, 1994).

3. Ibid.

4. National Park Service, "Wildland Fire," on "The Official Website of Yellowstone National Park"; www.nps.gov/yell/nature/fire; accessed September 5, 2005.

5. D. L. Azuma, J. Donnegan, and D. Gedney, *Southwest Oregon Biscuit Fire*, U.S. Forest Service Research Paper PNW-RP-560 (Portland, Oreg.: U.S. Forest Service, Pacific Northwest Research Station, 2004).

6. "Yellowstone: Shaped by Fire"; www.pbs.org/edens/yellowstone/shaped .html; accessed September 12, 2005.

7. C. Smith, *Media and Apocalypse: News Coverage of the Yellowstone Forest Fires, Exxon Valdez Oil Spill, and Loma Prieta Earthquake* (Westport, Conn.: Greenwood, 1992).

8. Ibid.

9. C. Smith, "Media Coverage of Fire Ecology in Yellowstone after 1988," in

The Ecological Implications of Fire in Greater Yellowstone: Proceedings of the Second Biennial Conference on the Greater Yellowstone Ecosystem, ed. J. Greelee (Fairfield, Wash.: International Association of Wildland Fires, 1996), 25–34.

10. J. K. Brown, "Introduction" and "Fire Regimes," in *Wildland Fire in Ecosystems: Effects of Fire on Flora*, ed. J. K. Brown and J. K. Smith, U.S. Forest Service General Technical Report RMRS-GTR-42, vol. 2 (Ogden, Utah: U.S. Forest Service, Rocky Mountain Research Station, 2000).

11. W. W. Covington and M. M. Moore, "Southwestern Ponderosa Forest Structure: Changes Since Euro-American Settlement," *Journal of Forestry* 92 (1994): 39–47.

12. J. K. Brown, "Could the 1988 Fires in Yellowstone Have Been Avoided Through Prescribed Burning?" *Fire Management Notes* 50, no. 4 (1989): 7–13.

13. D. J. Parsons and S. J. Botti, "Restoration of Fire in National Parks," in *The Use of Fire in Forest Restoration*, U.S. Forest Service General Technical Report INT-341 (Ogden, Utah: U.S. Forest Service, Intermountain Research Station, 1996).

14. M. G. Turner, W. H. Romme, R. H. Gardner, et al., "A Revised Concept of Landscape Equilibrium: Disturbance and Stability on Scaled Landscapes," *Landscape Ecology* 8, no. 3 (1993): 213–227.

15. W. H. Romme and D. G. Despain, "Historical Perspective on the Yellowstone Fires of 1988," *Bioscience* 39, no. 10 (1989): 695–699.

16. S. H. Millspaugh, C. Whitlock, and P. J. Bartlein, "Variations in Fire Frequency and Climate over the Past 17,000 Years in Central Yellowstone National Park," *Geology* 28 (2000): 211–214; http://geography.uoregon.edu/envchange/figures/millspaugh-etal-geology-2000-figs/millspaugh.pdf; accessed September 21, 2005.

17. G. A. Meyer and S. G. Wells, "Fire-Related Sedimentation Events on Alluvial Fans, Yellowstone National Park," *Journal of Sedimentary Research* A67, no. 5 (1997): 775–791.

18. M. G. Turner, W. H. Romme, and D. B. Tinker, "Surprises and Lessons from the 1988 Yellowstone Fires," *Frontiers in Ecology and the Environment* 1, no. 7 (2003): 351–358.

19. G. Wuerthner, *Yellowstone: A Visitor's Companion* (Mechanicsburg, Pa.: Stackpole Books, 1991).

20. D. G. Despain, *Yellowstone Vegetation: Consequences of Environment and History in a Natural Setting* (Boulder: Rinehart, 1990).

21. R. A. Marston and J. E. Anderson, "Watersheds and Vegetation of the Greater Yellowstone Ecosystem," *Conservation Biology* 5, no. 3 (1991): 338–346.

22. Despain, *Yellowstone Vegetation.*

23. Ibid.

24. Ibid.

25. D. McKenzie, A. E. Gedalof, D. I. Peterson, and P. Mote, "Climatic Change, Wildfire, and Conservation," *Conservation Biology* 18, no. 4 (2004): 890–900.

26. Millspaugh et al., "Variations in Fire Frequency."

27. M. G. Turner and W. H. Romme, "Landscape Dynamics in Crown Fire Ecosystems," *Landscape Ecology* 9 (1994): 59–77.

28. J. Neckels, B. Mutch, R. Wallace, et al., *Greater Yellowstone Area Fire Situation* (Billings, Mont.: Greater Yellowstone Coordinating Committee, 1988).

29. R. A. Hartford and R. C. Rothermel, *Fuel Moisture as Measured and Predicted During the 1988 Fires in Yellowstone Park*, U.S. Forest Service Research Note INT-396 (Ogden, Utah: U.S. Forest Service, Intermountain Research Station, 1991).

30. NPS, "Wildland Fire."

31. McKenzie et al., "Climatic Change."

32. E. A. Johnson and D. R. Wowchuck, "Wildfires in the Southern Canadian Rocky Mountains and Their Relationship to Mid-Tropospheric Anomalies," *Canadian Journal of Forest Research* 23 (1993): 1213–1222.

33. Turner et al., "Surprises and Lessons."

34. R. C. Rothermel et al., "Fire Growth Maps."

35. Ibid.

36. NPS, "Wildland Fire."

37. F. J. Singer, W. Schreier, J. Oppenheim, and E. O. Garton, "Drought, Fires, and Large Mammals: Evaluating the 1988 Severe Drought and Large-Scale Fires," *Bioscience* 39, no.10 (1989): 716–722.

38. Meyer and Wells, "Fire-Related Sedimentation Events."

39. M. J. McIntyre and G. W. Minshall, "Changes in Transport and Retention of Coarse Particulate Organic Matter in Streams Subject to Fire," in *The Ecological Implications of Fire in Greater Yellowstone: Proceedings of the Second Biennial Conference on the Greater Yellowstone Ecosystem*, ed. J. Greenlee (Fairfield, Wash.: International Association of Wildland Fire, 1996), pp. 59–76.

40. G. W. Minshall, T. V. Royer, and C. T. Robinson, "Response of the Cache Creek Macroinvertebrates During the First 10 Years Following Disturbance by the 1988 Yellowstone Wildfires," *Canadian Journal of Fisheries and Aquatic Sciences* 58 (2001): 1077–1088.

41. D. B. Tinker and D. H. Knight, "Fire and the Dynamics of Coarse Woody Debris in Yellowstone National Park" [conference abstract], *Yellowstone Science Supplement* 6, no. 2 (1998): 53.

42. M. A. Franke, *Yellowstone in the Afterglow: Lessons from the Fires* (Mammoth Hot Spring, Wyo.: Yellowstone National Park, Yellowstone Center for Resources, 2000); www.nps.gov/yell/publications/pdfs/fire/afterglow.htm; accessed September 15, 2005.

43. E. A. Johnson and G. I. Fryer, "Population Dynamics in Lodgepole Pine–Engelmann Spruce Forests," *Ecology* 70 (1989): 1335–1345.

44. Turner et al., "Surprises and Lessons."

45. Ibid.

46. Ibid.

47. W. H. Romme, M. G. Turner, R. H. Gardner, et al., "A Rare Episode of Sexual Reproduction in Aspen (*Populus tremuloides*) Following the 1988 Yellowstone Fires," *Natural Areas Journal* 17 (1997): 17–25.

48. Turner et al., "Surprises and Lessons."

49. Turner and Romme, "Landscape Dynamics."

50. D. H. Knight and L. L. Wallace, "The Yellowstone Fires: Issues in Landscape Ecology—A Landscape Perspective Is Necessary in Resolving the Difficulties of Natural Area Management," *Bioscience* 39, no. 10 (1989): 700–706.

FIRE ECOLOGY OF THE SIERRA NEVADA

1. N. K. Huber, *The Geologic Story of Yosemite National Park*, Bulletin 1595 (Washington, D.C.: U.S. Department of the Interior, U.S. Geological Survey, 1987).

2. Ibid.

3. M. Hill, *Geology of the Sierra Nevada* (Berkeley and Los Angeles: University of California Press, 1975).

4. J. W. van Wagtendonk, "Spatial Analysis of Lightning Strikes in Yosemite National Park," *Proceedings 11th Conference on Fire and Forest Meteorology* 11 (1991): 605–611.

5. N. L. Stephenson, "Reference Conditions for Giant Sequoia Forest Restoration: Structure, Process and Precision," *Ecological Applications* 9 (1999): 1253–1265.

6. J. W. van Wagtendonk and J. Fites-Kaufman, "Fire in the Sierra Nevada Bioregion," in *Fire in California Ecosystems*, ed. N. G. Sugihara, J. W. van Wagtendonk, J. Fites-Kaufman, et al. (Berkeley and Los Angeles: University of California Press, 2004).

7. Ibid.

8. C. N. Skinner and C. Chang, "Fire Regimes, Past and Present," in *Sierra Nevada Ecosystem Project: Final Report to Congress*, vol. 2 (Davis: University of California, Centers for Water and Wildland Resources, 1996); W. W. Wagener, "Past Fire Incidence in Sierra Nevada Forests," *Journal of Forestry* 59 (1961): 739–748.

9. T. M. Bonnicksen and E. P. Stone, "Reconstruction of a Presettlement Giant Sequoia–Mixed Conifer Forest Community Using the Aggregation Approach," *Ecology* 63 (1982): 1134–1168; J. W. van Wagtendonk, "Fire Suppression Effects on Fuels and Succession in Short-Fire-Interval Wilderness Ecosystems," in *Proceedings of the Symposium and Workshop on Wilderness Fire, November 15–18, 1983, Missoula, Mont.*, ed. J. E. Lotan, B. M. Kilgore, W. C. Fischer, and R. W. Mutch, U. S. Forest Service General Technical Report INT-182 (Ogden, Utah: U.S. Forest Service, Intermountain Research Station, 1985), pp. 119–126.

10. van Wagtendonk and Fites-Kaufman, "Fire in the Sierra Nevada Bioregion."

11. J. W. van Wagtendonk, "Spatial Patterns of Lightning Strikes and Fires in Yosemite National Park," *Proceedings 12th Conference on Fire and Forest Meteorology* 12 (1994): 223–231.

12. B. M. Kilgore, "The Role of Fire in Managing Red Fir Forests," *Transactions North American Wildlife and Natural Resources Conference* 36 (1971): 405–416.

13. Skinner and Chang, "Fire Regimes."

14. J. W. van Wagtendonk, "Large Fires in Wilderness Areas," in *Proceedings: Symposium on Fire in Wilderness and Park Management, March 30–April 1, Missoula, Mont.*, ed. J. K. Brown, R. W. Mutch, C. W. Spoon, and R. H. Wakimoto, U.S. Forest Service General Technical Report INT-GTR-320 (Ogden, Utah: U.S. Forest Service, Intermountain Research Station, 1995).

15. van Wagtendonk and Fites-Kaufman, "Fire in the Sierra Nevada Bioregion."

16. van Wagtendonk, "Spatial Patterns."

17. S. H. deBennedetti and D. J. Parsons, "Post-Fire Succession in a Sierran Subalpine Meadow," *American Midland Naturalist* 111 (1984): 118–125.

18. J. E. Keeley, "Reproductive Cycles and Fire Regimes," in *Proceedings of the Conference on Fire Regimes and Ecosystem Properties*, ed. H. A. Mooney, T. M. Bonnickson, N. L. Christensen, et al., U.S. Forest Service General Technical Report WO-26 (Washington, D.C.: U.S. Forest Service, 1981).

19. van Wagtendonk, "Large Fires."

20. van Wagtendonk and Fites-Kaufman, "Fire in the Sierra Nevada Bioregion."

21. van Wagtendonk, "Spatial Patterns."

22. van Wagtendonk and Fites-Kaufman, "Fire in the Sierra Nevada Bioregion."

23. A. Taylor and M. Beaty, "Climatic Influences on Fire Regimes in the Lake Tahoe Basin," *Abstracts Second International Wildland Fire Ecology and Fire Management Congress* (Sacramento: Association for Fire Ecology, 2003).

24. S. J. Smith and R. S. Anderson, "Late Wisconsin Paleoecologic Record from Swamp Lake, Yosemite National Park, California," *Quaternary Research* 38 (1992): 91–102.

25. R. S. Anderson and S. J. Smith, "The Sedimentary Record of Fire in Montane Meadows, Sierra Nevada, California, USA: A Preliminary Assessment," in *Sediment Records of Biomass Burning and Global Change*, ed. J. S. Clark, H. Cachier, J. G. Goldammer, and B. J. Stocks, NATO ASI Series 51 (Brussels: NATO, 1997), pp. 313–327.

26. Ibid.

27. Wagener, "Past Fire Incidence."

28. S. L. Stephens and B. M. Collins, "Fire Regimes of Mixed Conifer Forests in the Northern Sierra Nevada, California," in *Blodgett Forest Research Station, Research Symposium 2003: Abstracts, February 7–8* (Berkeley: University of California, Center for Forestry, 2003).

29. B. M. Kilgore and D. Taylor, "Fire History of a Sequoia–Mixed Conifer Forest," *Ecology* 60 (1979): 129–142.

30. T. W. Swetnam, "Fire History and Climate Change in Giant Sequoia Groves," *Science* 262 (1993): 885–889.

31. Ibid.

32. K. L. Hull and M. J. Moratto, *Archeological Synthesis and Research Design, Yosemite National Park, California*, Publications in Anthropology No. 21 (El Portal, Calif.: National Park Service, Yosemite, 1999).

33. M. K. Anderson, "The Fire, Pruning, and Coppice Management of Temperate Ecosystems for Basketry Material by California Indian Tribes," *Human Ecology* 27 (1999): 79–113.

34. R. S. Anderson and S. L. Carpenter, "Vegetation Changes in Yosemite Valley, Yosemite National Park, California, During the Protohistoric Period," *Madroño* 38 (1991): 1–13.

35. Anderson and Smith, "Sedimentary Record."

36. T. R. Vale, *Fire, Native Peoples, and the Natural Landscape* (Washington, D.C.: Island Press, 2002).

37. S. B. Show and E. I. Kotok, *Forest Fires in California, 1911–1920: An Analytical Study*, Department Circular 243 (Washington, D.C.: U.S. Department of Agriculture, 1923).

38. K. S. McKelvey and K. L. Busse, "Twentieth Century Fire Patterns on Forest Service Lands," in *Sierra Nevada Ecosystem Project: Final Report to Congress*, vol. 2.

39. H. H. Biswell, "Man and Fire in Ponderosa Pine in the Sierra Nevada of California," *Sierra Club Bulletin* 44 (1959): 44–53; R. J. Hartesvelt, "Effects of Human Impact on *Sequoia gigantea* and Its Environment in the Mariposa Grove, Yosemite National Park, California" (Ph.D. dissertation, University of Michigan, Ann Arbor, 1962).

40. H. W. DeBruin, "From Fire Control to Fire Management: A Major Policy Change in the Forest Service," *Proceedings of the Tall Timbers Fire Ecology Conference* 14 (1974): 11–17.

41. B. M. Kilgore and G. M. Briggs, "Restoring Fire to High Elevation Forests in California," *Journal of Forestry* 70 (1972): 266–271; J. W. van Wagtendonk, "The Role of Fire in the Yosemite Wilderness," in *Proceedings of the National Wilderness Research Conference: Current Research*, U.S. Forest Service General Technical Report INT-212 (Ogden, Utah: U.S. Forest Service, Intermountain Research Station, 1986).

42. McKelvey and Busse, "Twentieth Century Fire Patterns."

43. J. W. van Wagtendonk, K. A. van Wagtendonk, J. B. Meyer, and K. J. Paintner, "The Use of Geographic Information for Fire Management Planning in Yosemite National Park," *George Wright Forum* 19 (2002): 19–39.

44. A. C. Caprio, C. Conover, M. B. Keifer, and P. Lineback, "Fire Management and GIS: A Framework for Identifying and Prioritizing Fire Planning Needs," in *Proceedings of the Symposium Fire Ecology in California Ecosystems: Integrating Ecology, Prevention, and Management*, Miscellaneous Publication No. 1 (Sacramento: Association for Fire Ecology, 2002).

45. Skinner and Chang, "Fire Regimes"; A. C. Caprio, and P. Lineback, "Pre–Twentieth Century Fire History of Sequoia and Kings Canyon National Parks: A Review and Evaluation of Our Knowledge," in *Proceedings of the Conference on Fire in California Ecosystems: Integrating Ecology, Prevention, and Management, November 17–20, 1997, San Diego*, Association for Fire Ecology Miscellaneous Publication No. 1 (Sacramento: Association for Fire Ecology, 2002).

46. van Wagtendonk et al., "The Use of Geographic Information."

47. Ibid.

48. Ibid.

49. van Wagtendonk and Fites-Kaufman, "Fire in the Sierra Nevada Bioregion."

WILDFIRE MANAGEMENT
ON A HUMAN-DOMINATED LANDSCAPE

Text

1. R. W. Halsey, *Fire, Chaparral and Survival in Southern California* (San Diego, Calif.: Sunbelt Publications, 2004), p. 48.

2. Jones and Stokes Associates, *Sliding Toward Extinction: The State of California's Natural Heritage* (San Francisco: California Nature Conservancy, 1987).

3. C. D. Allen, M. Savage, D. A. Falk, et al., "Ecological Restoration of Southwestern Ponderosa Pine Ecosystems: A Broad Perspective," *Ecological Applications* 12 (2002): 1418–1433.

4. M. Savage and T. W. Swetnam, "Early 19th-Century Fire Decline Following Sheep Pasturing in a Navajo Ponderosa Pine Forest," *Ecology* 71 (1990): 2374–2378.

5. D. C. Odion, E. J. Fost, J. R. Strittholt, et al., "Patterns of Fire Severity and Forest Conditions in the Western Klamath Mountains, California," *Conservation Biology* 18 (2004): 927–936.

6. J. E. Keeley and CJ Fotheringham, "Historic Fire Regime in Southern California Shrublands," *Conservation Biology* 15 (2001): 1536–1548; ibid., "Impact of Past, Present, and Future Fire Regimes on North American Mediterranean Shrublands," in *Fire and Climatic Change in Temperate Ecosystems of the Western Americas*, ed. T. T. Veblen, W. L. Baker, G. Montenegro, and T. W. Swetnam (New York: Springer, 2003), pp. 218–262.

7. M. A. Moritz, "Spatiotemporal Analysis of Controls on Shrubland Fire Regimes: Age Dependency and Fire Hazard," *Ecology* 84 (2003): 351–361; M. A. Moritz, J. E. Keeley, E. A. Johnson, and A. A. Schaffner, "Testing a Basic Assumption of Shrubland Fire Management: How Important Is Fuel Age?" *Frontiers in Ecology and the Environment* 2 (2004): 65–70.

8. C. R. Clar, *California Government and Forestry* (Sacramento: California Division of Forestry, 1959); S. J. Pyne, *Fire in America: A Cultural History of Wildland and Rural Fire* (Princeton, N.J.: Princeton University Press, 1982).

9. Keeley and Fotheringham, "Historic Fire Regime"; ibid., "Impact of Past, Present, and Future Fire Regimes."

10. M. A. Moritz, et al. "Testing a Basic Assumption."

11. R. Schoenberg, R. Peng, Z. Huang, and P. Rundel, "Detection of Nonlinearities in the Dependence of Burn Area on Fuel Age and Climatic Variables," *International Journal of Wildland Fire* 12 (2003): 1–10.

12. J. E. Keeley, CJ Fotheringham, and M. Moritz, "Lessons from the 2003 Wildfires in Southern California," *Journal of Forestry* 102, no. 7 (2004): 26–31.

13. National Park Service, *Draft Environmental Impact Statement: Fire Management Plan* (Thousand Oaks, Calif.: Santa Monica Mountains National Recreation Area, 2004).

14. A. L. Westerling, A. Gershunov, D. R. Cayan, and T. P. Barnett, "Long Lead Statistical Forecasts of Area Burned in Western U.S. Wildfires by Ecosystem Province," *International Journal of Wildland Fire* 11 (2002): 257–266.

15. J. E. Keeley, "Impact of Antecedent Climate on Fire Regimes in Coastal California," *International Journal of Wildland Fire* 13 (2004): 173–182.

16. S. A. Mensing, J. Michaelsen, and R. Byrne, "A 560-Year Record of Santa Ana Fires Reconstructed from Charcoal Deposited in the Santa Barbara Basin, California," *Quaternary Research* 51 (1999): 295–305.

17. P. Odens, *The Indians and I: Visits with Dieguenos, Quechans, Fort Mojaves, Zumis, Hopis, Navajos and Piutes* (El Centro, Calif.: Imperial Printers, 1971).

18. L. A. Barrett, *A Record of Forest and Field Fires in California from the Days of the Early Explorers to the Creation of the Forest Reserves* (San Francisco: U.S. Forest Service, 1935).

19. W. S. Brown and S. B. Show, *California Rural Land Use and Management. A History of the Use and Occupancy of Rural Lands in California* (Berkeley, Calif.: U.S. Forest Service, California Region, 1944); D. Gomes, O. L. Graham Jr., E. H. Marshall, and A. J. Schmidt, *Sifting Through the Ashes: Lessons Learned from the*

Painted Cave Fire (University of California, Santa Barbara: Graduate Program for Public Historical Studies, 1993); J. E. Keeley, CJ Fotheringham, and M. Morais, "Reexamining Fire Suppression Impacts on Brushland Fire Regimes," *Science* 284 (1999): 1829–1832.

20. Keeley and Fotheringham, "Historic Fire Regime"; ibid., "Impact of Past, Present, and Future Fire Regimes."

21. U.S. Department of Commerce, Bureau of the Census, *Selected Historical Decennial Census and Housing Counts*; www.census.gov/population/www/censusdata/hiscendata.html; November 17, 2004, update.

22. Keeley and Fotheringham, "Historic Fire Regime"; ibid., "Impact of Past, Present, and Future Fire Regimes."

23. S. G. Conard and D. R. Weise, "Management of Fire Regime, Fuels, and Fire Effects in Southern California Chaparral: Lessons from the Past and Thoughts for the Future," *Tall Timbers Ecology Conference Proceedings* 20 (1998): 342–350.

24. J. E. Keeley, CJ Fotheringham, and M. Moritz, "Lessons from the 2003 Wildfires."

25. Ibid.

26. J. E. Keeley, "Chaparral Fuel Modification: What Do We Know—and Need to Know?" *Fire Management Today* 65, no. 4 (2005):11–12.

27. National Park Service, *Draft Environmental Impact Statement: Fire Management Plan* (Thousand Oaks, Calif.: Santa Monica Mountains National Recreation Area, 2004).

28. J. E. Keeley, "Postfire Ecosystem Recovery and Management: The October 1993 Large Fire Episode in California," in *Large Forest Fires*, ed. J. M. Moreno (Leiden, The Netherlands: Backhuys, 1998), pp. 69–90.

29. J. E. Keeley, CJ Fotheringham, and M. B. Baer, "Determinants of Postfire Recovery and Succession in Mediterranean-Climate Shrublands of California," *Ecological Applications* 15, no. 5 (2005): 1515–1534.

30. R. M. Rice, R. R. Ziemer, and S. C. Hankin, "Slope Stability Effects of Fuel Management Strategies: Inferences from Monte Carlo Simulations," in *Proceedings of the Symposium on Dynamics and Management of Mediterranean-Type Ecosystems*, ed. C. E. Conrad and W. C. Oechel, U.S. Forest Service General Technical Report PSW-58 (Berkeley, Calif.: U.S. Forest Service, Pacific Southwest Forest and Range Experiment Station, 1982); P. J. Riggan, S. E. Franklin, J. A. Brass, and F. E. Brooks, "Perspectives on Fire Management in Mediterranean Ecosystems of Southern California," in *The Role of Fire in Mediterranean-Type Ecosystems*, ed. J. M. Moreno and W. C. Oechel (New York: Springer, 1994), pp. 140–162.

31. Keeley, Fotheringham, and Moritz, "Lessons from the 2003 Wildfires."

32. J. Loomis, P. Wohlgemuth, A. González-Cabán, and D. English, "Economic Benefits of Reducing Fire-Related Sediment in Southwestern Fire-Prone Ecosystems," *Water Resources Research* 39, no. 9 (2003): 1–8.

33. Ibid.

34. J. E. Keeley, "Fire Management Impacts on Invasive Plant Species in the Western United States," *Conservation Biology*, in press, 2006.

35. Rice, Ziemer, and Hankin, "Slope Stability Effects."

36. Keeley, "Fire Management Impacts."

37. J. E. Keeley, M. B. Keeley, and CJ Fotheringham, "Alien Plant Dynamics

Following Fire in Mediterranean-Climate California Shrublands," *Ecological Applications* 15: 2109–2125.

38. J. E. Keeley, "Native American Impacts on Fire Regimes in Coastal California Ranges," *Journal of Biogeography* 29 (2002): 303–320.

39. Keeley and Fotheringham, "Historic Fire Regime"; ibid., "Impact of Past, Present, and Future Fire Regimes."

Box 1

1. California Department of Forestry and Fire Protection, Fire and Resource Assessment Program, *2003 Southern California Fires: New Assessments;* http://frap.cdf.ca.gov.

2. T. M. Bonnicksen, "Foresters Need Complete Set of Tools to Trim the Trees," op-ed, *San Francisco Chronicle,* August 19, 2004; www.foresthealth.org/pdf/BonnicksenOp.pdf.

3. J. E. Keeley, CJ Fotheringham, and M. Moritz, "Lessons from the 2003 Wildfires in Southern California," *Journal of Forestry* 102, no. 7 (2004): 26–31.

4. J. Steele, "Insurer Seeks Reparation, Class-Action Suit Pursued," *San Diego Union-Tribune,* July 18, 2004; www.signonsandiego.com/uniontrib/20040718/news_1m18claims.html.

Box 2

1. C. D. Allen, M. Savage, D. A. Falk, et al., "Ecological Restoration of Southwestern Ponderosa Pine Ecosystems: A Broad Perspective," *Ecological Applications* 12 (2002): 1418–1433.

2. J. E. Keeley, CJ Fotheringham, and M. Morais, "Reexamining Fire Suppression Impacts on Brushland Fire Regimes," *Science* 284 (1999): 1829–1832.

Box 3

1. M. J. Schroeder, M. Glovinsky, V. Hendricks, et al., *Synoptic Weather Types Associated with Critical Fire Weather* (Washington, D.C.: U.S. Department of Commerce, National Bureau of Standards, Institute for Applied Technology, 1964).

FIRE IN THE KLAMATH-SISKIYOU ECOREGION

1. D. A. DellaSala, "State of the Klamath Knot: How Far Have We Come and Where Are We Going," in *Proceedings of the Second Conference on Klamath-Siskiyou Ecology,* ed. K. L. Mergenthaler, J. E. Williams, and E. S. Jules (Cave Junction, Oreg.: Siskiyou Field Institute, 2004), pp. 2–9; D. A. DellaSala, S. B. Reid, T. J. Frest, et al., "A Global Perspective on the Biodiversity of the Klamath-Siskiyou Ecoregion," *Natural Areas Journal* 19 (1999): 300–319.

2. Ibid.

3. E. Frost and R. Sweeney, *Fire Regimes, Fire History, and Forest Conditions in the Klamath-Siskiyou Region: An Overview and Synthesis of Knowledge* (Washington, D.C.: World Wildlife Fund, 2000), www.worldwildlife.org/wildplaces/kla/pubs/fire_report.pdf; J. R. Odion, J. R. Strittholt, H. Jiang, et al., "Fire Severity Patterns and Forest Management in the Klamath National Forest, Northwest Cal-

ifornia, USA," *Conservation Biology* 18 (2004): 927–936; R. H. Whittaker, "Vegetation of the Siskiyou Mountains, Oregon and California," *Ecological Monographs* 30 (1960): 279–338.

4. Whittaker, "Vegetation of the Siskiyou Mountains."

5. D. Martinez, "Restoring Indigenous History and Culture to the Klamath-Siskiyou Ecoregion: Conservation, Restoration, and Wood Fiber Production in the Forest Matrix," in *Proceedings of the Second Conference on Klamath-Siskiyou Ecology*, pp. 140–147.

6. R. D. Willis and J. D. Stuart, "Fire History and Stand Development of a Douglas-Fir/Hardwood Forest in Northern California," *Northwest Science* 68 (1994): 205–212.

7. S. F. Arno and S. Allison Bunnell, *Flames in Our Forests: Disaster or Renewal?* (Washington D.C.: Island Press, 2002).

8. Willis and Stuart, "Fire History."

9. Ibid.

10. Ibid.

11. D. McKenzie, Z. Gedalof, D. L. Peterson, and P. Mote, "Climate Change, Wildfire, and Conservation," *Conservation Biology* 18 (2004): 890–902.

12. E. Frost, "Serpentine Fen Conservation Project, Summary of Phase III: Field Surveys for New Fens and Rare Plant Populations on the Siskiyou National Forest," unpublished report prepared for the World Wildlife Fund, 2002.

13. R. G. Coleman and A. R. Kruckeberg, "Geology and Plant Life of the Klamath-Siskiyou Mountain Region," *Natural Areas Journal* 19, no. 4 (1999): 320–340; Frost, "Serpentine Fen Conservation Project."

14. S. J. Pyne, *Fire in America: A Cultural History of Wildland and Rural Fire* (Princeton: Princeton University Press, 1982), p. 294.

15. D. A. DellaSala, D. M. Olson, S. Barth, et al., "Forest Health: Getting Beyond the Rhetoric to Restore Healthy Landscapes in the Inland Northwest," *Wildlife Society Bulletin* 23, no. 3 (1995): 346–356.

16. D. A. DellaSala, J. Williams, C. Deacon-Williams, and J. F. Franklin, "Beyond Smoke and Mirrors: A Synthesis of Forest Science and Policy," *Conservation Biology* 18 (2004): 976–986.

17. J. F. Franklin and J. Agee, "Scientific Issues and National Forest Fire Policy: Forging a Science-Based National Forest Fire Policy," *Issues in Science and Technology* 20, no. 1 (2003): 59–66; V. Rapp, U.S. Forest Service, Pacific Northwest Research Station, "Fire Risk in East-Side Forests," *Science Update* 9, no. 2 (2002): 12.

18. Rapp, "Fire Risk."

19. DellaSala et al., "Beyond Smoke."

20. N. L. Staus, J. R. Strittholt, D. A. DellaSala, and R. Robinson, "Rate and Pattern of Forest Disturbance in the Klamath-Siskiyou Ecoregion, U.S.A.," *Landscape Ecology* 17 (2002): 455–470.

21. J. F. Franklin and J. Agee, "Scientific Issues and National Forest Fire Policy; D. B. Lindenmayer and J. F. Franklin, *Conserving Forest Biodiversity: A Comprehensive Multiscaled Approach* (Washington, D.C.: Island Press, 2002).

22. Ibid.

23. Odion et al., "Fire Severity Patterns."

24. Staus et al., "Rate and Pattern"; J. R. Strittholt and D. A. DellaSala, "Importance of Roadless Areas in Biodiversity Conservation in Forested Ecosystems: A Case Study—Klamath-Siskiyou Ecoregion, U.S.A.," *Conservation Biology* 15, no. 6 (2001): 1742–1754.

25. J. D. Cohen, "Preventing Disaster: Home Ignitability in the Wildland-Urban Interface," *Journal of Forestry* 98, no. 3 (2000): 15–21; DellaSala et al., "Beyond Smoke."

26. A. J. Belsky and D. M. Blumenthal, "Effects of Livestock Grazing on Stand Dynamics and Soils in Upland Forests of the Interior West," *Conservation Biology* 11 (1997): 315–327; W. W. Covington, P. Z. Fulé, M. M. Moore, et al., "Restoring Ecosystem Health in Ponderosa Pine Forests of the Southwest," *Journal of Forestry* 95, no. 4 (1997): 23–29.

27. Ibid.

28. E. S. Jules, M. J. Kaufmann, W. Ritts, and A. L. Carroll, "Spread of an Invasive Pathogen over a Variable Landscape: A Non-Native Root Rot on Port Orford Cedar," *Ecology* 83 (2002): 3167–3181.

29. Strittholt and DellaSala, "Importance of Roadless Areas."

30. U.S. Forest Service, *Biscuit Fire Chronology, Siskiyou National Forest* (February 2003).

31. Ibid.

32. T. Ingalsbee, "Collateral Damage—The Environmental Effects of Firefighting: The 2002 Biscuit Fire Suppression Actions and Impacts," research paper, May 2004; www.fire-ecology.org/research.html; accessed June 6, 2005.

33. U.S. Forest Service/Bureau of Land Management, *The Biscuit Fire Recovery Project Draft Environmental Impact Statement* (Portland, Oreg.: U.S. Forest Service, Northwest Region, 2003); www.fs.fed.us/r6/rogue-siskiyou/biscuit-fire/feis.shtml.

34. Odion et al., "Fire Severity Patterns."

35. Conservation Biology Institute, "Ecological Issues Underlining Proposals to Conduct Salvage Logging in Areas Burned by the Biscuit Fire," unpublished report (Corvallis, Oreg.: Conservation Biology Institute, 2004).

36. J. Sessions, R. Buckman, M. Newton, and J. Hamann. *The Biscuit Fire: Management Options for Forest Regeneration, Fire and Insect Risk Reduction and Timber Salvage* (Corvallis: Oregon State University, College of Forestry, 2003); K. Durbin, "Unsalvageable," *High Country News*, May 16, 2005, p. 10; U.S. Forest Service/BLM, *Biscuit Fire Recovery Project Draft EIS*, pp. 1–8.

37. U.S. Forest Service/BLM, *Biscuit Fire Recovery Project Draft EIS*.

38. Ibid.

39. Odion et al., "Fire Severity Patterns."

40. Sessions et al., *Biscuit Fire*.

41. R. L. Beschta, J. J. Rhodes, J. B. Kauffman, et al., "Postfire Management on Forested Public Lands of the Western USA," *Conservation Biology* 18 (2004): 957–967; Conservation Biology Institute, "Ecological Issues"; D. B. Lindenmayer, D. R. Foster, J. F. Franklin, et al., "Salvage Harvesting Policies After Natural Disturbance," *Science* 303 (2004): 1303.

42. K. Harma and P. Morrison, "Analysis of Vegetation Mortality and Prior

Landscape Condition, 2002 Biscuit Fire Complex," unpublished report (Winthrop, Wash.: Pacific Biodiversity Institute, 2003).

43. G. W. Minshall, "Response of Stream Benthic Macroinvertebrates to Fire," *Forest Ecology and Management* 178 (2003): 155–161.

44. Beschta et al., "Postfire Management"; Conservation Biology Institute, "Ecological Issues"; Lindenmayer et al., "Salvage Harvesting Policies."

45. Sessions et al., *Biscuit Fire.*

46. Ibid.

47. A. B. Franklin, D. R. Anderson, R. J. Gutierrez, and K. P. Burnham, "Climate, Habitat Quality, and Fitness in Northern Spotted Owl Populations in Northwestern California," *Ecological Monographs* 70, no. 4 (2000): 539–590.

48. Franklin and Agee, "Scientific Issues and National Forest Fire Policy."

49. U.S. Forest Service/BLM, *Biscuit Fire Recovery Project Draft EIS.*

50. DellaSala et al., "Forest Health"; Lindenmayer and Franklin, *Conserving Forest Biodiversity;* D. Perry, *Forest Ecosystems* (Baltimore: John Hopkins University Press, 1994).

51. Ibid.

52. M. G. Turner, W. H. Romme, and D. B. Tinker, "Surprises and Lessons from the 1988 Yellowstone Fires," *Frontiers in Ecology and Environment* 1, no. 7 (2003): 351–358.

53. J. K. Agee, *Fire Ecology of Pacific Northwest Forests* (Washington, D.C.: Island Press, 1993).

54. J. D. Cohen, "Preventing Disaster"; DellaSala et al., "Beyond Smoke."

55. J. B. Kauffman, "Death Rides the Forest: Perceptions of Fire, Land Use, and Ecological Restoration of Western Forests," *Conservation Biology* 18 (2004): 878–882.

56. D. A. DellaSala, A. Martin, R. Spivak, et al., "A Citizens' Call for Ecological Forest Restoration: Forest Restoration Principles and Criteria," *Ecological Restoration* 21, no. 1 (2003): 14–23.

57. DellaSala et al., "Beyond Smoke."

58. DellaSala et al., "Citizens' Call."

59. The author would like to thank Dr. Dennis Odion, fire ecologist, for reviewing an earlier draft of this essay.

FIRE IN THE SOUTHWEST

1. C. D. Allen, "Ecological Patterns and Environmental Change in the Bandelier Landscape," in *Archaeology of Bandelier National Monument: Village Formation on the Pajarito Plateau, New Mexico*, ed. T. A. Kohler (Albuquerque: University of New Mexico Press, 2004), pp. 19–68.

2. J. Herron, "Where There's Smoke," in *Forests Under Fire: A Century of Ecosystem Mismanagement in the Southwest*, ed. C. J. Huggard and A. R. Gómez (Tucson: University of Arizona Press, 2001), p. 187.

3. Ibid.

4. C. D. Allen, U. S. Geological Survey Jemez Mountains Field Station, personal interview, April 12, 2003.

5. C. D. Allen, "Fire and Vegetation History of the Jemez Mountains," in *Water, Watersheds, and Land Use in New Mexico: Impacts of Population Growth on Nat-*

ural Resources, Santa Fe Region, ed. P. S. Johnson (Socorro: New Mexico Bureau of Mines and Mineral Resources, 2001), pp. 29–33.

6. S. J. Pyne, *Fire in America: A Cultural History of Wildland and Rural Fire* (Seattle: University of Washington Press, 1997), p. 520.

7. C. D. Allen; "Lots of Lightning and Plenty of People: An Ecological History of Fire in the Upland Southwest," in *Fire, Native Peoples, and the Natural Landscape,* ed. T. Vale (Washington, D.C.: Island Press, 2002), p. 164.

8. Pyne, *Fire in America,* p. 520.

9. W. Kupper, *The Golden Hoof: The Story of the Sheep of the Southwest* (New York: Knopf, 1945), p. 87.

10. Allen, "Ecological Patterns."

11. Ibid.

12. W. A. Dick-Peddie, *New Mexico Vegetation: Past, Present, and Future* (Albuquerque: University of New Mexico Press, 1993), p. 19.

13. A. W. Carson, "The New Mexico Sheep Industry 1850–1900," *New Mexico Historical Review,* January 1969.

14. Ibid.

15. G. Wuerthner, "Myth: Cattle Have Replaced the Bison," in *Welfare Ranching: The Subsidized Destruction of the American West,* ed. G. Wuerthner and M. Matteson (Washington, D.C.: Island Press, 2002), p. 11.

16. Allen, "Ecological Patterns."

17. Dick-Peddie, *New Mexico Vegetation,* p. 18.

18. Allen, "Ecological Patterns."

19. E. A. Tucker and G. Fitzpatrick, *Men Who Matched the Mountains: The Forest Service in the Southwest* (Albuquerque: U.S. Forest Service, Southwestern Region, 1972), p. 26.

20. B. P. Wilcox, J. Pitlick, C. D. Allen, and D. W. Davenport, "Runoff and Erosion from a Rapidly Eroding Pinyon-Juniper Hillslope," in *Advances in Hillslope Processes,* vol. 1, ed. M. G. Anderson and S. M. Brooks (New York: Wiley, 1996), p. 61.

21. L. Jacobs, *Waste of the West: Public Land Ranching* (self-published, 1991), p. 113.

22. Aldo Leopold's ideas on fire in the Southwest went through a rapid evolution between 1920 and 1924. At first he was opposed to "light burning" (essentially prescribed fire) as advocated by private foresters. He joined with those seeking to protect the Forest Service's total exclusion of fire. By 1924 he had completely reversed himself and was advocating removal of livestock and reintroduction of fire to southern Arizona in order to stop severe erosion and the encroachment of brush into former grasslands. His 1924 *Journal of Forestry* essay "Grass, Brush, Timber and Fire in Southern Arizona" could easily stand as the last word on the subject of fire and landscape change in the Southwest.

23. P. M. Leschak, *Ghosts of the Fireground: Echoes of the Great Peshtigo Fire and the Calling of a Wildland Firefighter* (San Francisco: Harper Collins, 2002), p. 6.

24. S. Pyne, *World Fire: The Culture of Fire on Earth* (Seattle: University of Washington Press, 1997), p. 186.

25. Allen, "Ecological Patterns."

26. C. D. Allen, "Changes in the Landscape of the Jemez Mountains, New Mexico" (Ph.D. dissertation, University of California, Berkeley, 1989), p. 250.

27. Pyne, *Fire in America*, p. 304.

28. M. Hoerling and K. Kumar, "The Perfect Ocean for Drought," *Science* 299 (2003): 691–694.

29. T. Ingalsbee, "Collateral Damage—The Environmental Effects of Firefighting: The 2002 Biscuit Fire Suppression Actions and Impacts" (May 2004), p. 2; http://FUSEE.org/ethics/docs/biscuit_suppression_copy.html.

30. Herron, "Where There's Smoke," p. 205.

31. Wuerthner, Part V introduction, *Welfare Ranching*, p. 261.

32. Ibid., Introduction, p. xiii.

FIRE IN THE EAST

1. D. K. Kennard, "Present-Day Wildfires," in *Encyclopedia of Southern Appalachian Forest Ecosystems* (Asheville, N.C.: U.S. Forest Service, Southern Research Station); www.forestryencyclopedia.net/Encyclopedia/Appalachian/Ecology/disturbance%20and%20succession/fire/historical_and_present-day_fire_regimes/present-day_wildfires.htm/document_view; accessed September 3, 2005.

2. W. Cronon, *Changes in the Land: Indians, Colonists, and the Ecology of New England* (New York: Hill and Wang, 1983).

3. W. Denevan, "The Pristine Myth: The Landscape of the Americas in 1492," *Annals of the Association of American Geographers* 82 (1992): 369–385; C. Kay and R. T. Simmons, *Wilderness and Political Ecology: Aboriginal Influences and the Original State of Nature* (Salt Lake City: University of Utah Press, 2002).

4. T. R. Vale, "The Pre-European Landscape of the United States: Pristine or Humanized?" in *Fire, Native Peoples and the Natural Landscape*, ed. T. Vale (Washington, D.C.: Island Press, 2002).

5. F. H. Bormann and G. E. Likens, "Catastrophic Disturbance and the Steady State in Northern Hardwood Forests," *American Scientist* 67 (1979): 660–669.

6. T. J. Fahey and W. A. Reiners, "Fire in the Forests of Maine and New Hampshire," *Bulletin of the Torrey Botanical Club* 8, no. 3 (1981): 362–373.

7. T. Parshall and D. Foster, "Fire on the New England Landscape: Regional and Temporal Variation, Cultural and Environmental Controls," *Journal of Biogeography* 29 (2002): 1305–1317.

8. U.S. Fish and Wildlife Service, "History of Southern Pine Ecosystems"; http://rcwrecovery.fws.gov/ecosystems.htm; accessed September 12, 2005.

9. J. K. Brown and J. K. Smith, eds., *Wildland Fire in Ecosystems: Effects on Flora*, U.S. Forest Service General Technical Report RMRS GTR-42, vol. 2 (Ogden, Utah: U.S. Forest Service, Rocky Mountain Research Station, 2000).

10. USFWS, "History of Southern Pine Ecosystems."

11. D. D. Wade and J. D. Lunsford, *A Guide for Prescribed Fire in the Southern United States*, U.S. Forest Service Technical Publication R8-TP 11 (Atlanta: U.S. Forest Service, Southern Region, 1989).

12. www.worldwildlife.org/wildworld/profiles/terrestrial/na/na0504_full.html.

13. Ibid.

14. http://nature.org/wherewework/northamerica/states/newyork/preserves/art11872.html.

15. http://wildwnc.org/trees/Pinus_rigida.html.

16. Brown and Smith, *Wildland Fire*.

17. G. Rouse, *Fire Effects in Northeastern Forests: Red Pine*, U.S. Forest Service General Technical Report NC-129 (St. Paul, Minn.: U.S. Forest Service, North Central Forest Experiment Station, 1998).

18. P. A. Quinby, "Self-Replacement in Old-Growth White Pine Forests of Temagami, Ontario," Forest Ecology and Management 41 (1999): 95–109.

19. R. P. Guyette, D. C. Dey, and C. McDonell, *Determining Fire History from Old White Pine Stumps in an Oak-Pine Forest in Bracebridge, Ontario*, Forest Research Report No. 133 (Sault Ste. Marie, Ontario: Ministry of Natural Resources, Forestry Research Institute, 1995).

20. www.smokeybear.com/natural_hickory.asp.

PART FOUR

LOGGING AND WILDFIRE

1. S. Pyne, *World Fire: The Culture of Fire on Earth* (Seattle: University of Washington Press, 1997).

2. C. C. Frost, "Presettlement Fire Frequency Regimes of the United States: A First Approximation," in *Fire in Ecosystem Management: Shifting the Paradigm from Suppression to Prescription*, ed. T. L. Pruden and L. A. Brennan, Tall Timbers Fire Ecology Proceedings, No. 20 (Tallahassee, Fla.: Tall Timbers Research Station, 1998), pp. 70–81.

3. D. J. McRae, L. C. Duchesne, B. Freedman, et al., "Comparisons Between Wildfire and Forest Harvesting and Their Implications in Forest Management," *Environmental Review* 9 (2001): 223–260; P. A. Quinby, F. McGuiness, and R. Hall, *Loss of Nutrients Due to Logging in the Lower Spanish Forest of Central Ontario*, Forest Landscape Baseline No. 13, Brief Progress and Summary Reports (Toronto: Ancient Forest Exploration and Research, 1996), www.ancientforest.org/flb13.html; accessed September 14, 2005.

4. R. Foster, D. H. Knight, and J. F. Franklin, "Landscape Patterns and Legacies Resulting from Large, Infrequent Forest Disturbances," *Ecosystems* 1, no. 6 (1998): 497–510.

5. National Park Service, "Fire Facts"; www.nps.gov/yell/technical/fire/factoid.htm; accessed September 14, 2005.

6. M. F. Jurgensen, A. E. Harvey, R. T. Graham, et al., "Impacts of Timber Harvesting on Soil Organic Matter, Nitrogen, Productivity, and Health of Inland Northwest Forests," *Forest Science* 43 (1997): 234–251.

7. M. D. Purser and T. W. Cundy, "Changes in Soil Physical Properties Due to Cable Yarding and Their Hydrologic Implications," *Western Journal of Applied Forestry* 7 (1992): 36–39.

8. J. A. Gent Jr., R. Ballard, A. E. Hassan, and D. K. Cassel, "Impact of Harvesting and Site Preparation on Physical Properties of Piedmont Forest Soils," *Soil Science Society of America Journal* 48 (1984): 173–177.

9. S. C. Trombulak and C. Frissell, "A Review of the Ecological Effects of Roads on Terrestrial and Aquatic Ecosystems," *Conservation Biology* 14 (2000): 18–30.

10. R. Beschta, C. Frissell, R. Gresswell, et al., "Wildfire and Salvage Logging: Recommendations for Ecologically Sound Post-Fire Salvage Management and Other Post-Fire Treatments on Federal Lands in the West"; www.saveamericasforests .org/congress/Fire/Beschta-report.htm; accessed September 14, 2005.

11. *Sierra Nevada Ecosystem Project: Final Report to Congress*, vol. 2, *Assessments and Scientific Basis for Management Options*, Wildland Resources Center Report No. 37 (Davis: University of California, Centers for Water and Wildland Resources, 1996).

12. Trombulak and Frissell, "A Review of the Ecological Effects of Roads."

13. M. P. Amaranthus, R. M. Rice, N. R. Barr, and R. R. Ziemer, "Logging and Forest Roads Related to Increased Debris Slides in Southwestern Oregon," *Journal of Forestry* 83 (1985): 229–233.

14. J. D. McCashion and R. M. Rice, "Erosion on Logging Roads in Northwestern California: How Much Is Avoidable?" *Journal of Forestry* 81 (1983): 23–26.

15. M. R. Kaufmann, C. M. Regan, and P. M. Brown, "Heterogeneity in Ponderosa Pine/Douglas-Fir Forests: Age and Size Structure in Unlogged and Logged Landscapes of Central Colorado," *Canadian Journal of Forest Research* 30, no. 5 (2000): 698–711.

16. D. S. Page-Dumroese, A. E. Harvey, M. F. Jurgensen, and R. T. Graham, "Organic Matter Function in the Inland Northwest Soil System," in *Proceedings: Management and Productivity of Western Montane Forest Soils*, ed. A. E. Harvey and L. F. Neuenschwander, U.S. Forest Service General Technical Report INT-280 (Ogden, Utah: U.S. Forest Service, Intermountain Research Station, 1991), pp. 95–100.

17. R. K. Mace, J. Waller, T. Manley, et al., "Relationships Among Grizzly Bears, Roads, and Habitat in the Swan Mountains, Montana," *Journal of Applied Ecology* 33 (1996): 1395–1404.

18. L. J. Lyon, "Road Density Models Describing Habitat Effectiveness for Elk," *Journal of Forestry* 81 (1983): 592–595, 613.

19. Mace et al., "Relationships Among Grizzly Bears."

20. Purser and Cundy, "Changes in Soil Physical Properties."

21. P. Amaranthus, D. Page-Dumroese, A. Harvey, et al., "Soil Compaction and Organic Matter Affect Conifer Seedling Nonmycorrhizal and Ectomycorrhizal Root Tip Abundance and Diversity," U.S. Forest Service Research Paper PNW-RP-494 (Portland, Oreg.: U.S. Forest Service, Pacific Northwest Research Station, 1996).

22. J. L. Gelbard and J. Belnap, "Roads as Conduits for Exotic Plant Invasions in a Semi-Arid Landscape," *Conservation Biology* 17 (2003): 420–432.

23. Y. Bergeron, P. J. H. Richard, C. Carcaillet, et al., "Variability in Fire Frequency and Forest Composition in Canada's Southeastern Boreal Forest: A Challenge for Sustainable Forest Management," *Conservation Ecology* 2 (1998), no. 2; www.consecol.org/vol2/iss2/art6; accessed September 14, 2005.

24. Associated Press, "Government Admits to Logging Losses in National Forests," June 10, 1998; http://forests.org/archive/america/govadmit.htm; accessed September 14, 2005.

25. S. F. Arno and S. Allison-Bunnell, *Flames in Our Forest: Disaster or Renewal?* (Washington, D.C.: Island Press, 2002).

26. J. K. Agee, *Fire Ecology of the Pacific Northwest Forests* (Washington, D.C.: Island Press, 1993), p. 33.

27. W. Hough, *Impact of Prescribed Fire on Understory and Forest Floor Nutrients*, U.S. Forest Service Research Note RN-SE-363 (Asheville, N.C.: U.S. Forest Service, Southern Research Station, 1981); www.srs.fs.usda.gov/pubs/644; accessed September 14, 2005.

28. W. W. Covington, P. Z. Fulé, M. M. Moore, et al., "Restoring Ecosystem Health in Ponderosa Pine Forests of the Southwest," *Journal of Forestry* 95 (1997): 23–29.

29. Arno and Allison-Bunnell, *Flames in Our Forest*.

30. D. J. Shinneman and W. L. Baker, "Nonequilibrium Dynamics Between Catastrophic Disturbances and Old-Growth Forests in Ponderosa Pine Landscapes of the Black Hills," *Conservation Biology* 11 (1997): 1276–1288.

31. T. T. Veblen, "Key Issues in Fire Regime Research for Fuels Management and Ecological Restoration," in *Proceedings of the Conference on Fire, Fuels Treatment and Ecological Restoration, Fort Collins, Colorado, April 16–28, 2002*, ed. P. N. Omi and L. A. Joyce, U.S. Forest Service Proceedings RMRS-P-29 (Fort Collins, Colo.: U.S. Forest Service, Rocky Mountain Research Station, 2003).

32. M. G. Turner, W. H. Romme, and D. B. Tinker, "Surprises and Lessons from the 1988 Yellowstone Fires," *Frontiers in Ecology and the Environment* 1 (2003): 351–358.

33. Bioscience, Special Issue on Yellowstone Fires edition, *Bioscience* 39, no. 10 (1989).

34. W. H. Romme, L. Floyd-Hanna, and D. D. Hanna, "Ancient Piñon-Juniper Forests of Mesa Verde and the West: A Cautionary Note for Forest Restoration Programs," in *Fire, Fuels Treatment and Ecological Restoration*.

35. Agee, *Fire Ecology*.

36. A. C. Caprio and T. W. Swetnam, "Historic Fire Regimes Along an Elevational Gradient on the West Slope of the Sierra Nevada, California," in *Proceedings of the Symposium on Fire in Wilderness and Park Management, Missoula, Montana, March 30–April 1, 1993*, ed. J. K. Brown, R. W. Mutch, C. W. Spoon, and R. H. Wakimoto, U.S. Forest Service General Technical Report INT-GTR-320 (Ogden, Utah: U.S. Forest Service, Intermountain Research Station, 1995).

37. NPS, "Fire Facts."

38. Pyne, *World Fire*, p. 186.

39. W. C. Bessie and E. A. Johnson, "The Relative Importance of Fuels and Weather on Fire Behavior in Subalpine Forests," *Ecology* 76, no. 3 (1995): 747–762.

40. B. M. Kilgore, "Restoring Fire to National Park Wilderness," *American Forests* (March 1975); www.nps.gov/seki/fire/pdf/bmk_af75.pdf; accessed September 14, 2005.

41. D. Shebitz, A. Andreu, M. Mytty, et al., "Smoke Infusion for Seed Germination in Fire-Adapted Species"; http://depts.washington.edu/propplnt/2003guidelines/group1/Smoke%20Infusion.htm; accessed September 14, 2005.

42. P. J. Dillon, L. A. Molot, and W. A. Scheider, "Phosphorous and Nitrogen Export from Forested Stream Catchments in Central Ontario," *Journal of Environmental Quality* 20 (1991): 857–864.

43. S. Wan, D. Hui, and Y. Luo, "Fire Effects on Nitrogen Pools and Dynamics in Terrestrial Ecosystems: A Meta Analysis," *Ecological Applications* 11, no. 5 (2000): 1349–1365.

44. M. G. Ryan, W. W. Covington, and W. Wallace, *Effect of a Prescribed Burn in Ponderosa Pine on Inorganic Nitrogen Concentrations of Mineral Soil*, U.S. Forest Service Research Note RM-464 (Fort Collins, Colo.: U.S. Forest Service, Rocky Mountain Forest and Range Experiment Station, 1986).

45. A. E. Harvey, M. F. Jurgensen, and R. T. Graham, "Fire-Soil Interactions Governing Site Productivity in the Northern Rocky Mountains," in *Prescribed Fire in the Intermountain Region: Forest Site Preparation and Range Improvements*, ed. D. M. Baumgartner, L. F. Neuenschwander, and R. H. Wakimoto (Pullman: Washington State University, 1989).

46. R. G. Lathrop, "Impacts of the 1988 Wildfires on the Water Quality of Yellowstone and Lewis Lakes, Wyoming," *International Journal of Wildland Fire* 4, no. 3 (1994): 169–175.

47. D. S. Coxson and M. Curteanu, "Decomposition of Hair Lichens (*Alectoria sarmentosa* and *Bryoria* spp.) Under Snowpack in Montane Forest, Cariboo Mountains, British Columbia," *Lichenologist* 34, no. 5 (2002): 395–402.

48. G. W. Minshall, J. T. Brock, and J. D. Varley, "Wildfires and Yellowstone's Stream Ecosystems," *Bioscience* 39 (1989): 707–715.

49. V. A. Saab and J. G. Dudley, *Responses of Cavity-Nesting Birds to Stand Replacement Fire and Salvage Logging in Ponderosa Pine/Douglas-Fir Forests of Southwestern Idaho*, U.S. Forest Service Research Paper RMRS-RP-11 (Ogden, Utah: U.S. Forest Service, Rocky Mountain Research Station, 1998).

50. J. F. Lehmkuhl, R. L. Everett, R. Schellhaas, et al., "Cavities in Snags Along a Wildfire Chronosequence in Eastern Washington," *Journal of Wildlife Management* 67, no. 1 (2003): 219–228.

51. R. E. Gresswell, "Fire and Aquatic Ecosystems in Forested Biomes of North America," *Transactions of the American Fisheries Society* 128, no. 2 (1999): 193–221.

AFTER THE SMOKE CLEARS

1. Wilderness Society/National Audubon Society, *Salvage Logging in the National Forests: An Ecological, Economic, and Legal Assessment* (Washington, D.C.: Wilderness Society, 1996).

2. E. Niemi, *Economic Issues Underlying Proposals to Conduct Salvage Logging in Areas Burned by the Biscuit Fire* (Eugene, Oreg.: ECONorthwest, 2003).

3. E. C. Lowell, S. A. Willits, and R. L. Krahmer, *Deterioration of Fire-Killed and Fire-Damaged Timber in the Western United States*, U.S. Forest Service General Technical Report GTR-PNW-292 (Portland, Oreg.: U.S. Forest Service, Pacific Northwest Research Station, 1992).

4. J. Sessions, R. Buckman, M. Newton, and J. Hamann, "The Biscuit Fire: Management Options for Forest Regeneration, Fire and Insect Risk Reduction and Timber Salvage" (unpublished report, College of Forestry, Oregon State University, Corvallis, 2003; www.cof.orst.edu/cof/admin/Biscuit%20Fire %20Report.pdf).

5. J. D. McIver and L. Starr, *Environmental Effects of Postfire Logging: Literature Review and Annotated Bibliography*, U.S. Forest Service General Technical Report PNW-GTR-486 (Portland, Oreg.: U.S. Forest Service, Pacific Northwest Research Station, 2000).

6. R. L. Beschta, J. J. Rhodes, J. B. Kaufman, et al., "Postfire Management on Forested Public Lands of the Western United States," *Conservation Biology* 18 (2004): 957–967.

7. Ibid.

8. R. Kattlemann, "Hydrology and Water Resources" in *Sierra Nevada Ecosystem Project: Final Report to Congress*, vol. 2, *Assessments and Scientific Basis for Management Options* (Davis: University of California, Centers for Water and Wildland Resources, 1996), pp. 855–920; http://ceres.ca.gov/ snep/pubs/web/ PDF/VII_C30.PDF.

9. U.S. Forest Service, *Biscuit Post-Fire Assessment* (U.S. Forest Service, Rogue River and Siskiyou National Forests, January 2003).

10. E. Niemi, personal communication, 2003.

11. C. Alkire, *Financial Losses from Logging on National Forests, FY 1993* (Washington, D.C.: Wilderness Society, 1994); R.W. Gorte, *Below-Cost Timber Sales: Overview*, Congressional Research Service Report 95-15 ENR (Washington, D.C.: Library of Congress, Congressional Research Service, 1994; E. Niemi, personal communication, 2003; J. Oppenheimer, *In the Red: National Forest Logging Continues to Lose Millions* (Washington, D.C.: Taxpayers for Common Sense, 2001).

12. J. F. Franklin, D. A. Perry, R. F. Noss, et al., *Simplified Forest Management to Achieve Watershed and Forest Health: A Critique* (Seattle: National Wildlife Federation, 2000); www.coastrange.org/documents/forestreport.pdf.

13. D. A. Perry and M. P. Amaranthus, "Disturbance, Recovery, and Stability," in *Creating a Forestry for the 21st Century*, ed. K. A. Kohm and J. F. Franklin (Washington, D.C.: Island Press, 1997).

14. D. H. Lindenmayer and J. F. Franklin, *Conserving Forest Biodiversity: A Comprehensive Multiscaled Approach* (Washington, D.C.: Island Press, 2002).

15. W. C. McComb and D. B. Lindenmayer, "Dying, Dead, and Down Trees," in *Maintaining Biodiversity in Forest Ecosystems*, ed. M. L. Hunter Jr. (Cambridge: Cambridge University Press, 1999), pp. 335–372.

16. R. L. Beschta et al., "Postfire Management"; Lindenmayer and Franklin, *Conserving Forest Biodiversity*; D. A. Perry, *Forest Ecosystems* (Baltimore: John Hopkins University Press, 1994).

17. R. L. Beschta, C. A. Frissell, R. G. Gresswell, et al., *Wildfire and Salvage Logging: Recommendations for Ecologically Sound Postfire Salvage Management and Other Postfire Treatments on Federal Lands in the West* (Eugene, Oreg.: Pacific Rivers Council, 1995); McIver and Starr, *Environmental Effects of Postfire Logging*.

18. M. A. Moritz, "Spatio-Temporal Analysis of Controls on Shrubland Fire Regimes: Age Dependency and Fire Hazard," *Ecology* 84 (2003): 351–361.

19. M. G. Turner and W. H. Romme, "Landscape Dynamics in Crown Fire Ecosystems," *Landscape Ecology* 9 (1994): 59–77.

20. J. K. Brown, E. D. Reinhardt, and K. A. Kramer, "Coarse Woody Debris: Managing Benefits and Fire Hazard in the Recovering Forest," U.S. Forest Service General Technical Report RMRSGTR-105 (Ogden, Utah: U.S. Forest Service, Rocky Mountain Research Station, 2003).

21. M. I. Borchert and D. C. Odion, "Fire Intensity and Vegetation Recovery in

Chaparral: A Review," in *Brushfires in California Wildlands: Ecology and Resource Management*, ed. J. E. Keeley and T. Scott (Fairfield, Wash.: International Association of Wildland Fire, 1995).

22. M. G. Rafael and M. L. Morrison, "Decay and Dynamics of Snags in the Sierra Nevada, California," *Forest Science* 33 (1987): 774–783.

23. J. F. Franklin and J. Agee, "Scientific Issues and National Forest Policy: Forging a Science-Based National Forest Fire Policy," *Issues in Science and Technology* 20 (2003): 59–66.

24. C. P. Weatherspoon and C. N. Skinner, "An Assessment of Factors Associated with Damage to Tree Crowns from the 1987 Wildfire in Northern California," *Forest Science* 41 (1995): 430–451.

25. S. Duncan, "Postfire Logging: Is It Beneficial to a Forest?" *Science Findings* 47 (Portland, Oreg.: U.S. Forest Service, Pacific Northwest Research Station, October 2002).

26. P. L. Andrews and R. C. Rothermel, "Charts for Interpreting Wildland Fire Behavior Characteristics," U.S. Forest Service General Technical Report INT-131 (Missoula, Mont.: U.S. Forest Service, Intermountain Research Station, 1982).

27. M. C. Grifantini, J. D. Stuart, and L. Foz III, "Deer Habitat Changes Following Wildfire, Salvage Logging and Reforestation, Klamath Mountains, California," in *Proceedings of the Symposium on Biodiversity of Northwestern California, Santa Rosa, Calif., October 28–30, 1991*, ed. R. Harris and D. C. Erman (Berkeley: University of California, Wildland Resources Center, 1992).

28. D. C. Odion, E. J. Frost, J. R. Strittholt, et al., "Patterns of Fire Severity and Forest Conditions in the Western Klamath Mountains, California," *Conservation Biology* 18 (2004): 927–936; D. B. Sapsis and C. Brandow, "Turning Plantations into Healthy, Fire Resistant Forests: Outlook for the Granite Burn," (California Department of Forestry and Fire Protection, Fire and Resource Assessment Program, 1997), http://frap.cdf.ca.gov/projects/granite_burn/gb.html; C. P. Weatherspoon, "Fire-Silviculture Relationships in Sierra Forests," in *Status of the Sierra Nevada: Sierra Nevada Ecosystem Project, Final Report to Congress*, vol. 2, *Assessments and Scientific Basis for Management Options* (Davis: University of California, Centers for Water and Wildland Resources, 1996), pp. 1471–1492; Weatherspoon and Skinner, "An Assessment of Factors."

29. Odion et al., "Patterns of Fire Severity."

30. J. Key, "Effects of Clearcuts and Site Preparation on Fire Severity, Dillon Creek Fire 1994" (master's thesis, Humboldt State University, Arcata, Calif., 2000).

31. J. E. Keeley and N. L. Stephenson, "Restoring Natural Fire Regimes to the Sierra Nevada in an Era of Global Change," in *Wilderness Science in a Time of Change Conference, May 23–27, 1999; Missoula, Mont.*, vol. 5, *Wilderness Ecosystems, Threats, and Management*, ed. D. N. Cole, S. F. McCool, W. T. Borrie, and J. O'Loughlin, U.S. Forest Service Proceedings RMRS-P-15-VOL-5 (Ogden, Utah: U.S. Forest Service, Rocky Mountain Research Station, 2000), pp. 266–299; W. H. Russell, J. McBride, and R. Rowntree, "Revegetation After Four Stand-Replacing Fires in the Tahoe Basin," *Madroño* 45 (1998): 40–46.

32. D. A. Perry, "Self-Organizing Systems Across Scales," *Trends in Ecology and Evolution* 10 (1995): 241–244.

33. M. G. Turner, W. H. Romme, and D. B. Tinker, "Surprises and Lessons from

the 1988 Yellowstone Fires," *Frontiers in Ecology and the Environment* 1, no. 7 (2003): 351–358.

34. Ibid.

35. J. R. Strittholt and H. Rustigian, *Ecological Issues Underlying Proposals to Conduct Salvage Logging in Areas Burned by the Biscuit Fire: Report by the Conservation Biology Institute* (Corvallis, Oreg.: Conservation Biology Institute, 2004); www.consbio.org/cbi/pubs/reports.htm.

36. S. G. Conard, A. E. Jaramillo, and S. Rose, *The Role of the Genus* Ceanothus *in Western Forest Ecosystems*, U.S. Forest Service General Technical Report PNW-GTR-182 (Portland, Oreg.: U.S. Forest Service, Pacific Northwest Research Station, 1985); C. C. Delwiche, P. J. Zinke, and C. M. Johnson, "Nitrogen Fixation by *Ceanothus*," *Plant Physiology* 40 (1965): 1045–1047.

37. K. A. Bode, "A Spatial Test of Mycorrhizal Facilitation of Vegetation Dynamics in the Coast Ranges of California (master's thesis, San Francisco State University, 1999); T. R. Horton, T. Bruns, and V. T. Parker, "Ectomycorrhizal Fungi in *Arctostaphylos* Patches Contribute to the Establishment of *Pseudotsuga menziesii*," *Canadian Journal of Botany* 77 (1999): 93–102.

38. W. I. Stein, *Regeneration Outlook on BLM Lands in the Southern Oregon Cascades*. U.S. Forest Service General Technical Report PNW-284 (Portland, Oreg.: U.S. Forest Service, Pacific Northwest Research Station, 1986); J. Walstad, M. Newton, and R. Boyd Jr., "Forest Vegetation Problems in the Northwest," in *Forest Vegetation Management for Conifer Production*, ed. J. D. Walstad and P. J. Kuch (New York: Wiley, 1987).

39. M. D. Busse, *Ecological Significance of Nitrogen Fixation by Actinorhizal Shrubs in Interior Forests of California and Oregon*, U.S. Forest Service General Technical Report PSW-GTR-178 (Albany, Calif.: U.S. Forest Service, Pacific Southwest Research Station, 2000).

40. C. H. Greenberg, D. G. Neary, L. D. Harris, and S. P. Linda, "Vegetation Recovery Following High-Intensity Wildfire and Silvicultural Treatments in Sand Pine Scrub," *American Midland Naturalist* 133, no. 1 (1994): 149–163.

41. T. O. Sexton, "Ecological Effects of Post-Wildfire Salvage-Logging on Vegetation Diversity, Biomass, and Growth and Survival of *Pinus ponderosa* and *Purshia tridentate*" (unpublished manuscript, on file with Department of Rangeland Resources, Oregon State University, Corvallis, 1994).

42. Lindenmayer and Franklin, *Conserving Forest Biodiversity*.

43. J. G. Blake, "Influence of Fire and Logging on Nonbreeding Bird Communities of Ponderosa Pine Forests," *Journal of Wildlife Management* 46, no. 2 (1982): 404–415; A. Haim and I. Izhaki, "Changes in Rodent Community During Recovery from Fire: Relevance to Conservation," *Biodiversity and Conservation* 3 (1994): 573–585.

44. McComb and Lindenmayer, "Dying, Dead, and Down Trees."

45. E. L. Caton, "Effects of Fire and Salvage Logging on the Cavity-Nesting Bird Community in Northwestern Montana" (Ph.D. dissertation, University of Montana, 1996); S. Hejl and M. McFadzen, "Maintaining Fire-Associated Bird Species Across Forest Landscapes in the Northern Rockies," Summary Report (Missoula, Mont.: U.S. Forest Service, Intermountain Research Station, 1998); S. M. Hitchcox, "Abundance and Nesting Success of Cavity-Nesting Birds in Unlogged

and Salvage-Logged Burned Forests in Northwestern Montana" (master's thesis, University of Montana, Missoula, 1996); V. Saab and J. Dudley, "Responses of Cavity-Nesting Birds to Stand-Replacement Fire and Salvage Logging in Ponderosa Pine/Douglas-Fir Forests of Southwestern Idaho," U.S. Forest Service Research Paper RMRS-RP-11 (Ogden, Utah: U.S. Forest Service, Rocky Mountain Research Station, 1998).

46. T. R. Torgersen, R. R. Mason, and R. W. Campbell, "Predation by Birds and Ants on Two Forest Insect Pests in the Pacific Northwest," *Studies in Avian Biology* 13 (1960): 14–19.

47. L. Hutto, "Composition of Bird Communities Following Stand-Replacing Fires in the Northern Rocky Mountains," *Conservation Biology* 9 (1995): 1041–1058.

48. McIver and Starr, *Environmental Effects*.

49. P. B. Durgin, "Burning Changes the Erodibility of Forest Soils," *Journal of Soil and Water Conservation* 40, no. 3 (1985): 299–301; L. F. DeBano, "The Effect of Fire on Soil Properties," in *Proceedings, Symposium on Management and Productivity of Western-Montane Forest Soils*, ed. A. C. Harvey and L. F. Neuenschwander, U.S. Forest Service General Technical Report INT-280 (Ogden, Utah: U.S. Forest Service, Intermountain Research Station, 1991), pp. 151–156.

50. S. M. Mackay and P. M. Cornish, "Effects of Wildfire and Logging on the Hydrology of Small Catchments near Eden, N.S.W.," in *Proceedings of First National Symposium on Forest Hydrology, May 11–13, 1982, Melbourne, Australia*, ed. E. M. O'Loughlin and L. J. Bren (Canberra: Australian Forest Council, 1982), pp. 111–117.

51. McIver and Starr, *Environmental Effects*.

52. R. A. Shakesby, D. J. Boakes, C. Coelho, et al., "Limiting the Soil Degradational Impacts of Wildfire in Pine and Eucalyptus Forests in Portugal: A Comparison of Alternative Post-Fire Management Practices," *Applied Geography* 16, no. 4 (1996): 337–355.

53. Beschta et al., "Postfire Management."

54. McIver and Starr, *Environmental Effects*.

55. Ibid.

56. J. L. Ebersole, W. J. Liss, and C. A. Frissell, "Restoration of Stream Habitats in Managed Landscapes in the Western USA: Restoration as Re-Expression of Habitat Capacity," *Environmental Management* 21 (1996): 1–14.

57. U.S. Forest Service and Bureau of Land Management, "Final Environmental Impact Statement: The Biscuit Fire Recovery Project," Publication #R6-RR-SNF-06 (U.S. Forest Service, 2004).

CONVENTIONAL SALVAGE LOGGING

1. C. Maser, *Our Forest Legacy: Today's Decisions, Tomorrow's Consequences* (Washington, D.C.: Maisonneuve Press, 2005).

2. Ibid.

3. Ibid.

4. The discussion of soil-rent theory is based on R. Plochmann, *Forestry in the Federal Republic of Germany*, Hill Family Foundation Series (Corvallis: School of Forestry, Oregon State University, 1968).

5. The discussion on the erroneous assumptions of the soil-rent theory is based on C. Maser, *Sustainable Forestry: Philosophy, Science, and Economics* (Delray Beach, Fla.: St. Lucie Press, 1994).

6. M. G. Turner, "Landscape Ecology: The Effect of Pattern on Process," *Annual Review of Ecological Systems* 20 (1989): 171–197.

7. D. J. Rapport, "What Constitutes Ecosystem Health?" *Perspectives in Biology and Medicine* 33 (1989): 120–132; D. J. Rapport, H. A. Regier, and T. C. Hutchinson, "Ecosystem Behavior Under Stress," *American Naturalist* 125 (1985): 617–640.

8. G. L. Hoxie, "How Fire Helps Forestry," *Sunset* 34 (1910): 145–151; S. J. Pyne, *Year of the Fires: The Story of the Great Fires of 1910* (New York: Viking, 2001).

9. Maser, *Our Forest Legacy.*

10. P. Bak and K. Chen, "Self-Organizing Criticality," *Scientific American,* January 1991, pp. 46–53.

11. Maser, *Our Forest Legacy.*

12. C. Maser and J. R. Sedell, *From the Forest to the Sea: The Ecology of Wood in Streams, Rivers, Estuaries, and Oceans* (Delray Beach, Fla.: St. Lucie Press, 1994).

13. Maser, *Our Forest Legacy.*

14. L. D. Harris and C. Maser, "Animal Community Characteristics," in *The Fragmented Forest,* ed. L. D. Harris (Chicago: University of Chicago Press, 1984), pp. 44–68.

15. Maser, *Sustainable Forestry;* C. Maser, J. M. Trappe, and R. A. Nussbaum, "Fungal–Small Mammal Interrelationships with Emphasis on Oregon Coniferous Forests," *Ecology* 59 (1978): 779–809.

16. J. G. P. Calvo, Z. Maser, and C. Maser, "A Note on Fungi in Small Mammals from the *Nothofagus* Forest in Argentina," *Great Basin Naturalist* 49 (1989): 618–620; A. W. Claridge, M. T. Tranton, and R. B. Cunningham, "Hypogeal Fungi in the Diet of the Long-Nosed Potoroo (*Potorous tridactylus*) in Mixed-Species and Regrowth Eucalypt Stands in South-Eastern Australia," *Wildlife Research* 20 (1993): 321–337.

17. C. Maser and J. M. Trappe, eds., *The Seen and Unseen World of the Fallen Tree,* U.S. Forest Service General Technical Report PNW-164 (Portland, Oreg.: U.S. Forest Service, Pacific Northwest Forest and Range Experiment Station, 1984).

18. Ibid.

19. Ibid.

20. C. Maser, "Salvage Logging: The Loss of Ecological Reason and Moral Restraint," *International Journal of Ecoforestry* 12 (1996): 176–178.

PYRO COWS

1. A. J. Belsky and D. M. Blumenthal, "Effects of Livestock Grazing on Stand Dynamics and Soils in Upland Forests of the Interior West," *Conservation Biology* 11, no. 2 (1997): 316–327; J. E. Freilich, J. M. Emlen, J. J. Duda, et al., "Ecologi-

cal Effects of Ranching: A Six-Point Critique," *Bioscience* 53, no. 8 (2003), 759–765.

2. M. A. Moritz, J. E. Keeley, E. A. Johnson, and A. A. Schaffner, "Testing a Basic Assumption of Shrubland Fire Management: How Important Is Fuel Age?" *Frontiers in Ecology and the Environment* 2, no. 2 (2004): 67–72; M. Savage, P. M. Brown, and J. Feddema, "The Role of Climate in a Pine Forest Regeneration Pulse in the Southwestern United States," *Ecoscience* 3 (1996): 310–318; G. K. Wuerthner, *Yellowstone and the Fires of Change* (Salt Lake City: Dream Garden Press, 1989).

3. J. K. Agee, *Fire Ecology of the Pacific Northwest Forests* (Washington, D.C.: Island Press, 1993), p. 323; A. J. Belsky and D. M. Blumenthal, "Effects of Livestock Grazing on Stand Dynamics and Soils in Upland Forests of the Interior West," *Conservation Biology* 11, no. 2 (1997), 316–327; D. J. Shinneman and W. L. Baker, "Nonequilibrium Dynamics Between Catastrophic Disturbances and Old-Growth Forests in Ponderosa Pine Landscapes of the Black Hills," *Conservation Biology* 11, no. 6 (1997): 1276–1288.

4. W. W. Covington and M. M. Moore, "Southwestern Ponderosa Forest Structure and Resource Conditions: Changes Since Euro-American Settlement," *Journal of Forestry* 92 (1994): 39–47.

5. E. A. Johnson, K. Miyanishi, and S. R. J. Bridges, "Wildlife Regime in the Boreal Forest and the Idea of Suppression and Fuel Buildup," *Conservation Biology* 15, no. 6 (2001): 1554–1557; J. E. Keeley and CJ Fotheringham, "History and Management of Crown-Fire Ecosystems: A Summary and Response," *Conservation Biology* 15, no. 6 (2001): 1561–1567; M. G. Turner, W. H. Romme, and D. B. Tinker, "Surprises and Lessons from the 1988 Yellowstone Fires," *Frontiers in Ecological Environment* 1 (2003): 351–358.

6. D. J. Shinneman and W. L. Baker, "Nonequilibrium Dynamics Between Catastrophic Disturbances and Old-Growth Forests in Ponderosa Pine Landscapes of the Black Hills," *Conservation Biology* 11, no. 6 (1997): 1276–1288; T. W. Swetnam, C. H. Baisan, and J. M. Kaib, "Forest Fire Histories of *La Frontera:* Fire-Scar Reconstructions of Fire Regimes in the United States/Mexico Borderlands," in *Vegetation and Flora of "La Frontera": Vegetation Change Along the United States-Mexican Boundary,* ed. G. L. Webster and C. J. Bahre (Albuquerque: University of New Mexico Press, 2001).

7. S. L. Stephens, C. N. Skinner, and S. J. Gill, "Dendrochronology-Based Fire History of Jeffrey Pine-Mixed Conifer Forests in the Sierra San Pedro Martir, Mexico," *Canadian Journal of Forest Research* 33 (2003): 1090–1101.

8. Agee, *Fire Ecology;* W. W. Covington, R. L. Everett, R. W. Steele, et al., "Historical and Anticipated Changes in Forest Ecosystems of the Inland West of the United States," *Journal of Sustainable Forestry* 2 (1994): 13–63.

9. J. F. Arnold, "Changes in Ponderosa Pine Bunchgrass Ranges in Northern Arizona Resulting from Pine Regeneration and Grazing," *Journal of Forestry* 48 (1950): 118–126; C. F. Cooper, "Changes in Vegetation, Structure and Growth of Southwestern Pine Forests Since White Settlement," *Ecological Monographs* 30 (1960): 129–164; M. H. Madany and N. E. West, "Livestock Grazing–Fire Regime Interactions Within Montane Forests of Zion National Park, Utah," *Ecology* 64 (1983): 661–667; J. E. Mitchell and D. R. Freeman, *Wildlife-Livestock-Fire Inter-*

actions on the North Kaibab: A Historical Review, U.S. Forest Service General Technical Report RM-222 (Fort Collins, Colo.: U.S. Forest Service, Rocky Mountain Forest and Range Experiment Station, 1993); R. S. Rummell, "Some Effects of Livestock Grazing on Ponderosa Pine Forest and Range in Central Washington," *Ecology* 32, no. 4 (1951): 594–607; M. Savage and T. W. Swetnam, "Early 19th Century Fire Decline Following Sheep Pasturing in a Navajo Ponderosa Pine Forest," *Ecology* (1990): 64: 661–667; R. Touchan, T. W. Swetnam, and H. D. Grissino-Mayer, "Effects of Livestock Grazing on Pre-Settlement Fire Regimes in New Mexico," in *Proceedings: Symposium on Fire in Wilderness and Park Management, Missoula, Montana,* U.S. Forest Service General Technical Report INT-GTR-320 (Ogden, Utah: U.S. Forest Service, Intermountain Research Station, 1995).

10. C. J. Bahre, "Human Impacts on the Grasslands of Southeastern Arizona," in *The Desert Grassland,* ed. M. P. McClaran and T. R. Van Devender (Tucson: University of Arizona Press, 1995).

11. Madany and West, "Livestock Grazing–Fire Regime Interactions"; R. S. Rummell, "Some Effects of Livestock Grazing."

12. Rummell, ibid.

13. Stephens et al., "Dendrochronology-Based Fire History."

14. C. D. Allen, M. Savage, D. A. Falk, et al., "Ecological Restoration of Southwestern Ponderosa Pine Ecosystems: A Broad Perspective," *Ecological Applications* 12, no. 5 (2002): 1418–1433; M. M. Larson and G. H. Schubert, *Root Competition Between Ponderosa Pine Seedlings and Grass,* U.S. Forest Service General Technical Report RM-54 (Fort Collins, Colo.: U.S. Forest Service, Rocky Mountain Forest and Range Experimental Station, 1969).

15. J. A. Belsky, "Viewpoint: Western Juniper Expansion—Is It a Threat to Northwest Arid Ecosystems?" *Journal of Range Management* 49 (1996): 53–59.

16. Agee, *Fire Ecology;* Arnold, "Changes in Ponderosa Pine Bunchgrass"; Savage and Swetnam, "Early 19th Century Fire Decline"; Touchan et al., "Effects of Livestock Grazing."

17. Touchan et al., ibid.

18. P. F. Hessburg, R. G. Mitchell, and G. M. Filip, *Historical and Current Roles of Insects and Pathogens in Eastern Oregon and Washington Forested Landscapes,* U.S. Forest Service General Technical Report PNW-327 (Portland, Oreg.: U.S. Forest Service, Pacific Northwest Research Station, 1994).

19. A. J. Belsky and J. L. Gelbard, *Livestock Grazing and Weed Invasions in the Arid West* (Bend: Oregon Natural Desert Association, 2000); W. D. Billings, "*Bromus tectorum:* A Biotic Cause of Ecosystem Impoverishment in the Great Basin," in *The Earth in Transition: Patterns and Processes of Biotic Impoverishment,* ed. G. M. Woodwell (New York: Cambridge University Press, 1990); R. N. Mack, "Invasion of *Bromus tectorum* into Western North America: An Ecological Chronicle," *Agro-Ecosystems* 7 (1981): 145–165.

20. S. J. Smith, "Viewpoint: Fuels Management—Is Livestock Grazing the Solution?" *Rangelands* 17, no. 3 (1995): 97.

21. K. H. Mayer, "The Effects of Defoliation on *Bromus tectorum* Seed Production and Growth" (master's thesis, Oregon State University, Corvallis, 2004).

22. J. F. Vallentine and A. R. Stevens, "Use of Livestock to Control Cheatgrass—

A Review," *Proceedings of the Symposium on Ecology, Management and Restoration of Annual Rangelands,* U.S. Forest Service General Technical Report INT-GTR-313 (Ogden, Utah: U.S. Forest Service, Intermountain Research Station, 1994).

23. S. Kimball and P. A. Schiffman, "Differing Effects of Cattle Grazing on Native and Alien Plants," *Conservation Biology* 17 (2003): 1681–1693.

24. E. W. Seabloom, W. S. Harpole, O. J. Reichman, and D. Tilman, "Invasion, Competitive Dominance, and Resource Use by Exotic and Native California Grassland Species," *Proceedings of the National Academy of Sciences* 100, no. 23 (2003): 13384–13389.

25. N. E. West and T. P. Yorks, "Vegetation Responses Following Wildfire on Grazed and Ungrazed Sagebrush Semi-Desert," *Journal of Range Management* 55 (2002):171–181.

26. B. F. Horn, "Animal Performance Under Drought: What Should Be Culled"; http://wyorange.net/Drought/anperf.html.

27. Montana Natural History Center, "Annual Patterns of Fire Occurrence"; www.northernrockiesfire.org/history/annual.htm.

PART FIVE

AVOIDING A NEW "CONSPIRACY OF OPTIMISM"

1. C. D. Allen, M. Savage, D. A. Falk, et al., "Ecological Restoration of Southwestern Ponderosa Pine Ecosystems: A Broad Perspective," *Ecological Applications* 12, no. 5 (2002): 1418–1433; see pp. 1418, 1420 for material referenced.

2. A. J. Belsky, A. Matzke, and S. Uselman, "Survey of Livestock Influences on Stream and Riparian Ecosystems in the Western United States," *Journal of Soil and Water Conservation* 54, no. 1 (1999): 419–431; T. L. Fleischner, "Ecological Costs of Livestock Grazing in Western North America," *Conservation Biology* 8 (1994): 629–644.

3. C. W. Hanselka, "Managing for Healthy Rangelands," *Cattleman,* April 2003; www.thecattlemanmagazine.com/issues/2003/0403/managingFor.asp.

4. U.S. Forest Service, Forest and Rangeland Management, *Timber Harvested on the National Forests [1995–2000],* issued December 24, 2002; www.fs.fed.us/forestmanagement/reports/sold-harvest/2000q4harv.htm. Pre-1995 timber harvest data are from the annual *Report of the Forest Service.*

5. The 190 million acres of federal land at increased risk for "extreme" wildfires is the acreage referred to by the proponents of the Healthy Forests Initiative, which became law in early 2004. See the White House fact sheet on that initiative, www.whitehouse.gov/ceq/hfi_12-02_wh_fact_sheet.pdf.

6. U.S. Forest Service, *Historical Fire Regimes by Current Condition Classes, Data Summary Tables* (Missoula, Mont.: U.S. Forest Service, Rocky Mountain Research Station, Fire Sciences Laboratory, February 15, 2000); www.taxpayer.net/govreports/forest/2-15-00FSfire.pdf.

7. U.S. Forest Service, "Healthy Forests Initiative: Fuels Accomplishments"; www.fs.fed.us/projects/hfi/May-2003/hfi-fuels-treatment-graphs.shtml.

8. P. Hirt, *A Conspiracy of Optimism: Management of the National Forests Since World War Two* (Lincoln: University of Nebraska Press, 1994).

9. R. O'Toole, "Multiple-Use Clearcuts," chap. 7 in *Reforming the Forest Service* (Washington, D.C.: Island Press, 1988).

10. Allen et al., "Ecological Restoration of Southwestern Ponderosa Pine Ecosystems," pp. 1418, 1420.

11. U.S. Forest Service, *Historical Fire Regimes*, Table 2b.

12. P. N. Omi and E. J. Martinson, *Effects of Fuels Treatment on Wildfire Severity*, final report submitted to the Joint Fire Science Program Governing Board, March 25, 2002 (Fort Collins: Colorado State University, Western Forest Fire Research Center, 2002), p. 1; www.cnr.colostate.edu/frws/research/westfire/FinalReport.pdf.

13. J. D. Cohen, *Reducing the Wildland Fire Threat to Homes: Where and How Much?* U.S. Forest Service General Technical Report PSW-GTR-173 (Albany, Calif.: U.S. Forest Service, Pacific Southwest Research Station, 1999).

14. J. D. Cohen, *Examination of the Home Destruction in Los Alamos Associated with the Cerro Grande Fire* (Missoula, Mont.: U.S. Forest Service, Rocky Mountain Research Station, Fire Sciences Laboratory, 2000); www.nps.gov/fire/download/pub_pub_examlosalamos.pdf.

15. J. D. Cohen, "What Is the Wildland Fire Threat to Homes?" (paper presented as the Thompson Memorial Lecture at Northern Arizona University, School of Forestry, Flagstaff, April 10, 2000); ibid., *Reducing the Wildland Fire Threat to Homes.*

16. S. Woodruff, "Racicot: Forest Policies a Failure," *Missoulian*, August 27, 2000; www.missoulian.com/articles/2000/08/27/export45583.txt.

17. California codes: Public Resources Code Section 4291 and Government Code 51182; Oregon: Forestland–Urban Interface Fire Protection Act of 1997.

18. The "2001 Fire Safe and Fire Insurance Guide" can be found at http://ci.monrovia.ca.us/city_hall/fire_department/fire_safe_insurance_guide2001.doc.

19. U.S. Department of Agriculture, U.S. Department of Interior, and White House Council on Environmental Quality, "Administrative Actions to Implement the President's Healthy Forest Initiative," Fact Sheet S-0504, December 11, 2002.

20. U.S. Forest Service, *Historical Fire Regimes.*

21. Ibid.

22. U.S. General Accounting Office, *Wildland Fire Management: Additional Actions Required to Better Identify and Prioritize Lands Needing Fuels Reduction*, GAO-03-805 (Washington, D.C.: USGAO, August 15, 2003), p. 18; www.endangered earth.org/opus/GAO-wildlandfire-mangt.pdf.

23. U.S. General Accounting Office, *Wildland Fire Management*; ibid., *Severe Wildland Fires: Leadership and Accountability Needed to Reduce Risks to Communities and Resources*, GAO-02-259 (Washington, D.C.: USGAO, January 2002), pp. 19–20; www.gao.gov/new.items/d02259.pdf; ibid., *Wildland Fire Management: Additional Actions Required to Better Identify and Prioritize Lands Needing Fuels Reduction*, GAO-03-805 (Washington, D.C., USGAO, August 2003), p. 5.

24. U.S. Forest Service, "Reducing Fire Hazard: Balancing Costs and Outcomes," *Science Update*, no. 7 (Portland, Oreg.: U.S. Forest Service, Pacific Northwest Research Station, June 2004), p. 8.

25. All percentages are based on the acres available for treatment after wilderness, roadless, nonforest, and understocked lands were removed from consideration; J. S. Fried, R. J. Barbour, R. D. Fight, et al., "Small-Diameter Timber Alchemy: Can Utilization Pay the Way Towards Fire-Resistant Forests?" in *Proceedings of the 2002 Fire Conference on Managing Fire and Fuels in the Remaining Wildlands and Open Spaces of the Southwestern United States*, ed. M. G. Narog, U.S. Forest Service General Technical Report PSW-GTR-189 (Albany, Calif.: U.S. Forest Service, Pacific Southwest Research Station, 2004).

26. C. L. Mason, K. Ceder, H. Rogers, et al., *Investigation of Alternative Strategies for Design, Layout and Administration of Fuel Removal Projects* (Seattle: University of Washington, College of Forest Resources, Rural Technology Initiative, July 2003), p. 33, Table 4.3.

27. U.S. Forest Service, "Reducing Fire Hazard," p. 7.

28. Ibid., p. 8.

29. C. E. Fiedler, C. E. Keegan III, S. H. Robertson, et al., "A Strategic Assessment of Fire Hazard in Montana," report submitted to the U.S. Forest Service, Pacific Northwest Research Station, September 29, 2001, p. 13, Table 7; www.fusee.org/ecology/docs/strategic_assessment_fire.pdf.

30. C. E. Fiedler et al., "A Strategic Assessment of Fire Hazard in New Mexico," final report submitted to the Joint Fire Sciences Program, U.S. Forest Service, Pacific Northwest Research Station, February 11, 2002, p. 14, Table 5.

MONEY TO BURN

1. S. J. Pyne, *Fire in America: A Cultural History of Wildland and Rural Fire* (Princeton: Princeton University Press, 1982), p. 263.

2. S. J. Pyne, *Vestal Fire: An Environmental History, Told Through Fire, of Europe and Europe's Encounter with the World* (Seattle: University of Washington Press, 1997), p. 58.

3. Ibid.

4. H. Graves, *Protection of Forest from Fire* (Washington, D.C.: U.S. Forest Service, 1914), p. 7.

5. Pyne, *Fire in America*, p. 196.

6. A. L. Schiff, *Fire and Water: Scientific Heresy in the Forest Service* (Cambridge: Harvard University Press, 1962), p. 115.

7. R. O'Toole, *Reforming the Forest Service* (Washington, D.C.: Island Press, 1988).

8. Ibid.

9. Ibid., p. 263.

10. S. J. Pyne, "Flame and Fortune," *New Republic*, August 8, 1994.

11. Ibid.

12. Chief F. A. Silcox, memo to regional foresters, May 25, 1935, on file at U.S. Forest Service, Fire and Aviation Management, Washington, D.C.

13. Pyne, *Fire in America*, p. 285.

14. Schiff, *Fire and Water*, pp. 25–26.

15. Ibid., pp. 29–44.

16. Ibid., p. 32.

17. Ibid., pp. 48–49.
18. Ibid., pp. 59–60.
19. Pyne, *Fire in America*, p. 290.
20. Schiff, *Fire and Water*, p. 101.
21. Ibid., p. 72.
22. Ibid, p. 56.
23. Ibid., p. 101.
24. Ibid., p. 110.
25. See, for example, United States Search and Rescue Task Force, *Wildland Fires: Average Number of Fires and Acres Burned by Decade* www.ussartf.org/wildland_fires.htm. The tables on this web page were originally posted on the National Interagency Fire Center's *Wildland Fire Statistics* web page, www.nifc.gov/stats/wildlandfirestats.html, but the NIFC has since removed the "acres burned by decade" table because it is unreliable.
26. D. W. MacCleery, *American Forests: A History of Resiliency and Recovery* (Washington, D.C.: U.S. Forest Service, 1992), p. 30.
27. U.S. Forest Service, *Forest Fire Statistics* (Washington, D.C: Forest Service, various years), an annual report published (with slightly varying titles) from 1931 to 1990.
28. Ibid., 1940.
29. Ibid., 1931–1990.
30. Ibid., 1940–1956.
31. Shiff, *Fire and Water*, p. 23.
32. R. A. Chase, "Planning the Fire Program for the Third Millennium," in *Proceedings of the Symposium on Wildland Fire 2000*, ed. J. B. Davis and R. E. Martin (Berkeley: U.S. Forest Service, 1987), p. 64.
33. S. Lundgren, "The National Fire Management Analysis System (NFMAS) Past 2000: A New Horizon," in *Proceedings of the Symposium on Fire Economics, Planning, and Policy: Bottom Lines*, ed. Armando González-Cabán and Philip N. Omi (Albany, Calif.: U.S. Forest Service, 1999), p. 72.
34. Pyne, *Fire in America*, p. 294.
35. National Interagency Coordination Center, *Incident Management Situation Report* (Boise: NICC, 2000), December 29, 2000; www.cidi.org/wildfire/0012/0004.html.
36. E. G. Schuster, "Analysis of Forest Service Wildland Fire Management Expenditures: An Update," in *Proceedings of the Symposium on Fire Economics, Planning, and Policy: Bottom Lines*, ed. Armando González-Cabán and Philip N. Omi (Albany, Calif.: U.S. Forest Service, 1999), pp. 43–44.
37. Ibid.
38. U.S. Forest Service, *Budget Explanatory Notes* (Washington, D.C.: USDA, 1990, 1991).
39. Ibid., 1982–2002.
40. Ibid., 1991–2005.
41. Ibid.
42. B. T. Hill, *The National Fire Plan: Federal Agencies Are Not Organized to Effectively and Efficiently Implement the Plan* (Washington, D.C.: GAO, 2001), p. 7.

43. National Incident Command Center, *Incident Management Report 26-Dec-03* (Boise: National Incident Command Center, 2003).

44. U.S. Forest Service, *Wildland and Prescribed Fire Implementation Guide* (Washington, D.C.: U.S. Forest Service, 1998), p. 36.

45. P. M. Leschak, *Hellroaring: The Life and Times of a Fire Bum* (St. Cloud, Minn.: North Star Press, 1994), p. 198.

46. Ibid., p. 67.

47. R. Nelson, *A Burning Issue: A Case for Abolishing the U.S. Forest Service* (Lanham, Md.: Rowman and Littlefield, 2000).

48. I evaluated state land management in R. O'Toole, *State Lands and Resources* (Bandon, Oreg.: Thoreau Institute, 1994), which is partly available online at http://ti.org/statelands.html.

49. R. O'Toole, *Run Them Like Businesses: Natural Resource Agencies in an Era of Federal Limits* (Bandon, Oreg.: Thoreau Institute, 1995); http://ti.org/business.html.

50. Forest Options Group, *Second Century Proposal* (Bandon, Oreg.: Thoreau Institute, 1998); http://ti.org/2c.html.

THE WAR ON WILDFIRE

1. T. Ingalsbee, "Money to Burn: The Economics of Fire and Fuels Management, Part One: Fire Suppression" (2000); www.fire-ecology.org/research/money_to_burn.html.

2. See S. J. Pyne, *Fire in America: A Cultural History of Wildland and Rural Fire* (Seattle: University of Washington Press, 1982); and D. Carle, *Burning Questions: America's Fight with Nature's Fire* (Westport, Connecticut: Praeger, 2002).

3. T. Ingalsbee, "Collateral Damage—The Environmental Effects of Firefighting: The 2002 Biscuit Fire Suppression Actions and Impacts" (2004); www.fusee.org/ethics/docs/biscuit_suppression_impacts.html.

4. E. E. Little and R. D. Calfee, "Environmental Persistence and Toxicity of Fire Retardant Chemicals, Fire-Trol GTS-R and Phos-Chek D75-R to Fathead Minnows, Final Report" (Missoula: U.S. Geological Survey, Columbia Environmental Research Center, 2002); www.cerc.cr.usgs.gov/pubs/center/pdfDocs/ ECO-04.pdf.

5. E. E. Little and R. D. Calfee, "The Effects of UVB Radiation on the Toxicity of Fire-Fighting Chemicals, Final Report" (Missoula: U.S. Geological Survey, Columbia Environmental Research Center, 2000); www.cerc.cr.usgs.gov/pubs/center/pdfDocs/ECO-02.pdf.

6. D. M. Backer, S. E. Jensen, and G. R. McPherson, "Impacts of Fire-Suppression Activities on Natural Communities," *Conservation Biology* 18, no. 4, (2004): 937–946.

7. G. E. Burdick and M. Lipshuetz, "Toxicity of Ferro- and Ferricyanide Solutions to Fish and Determination of the Cause of Mortality," *Transactions of the American Fisheries Society* 78 (1950): 192.

8. P. Janik, "Retardant Resume Work Order: FIRE-TROL Holdings, LLC," U.S. Forest Service memorandum dated April 20, 2000.

9. U.S. Forest Service, Fire and Aviation Management, "Briefing Paper: Issuing a Resume Work Order for FIRE-TROL Holdings, LLC Retardant Products," dated April 20, 2000.

10. Pyne, *Fire in America.*

11. U.S. Forest Service and Bureau of Land Management, *Biscuit Fire Recovery Project Final Environmental Impact Statement* (Rogue River/ Siskiyou National Forest, 2004); www.fs.fed.us/r6/rogue-siskiyou/biscuit-fire/feis.shtml.

12. T. Ingalsbee, "Fuelbreaks for Wildland Fire Management: A Moat or a Drawbridge for Ecosystem Fire Restoration?" *Fire Ecology* 1, no. 1 (2005): 85–99; www.fireecology.net/fe/VOL1/Ingalsbee.pdf.

13. Dr. Seuss, *The Lorax* (New York: Random House, 1971).

14. Ingalsbee, "Collateral Damage."

15. S. Devlin, "USFS Reports Fail to Answer Question About Backburn," *Missoulian,* October 7, 2000; D. Gadbow, "Residents Sue Over Bitterroot Fires," *Missoulian,* July 23, 2002.

16. J. Hughes, "Analysts: Suppression Fire Led to New Mexico Inferno," *Albuquerque Tribune* and Associated Press, May 27, 2000. See also J. Robertson, "Events Leading up to the Escape of the Frijoles Upper Units One and Five Prescribed Fire," *Cerro Grande Prescribed Fire Investigation Report* (National Park Service, U.S. Forest Service, et al., May 2000).

17. U.S. Forest Service and California Department of Forestry, *Accident Report: CDF Helitack Crew 404 Burnover, Tuolumne Fire, Stanislaus National Forest, September 12, 2004;* www.fire.ca.gov/php/fire_er_fatalities.php.

18. U.S. Forest Service, *Warner Fire Recovery Project Final Environmental Impact Statement* (Willamette National Forest, 2003).

19. See for example, C. Ambrose, "The 1999 Big Bar Fire Complex" (unpublished research paper, Citizens for Better Forestry, 2001); and Ingalsbee, "Collateral Damage."

20. USFS and BLM, *Biscuit Fire Recovery Project Final Environmental Impact Statement.*

21. Ingalsbee, "Collateral Damage."

22. U.S. Forest Service, Siskiyou National Forest, Biscuit Post-Fire Assessment, 2003.

23. Ibid.

24. B. Quinn, "30-Mile Fire Front Menaces Southwest Oregon Towns," *Portland Oregonian,* July 30, 2002.

25. Ingalsbee, "Collateral Damage."

26. S. J. Pyne, *Tending Fire: Coping With America's Wildland Fires* (Washington, D.C.: Island Press, 2004).

PART SIX

KEEP THE GREENFIRE BURNING

1. S. J. Pyne, *Fire: A Brief History* (Seattle: University of Washington Press, 2001).

2. T. C. Blackburn and Kat Anderson, eds., *Before the Wilderness: Environmental Management by Native Californians* (Menlo Park, Calif.: Ballena Press, 1993).

3. See, for example, R. Boyd, ed., *Indians, Fire, and the Land in the Pacific Northwest* (Corvallis: Oregon State University Press, 1999); and T. Vale, ed., *Fire, Native Peoples, and the Natural Landscape* (Washington, D.C.: Island Press, 2002).

4. H. Lewis, *Patterns of Indian Burning in California: Ecology and Ethnohistory* (Menlo Park, Calif.: Ballena Press, 1973).

5. N. Langston, *Forest Dreams, Forest Nightmares: The Paradox of Old Growth in the Inland West* (Seattle: University of Washington Press, 1995).

6. S. J. Pyne, *Fire in America: A Cultural History of Wildland and Rural Fire* (Seattle: University of Washington Press, 1982).

7. J. K. Agee, *Fire Ecology of Pacific Northwest Forests* (Washington, D.C.: Island Press, 1993).

8. D. Carle, *Burning Questions: America's Fight with Nature's Fire* (Westport, Conn.: Praeger, 2002).

9. Ibid.

10. Ibid.

11. See, for example, J. K. Brown and J. K. Smith, *Wildland Fire in Ecosystems: Effects of Fire on Flora*, U.S. Forest Service General Technical Report RMRS-GTR-42, vol. 2 (Ogden, Utah: U.S. Forest Service, Rocky Mountain Research Station, 2000); L. F. DeBano, D. G. Neary, and P. F. Ffolliott, *Fire's Effects on Ecosystems* (New York: Wiley, 1998); S. J. Pyne, P. L. Andrews, and R. D. Laven, *Introduction to Wildland Fire* (New York: Wiley, 1996); and J. K. Smith, *Wildland Fire in Ecosystems: Effects of Fire on Fauna*, U.S. Forest Service General Technical Report RMRS-GTR-42, vol. 1 (Ogden, Utah: U.S. Forest Service Rocky Mountain Research Station, 2000).

12. R. E. Martin and D. B. Sapsis, "Fires as Agents of Biodiversity: Pyrodiversity Promotes Biodiversity," in *Proceedings of the Symposium on Biodiversity of Northwestern California*, ed. H. M. Kerner (Berkeley: Wildland Resources Center, Division of Agriculture and Natural Resources, University of California, 1992).

13. See, for example, H. Biswell, *Prescribed Burning in California Wildlands Vegetation Management* (Berkeley and Los Angeles: University of California Press, 1989); and J. E. Deeming, "Effects of Prescribed Fire on Wildfire Occurrence and Severity," in *Natural and Prescribed Fire in Pacific Northwest Forests*, ed. J. D. Walstad, S. R. Radosevich, and D. V. Sandberg (Corvallis: Oregon State University Press, 1990), pp. 95–104.

14. J. D. Walstad and K. W. Seidel, "Use and Benefits of Prescribed Fire in Reforestation," in *Natural and Prescribed Fire in Pacific Northwest Forests*, pp. 67–80.

15. Biswell, *Prescribed Burning.*

16. R. G. Clark and E. E. Starkey, "Use of Prescribed Fire in Rangeland Ecosystems," in *Natural and Prescribed Fire in Pacific Northwest Forests*, pp. 81–91.

17. See for example, A. A. Brown and K. P. Davis, *Forest Fire: Control and Use* (New York: McGraw-Hill, 1973); C. Chandler, P. Cheney, P. Thomas, et al., *Fire in Forestry*, vol. 2, *Forest Fire Management and Organization* (New York: Wiley, 1983); Pyne et al., *Introduction to Wildland Fire.*

18. C. P. Weatherspoon, "Fire-Silviculture Relationships in Sierra Forests," in *Sierra Nevada Ecosystem Project Final Report to Congress*, vol. 2, *Assessments and Scientific Basis for Management Options* (Davis: Wildland Resources Center, University of California, 1996).

19. See, for example, Blackburn and Anderson, *Before the Wilderness.*

20. W. W. Covington and M. M. Moore, "Southwestern Ponderosa Forest Structure: Changes Since Euro-American Settlement," *Journal of Forestry* 92, no. 1 (1994): 39–47.

21. L. A. C. Weldon, "Dealing with Public Concerns in Restoring Fire to the Forest," in *The Use of Fire in Forest Restoration*, U.S. Forest Service General Technical Report INT-GTR-341, ed. C. C. Hardy and S. F. Arno (Ogden, Utah: U.S. Forest Service, Intermountain Research Station, 1996), pp. 56–58.

22. B. Leenhouts, "Assessment of Biomass Burning in the Conterminous United States," *Conservation Ecology* 2, no. 1 (1998); www.consecol.org/vol2/iss1/art1.

23. M. Fuller, *Forest Fires: An Introduction to Wildland Fire Behavior, Management, Firefighting, and Prevention* (New York: Wiley, 1991).

24. S. F. Arno and S. Allison-Bunnell, *Flames in Our Forest: Disaster or Renewal?* (Washington, D.C.: Island Press, 2002).

25. S. Pyne, *Year of the Fires: The Story of the Great Fires of 1910* (New York: Viking, 2001).

26. T. Ingalsbee, "Collateral Damage: The Environmental Effects of Firefighting: The 2002 Biscuit Fire Suppression Actions and Impacts"; found on the website of Firefighters United for Safety, Ethics, and Ecology, www.fusee.org/ethics/docs/biscuit_suppression_impacts.html.

27. S. Pyne, *World Fire: The Culture of Fire on Earth* (Seattle: University of Washington Press, 1995).

28. J. Turner, "The Quality of Wildness: Preservation, Control, and Freedom," in *Place of the Wild: A Wildlands Anthology*, ed. D. C. Burks (Washington, D.C.: Island Press, 1994), pp. 175–189.

29. Pyne, *Fire in America*.

30. M. Keifer, N. L. Stephenson, and J. Manley, "Prescribed Fire as the Minimum Tool for Wilderness Forest and Fire Regime Restoration: A Case Study from the Sierra Nevada, California," *Proceedings of the Wilderness Science in a Time of Change Conference*, vol. 5, *Wilderness Ecosystems, Threats, and Management*, ed. D. N. Cole, S. F. McCool, W. T. Borrie, et al., U.S. Forest Service Proceedings, RMRS-P-15, Vol. 5 (Ogden, Utah: U.S. Forest Service Rocky Mountain Research Station, 2000), pp. 266–269.

31. M. V. McGinnis, "Deep Ecology and the Foundations of Restoration," *Inquiry* 39 (1996): 203–217.

32. C. Miller, "Wildland Fire Use: A Wilderness Perspective on Fuel Management," in *Fire, Fuel Treatments, and Ecological Restoration: Conference Proceedings*, ed. P. N. Omi and L. A. Joyce, U.S. Forest Service Proceedings, RMRS-P-29 (Fort Collins, Colo.: U.S. Forest Service Rocky Mountain Research Station, 2003), pp. 379–385.

33. G. T. Zimmerman and D. L. Bunnell, *Wildland and Prescribed Fire Management Policy: Implementation Procedures Reference Guide* (Boise: U.S. Department of Agriculture and U.S. Department of Interior, 2002); www.fs.fed.us/fire/fireuse/wildland_fire_use/ref_guide.

SPRAWLING INTO DISASTER

1. T. Clark and S. C. Minta, *Greater Yellowstone's Future: Prospects for Ecosystem Science, Management, and Policy* (Moose, Wyo.: Homestead Publishing, 1994).

2. R. Rasker and B. Alexander, *Getting Ahead in Greater Yellowstone: Making the Most of Our Competitive Advantage* (Bozeman, Mont.: Sonoran Institute in conjunction with the Yellowstone Business Partnership, 2003), p. 7.

3. V. K. Johnson, "Trends in Rural Residential Development in the Greater Yellowstone Ecosystem Since the Listing of the Grizzly Bear, 1975–1998," *Yellowstone Science* 9, no. 2 (2001).

4. P. Hernandez, "Rural Residential Development in the Greater Yellowstone: Rates, Drivers, and Alternative Future Scenarios" (master's thesis, Montana State University, Bozeman, 2004).

5. Greater Yellowstone Coordinating Committee, *The Greater Yellowstone Area: An Aggregation of National Park and National Forest Management Plans* (Billings, Mont.: Greater Yellowstone Coordinating Committee, 1987).

6. R. D. Barbee and J. Varley. "The Paradox of Repeating Error: Yellowstone National Park from 1872 to Biosphere Reserve and Beyond," in *Proceedings of the Conference on the Management of Biosphere Reserves, November 27–29, 1984, Great Smokey Mountains National Park, Gatlinburg, Tenn.*, ed. J. E. Peine (Gatlinburg: National Park Service, Uplands Field Research Laboratory, 1984).

7. Targhee National Forest, *Jedediah Smith Wilderness Fire Management Plan* (U.S. Forest Service, Intermountain Region, 1997).

8. Gallatin National Forest, *Gallatin National Forest Fire Management Plan* (U.S. Forest Service, 2002).

9. Personal communication with Keith Birch, June 2001, and Gina Martin, July 2005, both of the Caribou-Targhee National Forest, Idaho Falls, Idaho.

10. Ibid.

11. National Academy of Public Administration, "Wildfire Suppression Strategies for Containing Costs" (September 2002), p. 8.

12. Rod Dykehouse, Bridger-Teton National Forest, Jackson, Wyoming, personal communication, August 2001 and July 2005.

13. National Interagency Fire Center, "Wildland Fire Statistics" table: "Suppression Costs for Federal Agencies"; www.nifc.gov/stats/index.html.

14. M. Benson, "Insurance Companies Take Closer Look at Fires," *Fort Collins Coloradoan*, May 6, 2001.

15. R. Coupal and A. Seidl, "Rural Land Use and Your Taxes: The Fiscal Impact of Rural Residential Development in Colorado," Agricultural and Resource Policy Report 03-02, Department of Agricultural and Resource Economics, Colorado State University, Fort Collins, May 2003; http://dare.agsci.colostate.edu/csuagecon/extension/docs/landuse/apr03-02.pdf.

16. American Farmland Trust, "Cost of Community Services Studies Fact Sheet," 2004.

17. Institute for Business and Home Safety, "Land Use Planning and Natural Hazard Mitigation," *Natural Hazards Mitigation Insights*, no. 1 (October 1998): 1.

18. T. Power, "Destroying Forests to Save Them: Rational Responses to the Summer 2000 Wildfires" (paper prepared for presentation at Boise State University, Boise, Idaho, October 19, 2000), p. 14; www.umt.edu/econ/papers/TmpWildfires.pdf.

BURNING DOWN THE HOUSE

1. G. E. Galloway Jr., "New Directions in Floodplain Management," *Water Resources Bulletin* 31 (1995): 353.

2. M. Davis, *Ecology of Fear: Los Angeles and the Imagination of Disaster* (New York: Metropolitan Books, 1998), p. 98.

3. Ibid., p. 99.
4. Ibid., p. 66.

THE COMMUNITY PROTECTION ZONE

1. J. D. Cohen, "Preventing Disaster: Home Ignitability in the Wildland-Urban Interface," *Journal of Forestry* 98, no. 3 (2000): 15–21; J. D. Cohen and B. W. Butler, "Modeling Potential Structure Ignitions from Flame Radiation Exposure with Implications for Wildland/Urban Interface Fire Management," in *Proceedings of the 13th Conference on Fire and Forest Meteorology, October 27–31, 1996, Lorne, Australia,* vol. 1 (Fairfield, Wash.: International Association of Wildland Fire, 1998), pp. 81–86.

2. J. B. Davis, "The Wildland-Urban Interface: Paradise or Battleground?" *Journal of Forestry* 88, no. 1 (1990): 26–31.

3. Cohen and Butler. "Modeling Potential Structure Ignitions."

4. J. D. Cohen, *Examination of the Home Destruction in Los Alamos Associated with the Cerro Grande Fire July 10, 2000* (Missoula, Mont.: U.S. Forest Service, Fire Sciences Laboratory, 2000); www.firelab.org.

5. Ibid.

6. J. D. Cohen and J. Saveland, "Structure Ignition Assessment Can Help Reduce Fire Damages in the W-UI," *Fire Management Notes* 57, no. 4 (1997): 19–23.

7. Three public agencies in the West provide information to homeowners on how to treat their homes and property to protect them from the threat of forest fire. The National Wildland/Urban Interface Fire Program (see www.firewise.org) and the California Department of Forestry and Fire Protection both recommend that homeowners remove hazardous fuels within 30 feet of the house. The Colorado Department of Forestry recommends that all flammable vegetation be removed from within 15 feet of the house and that a defensible space of reduced fuels extending 75 to 125 feet from the house also be created. The treatments described here surpass all of these and include additional recommendations by the U.S. Forest Service Fire Sciences Laboratory (www.firelab.com).

8. M. Beighley, "Beyond the Safety Zone: Creating a Margin of Safety," *Fire Management Notes* 55, no. 4 (1995): 21–24.

9. Cohen and Butler, "Modeling Potential Structure Ignitions." The calculations are based on a burn injury limit of 7 kW/m^2; see E. Braun, D. Cobb, V. B. Cobble, et al., "Measurement of the Protective Value of Apparel Fabrics in a Fire Environment," *Journal of Consumer Product Flammability* 7 (1980): 15–25; B. W. Butler and J. D. Cohen, "Firefighter Safety Zones: How Big Is Big Enough?" *Fire Management Notes* 58, no. 1 (1988): 13–16; and ibid., "Firefighter Safety Zones: A Theoretical Model Based on Radiative Heating," *International Journal of Wildland Fire* 8, no. 2 (1998): 73–77. Human burn injury limit is the amount of heat required to injure a firefighter not using a personal fire shelter, over the duration of a flame front during a forest fire.

10. Butler and Cohen, "Firefighter Safety Zones: A Theoretical Model."

11. Ibid.

12. H. E. Anderson and J. K Brown, "Fuel Characteristics and Fire Behavior Considerations in the Wildlands," in *Protecting People and Homes from Wildfire in*

the Interior West: Proceedings of the Symposium and Workshop, ed. W. C. Fischer and S. F. Arno, U.S. Forest Service General Technical Report GTR-INT-251 (Ogden, Utah: U.S. Forest Service, Intermountain Research Station, 1998), pp. 124–130; W. C. Schmidt and R. H. Wakimoto, "Cultural Practices That Can Reduce Fire Hazards to Homes in the Interior West," in *Protecting People and Homes from Wildfire,* pp. 131–140.

13. Cohen and Saveland, "Structure Ignition Assessment."

14. J. D. Cohen, "Reducing the Wildland Fire Threat to Homes: Where and How Much?" U.S. Forest Service General Technical Report PSW-GTR-173 (Albany, Calif.: U.S. Forest Service, Pacific Southwest Research Station, 1999).

15. U. S. Department of the Interior and U. S. Department of Agriculture, "Urban Wildland Interface Communities Within the Vicinity of Federal Lands That Are at High Risk from Wildfire," *Federal Register,* January 4 , 2001, pp. 751–777.

PART SEVEN

THE ULTIMATE FIREFIGHT

1. See Smokey's Vault; http://smokeybear.com/vault/default.asp.

2. See J. Elrod, "Mark Trail" [comic strip], *The Oregonian,* August 1, 2004, appearing in the Sunday *Oregonian* Comics and 175 other newspapers.

3. W. J. Kempton, J. S. Boster, and J. A. Hartley, *Environmental Values in American Culture* (Boston: MIT Press, 1993), as quoted in J. Sobel and C. Dahlgren, *Marine Reserves: A Guide to Science, Design and Use* (Washington, D.C.: Island Press, 2004).

4. See, generally, J. E. Williams and D. DellaSala, eds., "Special Section: Wildfire and Conservation in the Western United States," *Conservation Biology* 18, no. 4 (2004): 872–976.

5. Williams and DellaSalla, "Special Section."

6. *Merriam-Webster's 11th Collegiate Dictionary,* electronic edition; v. 3.0 (2003).

7. D. M. Backer, S. E. Jensen, and G. R. McPherson, "Impacts of Fire-Suppression Activities on Natural Communities," *Conservation Biology* 18, no. 4 (2004): 937–966.

8. J. D. Cohen, "Preventing Disaster: Home Ignitability in the Wildland-Urban Interface," *Journal of Forestry* 98 (2000): 15–21.

9. For information on Reddy Squirrel, see www.fseee.org/whosreddy.htm.

10. R. L. Beschta, J. J. Rhodes, J. B. Kauffman, et al., "Postfire Management on Forested Public Lands of the Western United States," *Conservation Biology* 18, no. 4 (2004): 957–967.

11. H. D. Thoreau, "Civil Disobedience," in *The Portable Thoreau,* ed. C. Bode, (New York: Viking Press, 1972), p. 121.

INDEX

Thoreau, H.D., quoted, 341
Tiller Fire, 71
timber, charred. *See* snags
timber harvest. *See* logging, commercial
timber harvest plans, conservatives'
dislike of, 79
timber rotation periods, 187–188
timber sales
marking of trees, ix–x
similarity to salvage sales, 192
in southwestern U.S., 164
see also logging industry; logging,
commercial; salvage logging
tornadoes, disaster relief funds, 312
trapping. *See* hunting, trapping, and
poaching
tree boles
removed by loggers, 181, 187
see also snags
tree plantations
disease-resistant seedlings, 191
distinguished from postfire succession,
197–198
diversity lacking in, 145–146, 187–
188, 197, 199
ecological concerns, 11, 182, 349
herbicide use, 187, 194, 199
Knutson-Vandenberg reforestation
fund, 255
logging industry justification for, 206
nonnative tree species planted in, 194
prescribed burning in, 291–292
Siskiyou Wild Rivers area, 144, 145
wildfires in, 71, 137, 144, 148–149,
185, 197, 243
Turner, Frederick Jackson, 47
type conversions from native shrubs to
alien herbs, 129–131

Udall, Congressman Mark, 71
urban areas/urban sprawl. *See* WUI
(wildland-urban interface)
communities
urban rube factor in media coverage,
64–65
U.S. Forest Service
10 a.m. policy, 135, 252, 255
Clarke-McNary fire protection districts,
253–254
distrust of, 78–79
Forest Fires Emergency Act, 222, 250–
261, 296

fuel-management policies, 239–241,
245
history, 228–229
Knutson-Vandenberg reforestation
fund, 255
let-burn policies, 255–256
management for multiple uses, 228–
229
postfire recovery in Siskiyou Wild
Rivers area, 143–144
prescribed burning, acceptance of,
253–254, 290
prescribed burning, resistance to, 252–
253, 288–290
pressured to increase timber harvest,
82, 228–229
wildfire-suppression policies, 135–136,
162, 164, 250–261, 262–282, 306
Utah
insurance for fire-prone areas, 237
prehistoric fire regimes, 154–158
regulations for building in fire-prone
areas, 236
see also southwestern U.S.; *specific sites
in Utah*

Wallop, Malcolm, 68
Warner Creek Fire, 274
Washington
regulations for building in fire-prone
areas, 236
see also Pacific Northwest; *specific sites
in Washington*
water infiltration
beaver-facilitated, 160
reduced by logging, 180
in soils burned by wildfire, 8, 201
water quality
degraded by firefighting, 265, 267–
268
see also sedimentation into waterways
Wawona, Miwok communities, 37–38
Weaver, Harold, 290
weeds. *See* invasive plant species
Weeks Act, 253
western U.S.
biological decomposition rates, 3, 166,
183
climate patterns, 183
congressional power of, 69
drought, 217
litter accumulation in forests, 119, 183

wildlife *(continued)*
  snags as habitat for, 5, 11, 81–82,
    188–189, 195, 200, 269, 292
  in temperate rainforests, 209
  see also hunting, trapping, and poach-
    ing; *specific animals*
wind
  Biscuit Fire and, 141
  blaze intensity and, 4, 10, 185, 196, 213
  Diablo winds, 121
  fire carried long distances by, 234
  Santa Ana winds, 90, 118, 121–124,
    126, 128, 131
  Sierra Nevada fires and, 104
  Yellowstone Park fires and, 97–98
Winema National Forest, salvage logging,
  199
wolves, xiii, 101, 160
woodpeckers, 189, 200
woody debris
  removed by wildfires, 4, 5
  slash left by logging, 119, 136, 181,
    187, 196–197, 201, 242, 293–294
  see also snags
WUI (wildland-urban interface) communities
  California chaparral wildfires and, 90,
    116–118, 130–131, 305–306
  community conservation plans, 308–
    309
  community protection zones, 286
  development, increased, 301–302
  development, limiting, 149–150, 236–
    238, 248, 306–307, 313–316,
    328, 339–340
  firefighting costs, 232–238, 285–286,
    304–306, 311–316, 339–340
  fire-safing homes, 29, 233–238, 248,
    286, 306–308, 317–323, 336–339
  fuel reduction strategies, 90, 113–115,
    149–150, 232–238, 247–248,
    286, 317–323
  Glenwood Springs Fire, 55, 58–59
  Greater Yellowstone Area, 285–286,
    301–310
  home ignition zones, 286, 307–308,
    310, 317–323
  increased development, 226–227
  insurance premiums for fire-prone
    areas, 150, 236–238, 248, 305–
    306, 310, 315–316, 339
  Klamath-Siskiyou ecoregion, 139

land-protection tools, 309–310
Los Alamos Fire, 65, 153–154, 162–
  163, 234, 257, 272, 313
media coverage of wildfires in, 54, 55,
  58–59, 64–65, 232, 336–337
prescribed burning and, 76, 79–80,
  126, 294–295, 322–323
responsibilities of property owners, 29,
  78, 84–85, 233–238, 248, 281,
  286, 307–308, 315–316, 317–
  323, 339–340
subsidized wildfire protection costs,
  286, 304–306, 311–316
thoughts on living in, 75–85
wildfire suppression costs, 113–114,
  120–121, 232–238, 248, 339–340
wildfire suppression policies, xiv–xv,
  29–30, 113–115, 232–238, 301–
  310, 339–340
Wyoming
  insurance for fire-prone areas, 237
  see also specific sites in Wyoming

Yellowstone Center for Resources, 70
Yellowstone National Park
  area covered by, 91
  geology, 95
  history, 91, 93
  livestock grazing in, 91
  lodgepole pine forests, 57, 64, 68, 89,
    92, 95, 100
  Native Americans' impact on land-
    scape, 34–39
  wildlife preservation role, 91, 101
  wolves reintroduced to, 101
Yellowstone National Park fires
  acres burned by, 91–92, 179, 184–185
  drought role, 96, 97–98, 100
  fire ecology, 95–96
  firefighters called to fight, 92
  fire regimes, 92–95, 101, 184
  impact on fire-management strategies,
    21–22, 68–70, 246, 256
  impact on watersheds, 99
  impact on wildlife, 98–99
  lightning role, 36
  media coverage of, 22, 55–58, 63, 64–
    65, 68–70, 91–93, 349
  prescribed burning, 92–93, 97
  quenched by snow, 6
  wildfire's role in shaping, 68, 94–95
  wildfire suppression, 93–94